Exploring the Ecology of World Englishes in the
Twenty-first Century

Exploring the Ecology of World Englishes in the Twenty-first Century

Language, Society and Culture

Edited by Pam Peters and Kate Burridge

University Press

Edinburgh University Press is one of the leading university presses in the UK. We publish academic books and journals in our selected subject areas across the humanities and social sciences, combining cutting-edge scholarship with high editorial and production values to produce academic works of lasting importance. For more information visit our website: edinburghuniversitypress.com

© editorial matter and organisation Pam Peters and Kate Burridge, 2021, 2023
© the chapters their several authors, 2021, 2023

Edinburgh University Press Ltd
The Tun – Holyrood Road, 12(2f) Jackson's Entry, Edinburgh EH8 8PJ

First published in hardback by Edinburgh University Press 2021

Typeset in 11.5/13 Monotype Ehrhardt by
Servis Filmsetting Ltd, Stockport, Cheshire

A CIP record for this book is available from the British Library

ISBN 978 1 4744 6285 3 (hardback)
ISBN 978 1 4744 6286 0 (paperback)
ISBN 978 1 4744 6287 7 (webready PDF)
ISBN 978 1 4744 6288 4 (epub)

The right of Pam Peters and Kate Burridge to be identified as the editors of this work has been asserted in accordance with the Copyright, Designs and Patents Act 1988, and the Copyright and Related Rights Regulations 2003 (SI No. 2498).

Contents

List of Figures and Tables	vii
List of Contributors	xi
Acknowledgement	xvi

1. Introduction: Exploring the Ecology of World Englishes in the Twenty-first Century: Language, Society and Culture
   Pam Peters and Kate Burridge ... 1

2. Platform Paper: Reflections of Cultures in Corpus Texts: Focus on the Indo-Pacific Region
   Edgar W. Schneider ... 15

3. Reflections of Afrikaans in the English Short Stories of Herman Charles Bosman
   Bertus van Rooy ... 46

4. *Susmaryosep!* Lexical Evidence of Cultural Influence in Philippine English
   Loy Lising ... 64

5. Cultural Keywords in Indian English
   Pam Peters ... 86

6. Lexicopragmatics between Cultural Heritage and Exonormative Second Language Acquisition: Address Terms, Greetings and Discourse Markers in Ugandan English
   Christiane Meierkord and Bebwa Isingoma ... 108

7 Cultural Relations? Kinship Terminology in Three Islands in
   the Northern Pacific   129
   Sara Lynch, Eva Kuske and Dominique B. Hess

8 Somewhere between Australia and Malaysia and 'I' and 'we':
   Verbalising Culture on the Cocos (Keeling) Islands   151
   Hannah Hedegard

9 Expressing Concepts Metaphorically in English Editorials in
   the Sinosphere   170
   Kathleen Ahrens and Winnie Huiheng Zeng

10 Ll Singapore English: The Influence of Ethnicity and Input   193
   Sarah Buschfeld

11 Across Three Kachruvian Circles with Two Parts-of-speech:
   Nouns and Verbs in ENL, ESL and EFL Varieties   215
   Tobias Bernaisch and Sandra Götz

12 Modality, Rhetoric and Regionality in English Editorials in
   the Sinosphere   238
   Pam Peters, Tobias Bernaisch and Kathleen Ahrens

13 Where Grammar Meets Culture: Pronominal Systems in
   Australasia and the South Pacific Revisited   260
   Kate Burridge and Carolin Biewer

14 Decolonisation and Neo-colonialism in Aboriginal Education   280
   Ian G. Malcolm

15 Modal and Semi-modal Verbs of Obligation in the Australian,
   New Zealand and British Hansards, 1901–2015   301
   Adam Smith, Minna Korhonen, Haidee Kotze and Bertus
   van Rooy

16 Privileging Informality: Cultural Influences on the Structural
   Patterning of Australian English   324
   Isabelle Burke and Kate Burridge

17 The Auckland Voices Project: Language Change in a
   Changing City   345
   Miriam Meyerhoff, Elaine Ballard, Helen Charters, Alexandra
   Birchfield and Catherine I. Watson

Index   369

Figures and Tables

FIGURES

5.1	Map of India	88
8.1	Map displaying the location of CKI in the world	155
8.2	Map displaying the layout of the islands	155
8.3	Proportions of first-person singular and plural pronoun forms across three age groups in the CKI data, and the average frequency of both forms for each group	160
8.4	Frequencies of collectivist indicator terms across three age groups in the CKI English data and the average frequency per speaker for each group	162
8.5	Proportions of collectivist and kinship indicator terms for six English varieties with the raw frequencies for each beneath	163
8.6	Frequencies of kinship indicator terms across the sexes in the CKI data and the average frequency per speaker for each group	164
9.1	Normalised ratios of metaphorical and literal tokens related to DEMOCRACY in Beijing, Hong Kong and Taipei editorial corpora	177
9.2	Normalised ratios of the top five frequent source domains associated with the target domain of DEMOCRACY in Beijing, Hong Kong and Taipei editorial corpora	179
9.3	Normalised ratios of metaphor references to particular countries in Beijing, Hong Kong and Taipei editorial corpora	181
10.1	Zero subjects by individual participant (Singaporean, English–ancestral, English–migrant/mixed	201

10.2	Non-standard realisations past tense marking (all types) by individual participant	202
10.3	Realisation of subject *it* (all types) by ethnicity	203
10.4	Past tense marking with regular verbs by ethnicity	204
11.1	Conditional inference tree for nouns	223
11.2	Conditional inference tree for verbs	224
11.3	Effect plot for the interaction between MEDIUM and STATUSREGION for nouns	227
11.4	Effect plot for the interaction between STATUSREGION and MEDIUM for verbs	229
12.1	Relative frequencies of 10 modal verbs in corpora for Beijing, Hong Kong and Taipei	246
12.2	Relative frequencies for nine quasi-modals in corpora for Beijing, Hong Kong and Taipei	249
12.3	Frequencies of seven core modals with first- and second-person subjects in corpora for Beijing, Hong Kong and Taipei	251
12.4	Conditional inference tree for modals *will/would* based on factors in Table 12.2	254
15.1	Distribution of *must* ptw in the three Hansards	306
15.2	Distribution of *HAVE to* ptw in the three Hansards	307
15.3	Distribution of *NEED to* ptw in the three Hansards	307
15.4	Distribution of *should* ptw in the three Hansards	308
15.5	Proportional frequency of first-person pronoun subjects with *must*	309
15.6	Proportional frequency of three categories of subjects with *must*	312
15.7	Proportional frequency of first-person pronoun subjects with *HAVE to*	316
15.8	Proportional frequency of three categories of subjects with *HAVE to*	317
15.9	Frequency of first-person pronoun subjects with *should*	318
15.10	Proportional frequency of three categories of subjects with *should*	319
16.1	Grammaticality of *This essay's due tomorrow and I've done bugger all'*	330
16.2	Grammaticality of *This essay's due tomorrow and I haven't done bugger all'*	331
17.1	Fieldwork locations for the Auckland Voices Project (2016–18)	349
17.2	Recordings collected in the Marsden-funded component	

	of the Auckland Voices Project (AKLV), the Auckland Libraries oral history archives (OH) and the Auckland Museum Tāku Tamaki (TT) project	352
17.3	The canonical New Zealand English vowel space, monophthongs compared with the vowels in read speech in Auckland Voices	355

TABLES

2.1	Hong Kong cultural terms	22
2.2	Singapore cultural terms	23
2.3	Indian cultural terms	23
2.4	New Zealand cultural terms	24
2.5	First-person singular vs plural usage	27
2.6	Collectivism-oriented indicator terms	28
2.7	Honorifics and address terms	29
2.8	Polite request phraseology as power distance indicators	30
2.9	Kinship terms as indicators of social relations	30
2.10	Terms signalling a Chinese culture connection	31
2.11	Summary of indicator terms for emotions	33
2.12	Summary of schematic indicator constructions	38
3.1	Indigenous language vocabulary with the English equivalents and raw frequency in the Oom Schalk subcorpus	52
4.1	Total number of occurrences of indigenous lexical items in written texts	69
4.2	Total number of non-printed text types and corresponding number of legitimate indigenous tokens	70
4.3	Total number of printed text types and corresponding number of legitimate indigenous tokens	72
5.1	Indian English words traceable to the Mughal regime	94
6.1	Greetings in the opening phases of face-to-face interactions	114
6.2	Greetings in the three data sets	115
6.3	Address terms in ICE-UG social and business letters	117
6.4	Address terms in the three data sets	119
6.5	Discourse markers in the three data sets	122
7.1	Selected kinship terms	138
7.2	Percentage of tokens for cousin- and sibling-related terms	139
7.3	Percentage of tokens for grandparent- and grandchild-related terms	140
7.4	Percentage of tokens for *mom* and *mother*	141

7.5	Percentage of tokens for courtship-related terms	142
7.6	Percentage of tokens for marriage-related terms	143
7.7	Percentage of tokens for adoption-related terms	143
7.8	Percentage of tokens for *family*	144
8.1	Demographic summary for the Cocos (Keeling) Islands Spoken English	158
8.2	Proportion of total pronoun frequencies that are first-person singular across Schneider's five nations and CKI	160
8.3	Frequency distributions for collectivist indicator terms in the CKI English data	161
8.4	Distributional frequencies for four kinship terms in six varieties of English	162
9.1	English editorials in the Sinosphere Corpus	174
9.2	List of lemmas searched for the target domain of DEMOCRACY	175
9.3	Frequencies of the topics related to DEMOCRACY in Beijing, Hong Kong and Taipei editorial corpora	175
Appendix 9.1	Cross-tabulation of cities and metaphor/literal DEMOCRACY	185
Appendix 9.2	Cross-tabulation of cities and source domains	186
10.1	A comparison of average length differences between KIT–FLEECE and FOOT–GOOSE	199
12.1	Sources for the English editorials in the Sinosphere Corpus	244
12.2	Categorisation of modals used in this research	244
12.3	Factors coded for *will* vs *would* for a multifactorial analysis of 1,080 corpus examples	252
15.1	Composition of the three Hansard corpora	304
15.2	The most common verbs collocating with *I should*, raw frequency and normalised frequency per 1,000 verbs	318
16.1	*Bugger* in the Old Bailey	337
17.1	Ethnic diversity in Auckland and in New Zealand according to the 2013 New Zealand Census	346
17.2	Age and social demographics in three Auckland communities	349
17.3	Speakers recorded for the Auckland Voices Project	351
17.4	Effect of following segment on older speakers' use of [ðə] in three Auckland communities	358
17.5	Effect of following segment on younger speakers' use of [ðə] in three Auckland communities	359

Contributors

Kathleen Ahrens is a Professor in the Department of English and Director of the Research Centre for Professional Communication in English at The Hong Kong Polytechnic University. Her current research focuses on the role of metaphors in political communication.

Elaine Ballard is a linguist and researcher in the Speech Science division of the School of Psychology at the University of Auckland, New Zealand. Her research interests lie in the discipline of bilingualism with a particular focus on language change and development in the multilingual communities of Auckland.

Tobias Bernaisch is Senior Lecturer at Justus Liebig University Giessen. His research focuses on South Asian Englishes with special emphasis on Sri Lankan English and potential epicentral constellations in the region, while he also currently studies genderlectal variation in World Englishes and in the history of the English language.

Carolin Biewer is the Chair of English Linguistics at the University of Würzburg, where she teaches corpus linguistics, historical linguistics, sociolinguistics and World Englishes. Her research focuses on language variation and change in East Asia, Australasia and the Pacific, particularly on the evolution and dynamics of South Pacific Englishes and Hong Kong English.

Alexandra Birchfield is a master's graduate of Victoria University of Wellington, New Zealand; research interests include relative clauses in

Auckland English, as well as issues in language and gender, historical sociolinguistics, and language contact.

Isabelle Burke is a postdoctoral researcher at Monash University, Australia. She is currently investigating changing metaphors and identities in the Australian vernacular, in addition to the linguistic expression of caused accompanied motion events in Australian English. Her research interests include grammatical change and ethnosyntax.

Kate Burridge is Professor of Linguistics at Monash University, Australia, and Fellow of the Australian Academy of the Humanities and of the Social Sciences. Her main areas of research are language change, the Pennsylvania German Anabaptist communities in North America, the notion of linguistic taboo, prescriptivism, and the structure and history of English.

Sarah Buschfeld is a Full Professor of English Linguistics (Multilingualism) at TU Dortmund University, Germany, after previous appointments at the Universities of Regensburg and Cologne. She has worked on postcolonial and non-postcolonial varieties of English, and in the fields of multilingualism, language acquisition (first and second), and language contact.

Helen Charters is an honorary research fellow in the School of Cultures, Languages and Linguistics at the University of Auckland, New Zealand. Her main research interest was the acquisition of syntax, but she has been retired for a few years and now focuses mainly on spinning and weaving.

Sandra Götz is a full Professor of English Didactics and Linguistics at Philipps University Marburg, Germany. Her research activities mainly focus on varieties of English around the word and learner Englishes. In two major ongoing projects she investigates the use of non-canonical syntax in South Asian varieties of English and spoken fluency in EFL, ESL and/vs. ENL.

Hannah Hedegard is a British postdoctoral researcher in the department of Modern English Linguistics at the University of Bern, Switzerland. Her current research foci are (1) language variation and change in Global Englishes and (2) applications of sociolinguistics in legal contexts, principally Language Analysis for the Determination of Origin (LADO).

Dominique B. Hess is a research associate at the Center for the Study of Language and Society (CSLS) at the University of Bern, Switzerland, currently working on a dialect/ethnolect project on youth language in Switzerland. Her research interests include sociolinguistics, (grammatical) language variation and change, varieties of English, studies of contact languages, as well as language planning and policy.

Bebwa Isingoma is a Senior Lecturer at Gulu University, Uganda. He obtained his PhD in English Linguistics at the University of Agder in 2013 and is an EU Marie Curie fellow (Freiburg Institute for Advanced Studies, 2018–19). His research areas include English linguistics, comparative syntax, (variational) sociolinguistics and Bantu linguistics.

Minna Korhonen is a research associate at the Department of Linguistics at Macquarie University, Australia. Her current research is on language variation and change in varieties of English, with a special focus on Australian English.

Haidee Kotze is Professor in the Department of Languages, Literature and Communication at Utrecht University, The Netherlands, where she holds the Chair of Translation Studies. Her research focuses on language variation and change in contact settings, with an emphasis on both the psycholinguistic and social conditions of language contact.

Eva Kuske currently works as a research associate at the Zurich University of Applied Sciences and teaches at the Center for the Study of Language and Society at the University of Bern, Switzerland. Her research focus is on variationist sociolinguistics, in particular phonetics and phonology, lesser-known varieties of English and regional English.

Loy Lising is a Lecturer in the Department of Linguistics at Macquarie University, Australia. She is a sociolinguist whose main research area of interest focuses on the investigation of multilingual practices in multilingual ecologies employing both ethnographic and corpus approaches.

Sara Lynch is a lecturer at the University of Lausanne and a researcher at the Center for the Study of Language and Society (CSLS) at the University of Bern, Switzerland. She is currently focusing on discourses of marginalisation in the Pacific. Her research interests include language variation and change, Critical Discourse Analysis, and Linguistic Anthropology.

Ian G. Malcolm is Emeritus Professor at Edith Cowan University, Australia, where, prior to his retirement (2003), he had been Professor of Applied Linguistics and inaugural Dean of the Faculty of Arts. He founded and led the Centre for Applied Language Research and continues with teams of Aboriginal and non-Aboriginal investigators to study Aboriginal English and its educational implications.

Christiane Meierkord holds the Chair of English Linguistics at the Ruhr-University of Bochum, Germany. She is author of *Interactions across Englishes* (2012) and co-edited *Ugandan English* (2016), with Bebwa Isingoma and Saudah Namyalo, as well as *World Englishes at the Grassroots* (2021), with Edgar Schneider. She currently researches English in post-protectorates and at the grassroots of societies.

Miriam Meyerhoff is Senior Research Fellow at All Souls College, and Professor of Sociolinguistics at the University of Oxford, UK. Her research focuses on the linguistic and social dimensions of language variation, especially in contexts of language or dialect contact. She works mainly in Vanuatu, but also Bequia (St Vincent & the Grenadines), Auckland (New Zealand), and Edinburgh and London (UK).

Pam Peters is a Fellow of the Australian Academy of the Humanities, and an Emeritus Professor in Linguistics at Macquarie University, Australia. She was Director of the University's Dictionary Research Centre 2001–7, and currently co-directs (with Kate Burridge) an international research project in Varieties of English in the Indo-Pacific.

Edgar W. Schneider is Emeritus Professor of English Linguistics at the University of Regensburg, Germany. Known best for his 'Dynamic Model' (*Postcolonial English*, 2007), he is an internationally renowned sociolinguist who has published many books and articles and lectured on all continents, including many keynote lectures. His current research seeks to establish the recognition of Englishes as a Complex Dynamic System.

Adam Smith is a Lecturer in the Department of Linguistics at Macquarie University, Australia. His main areas of research are language variation over time and across different regions, lexicography/terminography, and also the theory and practice of editing.

Bertus van Rooy is professor of English linguistics at the University of Amsterdam, The Netherlands, and extraordinary professor at North-West University, South Africa. His main field of interest is World Englishes, focusing on how new grammatical features arise and gain acceptance in settings of language contact. He also works on the syntax of Afrikaans.

Catherine I. Watson is an Associate Professor based in the Department of Electrical, Computer and Software Engineering at the University of Auckland, New Zealand. She is an acoustic phonetician, looking at speech spoken by human and machines, and has a specific focus on languages spoken in New Zealand. She has contributed to the field of sound change for over 20 years.

Winnie Huiheng Zeng is a PhD student in the Department of English at The Hong Kong Polytechnic University. Her research interests include corpus linguistics, critical metaphor analysis, language and gender, and political communication.

Acknowledgement

This research anthology is a fruit of the *Varieties of English in the Indo-Pacific* project, which was proposed by the Australian Academy of the Humanities to the Union Academique Internationale in 2015 and gained its endorsement. We are most grateful to both institutions for their support.

Pam Peters and Kate Burridge, Editors

CHAPTER I

Introduction: Exploring the Ecology of World Englishes in the Twenty-first Century: Language, Society and Culture

Pam Peters and Kate Burridge

1. PRELIMINARIES: AIMS AND THEMES OF THIS ANTHOLOGY

The papers in this collection are designed to connect two key issues at the forefront of research on World Englishes. One is language contact: how New Englishes develop in contact with the other languages used by multilingual speakers (Onysko 2016; Schreier and Hundt 2013); the other is the social context in which language contact takes place (Guy and Hinskens 2016). Both contact and context are embraced in linguistic ecology (Mühlhäusler 1996), and in current ecolinguistics (Fill and Penz 2017), where the focus is on languages in their social and individual environments.[1] Collectively, the papers will illustrate the interplay between the distinctive features of a regional English and its ecolinguistic environment, including contact with other languages in multilingual speech communities, and the social, cultural and political forces in the context that prompt varietal change and differentiation.

Ecological links between language, society and culture can be seen at different levels of language. The connections are most visible in the lexical features of World Englishes, in words borrowed from substrate or adstrate languages in their regional context. For example, content words such as *masala* in Indian English referring to a spice mix originated in the Persian-Arabic mix of languages in pre-British colonial India, while *veldt* for the elevated open grasslands of the South African environment comes from Afrikaans, the language of the first European colonial regime in the region.

Other kinds of lexical links to the context are there in lexicopragmatic borrowings, such as the words expressing social relations, especially kinship. These often large repertoires of terms represent the continuing strength of family ties in many postcolonial societies, in small islands of the Pacific or very large communities as in the Philippines. Conventional naming practices are maintained through loanwords or calques of them in Indian English (Kachru 1983) and in the use of compliments as preliminary greetings in Ugandan English.

At deeper levels of language construction, we find ecological connections in variations of modifications to morphosyntactic structures of English, especially in multilingual speech communities. The marking of the past tense with *–ed* is varied with zero suffix and also with the particle *finish* among children in Singapore, reflecting the mix of ethnicities in the community and the analytic and synthetic substrate languages they bring to it. We find local variants in the English pronoun systems in Norfolk Island English in unique first-person plural forms (*auwa, uklan*) and in Aboriginal English for both first- and second-person plural (*wefella, youmob*) – all of which reflect community perceptions of who are felt to belong and those outside it. These variants or additions to standard English morphosyntax are strongly connected with the linguistic and sociolinguistic ecology and illuminated by it. In spoken encounters, they can contribute to the construction of sociolinguistic identity.

With the subsystems of English syntax continually evolving, different trends and practices are emerging in World Englishes which seem to align with social and cultural differences in their respective contexts. There are marked differences in range of modals and semi-modals (from *will/shall* to *have to/be going to*) written into English editorials from different Chinese-speaking cities. These seem to correlate with the more and less authoritarian systems in their respective political contexts. They would also reflect sociolinguistic practices in each community: the extent to which English is used there in ordinary social interaction with its variable pragmatics. The changing proportions of English as a foreign language (EFL) and English as a second language (ESL) speakers is an important ongoing variable in different regional contexts. It has possible repercussions on English as a native language (ENL) usage in multilingual urban communities, for example New Zealand.

The ecological links between a particular regional variety and its context may of course be found at more than one level of language. There may be multiple linguistic features or variants that connect with the sociocultural makeup of the speech community, especially in outer- or expanding-circle Englishes. The ecolinguistic approach provides a coherent framework for analysing multiple parameters of variability in any regional English, rather than isolated linguistic variables. The goal of developing coherence in explaining a set of sociolinguistic variables can be achieved in several ways (Guy and Hinskens 2016). They include detailing the social, cultural and structural support for co-variation, as well as its perceptual salience. This invites a variety of methodologies for researching linguistic variation in context, using standard or customised corpora, sociolinguistic interviews and other empirical resources, and applying descriptive or inferential/multifactorial statistics as appropriate to the data.

2. LANGUAGE, CULTURE AND SOCIETY IN CROSS-CULTURAL ANALYSIS

This anthology begins with an invited paper in cultural linguistics by Edgar W. Schneider on 'Reflections of Cultures in Corpus Texts'[2] which is the stimulus and platform for the collection. He postulates three types of 'nexus' between language and culture inherent in individual regional varieties and offers a systematic way to analyse the different kinds of cultural contact or contextual influences to be seen in their linguistic constituents.

Nexus I: Cultural objects and practices: This recognises the nexus between language and culture in the words borrowed or rather introduced by speakers of regional varieties of English from other languages/cultures in their context – loanwords that are everyday expressions for referring to material objects and maintaining shared cultural practices. Some of these may be regarded as cultural keywords for their variety, capturing something of its essence and differentiating it from other varieties. Examples might be terms borrowed from indigenous languages for flora, foods, entertainment, dress.

Nexus II: Dimensions of cultures: This type of nexus focuses on attitudinal and behavioural parameters on which cultures round the world can vary, for example time orientation, power distance, expression of emotion. Associated with these sociological dimensions there are characteristic indicator terms, words or phrases, whose relative frequency provides a measure of the strength and salience of each dimension in a given variety. Their use can be performative, in that they project the attitudes and interactive behaviours that enact the mores of the speech community. Examples might be use of the first-person plural as an indicator of collectivism versus individualism or address terms such as *Sir/Madam* that mark high (or low) status in verbal encounters.

Nexus III: Structural schemas reflecting cultures: This nexus between language and culture involves the preference for particular syntactic structures (indicator constructions) that seem to represent a certain cultural orientation to agency or individuality. These pervasive orientations are expressed in quantitative differences in usage of the constructions they correlate with, their relative frequency of occurrence – or absence. An example might be the preference for passive structures that downplay the agency of the individual or for singular concord with collective nouns which underscores the unity of the whole – as indicators of more collectivistic cultures.

Schneider indicates that the three types of nexus between language and culture form a scale from concrete to abstract. The nexus 1 loanwords typically have tangible referents, or are instantiated in conventional verbal exchanges, whereas the nexus 2 indicator terms represent less tangible behaviours and attitudes expressed in extended discourse in the cultural context. The culturally preferred schematic structures – whether drawn, adapted or extended from the core English morphosyntax – are the most abstract manifestation of the culture and social orientations within it. He notes that the third category includes the more tenuous examples of the language–culture nexus, showing that linguistic rather than cultural explanations could be invoked to explain a particular regional preference.

Following Schneider's platform paper, the contributed papers form a set of case studies on the relationship between language, society and culture. In the following outline, they have been grouped into three sets roughly according to which of the three nexuses between language and culture each is most concerned with. The nexus groupings are not exclusive because several papers discuss data that relate to more than one of the nexuses. They also show how some language features (pronouns, for example) can be analysed from the point of view of the cultural dimension they support (nexus 2), or the way in which regional variants extend the syntactic paradigm as a schematic structure (nexus 3). The third and largest group of papers is ordered into two subparts, the first of which deals with morphosyntactic variations used in bi- or multilingual regional contexts, and the second with those in English-dominant contexts.

INTRODUCTION 5

NEXUS I PAPERS: CULTURAL OBJECTS AND PRACTICES (CHAPTERS 3–6)

This section is concerned with lexical borrowings from substrate or adstrate languages, which represent characteristic elements of the regional culture and its traditions. Rich admixtures of loanwords provide countless links with the cultural context for the communities of bi- and multilingual speakers where most World Englishes originate. The papers present data that include indigenous words, as well as those acquired through contact with earlier colonial powers in continuing usage by the speech community. The paper on South African English presents research on the wide range of Afrikaans words taken in from that earlier colonial phase, and some from Setswana. Philippine English similarly contains a variety of loanwords from Tagalog and other indigenous languages, as well as indigenised forms of Spanish loanwords that reflect the profound impact of Spanish colonialism on Philippine culture and society up to 1898. Twenty-first century Indian English includes words in contemporary semantic fields which are traceable to Persian and Arabic, again showing the durability of cultural traditions established under earlier colonial regimes. Some borrowings found in Ugandan English come from indigenous languages, functioning alongside those continuing from British colonial rule.

Bertus van Rooy's study 'Reflections of Afrikaans in the English Short Stories of Herman Charles Bosman' investigates linguistic contact between English and Afrikaans in South African literary writing. An electronic corpus of Bosman's short stories written between 1930 and 1950 shows how Bosman uses the medium of English to create Afrikaans characters in the Afrikaans cultural setting. His use of Afrikaans elements is deemed by literary critics to be more natural – less contrived – than others writing in the same genre and thus a fair reflection of the contact between Afrikaans and English in South African English. Afrikaans elements are visible in Bosman's use of Afrikaans proper names for different characters and hundreds of common nouns: words relating to local institutions, traditions and practices, as well as the social, natural and built environment. Other kinds of language–culture connections can be seen in Bosman's frequent use of Afrikaans terms of address in dialogues between characters and some subtle elements of his lexicogrammar and syntax which seem to calque underlying structures in Afrikaans.

Loy Lising's paper '*Susmaryosep!* Lexical Evidence of Cultural Influence in Philippine English' uses data from the ICE-Philippine corpus of English, focusing on indigenous words in the 13 written text types as established elements of contemporary Philippine English. She uses the Myers-Scotton (2006) classification of lexical borrowing into 'cultural' and 'core' borrowings to analyse the 400 tokens into a set of semantic categories that reflect material elements of the Philippine environment, culture, social relationships and traditions. The cultural borrowings for which there are no English equivalents far outnumber the core borrowings (which provide indigenous alternatives to available English words). Her examples of core borrowings show how they typically carry particular contextual connotations in the Philippine speech community which the English equivalents lack. Apart from the cultural and core borrowings in the ICE corpus data, Lising found a number of neologisms formed out of English or English+Tagalog elements – striking examples of how multilingual resources in the context are used to create new words that link Philippine English with the contemporary culture.

Pam Peters's paper on 'Cultural Keywords in Indian English' presents a diachronic approach to identifying cultural keywords, in a combination of historical lexicography and 21st century data from the GloWbE corpus. She focuses on Arabic and Persian words with long histories of use from the Mughal regime (approximately 1600–1800) which managed both India and Pakistan through a Hindi-Urdu contact language (Hindustani). It was also used under the British Raj until the partition of India in 1947. A sample of the long-lived Persian and Arabic words show ongoing language–culture connections in references to monetary and legal institutions, as well as traditional foods, costume and entertainment. But other colonial words designating once important roles in handling money and managing large households are now degraded or neutralised in proper names. Traditional terms of reference and address from Arabic are still widely used in online Indian English, to affirm shared social and cultural relationships; and though their connotations of respect or friendship are eroded, they continue to index such values in changing social contexts.

'Lexicopragmatics between Cultural Heritage and Exonormative Second Language Acquisition: Address Terms, Greetings and Discourse Markers in Ugandan English' by Christiane Meierkord and Bebwa Isingoma details the mix of colonial and indigenous elements in different kinds of interpersonal and discourse markers, in the ICE-Uganda corpus and the Web-UG corpus compiled from websites and blogs. Despite the elaborate tradition of greetings in African cultures, those they found in the two Uganda corpora were applications of conventional English 'Welcome'. A few indigenous examples of address terms were used, in Web-UG and written data from ICE, as signs of language contact in the multilingual speech community. The best evidence was found in a set of nine indigenous discourse markers in the internet data and spoken ICE data, with various interpersonal functions, in expressing individual attitudes (embedding surprise or scepticism in the information expressed), or else in criticising or eliciting empathy from listeners or readers. They are important evidence from east Africa of the way non-English discourse markers can be taken up into indigenised Englishes without drawing attention to themselves.

NEXUS II PAPERS: DIMENSIONS OF CULTURES (CHAPTERS 7–9)

The second type of language–culture nexus focuses on sociocultural parameters on which speech communities round the world are found to vary, such as their orientation to time, management of differences in power and status, connectedness with family or their expression of emotion. These sociological dimensions are expressed through characteristic indicator terms, whose relative frequency provides a measure of the strength and salience of each dimension in a given variety. The use of kinship terminology varies across time and space in different speech communities in response to different social structures and cultural values. These are the focus of the first two papers from small island communities in the Indian and western Pacific Oceans, while the third uses the terms used in metaphorical constructions of democracy in three different places in the Sinosphere, which seem to characterise their different political values and systems.

'Cultural Relations? Kinship Terminology in Three Islands in the Northern Pacific', authored by Sara Lynch, Eva Kuske and Dominique B. Hess, presents comparative data on the use of English family terminology on Kosrae, Saipan and Guam, based on a total of around 930,000 words of extended sociolinguistic interviews. The islands are unique in their cultural histories and social values, relatively more traditional in Kosrae in the west and more Westernised in Guam on the eastern side. The research focuses on familial relationships, analysed and compared with the relative frequencies of a set of 15 terms for family members. They included the surprisingly high frequency of references to grandparents and grandchildren in Guam (in comparison with those from Saipan and Kosrae) – despite its greater Westernisation. On the other hand, references to adoption were far more frequent in Kosrae than either Guam or Saipan, perhaps because it is the least urbanised of the three islands and children are shared because of the tendency for adults to go overseas to find work.

Hannah Hedegard's 'Somewhere between Australia and Malaysia and "I" and "we": Verbalising Culture on the Cocos (Keeling) Islands' presents a sociolinguistic study on the cultural dimension of collectivism in the indigenous community of the Cocos Islands between Australia and Malaysia, focusing on the use of *I* and *we*, along with other kinship and collectivist terms. Her corpus of 55 hours (around 320,000 words) of speech from 60 Cocos Malay speakers includes individuals in three age brackets corresponding to three generations and equal numbers of males and females. Compared with ICE data from other World Englishes, Cocos islanders make far more use of kinship terms such as *uncle*, *aunt*, *brother*, *cousin* than notionally collectivist cultures such as India. But among the islanders, the ratio of *I* to *we* was strongly stratified with the oldest islanders making far more use of *we* than *I*. The results for the use of collectivist terms such as *community*, *give*, *help* were similarly graded from older to younger islanders. The data suggests that a generational shift toward a more individualistic culture may be underway.

'Expressing Concepts Metaphorically in English Editorials in the Sinosphere' is the focus of research by Kathleen Ahrens and Winnie Huiheng Zeng. Their investigation of the metaphors relating to *democracy* is based on a corpus of early 21st century newspaper and magazine editorials from Hong Kong, Beijing and Taipei. They find marked differences in how and how often *democracy* is metaphorised in each city. The word is more frequently metaphorised in Beijing editorials than in either Hong Kong or Taipei, both of which use it literally more often. There are also differences in the metaphorical source domains used for *democracy*, in that Hong Kong writers made significantly more use of BUILDING while Taipei writers made it a JOURNEY. The metaphor of COMPETITION was used by writers in all three cities, but interestingly Beijing writers made more use of it than the other two. These different source domains for metaphorising *democracy* work rather like Schneider's indexical terms, reflecting different political orientations to the concept in three Chinese contexts.

INTRODUCTION 9

NEXUS III PAPERS: STRUCTURAL SCHEMAS REFLECTING CULTURES (CHAPTERS 10–17)

A third type of language–culture nexus can be found in formal and structural variants that seem to align with or represent cultural orientations (such as agency or individuality) and to underscore or downplay them. These pervasive preferences are expressed in quantitative differences in the selection of the morphosyntactic structures they correlate with. The eight case studies in this bracket in fact suggest two subsets to be recognised within the category:

- Nexus III.1 (Chapters 10–14) are papers that research variable use or adaptation of common English morphosyntactic structures, by bi- or multilingual (ESL and EFL) speakers in multilingual contexts. Their research focuses on variable, preferential or idiosyncratic use of elements of common grammatical systems, such as verb tense forms used in Singapore English, the ratio of nouns to verbs used across Asian varieties of English, the range of modal verbs in the Sinosphere, or pronoun usage in the South Pacific Islands and Australian Aboriginal English.
- Nexus III.2 (Chapters 15–17) are papers where typically monolingual speakers in English-dominant contexts develop new or marked patterns of usage within the common ENL structures. This can be demonstrated at the macro level with multidimensional diachronic analysis of lexicogrammatical variables in Australian and New Zealand Hansard records, or in microanalysis of informal variants in the Australian negation system, or the variable pronunciations of the article in New Zealand English.

Sarah Buschfeld's paper on 'L1 Singapore English: The Influence of Ethnicity and Input' focuses on the spoken English of children aged from 2 to 12 years from different ethnic backgrounds, based on sociolinguistic interviews. In her phonological data on vowel lengths, she found considerable variability in individual children, in a mix of longer and shorter realisations of the same vowel by the same child, even in successive utterances. Variable vowel lengths and variable rhoticity suggested inputs from both American and British English. There was no age-graded effect in their average vowel lengths. In morphosyntax, their realisations of the past tense and use of subject pronouns showed inputs from both colloquial and standard varieties of Singapore English and correlated with their ethnic affiliations with the Chinese and Indian communities. The morphological data suggest possible influences from substrate languages including Cantonese and Tamil. This research provides insights into the variability of children's language, reflecting the heterogeneity of the inputs in the Singapore speech community and the socio-ethnic matrix of the new variety.

'Across Three Kachruvian Circles with Two Parts-of-speech: Nouns and Verbs in ENL, ESL and EFL Varieties', by Tobias Bernaisch and Sandra Götz, is a statistical study of the grammatical properties of the English used by EFL and ESL speakers in Hong Kong, the Philippines and Singapore. Their data for ESL speakers comes from the relevant ICE corpora, and for EFL speakers in the International Corpus Network of Asian Learners of English. The study focuses on the ratio of words tagged as nouns or verbs in spoken and written data from the two speaker types in the three regions in the two corpora. It finds some overall regional differences in their linguistic cultures in so far as Hong Kong English tended to be more nominal in style and Philippine English more verbal. Yet the ratio of nouns to verbs used by ESL and EFL speakers was similar in all three regions. The research shows the complex interrelationships between region, medium and learner status, when based on abstract linguistic categories such as major word classes.

'Modality, Rhetoric and Regionality in English Editorials in the Sinosphere', by Pam Peters, Tobias Bernaisch and Kathleen Ahrens, examines the range of modal verbs in a corpus of newspaper editorials from 2016, published in Hong Kong, Beijing and Taipei. The paper uses inferential statistics to analyse the distributions of canonical modals and semi-modals, especially those with differing predictive force (*will*, *would*, *going to*). The study compares their frequency of use by writers in each city, and how they position themselves as they discuss future sociopolitical plans and prospects. The data show significantly different distributions for the predictive verbs in the three regions, with disproportionate use of *will* in the Beijing editorials and more equal use of *would* alongside it in Hong Kong and Taiwan editorials. Their combination of *will* and *would* provides flexibility in discussing the future and more nuanced expression of authority than in Beijing. The distribution of the predictive modals in the three Chinese states seems to reflect their different political and cultural contexts.

In 'Where Grammar Meets Culture: Pronominal Systems in Australasia and the South Pacific Revisited', Kate Burridge and Carolin Biewer examine the pronoun systems used in varieties of English in

Australia and South Pacific territories, drawing on fieldwork studies in the region. Although nonstandard pronominal forms are attested around the anglophone world (and thus angloversals), those found in this southern hemisphere region for the first-person plural are special to it (and thus areoversals). In Norf'k (Norfolk Island English), the pronouns *auwa/uklan* are used to affirm insider status in the island community and exclude outsiders; the dual inclusive plural form *hemi/himii*, meaning 'the two of us', again makes a special distinction in the pronoun system. Elsewhere – in the Cook Islands – the use of *we all* serves to indicate a collectivity (for example, that of a family) contrasting with the unmarked *we*, used to refer to the larger island community. These special first-person plural pronouns thus represent fine-grained linguistic constructions of social solidarity within these island cultures. Even where pronoun uses look similar to ENL, local functions reveal regional differences fostered by the local sociocultural context.

Ian G. Malcolm's paper 'Decolonisation and Neo-colonialism in Aboriginal Education' analyses the deconstruction of Aboriginal culture and Indigenous languages under colonial administration. As he describes it, Aboriginal Australians have faced dispossession of their lands and been subjected to practices, laws and language that contradict their culture. Legal and educational systems imposed by the dominant culture have worked to maintain colonial domination, that is, neo-colonialism. Yet these speakers have shown their resistance to colonialism, by adapting the English language to make it express an Aboriginal rather than a colonial worldview and affirming its nexus with their culture. He presents five elements of this reconceptualisation in the changed lexical and grammatical elements of Aboriginal English. New words for identifying themselves and their group identities are elements in affirming the decolonisation of Indigenous people. The paper argues that a bicultural approach to education is needed to counter neo-colonialism, affirm Indigenous culture and languages where possible, and otherwise develop a bidialectal approach using Aboriginal and Australian English in schools.

'Modal and Semi-modal Verbs of Obligation in the Australian, New Zealand and British Hansards, 1901–2015', by Adam Smith, Minna Korhonen, Haidee Kotze and Bertus van Rooy, contributes a longitudinal study of changes in the language of parliamentary discourse, focusing on the modals and semi-modals of obligation: *must*, *should*, *need to*, *have to*. The researchers use a large diachronic corpus of material from the three regional Hansards to compare the profiles of modal usage at five key points from the early 20th to 21st century. They find overall declining frequencies for *must, should* and *have to* in all three Hansards, but also remarkably high levels and peaks in Australian and New Zealand usage when the subject of the verb is *we* or *the Government*. Some of these co-occur with key points in national history, suggesting waves of collective sentiment in parliamentary rhetoric and setting national priorities. Other contextual factors – such as changing editorial conventions, and newer parliamentary practices in presenting speeches and broadcasting debates – may also have modulated the expression of obligation in individual Hansards over time.

'Privileging Informality: Cultural Influences on the Structural Patterning of Australian English' is Isabelle Burke and Kate Burridge's study of the evolution of taboo negators in current Australian English. They give evidence that phrases like *damn/bugger/fuck all* ('X-all') began life with an inherently negative value and do not represent an advanced stage in the 'Jespersen cycle' of negator renewal (Jespersen 1917). Their data comes from the University of Western Australia corpus of spoken Australian English, coupled with survey data on the acceptability of 'X-all' with and without an explicitly negated verb. The survey respondents rated the version without an explicit negator very positively, but dismissed the version with a negator as ungrammatical, commenting that the combination of *bugger all* with an explicit negator was 'double negation', and therefore unacceptable. While there is irony in their application of a formal English rule to informal grammar, they support the analysis of 'X-all' as a fully fledged marker of negation ('not'). The authors argue that this development was assisted by social and cultural pressures – the more informal character of Australian culture and its greater willingness to embrace colloquial styles.

'The Auckland Voices Project: Language Change in a Changing City', by Miriam Meyerhoff, Elaine Ballard, Helen Charters, Alexandra Birchfield and Catherine I. Watson, examines the impact of migration on Auckland English, focusing on the variable realisation of the definite article in New Zealand's largest and most multicultural city. Their research is based on conversational data from 70 people, male and female, younger and older, from three ethnographically distinct areas of the city. Their pronunciation of *the* was tested before a following vowel, in stressed or non-stressed NPs, to see if the standard [ði] was used rather than [ðə]. Multivariate analysis showed that [ə] is becoming more typical before vowel-initial NPs in all three areas of Auckland, even more so in South Auckland, which has been most ethnically diverse for the longest. Evidence also suggests [ə] is spreading rapidly among younger speakers in the other two communities. These pronunciation changes are thus associated with migration and higher levels of multilingualism in the community and support the claim that high levels of diversity in communities favour the emergence of new and distinct regional varieties.

3. A SYNOPSIS

The regional research data presented in all these papers have brought to light other kinds of language–culture connections than the three nexuses discussed in Schneider's original platform paper. While the three nexuses are all identified in synchronic data, some of the papers introduce a diachronic dimension for discussion, using lexicographic or generational data. They reflect cultural changes in the context and in the composition of the speech community. With social and ethnic changes come new kinds of linguistic variants not necessarily connected with the existing substrate or adstrate languages. Their impact can be seen in novel variants which may or may not disappear in the levelling process that takes place in the endonormativity of the variety. These dynamic processes are beyond the scope of this volume, but there are insights into them in the context of English in India, Singapore, Micronesia, Australia and New Zealand.

The papers in this collection have embraced the range of postcolonial English speakers from ENL to ESL and EFL, since all three types need now to be considered in English-using communities such as South Africa, India, Hong Kong and Singapore. The interplay between the EFL and ESL speaker types can be seen in the greater heterogeneity in papers on grammatical features of English in Singapore, Hong Kong, the Philippines and Taiwan. In the South Pacific and in Aboriginal Australia the interplay of speaker types helps to generate remarkable innovations in the schematic structures of English. Even in predominantly ENL communities in Australia and New Zealand, elements of standard grammar show local patterns of preference and innovation that reflect aspects of the social or multicultural context.

Broad differences among the World Englishes represented in this collection can be linked to the levels of multilingualism in the context and the types of language–culture nexus most visible. Those embedded in highly multilingual contexts, such as South Africa, Uganda, India and the Philippines, offer a wealth of lexical and lexicopragmatic innovations, compared with those where English is used in a stable bilingual or monolingual English-speaking community with more structured variants of the standard language. Although this is an artefact of the collection itself, it suggests other kinds of language–culture–society nexuses for further research. The diversity of World Englishes reflects their unique ecologies, whether they are in continuous contact with other languages through bi- and multilingual speakers or reflecting ongoing social trends in monolingual English-speaking communities.

NOTES

1. Compare the use of 'ecolinguistics' to refer to the concern with the language of environmental science, an entirely different field, as presented in Fill and Penz's *Routledge Handbook of Ecolinguistics* (2017).
2. This paper builds on some of the same data from an earlier paper (Schneider 2018) but it has been adapted to support the geographical range of World Englishes from the Indo-Pacific region discussed by other contributors to this volume.

REFERENCES

Fill, A. and Penz, H. (Eds.). (2017). *The Routledge handbook of ecolinguistics*. Routledge.

Guy, G. and Hinskens, F. (Eds.). (2016). Coherence, covariation, and bricolage [Special issue]. *Lingua, 172–173*, 1–146.

Jespersen, O. (1917). *Negation in English and other languages* (2nd ed.). Munksgaard.

Kachru, B. (1983). *The Indianization of English: The English language in India*. Oxford University Press.

Mühlhäusler, P. (1996). *Linguistic ecology: Language change and linguistic imperialism in the Pacific region*. Routledge.

Myers-Scotton, C. (2006). *Multiple voices: An introduction to bilingualism*. Blackwell.

Onysko, A. (Ed.). (2016). Modeling World Englishes from the perspective of language contact. *World Englishes, 35*(2), 196–220.

Schneider, E. W. (2018). Reflections of culture in corpus texts. *ICAME Journal, 42*, 25–60.

Schreier, D. and Hundt, M. (Eds.). (2013). *English as a contact language*. Cambridge University Press.

CHAPTER 2

Platform Paper: Reflections of Cultures in Corpus Texts: Focus on the Indo-Pacific Region

Edgar W. Schneider

1. INTRODUCTION: LINGUISTIC MANIFESTATIONS OF CULTURES

The relationship between language and culture seems an interesting but a difficult one. Languages operate in cultures and are the main means of manifesting and expressing them, so very obviously there must be some sort of an intrinsic relation. But it seems difficult to grasp, since 'culture' is a rather versatile, perhaps fuzzy notion that may relate to different objects, concepts and practices, while linguistics tends to focus more on tangible, relatively precisely defined units (such as phonemes, clauses or constructions). An increasing number of publications and activities over the recent past have somehow discussed the interface between culture and language, but on closer inspection much of this remains fairly abstract and theory-oriented, not primarily interested in looking into language forms and structures as such. The present paper sets out to systematise the question of the relationship between these two domains and to pin it down empirically by asking which observable formal representations of 'culture' in linguistic forms and structures exist and how they can be detected, employing a modern corpus-linguistic methodology.

The basic question for the relationship between cultures and language can of course be asked in very general terms, but here it will be applied and confined to the context of World Englishes, the newly grown stable varieties that colonial and postcolonial history have produced and which have been investigated and theoretically accounted for by a vigorous young subdiscipline of English linguistics (Schneider 2007, 2011;

Nelson et al. 2019; Kirkpatrick in press; Hundt et al. 2020). I investigate data from the International Corpus of English (ICE) project (see Section 3) and focus specifically on nations in the Indo-Pacific region, namely New Zealand (NZ), Hong Kong, Singapore and India.

The following section will discuss the notion of culture and some of its different meanings and manifestations and it will then briefly summarise earlier research on language and culture, with a special eye on studies of language forms. Most importantly, I will introduce, contextualise and explain the three main 'nexuses', intrinsic connections, between language forms and cultures which will then, after a brief survey of the methodology employed, constitute the backbone of the data analysis and discussion – namely, cultural objects, dimensions of cross-cultural analysis and syntactic constructions. They represent increasingly abstract ties, cultural representations in linguistic forms. It will be shown, in conclusion, that there is a correlation between this degree of abstractness and the strength of manifestations of cultures in language.[1]

2. BACKGROUND: LANGUAGE AND CULTURE – AND THE NEXUSES BETWEEN THEM

Cultural studies as a humanities discipline has grown to become a successful and influential scholarly branch over the last few decades (Assmann 2012). Its very object seems ill defined to some extent; however, the notion of culture itself is characterised by a high degree of fuzziness, versatility and underspecified semantics (Moran 2001; Hua 2013: ch. 11). It comprises aspects of time and space (relating it to disciplines such as history and geography), identity and memory, gender and social roles (that is, sociology, anthropology and psychology), arts and the media, and many more approaches and facets. Minkov (2013: 2, 9) explicitly states that 'culturology' encompasses a range of varying conceptualisations. Approaches and definitions map onto a cline from relatively concrete to highly abstract modes of understanding the notion. At the concrete end, there is a straightforwardly material 'culture-as-content approach' which looks into objects, artefacts, foods, customs, clothing, social hierarchies and so on (Hua 2013: 4) – a rather encyclopaedic, concrete way of understanding the notion. Relatively more intermediate is an understanding of sociopsychological, conventionalised and more abstract elements of culture (Minkov 2013: 38–60; Hua 2013: 86–7; cf. Moran 2001: 24–5), including meanings, rituals, taboos, institutions, values, norms, beliefs, attitudes, behaviours and the like. At the abstract end, culture has been defined as 'the collective programming of the mind that distinguishes the members of one group or category of people from another' (Hofstede 2001: 9). Broadly, these levels of understanding 'culture' relate to the three 'nexuses' to linguistic manifestations to be discussed in a moment: terms and objects, dimensions, and schematic constructions, respectively.

The relationship between culture(s) and language(s) has been the topic of some discussion in linguistics (not too much, though). To my mind, however, these discussions have tended to remain on a fairly abstract, generic or theoretical level. Reflections of cultures are commonly looked for and identified in cognition systems and pragmatic conventions but rarely in linguistic forms.

One of the oldest concepts that can be seen in this light is the theory of 'linguistic relativity', widely known also as the 'Sapir–Whorf hypothesis' after its main early proponents, which argues that the structure of a language shapes patterns of cognition in the community of speakers of that language (cf. Everett 2005: 623; Salzmann et al. 2012: 225–56; Hua 2013: 173–6; Leavitt 2015; Sharifian 2017: 111–22). It has been debated widely and in various formats. A strong version of 'linguistic determinism' held that linguistic structures actually firmly determine and constrain possible frames of thought in a community; this is no longer seriously assumed today. In contrast, the weak version of 'linguistic relativity', which suggests that language influences cognitive categories, is still under investigation. It seems to be valid in certain semantic domains, though only weakly. It seems obvious that there is some sort of an interrelationship between language and cognition, but it is not monocausal (and rather a chicken-and-egg type of problem) and clearly quite fuzzy. The Sapir–Whorf theory has triggered many debates which are essentially still ongoing and related to cognitive linguistics, but no real consensus has been reached so far.

Given that behavioural conventions in societies and modes of thinking and interaction are known to vary substantially across nations and cultures, it is not surprising that a largely applied practically oriented branch of this approach has emerged. Studies of 'intercultural communication' have investigated and describe mainly conversational routines and politeness issues, notably for business encounters (for example, Hua 2013). In practical terms, then, this approach results in the teaching of intercultural skills as an important component of teaching foreign languages in general (Byram 1997; Byram et al. 2001).

The interface between culture and language is the focus of a young branch known as 'cultural linguistics'. It features in an outline monograph (Sharifian 2017), a handbook (Sharifian 2015), an *International Journal of Language and Culture* (founded in 2016) and a growing body of other publications. Core concepts and approaches of this branch include 'cultural cognition' and its linguistic manifestations via 'cultural conceptualizations' (Sharifian 2011), 'cultural key words' (Hua 2013: 180–1; Levisen and Waters 2017), schemas, 'conceptual metaphors' (Wolf and Polzenhagen 2009), culture-specific conceptualisations and intercultural pragmatics, or embodiment. Overall, however, analyses in this domain remain fairly abstract, mostly explaining concepts and notions peculiar to specific cultures, often as based on specific key words. I find hardly any traces of a more solidly grounded empirical approach, as is typical of structural analyses in corpus linguistics. For instance, Sharifian (2017: 47) has a one-paragraph section on 'corpus-based analysis', in which a single, programmatic paper (Jensen 2017) is summarised. In sum, then, I do not think cultural linguistics in its current shape is ready to answer the question for possible linguistic (that is, formal) manifestations of cultures comprehensively, beyond abstract concepts such as cultural cognition, conceptualisations and key words (which are valuable in themselves, of course).

Serious attempts at connecting linguistic forms and structures with possible cultural roots have remained rare so far. In World Englishes research in particular a small number of scholars have empirically investigated structural preferences as reflections of cultural differences; some of these will be outlined in Section 4.3. For example, Olavarría de Ersson and Shaw (2003) showed that Indian English prefers certain structures over others and interpreted this as motivated by cultural differences when compared with Britain and British English; and Mukherjee and Bernaisch (2015) investigated 'linguistic acculturation' by filtering out certain noun–verb co-occurrence relationships in South Asian Englishes employing statistical techniques.

In the present paper, connections ('nexuses') between cultures and language forms will be sought for and established on three different increasingly abstract levels, in line with the fundamental definitions of 'culture' referred to above.

The first, most straightforward nexus analyses cultural terms and objects referred to in texts from specific regions, those directly evident manifestations of cultures, in line with 'naive' assumptions of what constitutes a culture. Hua (2013: 4) calls this the 'culture-as-content approach', which highlights the 'four Fs', that is, 'food, fairs, folklore, facts': typical objects and artefacts; food and clothes; social roles, values and the like. In language contact settings, and consequently in many localised varieties of English, such terms are typically not translated but rather borrowed from indigenous languages to denote the objects in question.

The second nexus investigates reflections of 'dimensions of cultures' as posited in the sociopsychological discipline of 'cross-cultural analysis'. The central idea of this approach is that differences between cultures can be captured along specific 'dimensions', which reflect consistent thematically ordered attitudes and values in a society. Results of such studies report broad regional sociocultural tendencies, often as scales or index values of a dimension relative to a given society. A wide range of specific dimensions have been suggested and assessed across cultures, most importantly the one distinguishing individualist versus collectivist cultures (compare Section 4.2). I propose they find their linguistic manifestations through select 'indicator terms'.

The third, relatively most abstract nexus involves the question of whether cultures may also have an impact upon structural choices, that is, whether culturally based principles may motivate one construction more than a semantically equivalent other one. Obviously, this is more difficult to pin down and needs to be 'translated' into specific structural hypotheses which lend themselves to empirical testing. In other words, it is necessary to find or define 'indicator constructions' which are functionally equivalent, can be accounted for as motivated by varying cultural perspectives and can be directly quantified and compared.

3. METHODOLOGY

The methodological task at hand, then, consists of identifying and documenting correlations between cultural spaces and orientations on the one hand and linguistic forms which are defined as manifestations of cultures on the other. The latter have to be searched for in representative and comparable bodies of text, that is, systematically compiled electronic corpora. Both components, the cultural categories and the language forms regarded as representing them, need to be identified and decided on beforehand; I have done that based on earlier writings on the subject and some hypothesising of my own. Ideally, the correlations should be quantitatively assessed, that is, tested for statistical significance.

For cultures, the most evident reference domains are spaces of whatever magnitude. For practical reasons, the units in question are typically nation states, since for these it is relatively easiest to obtain data such as statistics, shared discourses or, as in the present case, text collections like the corpora representing English as used in NZ, Hong Kong, Singapore or India. National coherence, shared discourse spaces such as media or politics and processes of nation building forge fairly homogeneous mindsets and attitudes, that is, components of cultures. In addition, there are entities which may be significantly larger, shaped by geographical extension and proximity (so we may consider 'Asian' or 'Caribbean' cultures), by philosophical or religious formative influences (for example, Confucian, Muslim or Judeo-Christian cultures), and more.

In language, the correlates of culture need to be defined and identified. I propose that for cultural objects they can be identified fairly straightforwardly through the terms denoting them, while for the more abstract nexuses there is a need to consider, select and define indicator terms and indicator constructions which are supposed to reflect cultural orientations indirectly. These will be explained in greater detail in the respective sections.

Like many other comparative studies of World Englishes, this investigation mainly employs selected components of the International Corpus of English (ICE) project. ICE was initiated in the 1990s (Greenbaum 1996); its goal is the compilation of a large number of comparable electronic text collections representative of different national varieties of English, all designed equally in terms of size and text type composition. ICE corpora represent both speech and writing as well as various genres and styles, and the proportion of 60 per cent of spoken texts guarantees a strong presence of localised usage (since speaking is less strongly subject to the normative tendencies found in writing). Currently about a dozen corpora are available; more are being compiled (Hundt et al. 2019). For the present context, the focus on VEIP, I have chosen five ICE corpora, representing English as used in these countries, as typical of major cultural orientations: Great Britain (GB) (ICE-GB), representing a Western culture and also the baseline input variety in most postcolonial contexts; NZ (ICE-NZ), a nation in which the British culture has been re-rooted in a Pacific setting; and Hong Kong (ICE-HK), Singapore (ICE-Sing) and India (ICE-Ind) as three important Asian cultures, which may be taken to share an Asian collectivist orientation but also vary along important parameters: Singapore and Hong Kong represent two Chinese-dominated, Buddhist-influenced cultures, which have undergone varying degrees of modernisation and Westernisation; and India is a more conservative, non-Confucian, Hindu country.

Lexical search terms were mostly lemmatised; that is, I searched for inflectional variants of nouns and verbs as well, and sometimes (indicated in the specific instances below) I also pooled derivation forms and cognates belonging to different word classes but denoting the same concept (for example, *Jain/Jainism*; *promiscuous/promiscuity*). Frequencies were counted in AntConc (Anthony 2014), using the WordList and Concordance tools (the latter when context mattered for disambiguation or excluding unwanted instances). As far as was reasonably possible, non-target homograph forms were excluded, for example when homonyms (unwanted formally identical items) were returned or when polysemic uses (alternative meanings) different from the target concept came up. Hence, idiosyncratic inclusion or exclusion decisions in specific instances may entail a small fringe of uncertainty as to the precision of the figures reported, but on the whole the frequency relations are robust.

Frequency data and comparisons ideally call for statistical assessment, since we would like to know if distributions observed are likely to be products of chance (the random variability that we always find in natural systems) or of some causal relationship. In the present study, token frequencies of indicator terms in each of the three Asian corpora were statistically assessed by comparing them with data from British English, the parent variety representing Western (or British) culture. Fisher's Exact test (suitable for small token numbers), with Bonferroni correction and automatic adjustment of benchmark p values when several pairwise comparisons are conducted (Gries 2008: 243–4), was employed to compare token frequencies of indicator terms relative to their non-occurrences in each Asian corpus as opposed to the corresponding relationship in ICE-GB.[2] In the results tables, I indicate active levels in the conventional fashion by asterisks: $p < .001 = ***$; $p <. 01 = **$; and $p < .05 = *$.

4. NEXUSES BETWEEN LANGUAGE AND CULTURE

In this section, data from three different layers of analysis which potentially reflect cultural differences in language forms are discussed, ranging across increasingly abstract notions of culture and modes of linguistic expression.

4.1 Nexus 1: Cultural Objects and Practices

The first, most straightforward and obvious layer of manifestation of cultures are localised terms and objects, in line with a material 'culture-as-content' approach, as defined in Section 2. Cultural objects and customs (for example, artefacts, clothes, food, social roles, rituals and so on) can obviously be readily identified by the terms denoting them, typically words borrowed from indigenous languages. I have identified, compiled and selected such terms from both linguistic publications (for example, Schneider 2007) and other sources, including websites, on local cultures. Since such objects are embedded in local practice and language, it is hypothesised that these terms are largely restricted to their respective regions (and regional corpora), although the question is whether some such words for regionally distinctive objects have come to be known internationally and thus used more widely.

Table 2.1 Hong Kong cultural terms

Words searched for in ICE corpora	GB	NZ	Hong Kong	Singapore	India
dim sum 'Cantonese dish'	0	0	10*	0	0
triad 'organised crime syndicate'	0	0	13**	7	0
dragon boat 'HK watercraft'	0	0	3	1	0
red packet 'monetary gift'	0	0	1	5	0
Canto(-)pop 'Cantonese popular music'	0	0	4	0	0
mahjong 'Chinese game'	1	1	42**	3	0

* = $p < .05$; ** = $p < .01$; and *** = $p < .001$.

Table 2.1 shows the distribution of some terms associated with Hong Kong culture. Two of them (*dim sum* and *Cantopop*) are unique to Hong Kong in the ICE evidence; three (*dim sum, triad, mahjong*) occur statistically significantly more frequently than in ICE-GB. Shared Chinese cultural roots are reflected in occurrences of some terms in Singapore as well (*triad, dragon boat, mahjong* and, even more frequently, *red packet*). India shares none of these terms and GB only one token of *mahjong*, so local and Chinese culture are strong determinants of these items. A few more terms (*spirit money* 'bank notes on incense paper for offerings', *lucky money* 'monetary gift' and *mooncake* 'Chinese bakery product') were searched for but not found at all.

Table 2.2 Singapore cultural terms

Words searched for in ICE corpora	GB	NZ	Hong Kong	Singapore	India
hawker center/-re 'street food court'	0	0	0	11*	0
food court	0	0	0	1	0
Peranakan/s 'Chinese-Malay ethnicity'	0	0	0	16***	0
Singlish	0	0	0	34***	0
kiasu/ism 'strongly competitive'	0	0	0	42***	0
shiok 'delightful'	0	0	0	26***	0

* = $p < .05$; ** = $p < .01$; and *** = $p < .001$.

Interestingly enough, all the Singaporean cultural terms listed in Table 2.2 are unique to that nation state and do not appear in ICE texts elsewhere; in almost all instances the frequency differences are statistically significant.

Table 2.3 Indian cultural terms

Words searched for in ICE corpora	GB	NZ	Hong Kong	Singapore	India
namaste 'a greeting'	0	0	0	0	1
Jain/ism 'type of religion'	2	0	0	0	15*
lakh 'one hundred thousand'	0	0	0	0	66**
tikka 'type of food'	0	0	0	0	5
chutney/s 'type of sauce'	0	1	0	1	9*
ayurveda 'system of medicine'	0	0	0	0	3
sari 'female garment'	0	2	0	3	5
mughal/s 'emperor'	0	0	0	0	3

* = $p < .05$; ** = $p < .01$; and *** = $p < .001$.

Table 2.3 shows eight cultural terms typical of India (two more, *dhoti* and *lunghi*, were not found in the corpora). The most culturally distinctive one is *lakh*; two more statistically significantly distributed ones (which occasionally occur elsewhere as well, however) include *Jain* and *chutney*. Similarly, the terms *namaste*, *tikka*, *ayurveda* and *mughal* show corpus documentation only in India, though with small token numbers there too. *Sari* occurs in Singapore (where there is also an Indian community) and NZ as well.

Table 2.4 New Zealand cultural terms

Words searched for in ICE corpora	GB	NZ	Hong Kong	Singapore	India
kiwi 'kind of bird'	0	129***	4	1	0
kauri 'kind of tree'	0	16**	0	0	0
kea 'kind of bird'	0	5	0	0	0
tuatara/s 'kind of reptile'	0	5	0	0	0
waka 'canoe'	0	24**	0	0	0
whare 'house'	0	26	0	0	0
hangi 'pit oven'	0	9	0	0	0
mana 'prestige, standing'	0	39**	0	0	0
hongi 'traditional greeting'	0	1	0	0	0
pakeha 'person of European descent'	0	183***	0	0	0
all black/s 'New Zealand's rugby team'	0	120***	0	0	0

$* = p < .05$; $** = p < .01$; and $*** = p < .001$.

Cultural terms characteristic of NZ, 11 of which are displayed in Table 2.4, are mostly (except for the last one) Māori in origin, and almost exclusively (except for a small number of tokens of *kiwi*) found there only. In more than half of all instances the distribution is also statistically significant (as opposed to GB). The table shows how strongly NZ has embraced Māori culture as part of its national heritage.

Overall, the distributions observed in this section are extremely straightforward and focused. Terms for cultural objects, artefacts, conventions and practices are used almost exclusively locally, with a few exceptions: a small number of 'indicator terms' have spilled over across their original confines, are found in other corpora as well and show transnational diffusion. They have become internationalisms with a pointer function to local cultures. Cases in point include *kiwi*, *sari*, *triad* and others. On the whole, thus, and not surprisingly, cultural terms and objects turn out to be solid reflectors of cultures.

4.2 Nexus 2: Dimensions of Cultures

4.2.1 Theoretical and methodological background

The second main nexus between culture and language is inspired by the sociopsychological discipline of 'cross-cultural analysis' and builds upon the core notion of 'dimensions of culture'. These dimensions reflect coherent mindsets, as it were, reflect consistent thematically ordered attitudes and values shared by and typical of a society and culture. In practice, studies in this discipline are usually based upon psychological questionnaire data which systematically collect reactions to stimulus statements given by subjects from many different regions and cultures, sometimes also on the systematic observation of behaviour in communities. Typically, their results report broad regional sociocultural tendencies, often measured as scales or index values of a dimension relative to a society. The discipline has tended to have a strongly applied orientation, with an overall focus on organisational culture, managerial and leadership styles, and business-directed applications in cross-cultural behaviour.

The study of intercultural communication emerged as a branch of anthropology during and after the 1950s, originally in work by the American anthropologist Edward Hall (see Hall and Hall 1990). Hall developed the notions of 'high-context' vs 'low-context' cultures and other dimensions (including proxemics and monochronic vs polychronic time). A few decades later the discipline came to full bloom with the work by its key figure and best-known, most influential representative, the Dutch sociologist Geert Hofstede, who explicitly posited and studied 'dimensions of cultures' (for a useful summary, see Minkov 2013: 201–16). Hofstede ([1980] 2001) has been immensely influential in the social sciences; the book counts as a milestone and core reference of cross-cultural psychology to the present day and has been very often and widely referred to. Of course, it has also been criticised – for regarding nations as overly homogeneous entities, for instance, for mixing up attitudinal and behavioural dimensions, or for having relied on non-representative subject samples or insufficiently clear stimuli. In essence, however, Hofstede's ideas have been tested in and have inspired very many follow-up projects and a very large number of publications (more than 1,400 alone on the individualism–collectivism dimension, following House et al. 2004: 437). A huge follow-up initiative, involving 170 researchers and covering 61 societies, was the 'GLOBE' project (House et al. 2004; described in Minkov 2013: 310–29). But while cross-cultural psychology has grown to be a strong research tradition in sociology and business studies, it has had surprisingly little impact in the humanities and in linguistics. There is not a single reference to this school in *The Routledge Handbook of Language and Culture* (Sharifian 2015).

The linguistic correlate of these sociopsychological dimensions, I assume, is specific 'indicator terms' which semantically represent specific dimensions and thus tend to occur more frequently where their intensity is high. These words or phrases, assumed to indicate, reflect or be associated with the cultural domain or issue in question, have been culled from the literature on (cross-)cultural theory, from sociopsychological writings or similar sources. Obviously, these sets of indicator terms call for discussion and justification; they have been decided on and selected for the present study but in principle they could be expanded or alternated. For example, Minkov (2013: 426) states that 'pride is almost a sin' in Asian cultures and I translated this into the assumption that this cultural concept can be tested by the presence or relative frequency of the lexemes *proud* and *pride* – but clearly this assumption is open to questioning or critical examination.

4.2.2 *Individualism versus collectivism*

As the labels imply, in some societies the rights and desires of individuals take centre stage and are pursued energetically, while in others priority is given to the community's goals and needs, with individuals being integrated and primarily assuming the social roles assigned to them. This is Hofstede's (2001) most central, most uncontroversial dimension, one which has 'attained the status of paradigm in cross-cultural psychology' (House et al. 2004: 437); it has been stated that '[i]ndividualism and collectivism ... are without a doubt the most significant constructs in research on culture and psychology' (Kashima and Kashima 2003: 125). Commonly, Western societies are seen as valuing individualism while in Eastern and Asian cultures a collectivist community orientation is taken to prevail (Fang 2012: 28). East Asian languages and cultures are proclaimed to more or less avoid an 'I' (Minkov 2013: 428). Interestingly enough, an economic explanation for the emergence of these different orientations rooted in early human history has been suggested (Minkov 2013: 428–33): European-style societies have derived from hunter-gatherers and herders who had to compete for scarce land and hence the competitive strength of individuals constituted a decisive advantage for a community's survival. In contrast, pastoralism as practiced in Asia, especially the cultivation of rice requiring complex communal irrigation systems, is a labour-intensive, necessarily collective activity, so the reconciling and downplaying of possible differences, the blending in of individuals to community interests and structures, is of utmost importance. This is not a clear-cut distinction, however, but rather a graded phenomenon: the results by Hofstede and others typically yield not absolute or qualitative distinctions but index values.

There are very few extant linguistic applications of this line of thinking and of Hofstede's concepts in general. Uz (2014) documents a weak correlation of the frequencies of first-person singular and plural pronoun use in Google's Ngram database with Hofstede's individualism scores. Yu et al. (2016) also compare pronoun frequency data from Google's Ngram database. Across nine languages, they find British and American English, respectively, showing the highest rates of first-person singular pronoun usage, and Chinese the lowest in 1949, but one increasing substantially until 2008, showcasing the 'dynamics of cultural change' (2016: 310).

Table 2.5, extrapolating from these publications, tests the hypothesis that a higher proportion of first-person singular as opposed to first-person plural pronouns mirrors a higher degree of individualism.[3]

Table 2.5 First-person singular vs plural usage

Words searched for in ICE corpora	GB	NZ	Hong Kong	Singapore	India
Sum pronouns 1st SG	22,985	27,729	40,054	24,498	19,359
Sum pronouns 1st PL	6,921	9,845	12,570	9,476	9,845
% 1st SG out of total	76.9%	73.8%	76.1%	72.1%	66.3%

The results are largely in line with expectations: GB displays the strongest proportion of first-person singular pronouns (76.9 per cent of all first-person personal pronouns), taken to reflect an individualist orientation. Conversely, with a first-person singular proportion of only 66.3 per cent, India is the most collectivist nation, based on this statistic. Hong Kong ranks surprisingly high on individualism (76.1 per cent), but with a higher plural/collectivist proportion. NZ trails not too far behind on individualism (73.8 per cent), and Singapore is also close (72.1 per cent).

Table 2.6 reports the frequencies of eight collectivism-oriented indicator terms and the results strongly confirm the hypothesis of a more strongly collectivist orientation being reflected in the language use in Asian Englishes. The sum total of collectivist terms is highly significantly much lower than elsewhere in GB, and especially high in Hong Kong and Singapore, less so (but still) in India. The same applies to most of the individual expressions. New Zealand ranks in between – collectivist expressions are much more common than in GB but not as frequent as in the two southeast and east Asian city states. But in general in British English there is consistently less talk (with very few exceptions) about

Table 2.6 Collectivism-oriented indicator terms

Words searched for in ICE corpora	GB	NZ	Hong Kong	Singapore	India
tak*|took care of	9	7	70***	54***	79***
protect*	118	210	215*	186**	147
loyal*	19	28	27	13	28
harmon*	11	19	57***	43***	36**
sharing/-ed	49	78	77	131***	42
together	270	321	471***	350	259
concerned about	19	43	26	22	13
sensitive	3	41***	45***	29***	51***
Total	498	747	988***	828***	655***

Asterisks after numbers: * = $p < .05$; ** = $4 < .01$; and *** = $4 < .001$.
A single asterisk at the end of a word or stem: * = zero or more characters, in line with AntConc's wildcard search conventions. So, for example, *tak** covers *take*, *takes* and *taking*; *loyal** includes *loyal*, *loyalty*, *loyalties*, *loyalist*, and so on. In further examples (for example, in Section 4.2.5) '#' means 'any one word', and '@' means 'zero or one word'.

taking care of, *protection*, *loyalty*, *harmonising*, *sharing*, and being *together*, *concerned about* and *sensitive* than in the Indo-Pacific area and in Eastern (possibly Confucian-shaped) Asia in particular.

The robustness of these distributions and relationships can also be measured by calculating correlations. Hofstede (2001: 215) reports an 'individualism index value' for many countries; it is 89 for GB, 79 for NZ, 25 for Hong Kong, 20 for Singapore, and 48 for India. Calculating the Pearson correlation coefficient between these index values and the percentages of first-person singular pronouns yields a weak positive correlation ($r = .28$); the same coefficient between Hofstede's index and the frequency of collectivism indicators shows a strong inverse correlation of $r = -.78$. In other words, the indicator terms mirror a society's collectivist orientation quite convincingly and first-person pronoun usage also reflects individualism.

4.2.3 Power-related dimensions: solidarity and distance, relationship and politeness

Despite democratic ideals, human beings are unequal in many ways and this translates into power stratifications which are inherent to a society's social structure. Societies also differ substantially with respect to the dimension of 'power distance', 'the extent to which the less powerful members of organizations and institutions accept and expect that power is distributed unequally' (Hofstede 2001: xix). Hofstede measures power distance indices; within an overall range of 104 to 11, India scores 77, Singapore 74, Hong Kong 68, NZ 22, and GB 35 (2001: 87). This dimension is strongly inversely correlated with individualism (House et al. 2004: 441). Power and solidarity can be expressed in various ways – so I document indicator terms for status differences, terms of address and other forms of politeness, and kinship terms as a staple of social relations.

I counted sixteen putative indicator terms for high status differences (*beg*, *apologise*, *owe something to*, *kind of you*, *not worthy*, *embarrass**, *disgrace*, *obedient/-ce*, *authority*, *respect*, *told to*, *humble/y*, *respectfully*, *thank you indeed*, *esteemed* + N, *anxiously*) and three expressions of low status difference (*equal/s*, *at leisure*, *consult*). Results in this case appear mostly idiosyncratic and inconclusive, showing noteworthy tendencies only for a few words. For example, *respect* and *told to* occur consistently more frequently in the Asian corpora than in GB and NZ, while, conversely, *apologize/-ise* is more common in GB and NZ than in Asian texts, and derivatives of *embarrass* and *humble* in particular seem strongly British expressions which occur less frequently everywhere else.

Table 2.7 Honorifics and address terms

Words searched for in ICE corpora	GB	NZ	Hong Kong	Singapore	India
sir	194	363***	144***	355***	997***
madam/e	9	24	180***	31*	90***
respected	9	12	11	9	34**

* = $p < .05$; ** = $p < .01$; and *** = $p < .001$.

As Table 2.7 shows, honorifics and address terms stratify societies clearly in the expected direction. The traditional polite and distanced terms of address, *sir* and *madam*, are much more regularly used in the Asian societies now (with the exception of *sir* in Hong Kong), where such expressions of politeness appear to prevail more strongly than in a more egalitarian and democratic Western society; NZ consistently ranks in between (which may be a conservative trait). The word *respected* is very much typical of Indian usage, with two phraseological combinations, *dear respected* and '*respected* plus personal name or title', occurring in India exclusively.

Among indicator terms for politeness, three (*polite*, *impolite*, *courtesy*) occur not overly frequently and without regional preferences, but two others yield interesting results. Being *arrogant* seems more Western than Asian behaviour (11 tokens each in GB and NZ, between 4 and 6 elsewhere). Remarkably, the word *please* is used consistently more frequently across Asia (Hong Kong and Singapore 410*** tokens each; India 342***) than in GB (209) and NZ (183).

Table 2.8 Polite request phraseology as power distance indicators

Words searched for in ICE corpora	GB	NZ	Hong Kong	Singapore	India
would you	124	106**	208	90	110
why don't you	19	17	39	45	35
would like to	79	81	243***	126*	193**
ask you to	8	9	39	11	3
appreciate it if	2	2	3	7	0
Total	232	215***	532***	279	341**

* = $p < .05$; ** = $p < .01$; and *** = $p < .001$.

In line with the above results or politeness terms, Table 2.8 shows that phrases expressing polite requests, signalling power distance, are very typical of Asian Englishes: in practically all instances, and particularly for *why don't you* and *would like to*, the Asian varieties use them much more frequently. New Zealand in this case sides very clearly with GB, displaying a Western, reduced emphasis on overt expression of politeness.

Table 2.9 Kinship terms as indicators of social relations

Words searched for in ICE corpora	GB	NZ	Hong Kong	Singapore	India
uncle	13	30	39	53***	14
aunt/ie	31	41	76*	42	26
brother/s	59	148***	195***	121***	152***
cousin/s	35	36	39	21	60
Total	138	255*	349***	237***	252***

* = $p < .05$; ** = $p < .01$; and *** = $p < .001$.

Finally, as shown in Table 2.9, talking about one's relatives is also a mainstay of signalling culture-specific social relations, in this case of proximity (Kronenfeld 2015; Kachru and Smith 2008: 49–50, 108). In general, kinship terms are used significantly less often in GB – which is remarkable and may be taken to reflect the reduced importance of family bonds in Western cultures. Talking of *brother/s* in particular seems more common across Asia and in NZ. The usage of *uncle* peaks in Singapore, *aunt* in Hong Kong and *cousin* in India.

In sum, almost all of the above results consistently confirm the existence and expression of power differences and different degrees of their acceptance in societies. In general, Asian societies use more distanced and more polite expressions and more family-related expressions; Western usage is more egalitarian and less polite and also less focused on family relations.

4.2.4 *Chinese Culture Connection*

Chinese Culture Connection (1987), a multi-authored, large-scale study (also reported in Minkov 2013: 217–23) conducted in 23 countries, claims that 40 'values' essential to Chinese culture, reduced to four main dimensions (integration, Confucian work dynamism, human heartedness and moral discipline), have shaped some societies. It shows strong correlations with Hofstede's dimensions and the belief in Eastern societies being more strongly characterised by faith, obedience, hard work and thrift (Minkov 2013: 143; cf. Fang 2012). To assess this claim and its linguistic manifestations, I have tested 22 terms which supposedly reflect these 'Chinese' values. Seven of them that I find particularly interesting, and the sum total of all 22, are shown in Table 2.10; the others, with results being less clearly distributed or token numbers lower, were *spiritual, Yin Yang, faith, loyal(ty), forgive(ness), solidarity, patience, prudence, modest(y), humble/y, reputation, proud(ly)/pride, kindness, compassion* and *mercy*.

Table 2.10 Terms signalling a Chinese culture connection

Words searched for in ICE corpora	GB	NZ	Hong Kong	Singapore	India
thrift/y	0	0	3	5	5
piety	1	2	5	8	1
harmony	9	8	36*	32**	28*
tradition	74	30***	61	30***	90
hono(u)r	17	97***	123***	184***	263***
shame	29	24	17	5***	8**
ashamed	11	10	5	7	7
Total (all)	**396**	**424***	**491**	**495**	**680***

* = $p < .05$; ** = $p < .01$; and *** = $p < .001$.

The overall frequency clearly confirms the basic claim: the frequency of usage of these 'Chinese cultural' terms is consistently and significantly higher in Asia and lowest in GB, with NZ in between again. The highest value by far, however, is found in India – which suggests that these values are not predominantly Chinese but rather generally conservative, harmony-related (and collectivist, we may say) and to some extent Asian. Expressions where the individual frequencies show this East–Western cleavage quite clearly include *thrift/y*, *piety*, *harmony* and *hono(u)r*. The word *tradition* shows no clear orientation. In contrast, the fact that causing or feeling *shame* or being *ashamed* is strongly avoided in Asian societies is directly reflected in these words being used more commonly in GB and (less so) NZ.

4.2.5 Further dimensions

A few more cultural dimensions have been suggested in cross-cultural psychology and tested in this study. However, I report them only briefly and summarily here, mainly for reasons of space.

Some of the well-established dimensions, identified already in Hall's early work (see Hall and Hall 1990), have to do with how cultures negotiate time and space. The dimension of 'long-term orientation' captures 'the extent to which a culture programs its members to accept delayed gratification of their material, social, and emotional needs' (Hofstede 2001: xix–xx; similarly, p. 29), while in 'short-term orientation' contexts the immediate satisfaction of one's needs and desires is striven for. East Asian countries are stated to score high for long-term orientation; Western societies rank low (Hofstede 2001: 351; see also Minkov 2013: 390). Furthermore, attitudes towards things getting done in time can be either 'monochronic', with activities performed consecutively, according to schedules, with time being treated as a precious commodity and completing tasks being more important than social contacts involved, or 'polychronic', with activities performed simultaneously, with little attention to effectiveness and human relations being more important than sticking to schedules (Hall and Hall 1990: 13–17; Hua 2013: 188). I tested seven terms for long-term orientation (*persist**, *continuity*, *long-term*, *postpon**, *delay**, *later*, *lifetime*), four terms for short-term orientation (*immediate/ly*, *rush*, *short-term*, *soon*), and 10 expressions for monochronic time orientation (*one thing at a time, one thing after the other, subsequent/ly, schedule, complet* # @ task, don't/didn't/doesn't have * time, sav* * time, spend* * time, los* * time, wast* * time*). In short, while of course there are frequency differences and regional preferences for one or the other expression, no clear distributional tendencies are extant.

The dimension of 'high vs low context' relates to the amount of detail provided in a society on the background of a statement under discussion: in high-context cultures, including Asia, Africa and southern Europe, things are mentioned only indirectly and details are assumed to be familiar anyhow, while in low-context cultures (supposedly northern and central Europe and North America) there is a tendency to provide detailed background information and to mention things explicitly (Hall and Hall 1990: 6–10; Hua 2013: 96). I took the verb forms of *explain* and *inform* and the corresponding nouns to be indicators of low-context communication and find a distribution which runs counter to the expectation, with sum values being higher in Asia (Hong Kong 969, Singapore 848, India 639) than in NZ (615) or GB (592).

Cultures also differ in how emotions can be expressed in public – both in general as to the amount to which this is considered permissible and specifically with respect to their predominant directionality, positive or negative (cf. Minkov 2013: 345–9, after work by Kuppens et al. 2006). Minkov (2013: 347–8) claims that Asian cultures score relatively low on positive and high on negative emotions. The following terms were counted as indicators of this dimension: *happy/iness, cheerful*, grateful/itude, pleasant, content/ment; unhappy/iness, grief/ve, guilt/y, jealous/y, anger/gry, sad/ness, unpleasant* and *worry*. Table 2.11 offers summary results.

Table 2.11 Summary of indicator terms for emotions

Words searched for in ICE corpora	GB	NZ	Hong Kong	Singapore	India
Positive	296 (56%)	338 (46%)	484 (55%)	337 (55%)	372 (67%)
Negative	233 (44%)	389 (54%)	392* (45%)	276 (45%)	187 (32%)
Total	**529**	**727**	**876*****	**613**	**559**

* = $p < .05$; ** = $p < .01$; and *** = $p < .001$.

The results show that there are indeed more and less 'emotion-friendly' cultures: GB and India are relatively constrained, displaying less talk about emotions, while, in contrast, in Hong Kong this is very common. If emotions are talked about at all in India then these are predominantly positive ones, while NZ is the only country where negative emotion expressions constitute a slight majority.

Finally, work by Schmitt (2005) in particular shows that societies differ substantially in how they express 'sociosexuality', that is, conventional verbalisations of mating strategies, display of courtship and romantic closeness, emotional investment, attitudes to monogamy versus promiscuity and so on (cf. Carbaugh 2005: 61–8; Minkov 2013: 341–3). For this dimension I tested 13 indicator terms, of which eight (*sex, sexual, girlfriend, boyfriend, pregnant/cy, contraception/ives, naked, abortion*) showed some kind of significant distributions while five others did not and/or were rare (*sexy, premarital, promiscuous/ity, topless, nude/ity*). Some individual figures stand out but are mostly difficult to interpret. For example, in Hong Kong both *boyfriend/s* (128*** tokens; elsewhere up to 46) and *girlfriend/s* (43; elsewhere up to 27) are most frequently talked about, while, perhaps not surprisingly, in India *girlfriend* occurs only rarely (8**; 25 or more elsewhere). On the other hand, the word *contraception* occurs exceptionally frequently in India (51**; elsewhere up to 12). In NZ, the words *naked* (22 times; elsewhere max. 14) and *abortion* (34 times; elsewhere max. 17) occur exceptionally frequently. The overall readiness of societies to mention sexual topics also varies considerably: it is highest in Hong Kong, with a total of 421*** tokens of indicator terms for sociosexuality, in the middle range for NZ (295), Singapore (213) and India (209), and lowest, perhaps not surprisingly, in GB (172).

A general survey of the results in this section shows that the notion of cultural dimensions is a valid one with strong linguistic reflections; also, its operationalisation via indicator terms works well in very many instances. The important dimension of individualism versus collectivism is mirrored fairly directly in both pronominal and lexical choices. Power-related dimensions also determine language usage in several ways, notably address terms, politeness expressions and formulae, and talking about kinship. Reflections of 'Chinese Culture' impact also turn out to be fairly strong overall and for several individual notions, although the reasons for these choices appear to be more of a collectivist conservative Asian perspective on life rather than an exclusively Chinese origin. Finally, cross-cultural linguistic differences have also manifested themselves in the intensity and directionality of expressing emotions and the amount and topics of referring to sociosexual issues.

4.3 Nexus 3: Structural Schemas Reflecting Cultures

4.3.1 Outline and methodology

As the third nexus between culture and language, the even more abstract question is whether there might be reflections of culture in grammar, that is, whether preferences for specific linguistic patterns might be motivated by differences between cultures. Could relatively general schematic constructions (as defined in Hoffmann and Trousdale 2013) be possibly inspired or motivated by culturally based principles? There has been some discussion of such issues in general linguistics. See, for example, Everett (2005), who makes a strong claim of causality for an Amazonian language, suggesting 'that Pirahã culture severely constrains Pirahã grammar in several ways' (2005: 622), and the discussion contributions following this article; or Gladkova (2015) on 'ethnosyntax', speculating on 'grammatical constructions [which] are not semantically arbitrary and . . . related to broader cultural understandings' (2015: 33) – though without much empirical backing. With respect to English, this is largely uncharted territory, however.

The earliest publication speculating along such lines in World Englishes research is Olavarría de Ersson and Shaw (2003), who document varying complementation preferences of certain verbs between British and Indian English and view them as reflections of different world views and roles of the individual, profiled (also in a syntactically prominent position) in Western but backgrounded in Asian usage, 'an extraordinarily . . . direct connection between grammar and "culture"' (2003: 159). Mukherjee and Hoffmann (2006) have a similar hunch on a preference of Indian English for monotransitive recipientless constructions (2006: 154), but they remain essentially sceptical of such cultural explanations of syntactic preferences. Finally, an interesting, rather deeply reflected claim on the growth of culturally motivated constructions can be found in Burridge (2015). She posits a dependency relationship: 'Cultural preoccupations give rise to ways of thinking and . . . can then end up embodied in the grammar; habitual conversation practices . . . solidify into specific morphosyntactic constructions' (2015: 72). Her examples are the loss of the 'impersonal construction' (for example, *it worries me* vs *I worry*) and in general the disappearance of dative experiencers in Early Modern English, which, she thinks, is partly to be explained by 'the rise of the modern self-determining individual' (2015: 70).

The methodological challenge, then, is how to capture such abstract tendencies – if indeed they exist. First, I identified five different syntactic issues where cultural motivations for alternative linguistic modes of expression could be reasonably hypothesised, to be introduced and discussed in Section 4.3.2. Secondly, for each of these topics I defined a tightly circumscribed set of 'indicator constructions', alternative linguistic surface patterns which are functionally and semantically equivalent and where the choice of one or the other pattern is assumed to reflect or possibly to have been influenced by cultural schemes. Since abstract syntactic schemes allow an almost limitless set of lexical fillers it would hardly be possible to find them all in a corpus using corpus-linguistic search strategies. Therefore, I constrained searches to tightly circumscribed syntactic sequences which employ selected sets of high-frequency verbs and pronouns, mostly personal pronouns, as NP complements (for examples, see Section 4.3.2) – which can be searched for mechanically. In corpus-linguistic terms this means I obtain low recall (only a limited subset of all relevant examples) but high precision, that is, all and only the structures which meet the syntactic definition are returned (Lindquist 2009: 33). More importantly, this yields a controlled 'envelope of variation' in the sense of Labov's (1972) variation theory, all occurrences of the alternative choices which meet the definition and reflect the hypothesis which thus can be objectively tested.

4.3.2 *Hypotheses and results*

The supposedly culture-sensitive constructions submitted to corpus searches largely boil down to manifestations of the individualism vs collectivism dimension. Some constructions syntactically downplay the agent, the individual as a persona, and highlight collectivity as opposed to individuality through syntactic choices, for instance by leaving out the agent noun phrase altogether or placing it in an inconspicuous clause position. Others but equivalent ones, in contrast, may highlight precisely that agent person by placing him or her in a syntactically prominent position, for example in end-focus. The relationship between these options is then measured and interpreted. Of the five different structural frames which have been identified and which allow this kind of perspective and analysis, I report and discuss four but leave out one (end-focus with ditransitive verbs) to save space and since the results are largely indeterminate (see Schneider 2018).

1. Passives: In active sentences the agent appears as the subject of a clause. In passive clauses the agent may be given in a *by*+NP, but one of the discourse functions of passives is to camouflage agency by not providing a *by*-phrase, that is, not telling the recipient who or what carried out the predicated activity. Assuming that collectivist cultures tend to downplay individual agency, it may be hypothesised that these cultures use a higher proportion of passives, especially agentless passives without a *by*-phrase. All occurrences of eight prototypically monotransitive verbs (*tell, offer, support, help, beat, inform, admire, encourage*) were investigated.
2. Impersonal constructions: Inspired by Burridge's (2015) suggestions, a few impersonal constructions were investigated, assuming that they also downplay agency by making the human 'agent' of a mental process not an (active) subject but a (recipient) object or complement of it. Thus, the hypothesis here is that relatively more impersonal constructions should be found in collectivistic cultures.
3. Recipientless constructions: In the construction type 'verb + experiencer-object + finite *that*-clause', the recipient individual can be downplayed in World Englishes by omitting the person in the object/experiencer position (so that, for example, *inform [somebody] that . . .* becomes *inform that . . .*). Thus, it is hypothesised that there should be more recipientless constructions in collectivistic cultures (Mukherjee and Hoffmann 2006). The hypothesis was tested by searching for two high-frequency verbs (*assure, inform*) directly followed by a *that*-clause.
4. Verb concord with collective nouns: Collective nouns allow a choice between singular and plural verb forms (for example, *my family is/ are happy*). This choice reflects a difference in the conceptualisation of the respective nouns as either a holistic group or a multitude of individuals – a difference which obviously parallels the one between collectivist and individualist orientations. The hypothesis is thus that collectivist cultures tend to conceive groups holistically, as a collective singular with singular agreement: for example, N *is*, rather than made up of several or many individuals, and expressed as plural entities with plural agreement: for example, N *are*. The methodological procedure was to choose a set of appropriate nouns (*team, military, council, government, company, family, committee*) and a set of controlled verb forms which consistently show the morphological difference in number marking, that is, the primary auxiliaries *is/are* and *has/have*.

Table 2.12 Summary of schematic indicator constructions

Indicator constructions	Construction searched for in ICE corpora	GB	NZ	Hong Kong	Singapore	India
1. Passives	sum active	171	274	400*	372*	319*
	sum passive without *by*	21	16	35	22	20
	sum passive with *by*	5	18	10	2	4
2. Impersonal constructions	(pron) *worry*	4	7	18	4	5
	worry (pron)	8	15	6	7	1
	seems to me	48	38	21***	4***	4***
	occur to (pron)	10	6	11	2	7
3. Recipientless constructions	*assure/inform that*	0	0	4	4	16***
4. Collective concord	N Vsg	95	183	327	131	233
	N Vpl	25	19	34	16	18
	% sing.	79.2	90.6	90.6	89.1	92.8

* = $p < .05$; ** = $p < .01$; and *** = $p < .001$.

Table 2.12 puts together relevant data to assess the above hypotheses on potentially culturally sensitive indicator constructions. For the three different pattern types they can be summarised and interpreted as follows:

1. For passives, at first sight the frequency distributions do not confirm the hypothesis: passives occur relatively frequently in GB and actives predominate, contrary to expectation and statistically significantly, in the Asian countries. New Zealand occupies a rather neutral intermediate position. However, zooming in to details yields some observations which are in line with the hypothesis. Passives without a *by*-phrase, downplaying the agent, occur consistently more frequently in the Asian texts than in NZ, especially in Hong Kong. Consequently, passives with an explicit *by*-phrase, where the agent is highlighted by not only not being omitted but by being placed in end-focus, occur least frequently across Asia, especially in Singapore and India (and also in HK when calculating proportions).
2. Impersonal constructions (*worry* (pron), *seems to me*, *occur to*) tend to occur more commonly in native-English-speaking (L1) communities (GB and NZ), going against the hypothesis of cultural influence, that is, their being preferred in more collectivist cultures, where the expression of agency should be less prominent. In Table 2.12 this

shows up in the British and NZ preference for *worry* (pron), while the opposite preference is shown in the data for Hong Kong and India. Instead they prefer the direct agency pattern *someone worries*, which runs counter to the assumption associated with their collectivist culture. The results for impersonal *seems to me* are very strongly weighted towards the L1 countries and each of the three second-language (L2) countries is significantly different. As Schneider (2018: 124) also shows on the basis of the huge corpus of Global Web-Based English, the impersonal *seems to me* is very much an L1 construction, rarely picked up in L2-speaking communities. For *occur to someone* the distribution is similar, though less straightforward. Both patterns also occur with a fairly high frequency in Hong Kong. These contradictory findings do not support the cultural hypothesis.

3. The recipientless constructions analysed behave fully in line with the hypothesis: they do not occur in GB and NZ at all, where mentioning the recipient of *assure* and *inform* is obligatory. Meanwhile the recipientless construction occurs in the data from all three Asian countries, and is especially (and highly significantly) frequent in India. This finding (amid the small numbers) supports the hypothesis.

4. For collective concord, the evidence is mixed but in principle consistent with the hypothesis. Singular concord is highest in ICE data from India, and almost the default choice (around 90 per cent of the time) and similarly in Hong Kong and Singapore, all collectivist cultures. But NZ also shows this strong preference among southern hemisphere L1 users of English, perhaps because it is 'correct' in terms of traditional English grammar, an alternative hypothesis to consider. It is only in British data that the putatively individualistic plural concord pattern occupies a noticeably higher proportion of over one fifth of all instances.

In all these cases, a central question of course is whether there are really cultural factors at work which have a causal relationship to the distributions observed. This is a tentative hypothesis at best. Sometimes alternative explanations are available and perhaps more convincing. For impersonal constructions, complexity may be a central factor, since raising patterns are difficult and relatively marginal rules of English syntax, and perhaps second-language speakers tend to avoid them and similarly for passives. For (4), singular concord is known to be a more characteristically American English choice (Hundt 2006), so American English linguistic impact may be playing a role here.

Overall, given the abstract and tentative nature of the question asked and the methodological difficulty of pinning it down, it will not come as a surprise that the evidence for cultural impact on language is weakest here, for schematic constructions. There is some, however – enough to find the results noteworthy, I believe. Of the four pattern types reported, three show results which are in line with the hypothesis of potential cultural impact: (3) and (4) largely, and (1) possibly.

5. CONCLUSION

Three different increasingly abstract 'nexuses' between cultures and languages have been explored in this chapter, from the lexical-material (looking at cultural objects) via the lexical-conceptual (that is, cultural dimensions) to the structural-schematic level. Fundamentally, it can and has to be stated that there is positive evidence of some relationship for each of these nexuses, to varying extents and with possible caveats to be considered, but fundamentally all across the board. There is a clear correlation between the potential of observing cultural impact on language form and the abstractness of the level looked at. The more concrete the questions and observations, the stronger and more direct is the evidence; for abstract issues, in contrast, it is more elusive and difficult to discern. Cultural objects and artefacts mostly show direct and straightforward linguistic manifestations via the lexemes, often indigenous borrowings, denoting them. The less tangible nexus of cultural dimensions, as posited in cross-cultural psychology, also yields fairly convincing results much of the time – it is strong for many dimensions and indicator terms, though also weak to non-existent for others investigated. For schematic constructions, results are partial and tentative rather than definitive. But the hypothesis of cultural conventions at least having an impact on structural preferences in some contexts can reasonably be upheld and awaits further testing.

The varieties of English along the Asia-Pacific rim position themselves in interesting ways with respect to the research question and its manifestations – partly along lines to be expected, partly idiosyncratically and reflecting mixed cultural input. Not surprisingly, British English, the donor and benchmark variety, turns out to be most individualistic in some ways (for example, for first-person pronoun usage), but also socioculturally constrained in others (for example, with respect to talking about kinship, status expressions, emotions or sociosexuality, or using words like *embarrassed* and *ashamed*). In general and as expected, though with individual variability, the Asian countries show strong traces of Asian cultural attitudes, notably a collectivist orientation in their lexical choices and, tentatively, in some structural preferences. Singapore, for instance, very often stands between GB on the one hand and other Asian countries on the other, reflecting its dual Asian-cum-Western cultural orientation. Hong Kong tends to side with other Asian collectivist nations (for example, for collectivist indicator terms, polite phrases, kinship reference or use of emotion terms) but also shows signs of modernity and individualism (for example, in first-person pronoun usage, talk about emotions and sexuality, and impersonal constructions). India quite often shows a fairly conservative, collectivist orientation (for example, in using first-person pronouns, respectful address terms, supposedly 'Chinese' cultures value terms, and recipientless constructions). NZ very often stands in between (for example, for collectivism or expressing emotions), reflecting both its British roots fairly strongly preserved but also some impact of the country's Asia-Pacific location and neighbouring cultures, to be accounted for by culture contact and immigration.

NOTES

1. The present paper resembles and partly follows an earlier one in which I addressed roughly the same question from a slightly different angle (Schneider 2018). It is structured similarly and builds on some (though not all) of the same data but it adds new data and is tailored specifically to the VEIP context (Varieties of English in the Indo-Pacific project), and therefore looks mainly into Asia-Pacific nations.
2. Corpus sizes are factored in since the number of non-occurrences of a target form was defined as the number of words a corpus consists of minus the number of occurrences of the respective form. Essentially this adopts a procedure suggested and documented by Rayson (n.d.), except for employing Fisher's Exact rather than a log likelihood test. I am grateful to Thomas Brunner for having written an R script which consistently performed these calculations and tests.
3. All pairwise Fisher's Exact comparisons with GB except HK:GB are highly significant ($p < .000$).

REFERENCES

Anthony, L. (2014). AntConc (Version 3.4.4w) [Computer software]. Waseda University. <https://www.laurenceanthony.net/software> (last accessed 4 January 2021).
Assmann, A. (2012). *Introduction to cultural studies: Topics, concepts, issues.* Erich Schmidt-Verlag.
Burridge, K. (2015). The body, the universe, society and language: Germanic in the grip of the unknown. In R. La Polla and R. de Busser (Eds.), *The shaping of language: The relationship between the structures of languages and their social, cultural, historical, and natural environments* (pp. 45–76). John Benjamins.
Byram, M. (1997). *Teaching and assessing intercultural communicative competence.* Multilingual Matters.
Byram, M., Nichols, A. and Stevens, D. (Eds.). (2001). *Developing intercultural competence in practice.* Multilingual Matters.
Carbaugh, D. (2005). *Cultures in conversation.* Lawrence Erlbaum Associates.
Chinese Culture Connection. (1987). Chinese values and the search for culture-free dimensions of culture. *Journal of Cross-Cultural Psychology, 18*(2), 143–64.
Everett, D. (2005). Cultural constraints on grammar and cognition in Piranã: Another look at the design features of human language. *Current Anthropology, 46*(4), 621–46.
Fang, T. (2012). Yin Yang: A new perspective on culture. *Management and Organization Review, 8*(1), 25–50.
Gladkova, A. (2015). Ethnosyntax. In F. Sharifian (Ed.), *The Routledge handbook of language and culture* (pp. 33–50). Routledge.
Greenbaum, S. (Ed.). (1996). *Comparing English worldwide: The International Corpus of English.* Clarendon Press.
Gries, S. T. (2008). *Statistik für Sprachwissenschaftler.* Vandenhoeck & Ruprecht.
Hall, E. T. and Hall, M. R. (1990). *Understanding cultural differences.* Intercultural Press.
Hoffmann, T. and Trousdale, G. (Eds.). (2013). *The Oxford handbook of construction grammar.* Oxford University Press.
Hofstede, G. (2001). *Culture's consequences: Comparing values, behaviors, institutions and organizations across nations* (2nd ed.). Sage. (Original work published 1980).
House, R. J., Hanges, P. J., Javidan, M., Dorfman, P. W. and Gupta, V.

(2004). *Culture, leadership, and organizations: The GLOBE Study of 62 Societies*. Sage.

Hua, Z. (2013). *Exploring intercultural communication: Language in action*. Routledge.

Hundt, M. (2006). The committee has/have decided . . .: On concord patterns with collective nouns in inner- and outer-circle varieties of English. *Journal of English Linguistics, 34*(3), 206–32.

Hundt, M., Lehmann, H. M. and Schneider, G. (2019). International Corpus of English (ICE) [Online corpus]. University of Zurich. <https://www.ice-corpora.uzh.ch/en.html> (last accessed 4 January 2021).

Hundt, M., Schreier, D. and Schneider, E. W. (Eds.). (2020). *The Cambridge handbook of World Englishes*. Cambridge University Press. <https://doi.org/10.1017/9781108349406> (last accessed 4 January 2021).

Jensen, K. E. (2017). Corpora and cultural cognition: How corpus-linguistic methodology can contribute to cultural linguistics. In F. Sharifian (Ed.), *Advances in cultural linguistics* (pp. 477–505). Springer Nature.

Kachru, Y. and Smith, L. E. (2008). *Cultures, contexts, and World Englishes*. Routledge.

Kashima, Y. and Kashima, E. S. (2003). Individualism, GNP, climate, and pronoun drop: Is individualism determined by affluence and climate, or does language use play a role? *Journal of Cross-Cultural Psychology, 34*(1), 125–34.

Kirkpatrick, A. (Ed.). (in press). *The Routledge handbook of World Englishes* (2nd ed.). Routledge.

Kronenfeld, D. B. (2015). Culture and kinship language. In F. Sharifian (Ed.), *The Routledge handbook of language and culture* (pp. 154–69). Routledge.

Kuppens, P., Ceulemans, E., Timmerman, M. E., Diener, E. and Kim-Prieto, C. (2006). Universal intracultural and intercultural dimensions of the recalled frequency of emotional experience. *Journal of Cross-Cultural Psychology, 37*(5), 491–515.

Labov, W. (1972). *Sociolinguistic patterns*. University of Pennsylvania Press.

Leavitt, J. (2015). Linguistic relativity: Precursors and transformations. In F. Sharifian (Ed.), *The Routledge handbook of language and culture* (pp. 18–30). Routledge.

Levisen, C. and Waters, S. (Eds.). (2017). *Cultural keywords in discourse*. John Benjamins.

Lindquist, H. (2009). *Corpus linguistics and the description of English*. Edinburgh University Press.
Minkov, M. (2013). *Cross-cultural analysis: The science and art of comparing the world's modern societies and their cultures*. Sage.
Moran, P. R. (2001). *Teaching culture: Perspectives in practice*. Heinle & Heinle.
Mukherjee, J. and Bernaisch, T. (2015). Cultural keywords in context: A pilot study of linguistic acculturation in South Asian Englishes. In P. Collins (Ed.), *Grammatical change in English world-wide* (pp. 411–35). John Benjamins.
Mukherjee, J. and Hoffmann, S. (2006). Describing verb-complementational profiles of New Englishes: A pilot study of Indian English. *English World-Wide, 27*(2), 147–73.
Nelson, C. L., Proshina, Z. and Davis, D. (Eds.). (2019). *The handbook of World Englishes* (2nd ed.). Blackwell.
Olavarría de Ersson, E. and Shaw, P. (2003). Verb complementation patterns in Indian Standard English. *English World-Wide, 24*(2), 137–61.
Rayson, P. (n.d.). *Log-likelihood and effect size calculator*. <http://ucrel.lancs.ac.uk/llwizard.html> (last accessed 4 January 2021).
Salzmann, Z., Stanlaw, J. and Adachi, N. (2012). *Language, culture and society: An introduction to linguistic anthropology*. Westview Press.
Schmitt, D. P. (2005). Sociosexuality from Argentina to Zimbabwe: A 48-nation study of sex, culture, and strategies of human mating. *Behavioral and Brain Sciences, 28*(2), 247–75.
Schneider, E. W. (2007). *Postcolonial English: Varieties around the world*. Cambridge University Press.
Schneider, E. W. (2011). *English around the world: An introduction*. Cambridge University Press.
Schneider, E. W. (2018). The interface between cultures and corpora: Tracing reflections and manifestations. *ICAME Journal, 42*(1), 97–132. <https://doi.org/10.1515/icame-2018-0006> (last accessed 4 January 2021).
Sharifian, F. (2011). *Cultural conceptualizations and language: Theoretical framework and applications*. John Benjamins.
Sharifian, F. (Ed.). (2015). *The Routledge handbook of language and culture*. Routledge.
Sharifian, F. (2017). *Cultural linguistics*. John Benjamins.
Uz, I. (2014). Individualism and first person pronoun use in written texts across languages. *Journal of Cross-Cultural Psychology, 45*(10), 1671–8.

Wolf, H. and Polzenhagen, F. (2009). *World Englishes: A cognitive sociolinguistic approach*. Mouton de Gruyter.

Yu, F., Peng, T., Peng, K., Tang, S., Chen, C. S., Qian, X., Sun, P., Han, T. and Chai, F. (2016). Cultural value shifting in pronoun use. *Journal of Cross-Cultural Psychology*, 47(2), 310–16.

CHAPTER 3

Reflections of Afrikaans in the English Short Stories of Herman Charles Bosman

Bertus van Rooy

1. INTRODUCTION

Herman Charles Bosman (1905–51) was a bilingual English-Afrikaans author of short stories which represent Afrikaans characters, and he uses an Afrikaans internal narrator (storyteller) in most short stories. These stories reflect an ostensibly simple pastoral world full of racism towards Black South Africans and antagonism towards the English, but with an ironic twist in every story that exposes the duplicity, in a way where it remains ambiguous whether it is the implied author or the fictional Afrikaans narrator who turns the tale upside down. Bosman's narrative style of imitating oral narration (MacKenzie 1999) and political engagement (Wenzel 1999; MacKenzie 2003; Leff 2016) has received considerable attention from especially literary researchers. Researchers often remark about his language in passing but detailed analysis is limited. To get a flavour of the texts, the internal narrator in the following extract tells a part of the story where he and his friends meet a newcomer Englishman for the first time. The extract comes from the short story 'The Rooinek'.[1]

(1) The wagon rolled along and came to a stop in front of the house. [. . .] Then he walked up to where we were standing. He was dressed just as we were, in shirt and trousers and **veldskoens**, and he had dust all over him. But when he stepped over a thorn-bush we saw that **he had got socks on**. Therefore we knew that he was an Englishman.
Koos Steyn was standing in front of the door.

> The Englishman went up to him and held out his hand.
> 'Good afternoon,' **he said in Afrikaans**. 'My name is Webber.'
> Koos shook hands with him.
> 'My name is Prince Lord Alfred Milner,' Koos Steyn said.
> That was when Lord Milner was Governor of the Transvaal, and we all laughed. The **rooinek** also laughed.
> 'Well, Lord Prince,' he said, 'I can speak your language a little, and I hope that later on I'll be able to speak it better. I'm coming to live here, and I hope that we'll all be friends.'
> He then came round to all of us, but the others turned away and refused to shake hands with him. He came up to me last of all; I felt sorry for him, and although his nation had dealt unjustly with my nation, and I had lost both my children in the concentration camp, still it was not so much the fault of this Englishman. It was the fault of the English Government, who wanted our gold mines. And it was also the fault of Queen Victoria, who didn't like **Oom** Paul Kruger, because they say that when he went over to London **Oom** Paul spoke to her only once for a few minutes. **Oom** Paul Kruger said that he was a married man and he was afraid of widows. (emphases added)

The extract shows the use of Afrikaans lexis, such as *rooinek* ('red-neck', a pejorative term for the English in South Africa), *veldskoens* ('field-shoes', shoes made from raw animal skin) and Afrikaans kinship terms like *Oom* ('uncle', used not only for relatives but for men a generation or more older than the speaker) but, equally importantly, the extract suggests that the fictional encounter took place in Afrikaans, rather than English.

Afrikaans literary critics, such as Aucamp (1972) and Brink (1976), hold the view that in Bosman's writing, the Afrikaans language and culture are hidden beneath a very thin outer surface of English. Aucamp (1972: 65) speaks of the camouflaged Afrikaans, while Brink (1976: 43) refers to 'the syntactic patterns of Afrikaans [that] are evident just below the surface'. Bekker, however, problematises this consensus by noting that:

> there is actually very little evidence to show that there is much by way of dramatic attempt to 'calque' Afrikaans-like constructions onto the English of these short-stories. The effect, it would appear therefore, is mainly rendered effective by the use of Afrikaans character names (*Oom Schalk Lourens, Jurie Steyn, Chris Welman*),

Afrikaans place names (*Bekkersdal*, *Zastron*) and other words derived from Afrikaans (*withaak*, *krantzes*). (Bekker 2020: 8)

This chapter takes a closer look at the extent of camouflaged Afrikaans in Bosman's English. I concur with Bekker (2020) and earlier scholars on the importance of Afrikaans vocabulary for the evocation of an Afrikaans milieu. I want to pose the question of whether Brink's claim about the hidden Afrikaans syntax is not more valid after all, particularly in view of the finding of Coetzee (1981) that a contemporary of Bosman's, Pauline Smith, despite limited command of Afrikaans, nevertheless used this device. If Bosman's narrative technique was more sophisticated, beyond the deceptive surface simplicity (MacKenzie 2003), was his use of Afrikaans syntax not also more sophisticated, beyond the superficial disruption of English syntax that may at times border on the caricature in Smith and other outsiders attempting to portray their colonial Other through language?

Brink and Bekker also concur, if not in the specifics, then more generally, on the superficiality that vocabulary borrowings as device for evoking the colonial Other may have, but Brink (1976: 42), in a passage quoted by Bekker (2020: 2), highlights an important aspect that asks for inquiry into the authenticity of the representation of the Other. He notes that 'English writers in South Africa seemed interested in the land only for what local colour it could provide, with a number of **misspelt** *kopjes*, *sjamboks*, *veldtschoens* or *Vrouw Grobbelaars* thrown in for good measure'. This ties in with the concern raised by Coetzee (1981: 29–30) that, at times, Pauline Smith's representation of Afrikaans syntax is not realistic. Distorted syntax may reduce the characters to caricatures and stifle the potential of these characters to invite the reader to identify with them, as a necessary precondition for the social impact of the text.

The question of the extent of and authenticity in Bosman's vocabulary and grammatical reflections of the Afrikaans culture and language is the central question in this chapter. It ties in with the questions raised by Schneider in his platform chapter for this volume, where he inquires into strategies to reflect cultures in corpus texts. He proposes three levels of reflection, or nexuses, between language and culture: cultural objects, broader and more abstract dimensions of culture reflected in vocabulary, and grammatical constructions reflecting cultural differences. Schneider's methodology cannot be replicated in order to answer the question in this chapter, but I nevertheless draw inspiration from the broad direction and adjust it to the context of this investigation.

Corresponding to Schneider's first and second nexuses, I examine vocabulary in Bosman's oeuvre to determine the extent to which Bosman reflects culturally specific objects and practices as well as representations of Afrikaans culture at a more abstract level. Schneider's third nexus is more schematic grammatical structure. A number of candidate grammatical features of Afrikaans that appeared to be reflected in the English text in my reading are examined in more rigorous terms to determine if there is evidence for grammatical reflections of Afrikaans in the English text, something that Aucamp (1972) and Brink (1976) take as self-evident, but which Bekker (2020) rightly points out has not been demonstrated conclusively.

The selection of Bosman's work in this paper is motivated by his unique place in the South African literary landscape. Prior to the publication of Bosman's short stories, very few works published in English by South African authors were deliberately written for a local audience and about local material. The typical texts in the early colonial history exoticise the colony and reinforce the racial and colonial hierarchies of the 19th century. The most clearly defined genre from the period before Bosman was the imperial romance, with a hero that conquers the unknown but exotic landscape and its people. The best canonised example from this genre is Rider Haggard's *King Solomon's Mines* originally published in 1885 (Chrisman 2012).[2] MacKenzie (2012: 373–4), along with Gray (1989) and Leff (2016), points out that Bosman, unlike his contemporaries, such as Pauline Smith (or Olive Schreiner's *Story of an African Farm* half a century before him), consistently published his short stories in local literary journals and sought to establish a local literary tradition through his publication and involvement in a number of local publishing ventures. Brink (1976) similarly credits Bosman, alongside Alan Paton, with pioneering roles in the establishment of an indigenised South African English-language literary tradition.

The next section introduces the corpus and method of the study, before the two sets of results are presented.

2. METHODS

This study adopts a corpus linguistic method, complemented by close reading through a syntactic lens. Bosman's entire oeuvre, in both English and Afrikaans, was carefully edited for a centenary edition around 2001. This work was undertaken by a team of Stephen Gray, Craig MacKenzie and Leon de Kock and published in fourteen volumes from 1998–2005 (MacKenzie 2005). The editors followed a conservative approach to reconstruct the texts as closely as possible to the first originally published version (which is no longer publicly available), while correcting obvious typing mistakes and, in a few cases, grammatical errors. An upshot of this was that a modern electronic copy of the work of Bosman came into being, and this was generously made available to me by Craig MacKenzie. The focus of the present study is on the most well-known set of Bosman's short stories, those in which he uses a fictional narrator called Oom Schalk Lourens. This narrator tells these stories to an appreciative audience of people that one might presume includes (a fictional alter ego of) the author, roughly in the time when Bosman was a teacher in the Marico district, 1926, who in turn 'merely' records these stories in writing.

For the analysis of vocabulary, the wordlist and keyword functions in WordSmith Tools Version 8 (Scott 2020) was used. A subcorpus of the Oom Schalk stories, consisting of 52 stories that were available electronically, was made (electronic copies of the remaining eight could not be retrieved due to file conversion problems). A wordlist of the Oom Schalk subcorpus, amounting to 120,451 words, was made and analysed for lexical items that originated in South African languages other than English. These were mostly from Afrikaans, but some were from Setswana, the indigenous language spoken in the Marico area. The wordlist contains 6,724 unique tokens. For reasons of feasibility, all tokens that occurred at least three times were examined, leaving 3,024 tokens under examination. The non-English words, other than proper nouns, were listed and classified further and English cognates of these words were also extracted from the list to consider possible variation or competition in the selection between languages.

For the grammatical constructions, an initial close reading was done of a sample of stories from the early period (1930–1), the period during which Bosman lived in London (1934–40) and the final years of his life (1948–51). Grammatical features of interest were identified by hand and examples annotated manually on the text. This was followed by a corpus search, using WordSmith 8, on the entire Oom Schalk subcorpus, and parallel searches of the Ponelis Corpus of Spoken Afrikaans (data[3] from mid 1970s) and the 50 million-word Taalkommissiekorpus of contemporary written Afrikaans (2011) where that data was too sparse in the spoken corpus. The analysis of grammatical patterns was also supported by means of a keywords comparison in WordSmith 8, where the wordlist of the Oom Schalk subcorpus was compared with the subcorpus of fiction from the 1900s to the 1950s, the decades in which Bosman lived, extracted from the historical corpus of South African English (Wasserman 2014).

3. RESULTS

3.1 Vocabulary

The most prominent indigenous vocabulary items in the Oom Schalk Lourens stories are the names of characters, followed by place names. A total of 227 tokens were identified that denote non-English names, of which five refer to African characters (for example, Mosiga, Ndambe) and the remaining 222 tokens refer to Afrikaans characters. English characters are usually explicitly marked as English, as illustrated by the extract from 'The Rooinek' in the introduction to this chapter. The few African characters are also usually introduced in the text with a clear identification of the ethnic Otherness, as shown by example (2).

(2) I remember the last drum-man they had at the Mtosa huts outside Ramoutsa. His name was Mosigo. ('Bush Telegraph')

The geographical setting is equally clear from the place names. The word list reveals 38 tokens that denote South African places. These mostly carry Afrikaans place names (with some still recognisably Dutch in spelling, such as Zeerust and Drogedal), alongside a smaller number of African place names, such as Ramoutsa and Molopo.

Common nouns that are from Afrikaans or Setswana account for 96 of the tokens with a frequency of three or higher in the electronic corpus. These tokens cover a range of semantic domains. A summary of these terms and their English equivalents is given in Table 3.1, grouped into semantic domains.

Group identifiers are from Afrikaans and from African languages and reflect the racist practices of the time. They also clearly reveal that the focalising consciousness in these stories is Afrikaans. This ties in very clearly with the characterisation that Schneider (2007: 50) gives of literary creativity in a new variety of English, that it is 'rooted in the new culture', and Brink's (1976) notion that with Bosman, English became a language for local rather than metropolitan expression. Thus the singular

Table 3.1 Indigenous language vocabulary with the English equivalents and raw frequency in the Oom Schalk subcorpus

Domain	Afrikaans (and Setswana)	English
Peoples (Afr 423, Eng 103)	Indigenous people: *Kaffirs* (128), *kaffir* (108), *kaffir's* (3), *Mtotas* (13), *Bapedi* (12), *piccanin* (6), *hottentot* (4) English: *rooinek* (7), *rooineks* (3), *uitlander* (3) Afrikaners: *boer* (47), *boers* (18), *baas* (26), *burghers* (20), *burgers* (15), *Afrikaner* (10)	Indigenous people: *Black/s* (0) English: *(the) English*[a] (65), *Englishman* (25), *Englishmen* (4), *Englishman's* (1), *redcoats* (5), *red coat* (1), *redneck* (0) Afrikaners: *Dutch/Dutchman* (0), *boss* (0), *countryman/men* (0), *citizen* (1), *citizens* (1)
Church and religion (Afr 202, Eng 51)	*ouderling* (65), *ouderling's* (12) *predikant* (59), *predikant's* (5), *nagmaal* (42), *nagmaals* (5), *pastorie* (6), *dominee* (5), *Kerkbode* (3), *Vader* (0)	*elder* (15), *minister* (5), *communion* (1), *parsonage* (0), *reverend* (28), *Father* (2)
Military and history (Afr 184, Eng 8)	*Trek* (51), *trekked* (34), *trekking* (6), *veldkornet* (38), *veldkornet's* (6), *kommandant* (21), *commandants* (3), *volksraad* (18), *seksie* (4), *assegais* (3)	*Move out* (1), *moved out* (1), *(field) cornet* (0), *commandant* (0), *colonel* (0), *commander* (0), *(house of) assembly* (0), *parliament* (0), *section* (4), *throwing spear* (1), *spears* (1)
Landscape (Afr 183, Eng 13)	Trees: *Withaak* (21), *withaaks* (7), *karee* (4), *maroelas* (7), *kremetart* (5), *tamboetie* (4) Geological features: *koppie* (61), *koppies* (3), *donga* (16), *krantz* (15), *krantzes* (3), *bult* (5), *vlakte* (5), *vlaktes* (3), *rant* (4), *rante* (4), *vlei* (4) Animals: *aardvark* (3), *aasvoëls* (3), *koedoe* (3), *kwê(voël)* (3)	Trees: *umbrella thorn* (0), *karee* (4), *baobab* (0), *tambotie* (4) Geological features: *hill* (1), *hills* (1), *hillock* (0), *ditch* (0), *rockface* (0), *plain* (0), *reef* (0), *marsh* (0) Animals: *aardvark* (3), *vulture* (0), *kudu* (0), *(grey) lourie* (0)
House (Afr 114, Eng 34)	*voorkamer* (48), *voorhuis* (8), *stoep* (25), *riem* (16), *riempies* (9), *riempiestoel* (4), *rusbank* (4), *kombuis* (0)	*lounge* (0), *dining room* (2), *hall* (0), *porch* (0), *veranda* (3), *raw ox-hide thong* (1), *leash* (0), *couch* (0), *kitchen* (27), *kitchens* (1)
Life on the farm (Afr 65, Eng 27)	*veldskoens* (22), *veldskoen* (5), *kraal* (12), *miltsiek* (7), *rinderpest* (7), *sjambok* (5), *bywoner* (4), *inspanning* (3)	*shoe* (2), *sheep-camp* (1), *barbed-wire camp* (2), *miltsiek* (7), *rinderpest* (7), *whip* (7), *whips* (1), *subfarmer/sharecropper* (0), *harness/harnessing* (0)

Table 3.1 (cont.)

Domain	Afrikaans (and Setswana)	English
Food and drink (Afr 28)	*mampoer* (13), *biltong* (7), *dagga* (5), *beskuit* (3)	*rusk* (0)
Other (Afr 14, Eng 17)	*landdrost's* (11), *dorp* (3)	*magistrate* (3), *magistrate's* (2), *magistrates* (1), *town* (11)

[a] Excluding references to the English language.

kaffir and plural *kaffirs* occur more than 200 times, across more than half of all the texts.[4] The use of these derogatory (and, from the current perspective, hugely offensive) words, albeit in their 'English spelling', was typical at the time of writing and they also occur in other texts from the same period. MacKenzie (2005: 10) refers to various editorial practices over the years, in which the word has been edited out and replaced by less offensive terms like 'black', but for the centenary edition, he and his fellow editors chose to retain Bosman's original formulation.

Afrikaner(s) and *Boer(s)* are both used to denote the people of which Oom Schalk Lourens is a member, while *Boer* is never used in its dictionary sense of farmer (which would be spelled with lower case b). The Afrikaans word for citizens, *burgers* and slightly anglicised in spelling to *burghers* also occur, especially in the context of stories about the war, where they do contrast with the English who are *redcoats*. The English (people) are denoted by English (language) forms like the *English*, *Englishman* and *Englishmen* far more frequently than *uitlander* (literally out-landers, people from abroad) or the derogatory Afrikaans form *rooinek(s)*. The central concern of Oom Schalk with the English and the antagonism between the Afrikaner and the English is clearly shown by the use of these words, such as the following examples.

(3) Grieta Prinsloo was due to come back from the finishing school at Zeerust, where she had gone to learn **English** manners and dictation and other high-class subjects. (Willem Prinsloo's 'Peach Brandy')

(4) In those days we still called the **English** 'redcoats'. ('The Red Coat')

(5) Of course, that was a long time ago. It was before the Great Trek. But it seems that even in those days there was a lot of trouble between the Boers and **English**. It had a lot to do with

slaves. The **English** Government wanted to free the slaves . . . ('Bushveld Romance')

These citations give a sample of the way Oom Schalk sketches the relationship of 'his people' to the English. The potential for irony and social commentary is quite obvious in examples (3) and (5), as is often the case elsewhere too. People are principally classified as belonging to a particular ethnic group and the relations between ethnic groups are antagonistic at the macro scale. In individual stories, the exceptions are in focus, where individual characters such as Nongaas, Mosigo or the Englishman Webber are treated with far more humanity than the blanket group descriptions.

The space in the short stories is described by Afrikaans terms for features of the landscape, design of the house, life on the farm, and food and drink, which are more frequent than the corresponding English equivalents in most cases. These preferences, illustrated by examples (6) and (7), tie in with the first nexus that Schneider (this volume) identifies, in that the cultural objects of the rural Afrikaner life are presented in ways that reflect their uniqueness and otherness from the English perspective.

(6) From where I lay, with my head on the stone, I had a clear view of the road all the way up to where it disappeared over the **bult**.[5] ('Dream by the Bluegum')

(7) I remember the first time I made myself a pair of **veldskoens**[6] out of that blue sole. The stuff was easy to work with, and smooth. And all the time I was making the **veldskoens** I knew it was very wrong. And I was still more disappointed when I found that the blue sole wore well. If anything, it was even better than raw quagga hide. This circumstance was very regrettable to me. ('Camp-fires at Nagmaal')

The second nexus that Schneider (this volume) identifies is the more abstract dimensions of culture. Given the specificity of the texts, Schneider's analysis cannot be replicated in full; thus, even though first-person singular pronouns account for 71 per cent of all first-person pronouns (3,704 vs 1,516), a number that is in the same ballpark as the numbers for more collectivist cultures in Schneider's Table 2.5 (this volume), it may have to do with the types of stories told by Oom Schalk, and I would therefore not attach the same confident interpretation[7] to it as Schneider can for a much more balanced corpus like the International

Corpus of English (ICE). Nevertheless, the vocabulary in Table 3.1 points to evidence that more general and intangible aspects of Afrikaans culture, beyond objects, are also reflected in the short stories, and that a similar general cultural dimension can be extracted.

Afrikaans terms of address are used very frequently in reporting the speech of characters, especially kinship terms like *Oom* (although this is also used once in every story to identify the narrator by name – Oom Schalk Lourens) and *Neef*, but also a title like *Dominee* and the colloquial *kêrels*. Apart from *Uncle* that is used as a term of address five times in one short story ('Marico Moon'), and even there alongside '*Oom*' in the direct speech attributed to the same character, the English equivalents of these terms are absent as terms of address in these texts, although they are used in the narration. The strategic use of terms of address is illustrated by example (8).

(8) 'Certainly, I shall pray for your little girl's recovery,' the **predikant** said to Gertruida. 'Take me to her.' Gertruida hesitated. 'Will you – will you pray for her the Catholic way, **dominee**?' Gertruida asked.
Now it was the **predikant's** turn to draw back.
'But, Gertruida,' he said, 'you, you whom I myself confirmed in the Enkel-Gereformeerde Kerk in Zeerust – how can you now ask me such a thing? Did you not learn in the catechism that the Romish ritual is a mockery of the Holy Ghost?'
'I married Piet Reilly,' Gertruida answered simply, 'and his faith is my faith. Piet has been very good to me, **Father**. And I love him.'
We noticed that Gertruida called the **predikant** 'Father,' now, and not '**Dominee**'. ('Dopper and Papist')

The passage shows the use of three terms for a minister of the church: *predikant* (equivalent to *minister*, and not used as term of address but as vocational noun), *dominee* (equivalent to *reverend*, and used as term of address or as vocational noun), and *Father* (the English form, that is associated with the Catholic ministry in this passage). The narrator, Oom Schalk, consistently refers to the minister as a *predikant*, but in Gertruida's direct wording, she shifts from *dominee* to *Father* as terms of address for the minister.

Religious practices are clearly a persistent concern in the Oom Schalk stories. The texts do not deal with dogma so much as the duplicity of religious practices. The Afrikaans vocabulary items such as *nagmaal* ('holy communion', in 19 different texts), *ouderling* ('elder', 65 times in nine texts), reference to the Reformed Church (Gereformeerde Kerk) by its colloquial name *Doppers*, all signal the centrality of the church and religious practices in the milieu of the short stories.

The history of the Afrikaner, in particular the conflicts with both the English and the indigenous African groups, also receives ample attention, with the verb (and its derived noun) *trek* ('to move, relocate, migrate'), military ranks, and institutions like the house of parliament (*volksraad*, literally people's council) occurring throughout the texts, in preference to their English equivalents. Not only are the Afrikaans terms used but also the practices associated with these institutions are clearly conveyed. In typical Bosman style, though, the duplicity and contradictions are exposed as well, as illustrated by example (9).

(9) They made it illegal to hunt by lamp-light since the time a policeman got shot in the foot, this way, when he was out tracking cattle-smugglers on the Bechuanaland border.
The magistrate at Zeerust, who did not know the ways of the cattle-smugglers, found that the shooting was an accident. This verdict satisfied everybody except the policeman, whose foot was still bandaged when he came into court. **But the men in the Volksraad, some of whom had been cattle-smugglers themselves, knew better** than the magistrate did as to how the policeman came to have a couple of buckshot in the soft part of his foot, and accordingly they brought in this new law. ('The Love Potion')

Only by drawing on the cultural milieu of the Afrikaner, telling the stories through their eyes, is it possible for Bosman to create credible characters that inhabit this fictional world. The reader is invited to identify with these characters, and only if the reader does so is the stage set for Bosman's ironic twist, in which he exposes the duplicity of revered members of parliament, who themselves come from a less than honourable background. The elevated position that is ascribed to these characters is used to ultimately undermine their credibility and show them to be no different from the ordinary people, despite pretences to the contrary.

Bosman's use of vocabulary therefore indeed extends beyond the landscape and characters, as Brink (1976) suggests earlier writers did. He does not use the cultural lexicon of the Afrikaner simply to make fun of the characters or set up caricatures. Instead, he bestows an authenticity and humanity on them, which makes his criticism of cultural practices all the more effective. He would have sacrificed credibility had he presented his characters dressed up either as simpletons or in a thoroughly anglicised blazer.

3.2 Grammar

An important question that Bekker (2020) raises about the grammar of Bosman is the extent to which there is evidence for the claim (for example, by Aucamp 1972; Brink 1976) that he writes in camouflaged Afrikaans. This question ties in with Schneider's (this volume) third nexus, reflections of culture in grammar. In the case of a study of a single author, generalisations about an entire language or culture cannot be made, but to the extent that Bosman's aim was to evoke Afrikaans culture through the use of language, one can ask if he limited himself to vocabulary or also reflected Afrikaans through grammar. Three sets of grammatical constructions are considered: particle verb constructions, adverbial placement and verb-second word order.

English and Afrikaans both use particle verb constructions. These are verbs that collocate with a preposition-like particle to form a lexical unit. The particle verb combinations are often, but not always, equivalent across the two languages, opening up a space for creative reflection of Afrikaans particle verb combinations in English. When examining the texts manually, two different unusual particle combinations with the verb *think* were noticed, namely *think on* and *think out*, as illustrated by (10) and (11).

(10) Maybe Veldkornet Joubert could not think **out** a lot of nonsense to say just on the spur of the moment . . . ('Funeral Earth')
(11) While I was thinking **on** these lines, it suddenly struck me that Piet Reilly was now living on a farm about six miles on the Bushveld side of Sephton's Nek . . . ('Dopper and Papist')

Closer analysis of the corpus revealed that *think on* was a once-off coinage, but *think out* was used more widely, occurring eight times in the Oom Schalk subcorpus and a total of 23 times in the complete fiction corpus of Bosman. English conventionally uses the expression *a well thought out plan* or related constructions, which offers something of a bridge, but the Afrikaans particle verb combination *dink uit* is an entrenched combination with a clear set of semantics: one thinks out (that is, invents) plans, excuses, solutions or stories in Afrikaans, as confirmed by corpus analysis of Afrikaans, for example in (12).

(12) En ek dink 'n verskoning uit om nie sokker te speel nie.[8]
and I think an excuse out for not soccer to play not
'And I think out an excuse not to play soccer.'

The semantics of *think out* in Bosman's oeuvre, including the Oom Schalk subcorpus, corresponds very closely to the semantics of Afrikaans. Thus, his characters think out lies, things to say, this question or an answer. A marginal grammatical option in English is used more extensively by Bosman, while it also corresponds very closely in form and usage to the Afrikaans equivalent. Many other unusual verb and particle combinations, such as *think on*, are used once only. Thus, while Bosman coins expressions in English on the basis of Afrikaans, he is also sensitive to the degree of unusualness and seems to have preferred investing in those constructions that have some grammatical resonance in English already.

Various patterns of adverbial use were noticed in the texts, where word orders marginal to English (but not fully ungrammatical) are used more extensively in Bosman's writing, where such marginal examples resemble the dominant word order patterns of Afrikaans clearly.

(13) Months passed before I **again** saw Marthinus Taljaard . . .
('The Ferreira Millions')
Maande het verbygegaan voor ek **weer** vir Marthinus Taljaard gesien het.

An important syntactic difference between English and Afrikaans is that Afrikaans main clauses have a verb in second position, but all the other verbs and verb particles in final position, after the complements and adverbials other than clausal and optionally preposition phrases that may follow the verb-final position. Bosman exploits this option when he lets his characters break up the auxiliary and main verb sequences with adverbials. The outcome is typically marginal in English, but not completely ungrammatical, as the following examples show. A verbatim translation into Afrikaans will be fully grammatical and idiomatic, observing the correct placement of adverbials relative to the verb-final position.

(14) I was **only once** caught. ('Karel Flysman')
 'Ek is **net eenmaal** gevang.'
(15) He was **several times** acquitted. ('Romaunt of the Smuggler's Daughter')
 'Hy is **baie kere** vrygespreek.'

The final grammatical construction under consideration is the occasional use of topicalisation in combination with verb-second word order, which is conventional in Afrikaans but archaic at best in English. In Afrikaans declarative main clauses, there is always a verb in the second position, irrespective of what precedes the verb. In the unmarked case, the subject precedes the verb, but through topicalisation, an adverbial or a complement of the verb can occur in the clause-initial position, followed by the verb, and then the subject and the remainder of the clause. Bosman exploits the Afrikaans topicalisation with verb-second on occasion, as the following examples illustrate, with an Afrikaans translation[9] that is fully idiomatic.

(16) and in your heart **are** wild and fragrant fancies. ('Drieka and the Moon')
 'en in jou hart **is** wilde en geurige begeertes.'
(17) Inside the wagon-tents **sat** the women and children ... ('Ox-wagons on Trek')
 'Binne die watente **sit** die vroue en kinders.'
(18) down **would come** a shower of fine meal.[10] ('Sold Down the River')
 'neer **sou** 'n stortreën van fyn meel sif.'

In the case of copular constructions, as in (16), the inversion of subject and complement is not ungrammatical in English, if somewhat unusual, but the examples with lexical verbs in (17) and (18) are marked in English, while being fully grammatical and regular in Afrikaans. Bosman capitalises on a partial resemblance between the grammars of the two languages and then lets his characters choose the grammatical variant that is fully idiomatic in Afrikaans, giving the English an unusual ring.

4. CONCLUSION

Bosman uses English to reflect the Afrikaans world, including the culture and language of his characters. He selects Afrikaans vocabulary to represent the physical space and the cultural practices of his characters. He also exploits similarities between the grammars of Afrikaans and English to use English constructions that reflect the Afrikaans that are at the edges of the conventional in English. However, he seems to steer clear of distorted English syntax and, in that way, avoids caricatures that would undermine the credibility of his characters.

The grammatical strategy that Bosman's Oom Schalk stories reflect is consistent with quantitative cross-linguistic influence more than with qualitative cross-linguistic influence (CLI), along the lines proposed by Mougeon et al. (2005). Where qualitative CLI denotes the transfer of a structural pattern from language A to language B that is otherwise not present in language B, quantitative CLI refers to an increase in the frequency of constructions or a change in the contexts where choices are made between constructional variants. Such quantitative CLI has been shown to affect the grammatical relations between English and Afrikaans in both directions, such that they converge in their use of constructions (Kruger and van Rooy 2020; van Rooy 2020a, 2020b). It seems that Bosman adopted this strategy long before the two languages showed larger convergent movements, as Bekker (2020) also points out. Unlike the way his contemporary, Pauline Smith, used imitations of Afrikaans grammar (Coetzee 1981), Bosman does not distort Afrikaans, nor does he distort English particularly strongly, but exploits the margins of the possible. For a reader familiar with Afrikaans, as suggested by Aucamp (1972) and Brink (1976), this is sufficient to see the Afrikaans camouflaged underneath the surface of the English text.

NOTES

1. All textual material from Bosman's short stories is cited from the electronic corpus, and thus identified by the name of the short story. The stories are also available in print format in the volume *The Complete Oom Schalk Lourens Stories* edited by Craig MacKenzie (Bosman 2006).
2. Consideration of writing in Afrikaans and indigenous African

languages that predate Bosman fall outside the scope of this chapter, but these texts were very clearly written for a local audience.
3. Corpus originally transcribed by F. A. Ponelis in 1975 and 1976 from informal conversation and radio broadcasts, converted to electronic format by the present author. Not publicly available at the time of writing.
4. The taboo value of the 'K-word' is at least equal to but probably higher than the N-word in the USA.
5. Landscape: hill.
6. Life on the farm: veld-shoes or hide-shoes (Afrikaans *velskoen* 'hide+shoe' is more widely used than *veldskoen* 'field+shoe').
7. Despite my caution about the interpretation of the first-person pronoun numbers, if the same analysis is run on the Ponelis Corpus of Spoken Afrikaans, collected about 25 years after Bosman's death, the corresponding percentage of first-person singular pronouns is 72 per cent, thus very close to the Oom Schalk percentage. By contrast, replicating Schneider's analysis on the face-to-face conversations (S1A) from ICE-SA, collected in the mid 1990s (Jeffery 2003), shows that the first-person singular accounts for 80 per cent of the total first-person pronouns, suggesting even more individualism than ICE-GB (albeit for just one register, but this register is selected because of the attempt at orality in the Bosman stories).
8. A word-for-word gloss that reflects the Afrikaans word order and a translation are both provided.
9. In these examples, the English past tense is translated as present tense in Afrikaans, to correspond to the number of words in English. However, Breed (2013) reports that Afrikaans narration is indeed typically in the present tense and not the past tense.
10. Bosman uses 'meal' in the English, denoting flour, which is related to the Afrikaans form 'meel'.

REFERENCES

Aucamp, H. (1972). Gekamoefleerde Afrikaans: 'n Studie van H.C. Bosman. *Contrast*, *29*(8), 65–77.
Bekker, I. (2020). Literary reflections of early postcolonial English in South Africa. *World Englishes*, 1–14. <https://doi.org/10.1111/weng.12471> (last accessed 5 January 2021).

Bosman, H. C. (2006). *The complete Oom Schalk Lourens stories*. Ed. Craig MacKenzie. Human & Rousseau.

Breed, A. (2013). Die hedetyd is iets van die verlede: 'n taalkundige motivering vir die 'hedetydskryfkunstradisie' in Afrikaans [The present tense is something of the past: a linguistic motivation for the 'present tense writing tradition' in Afrikaans]. *Literator, 34*(2), 1–9.

Brink, A. P. (1976). English and the Afrikaans writer. *English in Africa, 3*(1), 35–46.

Chrisman, L. (2012). The imperial romance. In D. Attwell and D. Attridge (Eds.), *The Cambridge history of South African literature* (pp. 226–45). Cambridge University Press.

Coetzee, J. M. (1981). Pauline Smith and the Afrikaans language. *English in Africa, 8*(1), 25–32.

Gray, S. (1989). Herman Charles Bosman's use of short fictional forms. *English in Africa, 16*(1), 1–8.

Jeffery, C. (2003). On compiling a corpus of South African English. *Southern African Linguistics and Applied Language Studies, 21*(4), 341–4.

Kruger, H. and van Rooy, B. (2020). A multifactorial analysis of contact-induced change in speech reporting in written White South African English (WSAfE). *English Language and Linguistics, 24*(1), 179–209.

Leff, C. (2016). Herman Charles Bosman: A man of profound contradictions. *English in Africa, 43*(1), 109–29.

MacKenzie, C. (1999). *The oral-style short story in English: A.W. Drayson to H.C. Bosman*. Rodopi.

MacKenzie, C. (2003). 'Simple unvarnished tales'? A case of H.C. Bosman's writerly technique. *English Studies in Africa, 46*(2), 1–12.

MacKenzie, C. (2005). Editing Bosman's stories. *Current Writing, 17*(1), 1–13.

MacKenzie, C. (2012). The metropolitan and the local: Douglas Blackburn, Pauline Smith, William Plomer, Herman Charles Bosman. In D. Attwell and D. Attridge (Eds.), *The Cambridge history of South African literature* (pp. 360–79). Cambridge University Press.

Mougeon, R., Nadasdi, T. and Rehner, K. (2005). Contact-induced linguistic innovations on the continuum of language use: The case of French in Ontario. *Bilingualism: Language and Cognition, 8*(2), 99–115.

Schneider, E. W. (2007). *Postcolonial English: Varieties around the world*. Cambridge University Press.

Scott, M. (2020). WordSmith Tools (Version 8) [Computer software].

Lexical Analysis Software.

Taalkommissie van die Suid-Afrikaanse Akademie vir Wetenskap en Kuns. (2011). Taalkommissiekorpus 1.1 [Online corpus]. CTexT, North-West University. <http://viva-afrikaans.org> (last accessed 5 January 2021).

van Rooy, B. (2020a). Present-day Afrikaans in contact with English. In R. Hickey (Ed.), *English in multilingual South Africa: The linguistics of contact and change* (pp. 241–64). Cambridge University Press.

van Rooy, B. (2020b). Grammatical change in South African Englishes. *World Englishes*, 1–14. <https://doi.org/10.1111/weng.12470> (last accessed 5 January 2021).

Wasserman, R. (2014). *Modality on trek: Diachronic changes in written South African English across text and context* [Doctoral dissertation, North-West University].

Wenzel, M. (1999). Of history and memory: Re-reading selected stories by Herman Charles Bosman on the Anglo-Boer War. *Kunapipi, 21*(3), 106–10.

CHAPTER 4

Susmaryosep! Lexical Evidence of Cultural Influence in Philippine English

Loy Lising

1. INTRODUCTION

This paper, based on a 400,000-word corpus, investigates how culture permeates into and is reflected through language via the presence of lexicosemantic tokens from Tagalog and other Philippine languages in sentences that observe English grammar in Philippine English data. Lexical research on Philippine English, thus far, has shown innovative usage of existing vocabulary, the introduction of indigenous terms or concepts, the invention of hybrid forms, the enduring usage of words or phrases that are becoming obsolete in their variety of origin, and the borrowing of lexicosemantic items from donor Philippine languages, especially Spanish into English (see for example Peters 2020; Gonzales 2017; Fuchs 2017; Borlongan 2007; Bolton and Butler 2004; Bautista 1997). These studies, however, all set out to investigate lexical innovations in Philippine English. Somewhat different from these studies, this paper aims to examine what lexicosemantic tokens from Philippine languages continue to permeate in Philippine English as evidence of cultural influence as a consequence of language contact.

In foregrounding the notion of borrowing, I am reminded of Myers-Scotton's (2006) framework of 'core' and 'cultural' borrowings in understanding the attributes and behaviours of lexicosemantic items taken from a donor language that are borrowed and which then persist in the recipient language. The former are lexical elements that are borrowed despite the fact that equivalent elements already exist in the recipient language; communicative functions motivate their use. On the other hand, the latter are lexicosemantic items in the donor language that represent objects and concepts that do not have direct equivalents in the recipient language. It is this perspective that provides the framework for this paper.

2. LANGUAGE AND CULTURE REVISITED

To assess the cultural impact on Philippine English of lexicosemantic borrowings from Philippine languages, it is necessary to understand the languages and cultures that have influenced Philippine society thus far. It is, therefore, paramount in this section to sketch, albeit skeletally, the many linguistic and cultural influences that have helped shape Philippine society and by extension Philippine English. Very little is known of the country's linguistic ecology and language contact situations before the Spanish colonial period of 1565–1898 and American colonisation beginning in 1900 (Bernardo 2004). Scott (1984), however, provides us with a historical account based on palaeography and related publications. He gives an account of the influence of Sanskrit (through Malay), Fukien (Hokkien) Chinese and Malay particularly on Tagalog. Prior to the arrival of the Spaniards, Scott (1984: 42) reports that 'Manila was a bilingual community . . . its bourgeoisie speaking Malay as a second language'. So, in considering the 182 Philippine languages (Ethnologue 2020) as a reference point when looking at local language contact situations and how indigenous and settler languages may pervade Philippine English, it is also important to keep these earlier linguistic influences in mind. In particular, due to the Spanish colonisation that lasted over three centuries, one finds the rather ubiquitous presence of Spanish-derived words perfusing local languages. And especially in the data discussed later, one finds the evidence of this longstanding presence in the way these words use either Spanish or Tagalog orthography interchangeably, evidence of the indigenisation of some Spanish words.

Such influences are variably reported in studies by Bautista (1997), Borlongan (2007), Bolton and Butler (2004), Fuchs (2017) and Peters (2020). In their analyses of the printed text types in the Philippine component of the International Corpus of English, Bautista (1997) and Borlongan (2007) similarly found that persistent borrowings in Philippine English from local Philippine languages and Spanish reflected semantic categories of flora and fauna, food, politics, life and expressions. Because the aim of both these studies was to investigate lexical innovations, not cultural influence of local languages, their discussions simply account for the presence of these lexical items without attributions to the reasons for their enduring presence in Philippine English. Bolton and Butler (2004: 104), on the other hand, in reviewing previous lexical research in the Philippines came to the conclusion that the inventory of lexical items distinct from those in exonormative standards continues to mirror a 'colonial inventory of the tribes and products of the Philippine islands'. Peters's (2020) study is perhaps the most relevant to this paper in that she investigated the cultural borrowings present in the 2012 Corpus of Global Web-based English (GloWbE) data to explore the presence of Spanish-derived lexicosemantic tokens (found in an earlier study by Freer (1906)) to show the enduring influence of Spanish in Philippine English.

Most of the works mentioned focus on the lexicon of Philippine English and share in their observation of innovations through four specific means: (1) borrowings of words from indigenous items, (2) adaptation and formation of new words and new compounds patterned after the source English, (3) persistent use of words which may have become archaic in the source English and (4) prevailing use of Spanish-derived lexical items. However, none of them discusses these findings in relation to the relationship of language and culture. This makes the focus of this study unique and highlights its contribution to the ongoing conversation on the interplay of language and culture in language contact situations, especially in a multilingual ecology like the Philippines.

3. DATA AND METHODOLOGY

The data source used in this paper for the investigation of the 'manifestation forms of cultural objects' (Schneider 2018: 29) in Philippine English is the Philippine component of the International Corpus of English (ICE-PH) (Bautista et al. 2004). Like the rest of the components from other countries, ICE-PH constitutes 1,000,000 words derived from 500 written and spoken texts of 2,000 words each, which have been annotated for various pre-established linguistic features. Of significance in this paper are indigenous tokens originally annotated and marked as indigenous <indig>. These are either singular lexical items, phrases or clauses expressed in a language other than English. There are 200 written texts and 300 spoken texts in the corpus. For the purpose of this paper, only the 200 written texts of 400,000 words were included in the analysis. In his paper on forensic stylistics, McMenamin suggests that:

[s]tyle in written language reflects both a writer's conscious response to the requirements of genre and context as well as the result of his or her unconscious and habituated choices of the grammatical elements acquired through the long term experiential process of writing. (McMenamin 2010: 488)

The written texts, therefore, exhibit more 'habituated' and considered decision-making in writing and demand a level of formality that may be absent in spoken texts. Therefore, any lexicosemantic items borrowed from and unique to Tagalog or any other Philippine languages which are inserted into an English grammatical matrix sentence should be arguably considered part of the features of Philippine English. After all, contributors to the Philippine English corpus, like in other ICE corpora, were vetted and deemed legitimate speakers of the (Philippine English) variety.

Subsequent data analysis to tease out the lexicosemantic tokens involved a four-step process. First, through the use of the concordance facility in AntConc (Anthony 2017), the number of indigenous entries marked <indig> in each of the 17 written text types (for example, *student essays*, *social letters* among others) was noted for tabular presentation, as reflected in Table 4.1 in Section 4.

Second, a separate concordance search in each text type ensued to identify which texts within the text type (for example, W1A-001 to W1A-010 for *student essays*) bear the indigenous entries, which were then systematically analysed to determine if the sentence that has the <indig> mark-up symbol observes an English syntactic frame with a single lexicosemantic token from a Philippine language. This second step is important to establish that the usage is widespread and not simply a reflection of a participant's idiolect. Other sentences bearing the <indig> mark-up symbol were excluded from the succeeding step of the analysis if they exhibited one of these three behaviours: the lexical token identified as indigenous is a proper noun; it is a codeswitched sentence which neatly shifts at the phrase or clause level; or the sentence has a Tagalog grammatical matrix. The first and third exclusion rules should be straightforward and need no further explanation. The second rule was applied given that studies have shown that multilingual speakers often codeswitch the languages in their repertoire as a norm to achieve various communicative functions (see for example Bautista 2004; Lising et al. 2020). Codeswitches at distinct boundaries, also called smooth switching (Bautista 2004; Poplack 2004), are quite rich in the ICE and necessitate a separate analysis. Table 4.1 in Section 4 showcases two sets of numbers that show the original number of all tokens marked <indig> and the subsequent number after the exclusion rules were applied. Here are some examples of each of these three linguistic behaviours.

Lexical token is a proper noun:

(1) Science and mathematics organizations such as the Ateneo Chemical Society, **<indig> Samahang Pisika ng Ateneo </indig>** and the Ateneo Math Club organize symposia and talks to learn about theoretical developments and practical applications in specific fields of inquiry. (ICE-PHI:W2D-002#113:1) [Tagalog: *Ateneo Physics Organisation*]

Codeswitching at the phrase or clause level:

(2) Now, I decided to balance my diet **<indig> para indi man ko matam-an </indig>**. (ICE-PHI:W1B-002#53:2) [Hiligaynon: so that I won't overdo it.]

Tagalog grammatical matrix sentence:

(3) <quote> <indig> <it> “ Bink, ba't ayaw mong magpahawak kay Claire? ” </it> </indig> </quote> </p> (ICE-PHI:W2F-020#76:1) [Tagalog: Bink, why don't you like Claire to hold you?]

Third, the valid entries, those which have an English syntactic frame with one lexicosemantic token marked indigenous, were then noted and further analysed to determine if they are 'core' or 'cultural' borrowings following Myers-Scotton's (2006: 212) framework. Once the categories were determined, in the fourth and final step, the tokens were further examined to ascertain their semantic categories.

4. LEXICOSEMANTIC BORROWINGS ACROSS WRITTEN TEXT TYPES

The analysis of the cultural borrowings present in the ICE-PH corpus yielded the following results. The total number of indigenous items was tabulated to see at a glance how many there are and where these items are sited. Table 4.1 reflects the spread of indigenous words across the 200 texts in the written component of the ICE-PH. It is important to note that the last column in the table displays two sets of numbers. The first one accounts for the number of times the <indig> mark-up symbol was originally applied in the various texts by the ICE-PH team who put this corpus together, while the second number indicates the number of indigenous tokens post-analysis deemed suitable for the purpose of this paper: any singular lexicosemantic item or expression in a Philippine language embedded within an English grammatical matrix sentence. As shown in this table, of the 17 written text types, four are non-printed and 13 are printed text types. The four non-printed text types comprise 50 unedited texts of 2,000 words, while the 13 printed text types are made up of 150 texts of 2,000 words, which have most likely

Table 4.1 Total number of occurrences of indigenous lexical items in written texts

Written text category	Written text type and number of texts	Number of occurrences of indigenous items pre- and post-syntactic analysis
Non-printed		
Non-professional writing	Student essays (10)	[56; 8]
	Examination scripts (10)	[6; 3]
Correspondence	Social letters (15)	[242; 110]
	Business letters (15)	[32; 10]
Printed		
Academic writing	Humanities (10)	[113; 35]
	Social sciences (10)	[43; 30]
	Natural sciences (10)	[38; 32]
	Technology (10)	[35; 19]
Non-academic writing	Humanities (10)	[50; 24]
	Social sciences (10)	[77; 27]
	Natural sciences (10)	[47; 33]
	Technology (10)	[54; 42]
Reportage	Press news reports (20)	[126; 16]
Instructional writing	Administrative writing (10)	[8; 2]
	Skills and hobbies (10)	[100; 60]
Persuasive writing	Press editorials (10)	[23; 2]
Creative writing	Novels and stories (20)	[180; 103]
Total		[1,230; 556]

gone through some form of editing prior to their publication. The four non-printed text types originally had 336 tokens marked <indig> with only 131 tokens of these included in the final analysis. The printed texts originally had 894 <indig> tokens with only 399 of these considered in the final analysis.

Table 4.2, in particular, showcases the non-printed text types, the number of these text types that actually had indigenous lexicosemantic tokens in them and the number of legitimate tokens that were further analysed for their semantic categories.

Table 4.2 Total number of non-printed text types and corresponding number of legitimate indigenous tokens

Written text type and original number of texts	Number of texts with legitimate tokens	Number of legitimate indigenous tokens
Student essays (10)	3	8
Examination scripts (10)	3	3
Social letters (15)	13	110
Business letters (15)	1	10
Total (50)	20	131

It is important to discuss the data in Table 4.2 relative to the text types. While all of these text types are non-printed, it can be assumed from our knowledge of genres that some of them demand or can only allow certain linguistic features. For instance, in the case of student essays and examination scripts, because these are assessed written tasks, it is unlikely that students will use non-English expressions unless they are warranted in the texts. The 11 lexicosemantic tokens, therefore, that we see in these two text types are core and cultural borrowings that are assumed to be essential in highlighting the points made by the students in their essays. Here are examples of each:

(4) It is true, and I know readers will agree with me that the strategies of today's **<indig> <it> TRAPO </it> </indig>** are seduction of agents (citizens), suspicion and panic in the side of the agent, and manipulation of interest. (ICE-PHI:W1A-001#52:2)

(5) This will help eradicate the **<indig> “ pagsasamantala ” </indig>** of some big private establishments in terms of pricing. </p> (ICE-PHI:W1A-011#83:2)

Excerpt (4) above is a student essay and the use of the borrowed word *trapo*, which is a coinage, efficiently delivers the intended meaning in this sentence. *Trapo* as a new coinage straddles the linguistic behaviour of both core and cultural borrowings. It is a cultural blend of the English words *traditional* and *politician*. It is also a core borrowing from Tagalog meaning 'rag'. Excerpt (5), on the other hand, is an examination script that uses a cultural borrowing *pagsasamantala*. This is a cultural borrowing as the Tagalog word has no direct singular lexical equivalent in English and cuts to the chase of what needs to be expressed in a full clause: *taking advantage of someone else*.

The third non-printed text type, social letters, generates the greatest number of indigenous tokens. This is predictable in an informal personal piece of writing. While the 110 indigenous tokens are quite mixed, there are two linguistic behaviours that are interesting to highlight here: a preponderance of kinship terms and borrowings from non-Tagalog languages, Hiligaynon and Kapampangan, which is not seen anywhere else. The following exemplify these:

(6) During Mommy's birthday, <indig> Ate </indig> Gigi made tuna <foreign> sushi </foreign> and it was a hit. (ICE-PHI:W1B-008#17:1)

(7) Take care and do not make so much <indig> lagaw </indig> especially if you do not have company. (ICE-PHI:W1B-002#34:1)

(8) <indig> Ma </indig> and <indig> Atche </indig>, James was given 6 months. (ICE-PHI:W1B-003#73:2)

Excerpt (6) shows the use of the Tagalog kinship term *ate* (a token used to address an older sister). It is one of the many Tagalog kinship terms used in a few text types in the corpus and these will be discussed further in Section 5. The seventh excerpt demonstrates the presence of another Philippine language in the corpus, the Hiligaynon word *lagaw*, which means in this usage 'larking around'. Similarly, excerpt 8 also shows the use of yet another language, Kapampangan, in the form of the honorific *atche*, which bears the same meaning as *ate*.

The text type business letters is remarkable in that only one text (W1B-020) bears legitimate indigenous items and these all pertain to local types of banana as shown in the excerpt below.

(9) Compared with the <indig> lacatan </indig> variety, it takes two (2) years for the <indig> saba </indig> before

it is harvestable for the first time, while the <indig> lacatan </indig> variety can be harvestable in less than a year. (ICE-PHI:W1B-020#132:6)

Table 4.3, on the other hand, showcases the printed text types, the number of these text types that actually had indigenous lexicosemantic tokens in them, and the numbers of legitimate tokens and distinct tokens (types) that were further analysed for their semantic categories. The number of distinct types exhibits the diversity of indigenous items used throughout these particular text types.

Table 4.3 Total number of printed text types and corresponding number of legitimate indigenous tokens

Written text type and original number of texts	Number of texts with legitimate tokens	Number of legitimate indigenous tokens (distinct types)
Academic		
Humanities (10)	5	35 (20)
Social sciences (10)	5	30 (22)
Natural sciences (10)	4	32 (10)
Technology (10)	3	19 (7)
Non-academic		
Humanities (10)	7	24 (18)
Social sciences (10)	7	27 (15)
Natural sciences (10)	4	33 (26)
Technology (10)	5	41 (15)
Press news reports (20)	12	17 (14)
Administrative writing (10)	2	2 (2)
Skills and hobbies (10)	7	61 (36)
Press editorials (10)	1	2 (2)
Novels and stories (20)	16	76 (50)
Total	78	399 (237)

The indigenous tokens in the 13 printed text types vary across different semantic categories which will be discussed in Section 5. The two text types in this printed category that warrant some remarks are novels and stories, and skills and hobbies as they generated the greatest number of indigenous tokens following social letters. In skills and hobbies, there is a rich presence of indigenous terminologies pertaining to arts and crafts and plant variants, topics consistent with the genre of this text type. On the other hand, in novels and stories, there is a high volume of Tagalog kinship and honorific terms in reference to a range of relationships: unrelated older man (*mang*), older woman (*aling*); one's father (*tatay*) and mother (*nanay*); older brother (*kuya*) and older sister (*ate*); and one's godfather to one's child (*pare*), which can also be used simply as a term of endearment for a close male friend. I will now discuss the relevant semantic categories.

5. INDIGENOUS LOANWORDS: CULTURAL BORROWINGS

As explained in Section 3, the legitimate indigenous tokens identified as 'core' or 'cultural' borrowings were further analysed to ascertain their semantic categories. This section discusses the six semantic categories identified to which the 'cultural' borrowings found in the data belong.

5.1 Arts, Crafts and Costumes

This semantic category, which is similar to Piao et al.'s (2005) 'arts and crafts' category, refers to cultural borrowings that reflect indigenous handiworks and Filipino traditional clothing. Excerpts (10), (11) and (12) exemplify this.

(10) A red <indig> <it> tampipi </it> </indig> goes well with a <indig> capiz </indig> star. </p> (ICE-PHI:W2D-015#16:1)
(11) <indig> <it> Sinamay </it> </indig> is the in thing for wrapping gifts, whether the material is used as wrapper or ribbon. </p> (ICE-PHI:W2D-015#7:1)
(12) With a pair of sharp scissors she shredded each <indig> barong Tagalog </indig>, each <indig> camisa de chino </indig>, each long-sleeved shirt, each pair of trousers, until there was a waist-high pile of shredded fabric on the floor. </p> (ICE-PHI:W2F-005#42:1)

Excerpt (10) has two cultural indigenous tokens, *tampipi* and *capiz*. *Tampipi* is a small trunk for clothes made from local materials such as palm leaves or bamboo, while *capiz* (follows Spanish orthography and is spelt *kapis* in Tagalog) refers to the placuna shell often used for lamp shades and window panes.[1] Excerpt (11) uses the indigenous word *sinamay*, which is a type of coarse cloth from abaca fibres. Excerpt (12), on the other hand, shows the use of *barong* and *camisa de chino*; the former is a Tagalog word referring to a garment made from native pineapple fibres and often used in formal events, while the latter is a Spanish-derived term for a kind of shirt that has no collar.

5.2 Flora and Fauna

This semantic category, which is also reported in Bautista (1997), has the greatest number of cultural borrowings. Like in Bautista (1997), this category contains lexicosemantic tokens reflective of the rich natural resources of this tropical archipelago. The entries in this category reveal varieties of indigenous animals, vegetables and fruits – the excerpts below show *bangus* 'milkfish', *sitao* 'string bean', and *paho* 'a species of Philippine mango'.

(13) There's now a way to transport live <indig> <it> bangus </it> </indig>. (ICE-PHI:W2B-033#107:2)
(14) Biotech has already produced commercially Nitro Plus fertilizer specifically for such legumes as peanut, mungbean, cowpea, pole <indig> <it> sitao </it> </indig> and soybean. (ICE-PHI:W2B-038#11:1)
(15) This is often confused for <indig> paho </indig>. (ICE-PHI:W2A-030#45:1)

5.3 Food and Beverages

This semantic category is one of those in which we would expect to find cultural practices embodied in borrowed words. Excerpts (16) and (17) give us a peek at the kinds of Tagalog borrowings present in the data.

(16) He brewed us some coffee, cooked some <indig> tocino </indig> & we brought <indig> ensaymada </indig>. (ICE-PHI:W1B-002#129:3)
(17) <quote> “ He has a knife! ” </quote> thought Alberto, the realization jolting him and reaching his <indig> <it> tuba </it> </indig> - numbed mind. (ICE-PHI:W2F-012#82:1)

Excerpt (16) showcases *tocino* and *ensaymada* – both Spanish-derived words with the former used with Spanish orthography (Tagalog spelling *tosino*), which refers to cured meat, and the latter with Tagalog orthography (Spanish spelling *ensaimada*), which means a 'puffed cake', both Philippine delicacies. In addition, the cultural borrowing in excerpt (17) shows the use of *tuba*, a native wine made from the nipa palm tree.

5.4 Music and Entertainment

This semantic category, also similar to Piao et al.'s (2005) music, sports and entertainment category, shows cultural borrowings that reflect indigenous words pertaining to different forms of music and musical instruments and various kinds of entertainment people engage in.

(18) Throughout the day, as the household goes about its routinary chores and activities, one may hear snatches of a tender <it> <indig> panhimaturog </indig> </i> or lullaby as a mother cradles the baby in her arms, rhythmical <it> <indig> pakonsuelo </indig> </it> sung by <indig> Lolo </indig> or <indig> Lola </indig> to amuse the children, and a sad <it> <indig> logo-logo </indig> </it> or song of disappointment and world-weariness as a mother busies herself in the kitchen, mends clothes or weaves a hat when housework is done. </p> (ICE-PHI:W2A-010#10:1)

(19) The cockpit owner inspected the <indig> <it> tari </it> </indig> himself and ruled it legal because it had the same dimensions as the opponent's knife. (ICE-PHI:W2F-013#76:1)

The interesting thing about excerpt (18) is that the music-related lexical items used here, while all cultural borrowings, are not from Tagalog but from Bikol, another Philippine language. They are terms used to refer to specific genres of songs: a lullaby (*panhimaturog*), an entertaining song (*pakonsuelo*) and a love song of resentment (*logo-logo*). The kinship items present in excerpt (18) will be discussed later. In excerpt (19), *tari* is used to refer to the metal spur attached to a cock during cockfights, a very popular form of entertainment during weekends or fiesta (a religious festival), especially in the rural areas.

5.5 Politics and Governance

This semantic category, also similar to Piao et al.'s (2005) government and the public domain, shows (as in Bautista 1997; Bolton and Butler 2004; Borlongan 2007) a very high occurrence of the word *barangay* 'smallest unit of government', as in excerpt (20).

(20) There are some 7 <indig> barangays </indig> said to be on the paths of the Boac and Makulapnit rivers. (ICE-PHI:W2E-002#20:1)

5.6 Social Relationships, Kinship Terms and Traditional Expressions

This semantic category has the greatest number of cultural borrowings. In this category, what are showcased are two practices: the use of appellations that signal respect and social relationships and the use of kinship terms that signal one's blood relationship with the addressee. There are many kinship words in Philippine society across different languages, but the ones present in the ICE data are largely Tagalog with an offering from Kapampangan as pointed out below: those that address grandparents as in excerpt (18) above (*lolo* for grandfather and *lola* for grandmother – both Spanish-derived from *abuelo* and *abuela* transformed into Tagalog by keeping and reduplicating the last syllable); those that address parents (*tatay* for father and *nanay* for mother); those that address aunts and uncles (*tito* for uncle and *tita* for aunt); those that address older siblings (*kuya* for older brother and *ate* for older sister with an entry in Kapampangan (*atche*) as shown in excerpt (21)); those used to address unrelated older people simply to attribute respect (*mang* for an older male and *aling* for an older female).

(21) <indig> Atche </indig>, this is a must see for you! (ICE-PHI:W1B-011#108:1)

In addition to all these, there are also borrowed lexicosemantic tokens to indicate one's social relationship to another person that are unique to the language. Similar expressions may exist in English, but these expressions need to be in phrase forms, not a singular lexical item, as the following examples show: *barkada*, *balae* and *ninang*. *Barkada* is often used to refer to one's group of close friends who are always there for one another and is believed to be derived from the Spanish word *barcada* meaning 'boatload', perhaps in reference to the friendship forged while travelling at sea. *Balae* is the Tagalog term in reference to the parents of your son- or daughter-in-law and signals your newly acquired social relationship. The final lexical item, *ninang*, serves both as the term to indicate one's role as a godmother at someone's religious baptism or wedding, and at the same time, as an honorific term of address to one's godmother.

Excerpt (22), on the other hand, which uses the word *pasalubong*, reflects a cultural tradition of buying a friend or a loved one a token especially during one's travel as a way of expressing thoughtfulness; the English words *gift* or *present* do not quite capture the essence of the gesture. By extension, the act itself is still indicative of one's social relationship.

(22) But if you do come home even later on, he said not to forget to give his brother a call before, regarding to the <indig> pasalubong </indig> if there are any. </p> (ICE-PHI:W1B-001#75:1)

The examples in excerpts (23), (24) and (25) exemplify traditional expressions/interjections which have no direct English equivalent. *Basta* in excerpt (23) is a Spanish-derived adverb indicative of an acceptance of the writer's faithful/fateful declaration regardless of possible contradicting circumstance. In excerpt (24), *sayang* invites us to be empathetic with the writer who has failed to take advantage of an opportunity to rendezvous with someone as planned; it can be equated to the English expression, *What a pity!*. Finally, the interjection in excerpt (25), *Bahala na!*, is a common fatalistic expression one hears when people are at their wits' end and are not quite certain what measures to take to find a solution to an existing problem. They, therefore, take the view to just leave things as they are and hope things will somehow work out. Anecdotally, the expression is said to be originally expressed as *Bathala na!* (de Jong 2011). *Bathala* is an indigenous appellation for God.

(23) <indig> Basta </indig> I'm so thankful to God and I'm so happy. (ICE-PHI:W1B-002#73:2)
(24) To Mon Llenado, <indig> sayang </indig>, I was looking forward to meeting you again after more than 30 years! (ICE-PHI:W1B-014#109:5)

(25) Finally, he threw his hands up in the air, sighed, <quote> “ <indig> <it> Bahala na! </it> </indig> - - What the hell-- ” </quote> and applied makeup and powder on Alvarez's face. (ICE-PHI:W2F-011#11:1)

As discussed above, cultural borrowings are lexicosemantic items that are derived from local and other Philippine languages and have no equivalent in English. One of the significant findings shown in this section is the rich presence of Spanish-derived words in the data. In addition, investigating the kinds of cultural borrowings present in the data yielded six semantic categories that reveal the sites of these borrowings.

6. INDIGENOUS ALTERNATIVES: CORE BORROWINGS

The other borrowed items that permeate English grammatical matrix sentences are 'core' borrowings, which are lexicosemantic items that have English equivalents. However, as the examples below show, while English equivalents do exist, the indigenous alternatives are imbued with special connotations, which are lost once translated into English.

(26) Of course, the most show-biz term of all was reserved for the lead character: If Estrada has ordained himself a hero, it is in the cinematic sense of the term, that of <indig> <it> bida </it> </indig>. (ICE-PHI:W1A-005#14:1)

In excerpt (26), *hero*, the English equivalent of *bida*, is already featured at the beginning of the sentence, yet its Tagalog equivalent is utilised for emphasis later. The English word *hero* has a positive denotation. And while the Tagalog word *bida* is the same, it can also have a negative connotation when used to refer to someone who may not necessarily deserve the title.

(27) The term <mention> <it> popular </it> </mention> in our subject matter brings to mind the divide between the historically important local personalities and the “ significant ”, faceless <indig> <it> masa </it> </indig>. (ICE-PHI:W1A-009#68:1)

In excerpt (27), the Tagalog word *masa* is used instead of its English equivalent *masses*. While *masses* does equate in meaning to *masa*, it does not achieve the same dramatic effect as the Tagalog word *masa*, which is conceptually loaded with images of the strength of the silent majority.

(28) And they are the following: Teopista (gardener/ **<indig> lavandera </indig>**), Rosalie (all around house help), and Liselle(**<indig>yaya</indig>**).(ICE-PHI:W1B-001#109:1)

In this excerpt, we also see the use of 'core' borrowings of Spanish-derived *lavandera* (washerwoman; spelt in Tagalog as *labandera*) and *yaya* (housemaid), and while the English equivalents exist, they are less familiar and are rarely used in a Philippine context.

(29) The doctors back home took long breaks, napping or having **<indig> merienda </indig>** while the patients waited for them in the operating room. (ICE-PHI:W2F-006#202:1)

Finally, the use of the Spanish-derived *merienda* in excerpt (29) is more accurate than the English equivalent *snack* as the former is perfused with cultural connotations and multiplicity of meaning absent in the word *snack*. These connotations pertain to the kinds of food on offer and the frequency with which they are enjoyed. In Philippine society, *meriendas* are usually especially prepared and richer than English *snacks* – they are often expected mid-morning and mid-afternoon and are reference points for other social activities in the day such as *siesta*, an afternoon nap which customarily follows the afternoon *merienda*.

The 'core' borrowings discussed here, while also available in English, are necessary as they fulfil richer connotations that achieve the desired communicative meaning. The fact that these were marked as indigenous <indig> in the data signals a monolingual expectation of how Philippine English sentences should look.

It is important to note here that such rich embedding of either 'core' or 'cultural' lexicosemantic borrowings from Philippine languages is actually a communicative practice that is the norm in multilingual contexts.

7. LEXICAL INNOVATIONS: FRAMED BY PHILIPPINE CULTURE

While the original intention of this paper is to investigate the kinds of lexicosemantic borrowings present in the ICE-PH written data and to probe whether they are core or cultural borrowings consistent with Myers-Scotton's (2006) framework, the analysis yielded an in-between category: neologisms. In this paper, neologisms are (newly) coined words which reflect different linguistic creativity and serve various communicative functions. These coinages are linguistic innovations that reveal cultural framing of objects and ways of doing things. The first of these are creative transformations of names of objects (as exemplified in excerpt (30)). The second are indigenous expressions which can be associated to some stock English expressions but the connotations get lost in translation as the appellations are distinct to the cultural milieu of the expressions (excerpt (31)). Finally, the third category are portmanteaus that show ingenious cultural innovations (excerpts (32), (33) and (34)), which help deliver the overall message with a brevity that cannot be captured in English only.

The first kind of innovations is exemplified in this lexical item: *jeepney*. *Jeepney* in excerpt (30) is an interesting lexical item. Based on the US military *jeep*, *jeepney* (also referred to in Tagalog as *dyip* or *dyipny*) has shifted to mean a type of bus (interestingly, this meaning is found in the English word *jitney (bus)*).

(30) These include not only <indig> **jeepneys** </indig> and buses but even privately owned cars stalled in congested traffic. (ICE-PHI:W2A-035#82:1)

The second category of linguistic innovations reinforces the need to occasionally use culturally borrowed lexicosemantic tokens from Tagalog in an English sentence as they mirror social realities unique to Philippine society. These sometimes have a close English equivalent but such does not quite mirror the Philippine setting. The lexicosemantic token in excerpt (31), *kuwentong kutsero*, can be glossed as 'stories of coachmen' but is used to mean 'made-up stories'. Its closest English equivalent is *cock and bull story*.

(31) This is <indig> **kwentong kutsero** </indig>. (ICE-PHI:W2E-002#19:1)

The final set of linguistic innovations are portmanteau words: *telebabad* in excerpt (32), *trapo* in excerpt (33) and *susmaryosep* in excerpt (34). All depict a highly creative morphological blend of two to three words to arrive at the new expression. The linguistic innovations in this category show two patterns: a hybrid blend of Tagalog and English words (32) to form a new Tagalog word and a morphological blend of English words to form a Tagalog word (33) and (34).

(32) But Rivera said there is basis to PLDT's argument that phone metering will discourage <indig> “ telebabad, ” </indig> or the extended and unproductive use of a telephone unit. </p> (ICE-PHI:W2C-014#44:2)

(33) In this unique vocabulary of Philippine politics, it is not, of course, the <indig> <it> trapo </it> </indig>'s cleaning power, but its natural affinity with dirt, that is recalled when applied to politicians. (ICE-PHI:W2B-012#4:1)

(34) <indig> Susmaryosep </indig>, you know we can't afford that. (ICE-PHI:W2F-006#66:1)

Excerpt (32) shows a creative lexical item, *telebabad*, which is a hybrid of English *telephone* and Tagalog *babad* ('to saturate one's self in an activity'), and from such clipping emerges the new Tagalog word. *Trapo* (excerpt (33)), on the other hand, is a creative blend of two English words (*traditional* and *politician*) to form a Tagalog word that has a derogatory connotation when used in reference to (corrupt) politicians. Similarly, in excerpt (34) we find the English (religious) names of Jesus, Mary and Joseph clipped to create the Tagalog expression *Susmaryosep!*. It is often used as an interjection to indicate either surprise, dislike or disapproval as in excerpt (34) where the meaning of its use in the sentence can be interpreted as a reprimand for someone who has asked the impossible.

These lexical innovations described and exemplified above show how necessary they are in Philippine English to capture and reflect cultural artefacts and ways of being and doing distinct in Philippine society. Some of these have been mentioned in earlier studies (Bautista 1997; Bolton and Butler 2004; Borlongan 2007; Fuchs 2017; Peters 2020) but mostly through the lens of linguistic innovation, not as lexicosemantic evidence of cultural influence in Philippine English.

8. CONCLUSIONS

This paper set out to investigate the kinds of lexicosemantic borrowings evident in language-contact situations like the Philippines through the analysis of the 400,000-word ICE-PH written component. What provides us with a kaleidoscope of linguistic influences on Philippine English is the rich ethnolinguistic history of the country with its 182 languages and its many linguistic and cultural influences – from earlier language contacts such as the Sanskrit-through-Malay influence, the Fukien Chinese impact of the early Chinese settlers, and the Malay effect given that it was the lingua franca of business and trade in the Southeast Asian region pre-Spanish era (Scott 1984).

What the analysis in this paper has shown is that there is indeed a rich collection of lexicosemantic borrowings present in the 200 ICE-PH written texts marked <indig> in the original transcription as attested to by the numbers presented in Section 4 of this paper. This confirms what Schneider has proposed: these lexical borrowings are 'manifestation forms of cultural objects' (2018: 29) and signal the indigenous cultural influence on Philippine English. It needs to be highlighted here that the more than three centuries of Spanish occupation are quite evident in the lexicosemantic items found in the data.

Most of the lexicosemantic borrowings fit into either the 'core' or 'cultural' borrowing category proposed by Myers-Scotton (2006). The lexicosemantic 'cultural' borrowings fall into six semantic categories, while the 'core' lexical borrowings fulfil various communicative functions and are enriched with connotations otherwise absent in their English equivalent. In addition, however, there is also a rich presence of neologisms, a category beyond the Myers-Scotton framework.

Some key observations that need to be made based on the findings include the politics of rendering lexical borrowings 'indigenous' and the implications of the limited presence of indigenous languages in Philippine English as attested to by the ICE-PH written data. In regard to the first point, what seems evident is that the lexicosemantic items discussed in Sections 4, 5, 6 and 7 serve a fundamental purpose of achieving the various communicative goals of the relevant utterances. The transcription protocol adhered to by the team in marking these lexical items 'indigenous' was consistent with what was required by Greenbaum (1991) in putting together an English component representative of the kind of English spoken in the Philippines for the ICE project. What seems obvious now though is that the ultimate goal of producing this English representation in the process ignored the norm in multilingual contexts where borrowing and codeswitching characterise communicative exchanges. Calling attention to these lexicosemantic items as 'indigenous' renders their presence a deviation from the 'norm'.

The second point that is important to raise here is that, as evidenced by the examples provided, speakers of Philippine English use English alongside other languages in their repertoire and these indigenous languages naturally influence the way English is used (Gonzales 2017). The protocol for participant choice employed in gathering samples of written and spoken texts for the ICE was anchored on the participants' English proficiency. What seems obvious in the ICE-PH data is that a significant number of participants who contributed to the corpus were largely Manila-based (Tagalog speakers), which limited the inclusion and presence of other Philippine languages that would otherwise have been present in the corpus, as attested to by the few examples that have been presented. The inclusion of speakers of other Philippine languages, I would imagine, would also mean the inclusion of richer lexicosemantic borrowings from other Philippine languages, which would be more revealing of the extent of the rich relationship between language and culture in the Philippines.

NOTE

1. All definitions of Tagalog words are taken from Vito C. Santos's (1988) *Vicassan's Pilipino–English Dictionary*.

REFERENCES

Anthony, L. (2017). AntConc (Version 3.5.0) [Computer software]. Waseda University. <https://www.laurenceanthony.net/software> (last accessed 4 January 2021).

Bautista, M. L. S. (1997). The lexicon of Philippine English. In M. L. S. Bautista (Ed.), *English is an Asian language: The Philippine context* (pp. 49–72). The Macquarie Library.

Bautista, M. L. S. (2004). Tagalog-English code-switching as a mode of discourse. *Asia-Pacific Education Review*, 5(2), 226–33. <https://doi.org/10.1007/BF03024960> (last accessed 5 January 2021).

Bautista, M. L. S., Lising, J. L. and Dayag, D. T. (2004). *The Philippine Corpus (International Corpus of English)*. Department of English and Applied Linguistics, De La Salle University-Manila.

Bernardo, A. B. I. (2004). McKinley's questionable bequest: Over 100 years of English in Philippine education. *World Englishes, 23*(1), 17–31.

Bolton, K. and Butler, S. (2004). Dictionaries and stratification of vocabulary: Towards a new lexicography for Philippine English. *World Englishes, 23*(1), 91–112.

Borlongan, A. M. (2007). Innovations in Standard Philippine English. In C. C. Mann (Ed.), *Current Research on English and Applied Linguistics: A De La Salle University Special Issue*, 1–36.

De Jong, R. (2011). Mindanao, 'Bahala na', the Filipino way. *Things Asian*, 21 January. <http://thingsasian.com/story/mindanao-%E2%80%9Dbahala-na%E2%80%9D-filipino-way> (last accessed 5 January 2021).

Ethnologue: Languages of the world (2020). *Philippines*. <https://www.ethnologue.com/country/PH> (last accessed 5 January 2021).

Freer, W. (1906). *The Philippine experience of an American teacher*. Scribner.

Fuchs, R. (2017). The Americanisation of Philippine English: Recent diachronic change in spelling and lexis. *Philippine ESL Journal, 19*, 64–87.

Gonzales, W. D. W. (2017). Language contact in the Philippines: The history and ecology from a Chinese-Filipino perspective. *Language and Ecology, 1*(2), 185–212.

Greenbaum, S. (1991). ICE: The International Corpus of English. *English Today, 7*(4), 3–7.

Lising, L., Peters, P. and Smith, A. (2020). Code-switching in online academic discourse: Resources for Philippine English. *English World-Wide, 41*(2), 131–61. <https://doi.org/10.1075/eww.00044.lis> (last accessed 5 January 2021).

McMenamin, G. R. (2010). Theory and practice of forensic linguistics. In M. Coulthard and A. Johnson (Eds.), *The Routledge handbook of forensic linguistics* (pp. 487–507). Routledge.

Myers-Scotton, C. (2006). *Multiple voices: An introduction to bilingualism*. Blackwell.

Peters, P. (2020). Cultural keywords in Philippine English. In K. Allan (Ed.), *Dynamic language changes: Looking within and across languages* (pp. 225–40). Springer.

Piao, S. S., Rayson, P., Archer, D. and McEnery, T. (2005). Comparing and combining a semantic tagger and a statistical tool for MWE extraction. *Computer Speech and Language, 19*(4), 378–97.

Poplack, S. (2004). Code-switching. In U. Ammon, N. Dittmar, K. J. Mattheier and P. Trudgill (Eds.), *Sociolinguistics/Soziolinguistik: An international handbook of the science of language* (2nd ed.; pp. 589–96). Walter de Gruyter.

Santos, V. C. (1988). *Vicassan's Pilipino–English dictionary*. National Book Store.

Schneider, E. W. (2018). The interface between cultures and corpora: Tracing reflections and manifestations. *ICAME Journal, 42*(1), 97–132. <https://doi.org/10.1515/icame-2018-0006> (last accessed 4 January 2021).

Scott, W. H. (1984). *Prehistoric source materials for the study of Philippine history*. New Day Publishers.

CHAPTER 5

Cultural Keywords in Indian English

Pam Peters

1. INTRODUCTION

Cultural keywords have been examined in several different disciplines of the humanities, using different approaches and finding larger and smaller sets of them. In Raymond Williams's original conception ([1976] 1983), they formed a large vocabulary of around 120 words (mostly nouns and adjectives), reflecting aspects of British English culture, society and its institutions with which he engaged. At the other end of the scale, Anna Wierzbicka (1997) focused on the contrasting semantics of a single keyword or rather key sociocultural concept (for example, *freedom*, *friendship*) in different European languages. Her selection of these words, and of culturally and socially significant words for 'talking' in Australian English, was based on intuition and observation.

Since then research on cultural keywords has expanded with the use of corpus-based methodologies. Paul Rayson (2008) applied statistical methods (Wmatrix)[1] to a corpus of British political publications from which he distilled high-frequency keywords in 20 different semantic fields. He found that different inventories of keywords seemed to reflect the differing 'cultures' of the ruling and opposition political parties. Other corpus linguists (Mukherjee and Bernaisch 2015) extracted high-frequency keywords from a corpus of newspapers in three South Asian Englishes (Indian, Pakistani and Sri Lankan Englishes). They found that South Asian Englishes shared numerous keywords in 15 semantic fields, but remarkable differences when drilling down to the verbs with which they most often collocated. Thus, *government* was found to be less often construed positively in Indian English than the other two, but more often construed neutrally (Mukherjee and Bernaisch 2015: 428). These corpus-based research studies suggest that well-used words seem to reflect the culture that generates them, and to correlate with the sociopolitical contexts of their use.

All four previous studies used synchronic material in supporting the case for their cultural keywords. The question of whether cultural keywords might endure through different historical phases of the society and its language was not part of their inquiry. Yet it does seem pertinent to establishing the cultural keyness of particular words that their usage should persist in the speech community over time and perhaps through major social and political changes in the language ecology. The longevity of such words would then be part of the demonstration that they function as cultural keywords in the longer term, as well as the extent to which they express or align with specific sociocultural values embedded in the community, even if their meanings change somewhat over time. Regional Englishes in their pre- and post-colonial phases present particularly interesting contexts in which to research the persistence of putative cultural keywords – if suitable diachronic data can be found.

In the case of Indian English, there are older dictionaries of Anglo-Indian from the 19th and early 20th centuries and recent ones of Indian English published before and after 2000. Their lexicographical records allow us to trace the usage of some distinctive and long-lived words of Indian English in different semantic fields, along with changes in their semantics. The status of these items as cultural keywords can be measured by their usage in the Indian component of the GloWbE corpus (Davies 2013). Their survival, with or without changes of meaning, is evidence of how much sociocultural investment there is in them – as cultural keywords of Indian English and as evidence of more than one of the nexuses between language, culture and society postulated in Schneider's platform paper (Chapter 2 in this volume).

2. INDIA'S COLONIAL PAST: THE MUGHAL LEGACY THROUGH HINDUSTANI

The Indian subcontinent is bordered by major mountain ranges to the north, but subject to invasion by aggressive neighbours beyond, notably the Mughals of south-central Asia. Their military intrusions, backed by early use of gunpowder, culminated in the formation of the Mughal empire in India which lasted from about 1526 to 1740. In its greatest

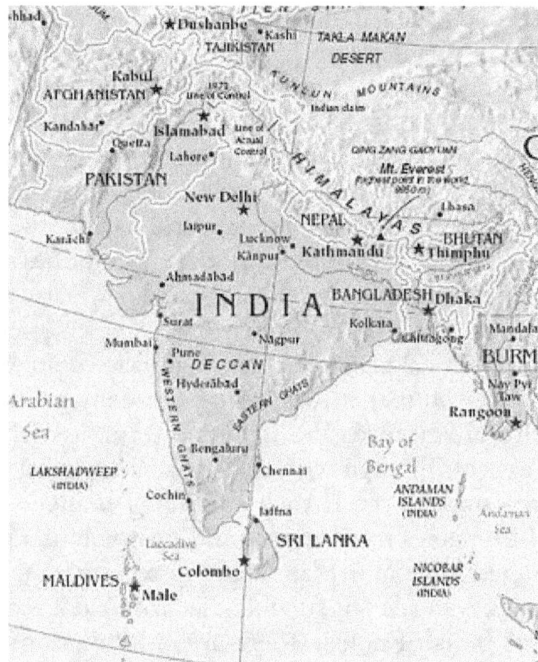

Figure 5.1 Map of India. A colour copy of this figure is available on the EUP website: edinburghuniversitypress.com/EcologiesofWorldEnglishes

extent, 'Hindustan' as it was known in Persian, stretched across northern India from modern day Pakistan to Bangladesh (see Figure 5.1). During the Mughal regime, India achieved very substantial economic prosperity in agriculture and manufacturing, allied with strong fiscal administration and management of the resources through regional rulers (*rajahs*, *nawabs*) and their powerful agents in regions across the country (*sarkars*).

The Mughals established Persian-Sanskrit as the language of government in Hindustan and Arabic with Islamic practice in religion. The local languages (Prakrits) were thus infused with Persian, Sanskrit and Arabic words, forming the lingua franca known as Hindustani which emerged as the common language for people living in northern and western India. Earlier forms of Hindi and Urdu also absorbed Persian, Sanskrit and Arabic words, resulting in their 'Persianisation' and 'Sanskritisation' (Lange 2020: 239) under the Mughal regime. The contact between language and cultures also prompted a flowering of Persian-style culture in literature, the arts and architecture, of which the Taj Mahal is the most renowned example.

The Hindustani language that developed under the Mughal empire as an administrative tool was subsequently taken up by the British, first in the 18th century in areas managed by the East India Company and subsequently under the British imperial Raj from 1858. It enabled the British to communicate with their subjects across northern India as well as what is now Pakistan. The Hindustani language was common to both and could be translated into the Devanagari (Nagari) for those literate in Hindi, and Arabic script for those literate in Urdu. The role of the *munshi* as translator and scribe of other languages was significant in Mughal government and continued under British rule, identified also as a native teacher of languages, especially Arabic, Persian and Urdu (Yule and Burnell [1886] 1903).

The role of Hindustani as a common Indic language under British rule was deconstructed with the partition of India after World War II.[2] The separation of India and Pakistan gave each country motivation to intensify Hindi–Urdu differences in their respective national languages, rather than maintain a common language. India's official (national) language is now Hindi, with 21 others 'scheduled' in the Constitution as the official languages of individual states, especially in southern India. English was to have been phased out after Independence (1947) but is still mandated as an official language for communication between states (especially in southern India) whose official language is other than Hindi. In socially stratified India, it is also a neutral language for the most disadvantaged people (Lange 2020: 247).

3. INDIAN ENGLISH, OLDER AND NEWER

The evolution of Indian English was a slow product of the colonial era, with only slight contact in its 'foundation' phase in the 17th century. Its exonormative phase is dated (Schneider 2007: 163–5) from c. 1757 to c. 1905, from when entrepreneurial trading companies, especially the East India Company, began to develop trading posts on the east coast around Bengal. They maintained 'company rule' over the areas inland which supplied them with manufactured goods with mini-armies of their own. From 1813, the East India Company was made responsible for Indian education and conserving the Indian cultural heritage. The imperative to educate Indians in English crystallised only through Thomas Macaulay's manifesto (known as 'Macaulay's minute') and the English Education Act 1835, which mandated that the British should proceed to educate a class of Indians to act as agents of the British Crown, and as intermediaries in the imperial administration. Thousands of elementary and secondary schools were opened to train Indian men for the civil service and universities opened in Calcutta, Bombay and Madras. As the administrative language of the British Raj from 1858 to 1947, English was introduced across multilingual India, from east to west and from north to south.

The English used by educated Indians was based on exonormative principles taught in the classroom, giving it a distinctly bookish flavour, once referred to as Babu English. Some of it can be found in elaborate phraseologies transferred by Indian speakers as polite and respectful English: 'May I know your good name?' As multilingual users of English, they found English calques for essential expressions from their other languages as the context required and otherwise spoke Hindi, Urdu or other Indian languages for practical and social purposes. Regular contact between Indian languages and English continued in code-switched Indian English through its lengthy exonormative phase, continuing until 1905 (Schneider 2007: 165). It naturally facilitated the transfer of many kinds of 'content' words into Indian English – for example, those relating to Indian foods: *chutney, dahl, naan*; Indian dress: *dupatta, jodhpurs, sari*; and occupational roles from the *dhobi* and *rickshaw wala* to the *nawab* – characteristic elements of Indian culture and lifestyle.

The evolution of Indian English from exonormativity to nativisation is a 20th century phenomenon, contemporary with the nationalistic movements of the first two decades. Some commentators (for example, Kachru 1983: 23) associate it with English becoming a second rather than foreign language, a process that is reflected in evidence of extensive code-mixing and code-switching between English and Hindi before and after Independence in 1947 for practical or expressive purposes. Examples abound, in mixed compounds such as *ghat road, gobar gas, rail rooko* as well as switching from Hindi to English at the boundaries between phrases, clauses or sentences:

(1) Reepu tappa kundaa vellaali. We must check the title deeds tomorrow. 'We must go tomorrow'. (Sailaja 2009: 91)

This mixed English first dubbed 'Hinglish' in the 1960s (*Oxford English Dictionary* online 2010) is an important code of communication alongside the official languages. While its usage has yet to be quantified (Anderson-Finch 2011), statistical modelling suggests that Hinglish is a significant 'species' in the dynamics of India's language ecology (Parshad et al. 2016). The acceptance of mixed code as a resource for upskilling of non-Hindi speaking workers is reflected in the teaching of 'job-related English' (Schilk et al. 2012: 141). It is also a recognised resource for Indian identity construction. Its histrionic form is registered in flamboyantly mixed dialogue of characters in Indian English fiction who excel in 'performing Bombay' (Muthiah 2012). Like Babu English, it aims to impress, but the medium is bilingualised rather than exotic English. It demonstrates the traditional and ongoing readiness of multilingual Indians to take in words from other languages in everyday interactions.

4. SOURCES ON INDIAN ENGLISH FROM THE 19TH CENTURY ONWARDS: DICTIONARIES AND LARGE COMPUTERISED CORPORA

Successive dictionaries of Anglo-Indian and Indian English help us to trace the passage of indigenous words borrowed from the various languages used in the Indian subcontinent before the British Raj. One very substantial collection of non-English words used in the British administration was compiled by Wilson (1855): his *Glossary of Judicial and Revenue Terms: and of Useful Words Occurring in Official Documents Relating to the Administration of the Government of British India* (728 pp.). It was published 'under the Authority of the Honourable Court of Directors of the East-India Company', where he was librarian. It contains a plethora of words compiled from Indian primary and secondary sources, often with multiple definitions and alternative forms, all keyed to their Arabic, Persian, Sanskrit or other Indian etyma. Wilson's early record of Anglo-Indian vocabulary makes it an invaluable source. It is larger in scope than the better known *Hobson-Jobson: A Glossary of Colloquial Anglo-Indian Words and Phrases* (Yule and Burnell [1886] 1903). But *Hobson-Jobson* repays readers with its range of words from informal Indian English, its citational material from many sources, including English and other foreign languages, and etymologies from Hindustani, Sanskrit, Persian and Arabic.

Two 21st century dictionaries provide fresh insights into the longevity of these Mughal loanwords in modern Indian English. One is the *Macmillan Comprehensive Dictionary* (2006), a learner's dictionary based on an Australian model (the *Macquarie Dictionary*).[3] It includes 2,175 words of current Indian English headwords (Lambert 2020: 423), defined and annotated within the main word list. The *Macmillan* provides etymologies that trace the Indianisms listed to their origins in Sanskrit, Persian, Arabic or Hindi. Another useful contemporary dictionary is Uwe Carls's posthumous *Dictionary of Indian English* (2017) edited by his colleagues, which contains 3,200 Indianisms, though its etymologies mostly indicate only the language of final transmission into English. The longer histories of Indian English words can still be traced with the help of the older dictionaries mentioned above, plus Ivor Lewis's *Sahibs, Nabobs and Boxwallahs* (1991). It focuses on the etymologies of Anglo-Indian and Indian English loanwords, showing their derivations from Old Persian, Sanskrit or Arabic etyma, interconnected with earlier forms of Hindi and Urdu as well as Hindustani (the contact language used under both Mughal and British imperial regimes). Words of ancient lineage can thus be distinguished from loanwords acquired from post-Independence contact between English and Hindi.

Dictionaries not uncommonly include a few old-fashioned words, because they typically develop their headword lists by piggybacking on earlier dictionaries (Lambert 2012, 2018). In order to double-check the continuing usage of Anglo-Indian words in 21st century Indian English, we turn to the large Indian English segment of the GloWbE corpus (96 million words), compiled out of internet material from 2012. This Indian English corpus consists of both institutional websites and blogs, that is, both edited and unedited texts, thus a useful mix of standard and more informal discourse to cover the lexical legacy of Anglo-Indian in modern Indian English. The ratio between the two types of language in GloWbE is about 50:50, in Loureiro-Porto's estimate (2017). GloWbE is large enough and diverse enough in its content to capture colloquial and standard written vocabulary, as well as words with more specialised applications.

5. WORDS DOCUMENTED IN DICTIONARIES AND THE GLOWBE SUBCORPUS OF INDIAN ENGLISH

In what follows, we examine the relative frequencies of a set of Indian words with Persian, Sanskrit, Prakrit and Arabic derivation – ones listed in the early dictionaries of Anglo-Indian, Wilson's large *Glossary* (1855) and *Hobson-Jobson* ([1886] 1903), as well as modern dictionaries of Indian English, namely *Macmillan Comprehensive Dictionary* (2006) and Carls's

Dictionary of Indian English (2017). It must be said that the modern coverage of Indian English vocabulary is partial. In the *Macmillan* the Indian words are embedded in an exogenous matrix, while Carls's dictionary contains Indianisms only, rather than a full lexicon of Indian English usage (Peters in press), but both provide a subset of Indian English vocabulary which could include cultural keywords.

All words included in Table 5.1 were acquired by early language contact: borrowed directly from written Sanskrit into modern Indian languages (*tatsama*) or passed down from Persian in Old and Middle Indo-Aryan (*tadbhava*) in spoken Prakrits (Lambert 2012: 298). Some words of Arabic origin were taken into Old Persian and others later on into Hindustani and spread across India that way, as shown by their position in the likely transmission sequence. All three types are shown in Table 5.1, based on the etymologies of Wilson (1855), *Hobson-Jobson* ([1886] 1903), Lewis (1991) and Carls (2017), as far as they converge. The words are a small set of 20 from the numerous candidate words, representing a range in terms of their frequencies and the semantic fields they inhabit. They illustrate the different kinds of cultural keywords in Indian English whose histories provide a record of usage from the Mughal period to the present day.

Table 5.1 presents a miscellany of long-lived words with variable levels of usage in 21st century Indian English, as indicated by their frequencies in GloWbE. The three out of the four highest counts are for words relating to the ancient reckoning system still used in India today (*crore, lakh, rupee*), interleaved with several that today mostly function as titles and forms of address (*baba, sahib, bhai*). Their high frequencies bespeak their continuing importance in Indian life today. But other lower frequency items are also significant as more specialised words in particular semantic fields, which still reference material or structural aspects of contemporary Indian culture and society. The semantic fields in which these enduring words of Indian culture reside include six of those identified in Piao et al.'s (2005) research.[4]

6. KEYWORDS WITH CULTURAL CONTENT

The cultural keywords which can be identified with Piao et al.'s (2005) semantic fields are discussed below in this section. Others which do not align easily with them, particularly those used in interactive discourse, are discussed in Section 7.

Table 5.1 Indian English words traceable to the Mughal regime

Spellings found in GloWbE	Etymologies: Wilson, Hobson-Jobson, Lewis, Carls	Current meanings listed in modern Indian English dictionaries (Macmillan Comprehensive, Dictionary of Indian English)	Freq. in GloWbE IndE corpus[a] in 96 m. words
crore	Prakrit *krodi* > (Hindustani *karor* > Hindi	10 million	11,663
lakh, lac	Sanskrit *laksha* > Hindustani > Hindi	100,000	7,305
baba	Turkish 'father' > Persian > Hindi	a father or grandfather; a form of address to a (grand) father or any old man; a holy man or title of respect for one	4,391
rupee	Sanskrit *rapya* > Hindi	a unit of currency in India	2,450
sahib, saheb, sahab	Arabic > Persian > Urdu/Hindi	a respectful title for a European man; a form of address placed after a person's name, or the name of a position held	2,384
bhai	Sanskrit *bhratr* > Hindi	a brother; an affectionate form of address to a man, added to first or last name	1,377
babu	Prakrit > Bengali > Hindustani > Hindi	a form of address added to a man's first or last name; an office worker	1,008[a]
masala	Persian > Hindustani > Urdu	seasoning or spices; spiced food; a film or book that uses exciting or shocking material; sensational, titillating, risqué	904
sarkar	Persian > Hindustani > Urdu	the government; a broker [in Bengal]; steward in a rich Bengali household	504[a]
chai	Persian (orig. Chinese) > Hindustani > India-wide	tea	335
yaar, yar	Arabic > Persian > Urdu	a friend, a form of address to a friend	269
haveli	Arabic > Hindustani > Urdu	large, impressive house with surrounding land; estate	176

Spellings found in GloWbE	Etymologies: Wilson, Hobson-Jobson, Lewis, Carls	Current meanings listed in modern Indian English dictionaries (Macmillan Comprehensive, Dictionary of Indian English)	Freq. in GloWbE InDE corpus[a] in 96 m. words
havala, hawala	Arabic > Hindustani > Hindi	an informal system for transferring money through non-traditional channels, especially the illegal exchange of foreign money	172
shroff, saraf	Arabic saraf > Hindustani > Hindi	a person who owns or manages a bank, or exchanges currency	159[a]
salwar, shalwar	Persian > Hindustani > Urdu	a pair of loose pleated trousers, tight at the ankles	153
bibi, beebi	Persian > Hindustani > Urdu	one's wife; respectful form of address to a woman	149[a]
tamasha	Arabic > Persian > Hindustan > Urdu	a type of popular theatre in western India; a spectacle; an absurd or badly organised event; a fuss	111
munshi	Arabic > Hindustani > Urdu	secretary; reader; interpreter/translator	75[a]
adalat	Arabic > Hindustani > Hindi	court of law	70
sabzi, sabji	Persian > Hindustani > Hindi	vegetables; a vegetable dish	63

[a] This total includes uses of the word as a proper noun/surname.

6.1 Monetary System: *crore, lakh, hawala, shroff, sarkar*

In the transition from the Mughal regime to the British Raj, many words for elements of the financial system were taken into Hindustani and the contemporary varieties of Urdu and Hindi. Many were recorded in Wilson's very large *Glossary* (1855) as part of the Anglo-Indian repertoire and carried forward into modern Indian English. The GloWbE corpus shows that the strongest survivors in 21st century Indian English are words for very large numbers (*crore* for 10 million and *lakh/lac* for 10,000), as well as *rupee*.[5] In GloWbE Indian English, *CRORE* and *LAKH* are usually attached to sums of money but also used for quantifying other things. Both usages are illustrated in the following examples:

(2) There are 75 *crore* people who individually spend Rs 150 per month on their mobile phone
(3) Universities like Mumbai and Pune have on an average 5 *lakh* students.

A much less conspicuous element of the Mughal monetary system is *HAWALA/HAVALA*, traceable to the Arabic word for a 'promissory note', and originally a system for transferring money through a network of brokers. It now refers to a system for avoiding traditional banking, associated with illegal operations and money laundering:

(4) received a tip off that unaccounted cash, suspected to be *havala* money

The illegality of modern *hawala* is spelled out as a serious crime under the Foreign Exchange Management Act (FEMA) 1999 and Prevention of Money Laundering Act 2002, according to another citation in GloWbE, which would explain its relatively low usage in the 21st century.

The shadowy connotations of the informal banking networks would also explain the low frequencies of professions associated with them in the past – notably, *SHROFF/SARAF* 'money changer'. It hardly appears at all as a common noun in GloWbE data: almost all instances are as a surname. The same goes for *SARKAR*, often glossed as 'broker', but used under the Mughal regime for a regional domain of government as well as its appointed executive. Like *shroff*, the GloWbE citations for *sarkar* are mostly as proper nouns, where its notoriety is presumably neutralised. The few examples of the use of *sarkar* as a common noun carry negative connotations:

(5) Manmohan's[6] '*sarkar*' will end its term in 2014 and a huge chunk of money from the national exchequer will go for holding the general election
(6) Soon, the affairs that you have with your rich advertisers and extortionist *sarkar*, will disillusion your readers. You should actually take formal divorce from your readers

The transition of cultural keywords from common to proper nouns is also to be seen in some of the terms discussed in Sections 6.2 and 7 below.

6.2 Civil Administration: *munshi, babu, adalat*

Three other words traceable to earlier Indian regimes capture roles in the civil administration, especially those of *MUNSHI*, the secretary, and *BABU*, the general office worker. The *munshi* was originally a translator of official documents from Persian under the British Raj, whereas in the present day it is an office worker able to read and write English, but rather low on the professional scale:

(7) You couldn't get a Govt. job or a teaching job unless you passed your *Munshi* exams.
(8) I'm a sociologist and I have served as a kind of assistant *munshi* to Teesta Setalvad and RB Sreekumar (former Director General of Police, Gujarat)

Another term for the modern Indian office worker is *babu*, stemming from its earlier use as the general title for a man (equivalent to *Mr* or *Esq*.). Its use as a term of reference can be pejorative, of a worker unable to exercise much discretion or autonomy, as the following citations show:

(9) A *babu* will not fetch tea for the boss since that is the chaprasi's job.
(10) Why hasn't the project taken off? Short answer: a *babu* is in charge, with little or no expertise in managing projects of this size.

Babu English likewise depreciates the quality of English used by such office workers, and is a byword for unreadable English:

(11) This used to be called *babu* English. If editors knew better, they'd toss the piece back at the writer.

The Arabic word *ADALAT* 'court' stands out among the surviving administrative words as having preserved its essential semantics to the present day. This is preserved in the formal names of courts, from the *Sadr Adalat*, the Chief Court of Civil Judicature, established in 1802, to the recently established the *Lok Adalat* 'People's court', given statutory status under the Legal Services Authorities Act 1987. In these official contexts, *adalat* maintains its reputation as the bastion of Indian law. Not so admirable is its use in the combination *jan adalat*, explained in a GloWbE citation as: 'a kangaroo court in which radicals hold a people's meeting' – where they take the law into their own hands and conduct summary executions of individuals that represent government authority.

Both sets of words discussed above preserve elements from India's colonial past in 21st century Indian English. For better, for worse, they reflect the content of its culture and society, persisting through two different phases of its colonial history.

6.3 Material Culture from Food to Fashion: *chai, masala, sabzi; tamasha, haveli, shalwar*

Several of the ancient words preserved in modern Indian English relate to India's favourite food and drink. *CHAI/CHA/CHAR* are the Hindustani forms of the original Chinese word for 'tea', which remains popular in India, both as a beverage and a place (*the chai shop*) where people drink together and socialise. The practice of social tea drinking is still strong, witnessed in the following citation from GloWbE:

(12) done on the spur of the moment: like going for a *chai* and cream roll at 3 in the morning; or going for a movie

While classical *chai* (dark tea, water with milk and sugar) is central to modern Indian culture, it can be varied and spiced up as *masala chai* for greater stimulation:

(13) Hot masala *chai* helped pep our spirits and senses.

MASALA itself, a Persian-Arabic loanword, has been central in Indian cuisine since the early 19th century (*Oxford English Dictionary* online 2010) as a generic word for spices, and more particularly spiced dishes. A modern online example has it in the following menu:

(14) Egg bhurji or *masala* vegetarian omelette for course two

The Indian diet is still largely vegetarian, helped by the great variety of vegetables that can be grown on the land there, and so *SABZI* 'vegetables' (in northern India) or *SABJI* (eastern/central India) are essential ingredients to be bought from the *sabzi mandis* 'vegetable markets'.

(15) The western diets lack the great Indian concept of Dal, *Sabji*, Roti as the major meal which incorporates a lot of fibre

Non-traditional applications of *sabzi/sabji* keep it current along Western fast-food lines in sandwiches:

(16) different sandwich fillings . . . you can stuff with potato *sabzi* or punjabi chana with some onion rings, tomato slices and some mint chutney . . .

While those terms all continue in traditional Indian gastronomy, *MASALA* has extended its reach into the entertainment world. Since the 1970s (*Oxford English Dictionary* online 2010), it has become a byword for a type of movie which is sensational and 'spicy', that is, sexually daring, designed to stir the emotions. Its elements are predictable, as spelled out by a film reviewer:

(17) It has all the elements of a Bollywood *masala* film -- romance, mystery, suspense and action

That the *masala* movie is not for serious filmmakers is clear from a reviewer's comment:

(18) It is not a *masala* film and the subject is controversial and real.

Meanwhile the Indian *TAMASHA*, an autochthonous form of popular entertainment, continues as a singing and dancing spectacular in western India. It can also be applied to rather extravagant kinds of stage performances, as in:

(19) Evam's Stand Up *Tamasha* was courageously in-your-face. . . . The only way comedy can grow

But *tamasha* has also become a general word for real life melodrama in public or private, especially the '**tamasha** that accompanies politics, with its recognizable election pitch to the mass population':

(20) the only link of the governing class with the populace was the 5 yearly *tamasha* called elections.

Domestic melodrama can also be seen as *tamasha:*

(21) He used to spy on her ... go to her home drunk and create *tamasha* ... flaunt his (non existent) ... underworld connections

Thus *tamasha* still channels the ancient sense of emotion-stirring popular entertainment, if only as a negative reflection on modern everyday life.

Another modern souvenir of India's earlier cultural history is *HAVELI*, an ancient Arabic word for a very large mansion and the estate attached to it. Some remain in contemporary India but no longer as the residences of large wealthy families where several generations lived together. The citations from GloWbE reflect the transition of the *haveli* from domestic to touristic uses:

(22) He had heard tales about a 40-room *haveli*, his family's ancestral home
(23) The hotel we stayed at was a converted *haveli*, well maintained with spacious grounds

Other citations mention a *haveli* in a state of decrepitude or ruin – adding negative associations to a word once charged with power and prosperity.

Among the ancient words relating to material culture that have survived in Indian English is *SALWAR/SHALWAR*, based on the Persian word *šalwār* for the traditional loosely pleated trousers originating in northern India as men's dress, and sometimes referred to as 'Pakistani fashion', hence a GloWbE citation that:

(24) Osama was wearing *shalwar* kameez when he was killed

Salwar kameez refers to a suit consisting of *salwar* trousers and a matching shirt (*kameez*). Indian women now also wear *salwar kameez* as fashionable dress, made in colourful fabrics with matching scarf, and no longer necessarily loose-fitting. It is a widely worn alternative, according to this GloWbE citation:

(25) now a days *Salwar* or Churidar is common all over India along with Western Style.

Material elements of Indian traditional culture are conserved in all three groups of words discussed above – for better, for worse. In cases like *masala*, the word has acquired lively new denotations and the *salwar* is a good deal more colourful than in its original form – both reflecting 20th century Western influence. In others, the word's connotations have become increasingly pejorative, as with *babu, hawala, tamasha*. The few that have retained their original meanings (for example, *crore, lakh*) are tied to numerical values still used in Indian accounting rather than the Western benchmarks of *thousand, million*. Likewise, the word *sabzi*, the essential component of the Indian vegetarian diet, retains its core meaning today. These words particularly suggest themselves as keywords of Indian English because they have survived through different phases of Indian colonial history, with some changes in their semantics.

7. INTERPERSONAL TERMS OF REFERENCE AND ADDRESS: *BABA, SAHIB, BHAI, BABU, YAAR, BIBI*

Among the ancient words still used in online Indian English are six that serve as terms of reference and especially as forms of address – as titles or honorifics. In their usage they affirm positive social relations with the addressee or third person referred to. They are residues of the intricate networks of familial and kinship terms that continue in modern Indian English, often with extended denotations or connotations (Kachru 1983: 117–18).

The most frequent of these terms in the GloWbE Indian English corpus is *BABA*, traceable to a Turkish word for *father*, and modern learner's dictionaries still record it with that meaning. But in modern Indian English usage as represented in GloWbE Indian English, it is overwhelmingly used in reference to a holy man who can be invoked in prayer as one's personal divinity:

(26) May *Baba* bless you, your pregnancy time and have a cute healthy baby.

This exclusively religious use of the word in Indian English contrasts with its continuing use in Pakistani English to refer to one's earthly parent. The difference is striking and aligns interestingly with Mukherjee and Bernaisch's (2015: 431) finding that the language associated with religion in Indian, Pakistani and Sri Lankan Englishes was the least shared of all the keywords they investigated.

The most striking case of continuing usage of Persian-Arabic terms of reference is *SAHIB* (also spelled *SAHEB, SAHAB*), originally (in Hindustani) a respectful form of address to a European and now added as a polite postnominal to the surname of any man referred to. Countless examples of this can be found in GloWbE:

(27) perhaps the best modern authority on Urdu meter. Faruqi *Sahib* was kind enough to prepare extensive notes

Sahib is now also attached to the name of a profession. As noted in one citation, it can be used along with a title such as *Doctor sahib* or *Professor sahib*. GloWbE data suggest it may be similarly used in third-person reference, ironically or otherwise:

(28) My deepest sympathies to our new cartoonist *sahib*. I wish him luck

Another term of address well used in modern Indian English is *BHAI*, descended via Hindustani from Sanskrit *bhratr*. While still used in its strictly familial sense, it is also widely used in 'brotherly' discourse outside the family, for example, among students:

(29) But why are you so worried, *bhai*.

Bhai is also readily used in third-person references to members and heroes of the cricket fraternity, and other kinds of following:

(30) a tall guy and can play the pull shot really well. Viru *Bhai* is a good cutter of the ball.
(31) Imran *bhai* never demanded respect, everybody gave him respect
(32) . . . would watch all Salman *bhai*'s films and copy his actions and dream of becoming an actor

As in those examples, *bhai* is generally attached as a postnominal to the first name of the person referred to.

An alternative term to be used between acquaintances is *YAAR/ YAR* 'friend' stemming from Arabic, according to Wilson (1855), which confirms its ancient origins.[7] Lange (2009) found it unevenly represented in her corpus: it was used rather more by women than men aged between 18 and 25 and in private rather than public conversations. She also noted that its distribution across speakers' mother tongues was patchy rather than regional (used disproportionately by L1 speakers of Kannada, Marathi and English). Two examples from the GloWbE Indian English suggest intimate contexts of communication:

(33) Oh no *yar*! Why should I convey him the innate [sic] feelings of my best friend . . .
(34) Chill *yaar*, don't stress, I've had just two drinks, I am totally . . .

Lange also noted that *yaar* can be used as a discourse marker at the end of a declarative or exclamatory clause, where it serves to emphasise the speaker's stance or attitude (Lange 2009: 218), and there are some likely instances of this in GloWbE, including:

(35) Boss, we are all human beings *yaar*.

This extended use of *yaar* as a discourse marker rather than for interpersonal address suggests another evolutionary path for *yaar*, extending its usage in modern Indian English discourse.

BIBI is the only surviving form of address specifically for women among the keyword candidates drawn from the network of earlier kinship terms. In fact, it has gone through major semantic changes in its recorded uses. It originally referred to one's wife, but then became the byword for a mistress or sex worker (*Oxford Advanced Learner's Dictionary*, Indian Supplement 1995). In modern Indian English, it is mostly used as a respectful term for referring to a woman. It can be attached as a postnominal to the first name:

(36) Nissa *Bibi*, 40, carries a mobile phone on an orange ribbon round her neck in the hope that her sister Shahina *Bibi* . . . [will call]

or used as an honorific prenominal with the full name of leaderly women, for example:

(37) His widow, *Bibi* Amarjit Kaur, and another member of the Jatha, *Bibi* Harsharan Kaur, had immediately entered the sanctuary of the Golden Temple;

The inclusion of data from GloWbE blogs brings to light these respectful usages of ancient words in modern Indian English. They illustrate the very high priority put on maintaining social relations and solidarity with others in the Indian community, perhaps indeed because of its very diverse makeup: 'displaying the highest degree of ethnic, linguistic and religious diversity' (Mukherjee and Bernaisch 2015: 416). To some observers, the routine use of familial, friendly or respectful forms of address seems artificial or 'fictive' (Sailaja 2009: 86). Their performative nature is acknowledged in the GloWbE citation:

(38) He's now '*Yaar*', '*Bhai*' and '*Baba*', and I slap him on the back.

But this does not gainsay the continuing importance of these terms in expressing friendship and respect in India's now less structured society. The traditional titles that once indexed politeness still hint at it as a reference value, even in casual or pejorative usage. As terms of reference and forms of address they continue to fulfil the cultural need to confirm 'shared norms of social interaction' (Lange 2020: 240).

8. CONCLUSION

Using historical and contemporary dictionary evidence in combination with corpus data, it is possible to document some of the longest-lived words in a variety of English that has evolved in a multilingual society. The usage of these words embeds both traditional and contemporary values of the host society and some continuing elements of its material culture. Such keywords have diachronic depth to set alongside their contemporary frequencies of usage.

Among the several semantic sets discussed, the terms relating to money (*crore*, *lakh*, *rupee*) are the most stable in meaning and frequent in usage,[8] whereas the most frequent forms of address and terms of reference (*baba*, *sahib*) and (*bhai*) have shifted in their denotations while retaining their essential connotations of respect. The monetary set represent the first nexus discussed by Schneider (this volume), and the terms of address his second nexus, as local indicator terms of social dimensions in Indian English discourse. All of them continue to index Indianness for speakers of English.

NOTES

1. For details of the Wmatrix method for identifying words in 21 semantic fields identified in USAS, the UCREL Semantic Analysis System developed at Lancaster University (UK), see Piao et al. (2005).
2. A mixed vernacular consisting of Hindi and Urdu elements is still spoken on the street, where they often 'merge and intersect to the point of being indistinguishable' (Cayla and Elson 2012: 297). In broad spectrum marketing, Indian advertisers are faced with appealing both to the 'vernacular Indian' consumer as well as the educated, anglophone Indian.
3. Thanks to Alison Moore, Chief Editor of the *Macquarie Dictionary* at Macmillan Australia in Sydney, for access to the *Macmillan Comprehensive Dictionary*.
4. They include: numbers and measurement, money and commerce, government and the public domain, food and farming, entertainment, architecture.
5. Mostly when referring to the rupee as a currency, as in 'that crazy fall in the **rupee** against the dollar lately', not counting the ubiquitous abbreviation for rupee: Rs.
6. A reference to Manmohan Singh, India's prime minister 2004–14.
7. It is not, however, included in Hobson-Jobson. The earliest citation in the OED is from the 20th century.
8. The durability of currency terms as cultural keywords in Indian English is matched in Philippine English (Peters 2020).

REFERENCES

Anderson-Finch, S. (2011). More than the sum of its parts: Hinglish as an alternative communicative resource. In R. Kothari and R. Snell (Eds.), *Chutnefying English: The phenomenon of Hinglish* (pp. 53–70). Penguin Books.

Carls, U. (2017). *A dictionary of Indian English*. Ed. P. Lucko, L. Peter and F. Polzenhagen. Leipziger Universitätsverlag.

Cayla, J. and Elsen, M. (2012). Indian consumer Kaun Hai? The class-based grammar of Indian advertising. *Journal of Macromarketing, 32*(3), 295–308.

Davies, M. (2013). *Corpus of Global Web-Based English: 1.9 billion words from speakers in 20 countries (GloWbE)*. <https://www.english-corpora.org/glowbe/> (last accessed 6 January 2021).

Kachru, B. (1983). *The Indianization of English: The English language in India*. Oxford University Press.

Lambert, J. (2012). Beyond Hobson Jobson: Towards a new lexicography for Indian English. *English World-Wide, 33*(3), 292–320.

Lambert, J. (2018). Anglo-Indian slang in dictionaries on historical principles. *World Englishes, 37*(2), 1–13. <https://doi.org/10.1111/weng.12291> (last accessed 6 January 2021).

Lambert, J. (2020). Lexicography and World Englishes. In D. Schreier, M. Hundt and E. Schneider (Eds.), *Cambridge handbook of World Englishes* (pp. 408–35). Cambridge University Press.

Lange, C. (2009). Where's the party yaar! Discourse particles in Indian English. In T. Hofmann and L. Siebers (Eds.), *World Englishes: Problems, properties and prospects* (pp. 207–25). John Benjamins.

Lange, C. (2020). Indian English. In D. Schreier, M. Hundt and E. Schneider (Eds.), *Cambridge handbook of World Englishes* (pp. 236–62). Cambridge University Press.

Lewis, I. (1991). *Sahibs, nabobs and boxwallahs*. Oxford University Press.

Loureiro-Porto, L. (2017). ICE v. GloWbE: Big data and corpus compilation. *World Englishes, 36*(3), 448–70.

Macmillan Comprehensive Dictionary. (2006). Macquarie Library.

Mukherjee, J. and Bernaisch, T. (2015). Cultural keywords in context: A pilot study of linguistic acculturation in South Asian Englishes. In P. Collins (Ed.), *Grammatical change in English world-wide* (pp. 411–36). John Benjamins.

Muthiah, K. (2012). Performing Bombay and displaying stances: Stylised Indian English in fiction. *English World-Wide, 33*(3), 264–91.

Oxford Advanced Learner's Dictionary. (1995). (5th ed. with Indian English supplement). Oxford University Press.

Parshad, R., Bhowmick, S., Chand, V., Kumari, N. and Sinha, N. (2016). What is India speaking? Exploring the 'Hinglish' invasion. *Physica A: Statistical Mechanics and its Applications, 449*(C), 375–89.

Peters, P. (2020). Cultural keywords in Philippine English. In K. Allan (Ed.), *Dynamics of language changes*. Springer Nature. Manuscript submitted for publication.

Peters, P. (in press). Pluricentricity and codification. In D. Perez, M. Hundt, J. Kebateh and D. Schreier (Eds.), *English and Spanish in interaction*. Cambridge University Press. Manuscript submitted for publication.

Piao, S., Rayson, P., Archer, D. and McEnery, T. (2005). Comparing and combining a semantic tagger and a statistical tool for MWE extraction. *Computer Speech and Language, 19*, 378–97.
Rayson, P. (2008). From key words to key semantic domains. *International Journal of Corpus Linguistics, 13*(4), 519–49.
Sailaja, P. (2009). *Indian English*. Edinburgh University Press.
Schilk, M., Bernaisch, T. and Mukherjee, J. (2012). Mapping unity and diversity in South Asian English lexicogrammar: Verb-complementational preferences across varieties. In M. Hundt and U. Gut (Eds.), *Mapping unity and diversity world-wide: Corpus-based studies of new Englishes* (pp. 137–66). John Benjamins.
Schneider, E. (2007). *Postcolonial English: Varieties around the world*. Cambridge University Press.
Wierzbicka, A. (1997). *Understanding cultures through their keywords: English, Russian, Polish, German, and Japanese*. Oxford University Press.
Williams, R. (1983). *Cultural keywords*. Fontana Press. (Original work published 1976).
Wilson, H. H. (1855). *A glossary of judicial and revenue terms: and of useful words occurring in official documents relating to the administration of the government of British India, from the Arabic, Persian, Hindustaání, Sanskrit, Hindí, Bengálí, Uriya, Maráthi, Guzaráthi, Telegu, Karnáta, Tamil, Malayálam, and other languages*. W. H. Allen.
Yule, H. and Burnell, A. (1903). *Hobson-Jobson: A glossary of colloquial Anglo-Indian words and phrases*. J. Murray. (Original work published 1886).

CHAPTER 6

Lexicopragmatics between Cultural Heritage and Exonormative Second Language Acquisition: Address Terms, Greetings and Discourse Markers in Ugandan English

Christiane Meierkord and Bebwa Isingoma

1. INTRODUCTION: CULTURE, LANGUAGE AND POST-PROTECTORATES

Studies of cultures and their languages, or varieties thereof, have investigated forms of address, greetings and discourse markers contrastively, for instance in the fields of ethnology and anthropology (for example, Hymes 1974). Similarly, comparisons of varieties of English indicate that cultural background impacts strongly on how speakers and writers greet and address their interlocutors and express stance. Ever since Braj Kachru (1977) put forward his notion of nativisation of English, the World Englishes paradigm has convincingly demonstrated that the varieties that have developed across the world have very different conventions as regards the influence of their speakers' cultures on the way they use English. In fact, '[p]atterns of expressing politeness, apologies, compliments and face-saving devices are often carried over from L1 [first language] practices to New English [sic]' (Mesthrie and Bhatt 2008: 141). Mesthrie and Bhatt (2008: 144) point out that 'there is a strong relationship between the forms that English manifests and its speakers' perceptions of reality and the nature of their cultural institutions', leading to differences in discourse patterns, uses of discourse particles and realisations of speech acts. Although discourse features have not received as much attention as aspects of grammar, the lexicon and phonology, the field has occupied a prominent place, having been brought to the fore by Yamuna Kachru (for example, Kachru 1991, 1992). Not only have these been discussed as differing across languages and varieties of English, but also these are areas where second-language (L2) varieties of English frequently use borrowed or calqued expressions to express concepts that seem to differ from those that the L1 varieties, particularly British and American English, have at their disposal.

Typically, examples, including those in Schneider (this volume), tend to come from L1 and L2 Englishes. This chapter discusses how culture is reflected in a post-protectorate variety, Ugandan English (UgE), which as Mesthrie and Bhatt (2008: 9) argue, 'may well have a status intermediate between ESL [English as a second language] and EFL [English as a foreign language] territories'. Given the fact that, (a) as a protectorate, Uganda never witnessed a significant settler population in the sense of Schneider (2007) and (b) English is still largely acquired through formal instruction following an exonormative British model, it is likely that the L2 acquisition process constitutes a significant factor that, besides culture, influences how greetings, address terms and discourse markers are employed.

In fact, starting from the 1970s and 80s onwards, research in the field of interlanguage pragmatics, that is, the use of a language by learners, established that an individual's first language and culture influence the way they perform individual speech acts through pragmatic interference (see the papers in Blum-Kulka et al. 1989) but also revealed that besides L1 influence, L2 acquisition processes constrain the way speakers use language. Corpus linguistic analyses of authentic language data allow us to better assess the degree to which varieties differ and also to assess whether individual features are reflections of culture or results of second language acquisition processes.

2. UGANDAN ENGLISH

English was introduced to Uganda at the end of the 19th century, when, following the arrival of Sir Henry Morton Stanley in the area in 1874, Anglican and Catholic missionaries established themselves and soon started schools and when administrative personnel arrived after the British Government declared a protectorate over Buganda in 1894 (Meierkord 2016). However, due to Uganda's status as a protectorate, where land purchases were not permitted, there were hardly any British settlers in the area and English was initially acquired by a very restricted social elite, through formal learning in missionary and later government schools (see Meierkord 2016 for a detailed discussion of the history of English in Uganda).

Today, English is the main medium of instruction in Uganda's schools and the sole medium at the secondary and tertiary levels of education, being used by individuals with very different cultural and ethnic backgrounds. Uganda is home to 65 cultures, as recognised in the Constitution of the Republic of Uganda together with The Constitution (Amendment) Act, 2005. Many of these have their own language, whilst others share a language (for example, the ethnic groups of the Banyaruguru, Bahororo and Bakiga, who all speak Rukiga), and Ethnologue (Eberhard et al. 2019) identifies 41 living indigenous languages for Uganda. These belong mainly to three language families, into which they fall as follows:

> Bantu languages (for example, Luganda): 66.4 per cent,
> Nilotic languages (for example, Ateso): 27.2 per cent, and
> Central Sudanic languages (for example, Lugbara): 6.3 per cent.
> (Simons and Fennig 2017)

In addition, there are minority languages including Kiswahili, Nubi, a few Kuliak languages and various immigrant languages, most notably those spoken by Uganda's Asian community (mostly Gujarati and Punjabi), and a total of 3,235 individuals from the UK, the US, Canada and Australia, as per the 2014 census (Namyalo et al. 2016: 27; Isingoma and Meierkord 2019: 295). English has become a very widespread language, spoken by large parts of Uganda's population, due to the fact that English is the main medium of instruction in a school system offering seven years of free universal primary education.[1] It seems to be justified to estimate that those 15.4 per cent of Uganda's population who have attained the ordinary level of education (Uganda Bureau of Statistics 2016: 26) have also attained an intermediate level of proficiency in English. As regards their religious background, most Ugandans are Christians of various denominations, but 13.7 per cent are Muslims (Uganda Bureau of Statistics 2016: 19), which may be reflected in greetings or address terms originating in Arabic.

Whilst research into UgE is still in its infancy, there has been a lot of activity in recent years (see the papers published in Meierkord et al. 2016; Ssempuuma 2018; Isingoma 2013, 2014a, 2014b; Nassenstein

2016; Isingoma and Meierkord 2019). The results of these investigations point to the fact that UgE is a variety that is distinct from its 'neighbour', Kenyan English. Individual sections of these publications also include discussions of how individual address terms, greetings and discourse markers are used in this variety.

The following sections provide accounts of how greetings, address terms and discourse markers expressing stance have been studied, particularly with relation to African cultures and varieties of English, before their use in written and spoken UgE is discussed based on the following three data sets. The written part of the Uganda component of the International Corpus of English (ICE-UG [W200]) has strictly followed the design laid out in Nelson (1991) and contains 431,776 words, including extra corpus material. The spoken data collected for ICE-UG until the time of writing (here referred to as ICE-UG [S131]), consists of 361,852 words from the text categories of face-to-face conversations, telephone conversations, unscripted speeches and broadcast talks. Finally, Web-UG is a corpus of web-based writings (mainly websites and blogs), collected using Sketch Engine (Kilgarriff et al. 2014; see Isingoma and Meierkord 2019: 311 for details) and totalling approximately 12.3 million words.

3. GREETINGS

The speech act GREET is a typical illocution in the opening phases of British English conversations (Edmondson and House 1981: 201) and has often been studied as being ritual and phatic routine formulae lacking propositional content. However, Duranti cautions his readers to be open to various types of conversational openings being greetings:

> Although some speech communities have activity-specific items that are used only for greetings (the American English 'hi!' and the Italian 'ciao', for example), the existing literature shows that many communities do not have such expressions, and what people say during greetings might be identical to what is being said during other kinds of speech activities, the English 'how're you doing?' being an example of such a type. (Duranti 1997: 67)

In his account of Samoan greetings, Duranti documents that one of the four forms is in fact an extension of complimenting, with *malo* translating into *congratulations*. Also, Samoan greetings are not necessarily expressive speech acts in the sense of Searle (1976), thus not having propositional content, but they can be used to 'accomplish various social acts, including searching for new information and sanctioning social behavior' (Duranti 1997: 63).

Studies investigating African languages and cultures emphasise the special importance of greetings (for example, Akindele 2007; Igboin 2012). As Akindele explains for the Basotho community of Southern Africa:

> in every context or situation, greetings are expected: when a person enters a house, he/she is expected to greet people in the house; on the street people are expected to greet each other. Traditionally, one is expected to greet everyone met in the street. (Akindele 2007: 2)

Greetings serve to facilitate interpersonal relationships and maintain rapport and comfort among the community. In Sesotho, another South African language, greetings depend on the time of the day, the formality of the situation and the age of the interlocutor. However, Akindele also finds that the practice is in transition and that, due to contact with Western culture, people no longer greet everybody, 'especially in urban areas where people are only concerned about those who are close to them' (2007: 2).

For the Nigerian context, Igboin (2012) explains that, traditionally, Yoruba greetings differ depending on the time of the day, the season, social factors and even professions. However, Oumarou (1997), similar to Akindele (2007), finds that greetings have become shorter in urban areas. In addition to such generational changes, Odebunmi (2013) explains that traditional Yoruba greetings are often in conflict with greeting practices established in modern society, that is, in doctor–patient encounters in hospitals, where they are more constrained by the norms of the medical institution and a Western cultural orientation.

Similarly, Agyekum's (2008) investigation into Akan greetings in Ghana documents that greetings range from simple to complex, that is, long and elaborate, and that, not surprisingly, there are informal but also formal and ceremonial greetings. Traditionally, greetings also differ as regards the day of the week, the time and the clan. Moreover, there are special forms of greeting for a number of individual situations (for example, when in a public bath) or with individual addressees (for example, to a blacksmith). Generally, greetings are 'used to negotiate status relationships' (Agyekum 2008: 504), and it is unacceptable not to greet. Like Igboin (2012), Agyekum also observes considerable change in greeting behaviour. As traditional greetings have become archaic and 'most people in the cities use the English greetings *Good morning, afternoon, evening* etc.' (Agyekum 2008: 509), knowledge of traditional greetings and responses is mainly found in rural settings today.

For the Ugandan context, Isingoma (2014a: 97) mentions that Runyoro-Rutooro greetings tend to be lengthy, requiring the speaker to show concern with the various aspects of the addressee's life. As he explains:

> [i]n Ugandan cultures, it is customary to first compliment someone before asking how he/she is, even when the addressee is actually doing nothing at the time of being complimented. The speaker assumes that the addressee must have done/be doing something productive, so he/she deserves the compliments. (Isingoma 2016: 167)

The practice is deeply rooted in various Ugandan languages. Whilst *gyebaleko* is the expression used in Luganda, *ogyebale* is used in Runyoro, Rutooro and Lusoga. In Acholi, which as a Nilotic language belongs to an entirely different language family, it is *apwoyo*.

For World Englishes, Mesthrie and Bhatt notice the transfer of L1 norms in greetings, in their case of *handfolded Namaskar!* at the opening of an email (2008: 142). Such transfer is also reported in Isingoma (2016), who explains that Ugandans use the greeting *Well done!*, which is calqued from the Bantu languages' *gyebaleko* discussed above.[2]

Searches in Web-UG produced a number of hits for *well done*, at the beginnings of posts to internet forums. However, none of these could be identified as genuine greetings but were speech acts of praise in reaction to a past performance or activity by the addressee. Further, neither of the indigenous greetings, *gyebaleko* from Luganda, *ogyebale/mugyebale* from Lusoga and Runyankole-Rukiga, or *agandi* and *ngoni* ('How are you?') from Runyankole-Rukiga and Lugbara respectively were attested in the data. Also, Kiswahili greetings such as *jambo*, *salama* or *habari* are not attested. However, there are four instances of *Namaste*, one of *Assalamu aleikum* and one of *Salam*.

To explore English greetings in UgE, we scrutinised the beginnings of the face-to-face dialogues, obtained through semi-structured ethnographic interviews. The recordings contain a total of 27 greetings at the beginning of the recorded conversations (shown in Table 6.1). Many of these consisted of a WELCOME in the sense of Edmondson and House (1981: 98). Interestingly, the exact phrasing varies between *Welcome once again*, as in British or American English, and expressions such as *I welcome you to this conversation* and *Once again, you're welcome to this talk*. It is particularly the latter which is frequently encountered in Uganda, resembling the typical reaction to a THANK in British English.

Table 6.1 Greetings in the opening phases of face-to-face interactions

Item	N
(Good) morning (once again)	2
Welcome	7
I welcome you	8
You're / You are welcome	10

A subsequent search in Web-UG yielded a total of 11 phrases, all of which occurred in the chat of a religious community. *You're / You are welcome* was used nine times as a GREET, *You are welcome to NP* (for example, the brotherhood of Illuminati) 10 times. The use of *You are welcome* as a greeting is illustrated in examples (1) and (2).[3]

(1) THE SPEAKER: Honourable members, in the public gallery we have teachers and pupils of Achievers Pride Education Centre; they are represented by hon. Sseggona and hon. Seninde. They are from Wakiso District, **you are welcome**. (Applause) (from Web-UG)

(2) Ladies and Gentlemen . . . **you're very welcome**. I'll start by introducing myself . . . that I'm the richest man in this room (from ICE-UG [S1 31])

The phrase *I welcome you* is used twelve times as a GREET and *we welcome you* occurs twice, while *Welcome to* has 78 hits and *Welcome* on its own 20. In sum, the uses of *You're welcome* are comparatively infrequent in the written data, where the form *Welcome to* is more prevalent.

At the same time, speakers and writers use the conventional Ll English greetings *Good morning* (24 in Web-UG), *Good evening* (nine in Web-UG) and *Good afternoon* (nine in Web-UG), albeit sparingly. In web-based communication, there is furthermore an overwhelming use of the more informal *Hello* (573 in Web-UG) and *Hi* (544 in Web-UG), which seems to reflect the globalisation of informal forms of GREETs. On the other hand, *Greetings*, which is considered 'old use' or an 'old-fashioned' way of saying *Hello*, occurs 33 times in Web-UG. Finally, greetings making use of the explicit speech act verb *greet* make up 18 instances in the form of *I greet*. . . .

Greetings were comparatively infrequent in the ICE-UG data, both written and spoken (the data reported for the interview starts were not contained in the transcribed parts), as Table 6.2 shows.[4]

Table 6.2 Greetings in the three data sets

Item	Web-UG	ICE-UG [W200]	ICE-UG [S131]
Hello	573	9	6
Hi	544	8	0
Welcome	20	5	1
I/we welcome you	14	0	7
You are welcome	19	0	3
Welcome to	78	4	0
Good morning	24	1	2
Good afternoon	9	0	0
Good evening	9	0	2
Greetings	33	4	0
I greet you	18	2	0

In sum, the data reveal a strong preference for English greetings, which, however, sometimes have forms and semantics that differ from those of the corresponding Ll greetings, in the case of *You're welcome/ You are welcome*, which seem to be influenced by the British English response to *Thank you*, or are considered archaic in Ll Englishes.

4. ADDRESS TERMS

Another area through which politeness and deference have been said to be encoded in languages, and that also constitutes part of nexus 2, is address terms.[5] Typically, these cater for social hierarchies based on sex, age and status but also kinship. Braun's (1988: 9–11) seminal work lists the following as nominal expressions (that is, excluding pronouns) of address: names, kinship terms, forms of address equivalent to *Mr* or *Ms*, titles, abstract forms such as *Your Majesty*, terms of profession or occupation, terms indicating relationships such as *friend* or *neighbour*, endearment terms and forms defining the addressee in relation to another person such as *son of Abdullah*.

For African contexts, Oyetade (1995) explains that Yoruba speakers address their interlocutors through pronouns, names (personal or praise name, full formal name or surname only), kinship terms, titles or occupational names. As Lüpke and Storch (2013: 99) clarify, several African languages also have more or less complex honorific systems, reflecting social hierarchies, as well as avoidance languages. For example, in Cameroon, using personal names 'is not only disrespectful but also a sign that they have no honor to merit the respect that goes with not calling their names' (Anchimbe 2011: 1472). Using instead kinship terms, professional titles, duty and hereditary titles (such as *honourable* or *president*) or social titles (for example, *manyi*, meaning 'mother of twins') is 'an important social interactional facet of the Cameroonian community' (Anchimbe 2011: 1482). As regards kinship terms, Wolf and Polzenhagen (2009: 72) point out that kinship in African cultures is typically not modelled on the prototypical Western nuclear family. Rather it contains 'a set of other "socially recognised relations"' (Wolf and Polzenhagen 2009: 75) which have traditionally been established in the local village community. Avoidance languages are often gendered languages, requesting married women to avoid addressing (Lüpke and Storch 2013: 106–7) their husband and his family's male members by their names.[6]

For World Englishes, Mesthrie and Bhatt (2008) document the use of address terms that cater for asymmetric power relations, in their case the use of *Respected Sir* to address the recipient of an email in Indian English, and explain that this serves to 'minimise the threat to face and to express polite behaviour' (2008: 142), a practice also attested by Bamgbose (1992) for Nigerian English. Awonusi (1990: 34) states that 'Nigerians not only relish deferential titles but also those of occupation or both at the same time', yielding, for example, *Chief X*, *Engineer X* or even multiple titles such as *Alhaji Dr. X*. Mesthrie and Bhatt (2008: 142) also notice that, as 'part of a structured system of "expressing respect" in the South Asian context', the actual name of the recipient is frequently avoided.

Several studies have emphasised the use of kinship terms in African varieties of English to refer to non-kin. Gough (1996: 64) explains that in Black South African English *mama* is employed with reference to a senior woman. Similarly, and in general for African Englishes, Schmied (2008: 465) points out that the reference of kinship terms is related to social features of 'seniority (age), solidarity, affection and role-relations', for example leading to the use of *auntie* towards an older sister to cater for her higher status.

Due to the limited size of the social and business letters categories in ICE-UG [W200], these lent themselves to an exploratory hand search, which revealed that address forms differ crucially between social and business letters (see Table 6.3). Whilst in the former the use of the addressee's personal name is the major strategy, business letters, not unexpectedly, have a clear preference to use *Sir* or *Sir/Madam*. Interestingly, there are 36 instances in which business letters make do without any address at all. The preference for more informal address forms in the social letters is, most likely, a result of the level of acquaintance between the writer and the addressee. In cases where the relation is not one of friendship, authors use more formal forms of address, typically containing titles.

Table 6.3 Address terms in ICE-UG social and business letters

Type of address	*Social letters*	*Business letters*
Personal name (PN)	68	0
Full PN	0	2
Mr + PN	0	2
Mr + Full PN	0	1
Mother/mum	3	0
Brother	2	0
Sir	4	38
Sir/Madam	0	38
Madam	0	8
Professor	5 (3 of which *Prof.*)	0
Dr. + PN	9	0
Pastor	4	0
Bishop	0	2
Lord/Lordship	0	4 *Lord*, 3 *Lordship*
Worship	0	2
none	5	36
parent(s)/guardian(s)	0	6
mukwano (address term for a very dear friend or girl-/boyfriend)	6	0

PN means a personal name.

In addition to the items collected in Table 6.3, there were single instances in the social letters of *Dear Deputy Vice-Chancellor Sir* and *mukama*, whilst in the business letters isolated instances of *MLEN*[7] *family* and *Madam Speaker* occur.

Several of the individual address forms were also found in Web-UG: *Sister* has a total of 16 hits for address term uses, with seven of these being single uses of *sister* and nine being *sister* in combination with a personal name (PN). A large number of these seem to occur in posts within a religious community. Relatedly, *brother* has a total of 34 hits, most of them occurring alone (28), and another six together with a PN. Often, these were used in posts in advice blogs, and in contrast to what is the case with *sister*, only five occurred in religious contexts.

(3) Go cry to your mother about this, **brother**. Leave the poor sweet, innocent ladies alone!
(4) **My brother Eric Sabiiti**, with you and Jennifer Angeyo at the helm of the legal department at the Electoral Commission, Uganda needs fervent prayers.

In addition, there are 13 hits of the more informal *bro* in the data, eight of these without a PN and five with a PN. The Kiswahili word *ndugu* occurs three times, but *aunt(ie)* not at all.

Titles are also attested with some frequency: *Doctor* in 88 cases, mostly in posts and letters sent in to a medical column, *Mr. President* with 42 hits (but none of *President* alone for address) and *Professor* 15 times, in blogs and chats. Titles of occupation like *Chief* or *Engineer*, as reported from Nigerian English, had no hits. However, the Kiswahili *afande* ('soldier of high rank') was used in three instances in ICE-UG [W200] and seven times in Web-UG, together with a personal name.

Standard (British) English address forms such as *Sir* and *Madam* are, at the same time, frequent in Web-UG: *Sir* is attested 25 times and an additional 19 as *Mr. Speaker, Sir* (from the Hansards; at times without punctuation and no upper case), whilst *Madam* has four hits on its own but 183 as *Madam Speaker* (resulting from the fact that since 2011 the Speaker of Parliament has been a lady) and another two as *Madam chair*.

(5) Mr. Museven **Sir**, our dear president, you have an attractive personality and surely you are a charismatic leader. (Web-UG)

Crucially, the corresponding L1 equivalents are only rarely used with *ssebo* ('Sir') occurring three times (of which one is *Ssebo President*) and *nyabo* ('Madam') twice in Web-UG. Both are used in Luganda as well as in Runyankole-Rukiga.

(6) If she brings her toothbrush, *ssebo* you are finished. Begin planning to buy food for two. (Web-UG)
(7) *Nyabo*, i cant say i like you or i hate you but your life stories in papers sucks. (Web-UG)

There are no uses of the L1 address terms equivalent to *Sir* and *Madam* used in the other major languages spoken in Uganda, that is, of *isebo/sebo* and *inhabo* from Lusoga, *ata mva* and *ata za* from Lugbara, or *ladit* and *lamego* from Acholi.

In ICE-UG, address terms are rather infrequent, save for the social and business letters reported on above, as summarised in Table 6.4.

Table 6.4 Address terms in the three data sets

Item	Web-UG	ICE-UG [W200]	ICE-UG [S131]
Mister/Mr	0 in first 1,000	0	2
Mister/Mr. + PN	2/0 in first 1,000	2	3
Mister/Mr + Full PN	0/0 in first 1,000	1	0
mother	6 in first 1,000	6	0
mum/mom	3/3	2/0	0/0
father	0	1	0
brother	34	2	0
bro	13	0	0
sister	16	0	0
Sir	44	42	0
Madam	187	8	1
Professor	15	3 (one *Prof.*)	7
Doctor/Dr	88	0/0	0
Doctor/Dr + PN	0	1/9	3
Pastor	11 + PN	4	0
Bishop	3 + PN	2	0
Lord(ship)	8/6	4/3	0
mukwano	0	9	0
President	42	0	0
ndugu	3	0	0
afande	7	3	0
(s)sebo	3	0	0
(n)nyabo	2	0	0

Similar to the case with greetings, UgE has a clear preference for English phrases but adapts their semantics and pragmatics to the local context and has uses which, at times, seem archaic and formal. Potentially, the overuse of individual terms in teaching material explains such uses, at least partially.

5. DISCOURSE MARKERS

At an expressive and social level, discourse markers function 'to display personal and social identities, to convey attitudes and perform actions, and to negotiate relationships between self and other' (Maschler and Schiffrin 2015: 189).[8] As such, they would also be one further constituent of nexus 2. Discourse marker systems are typically language-specific and a particular marker in one language rarely has an exact equivalent in another (for example, Rossari 1996; Ariel 1998). As such, they cannot easily be substituted and, in fact, studies of bilingual discourse have documented that 'bilinguals very often switch languages when verbalizing discourse markers', either 'highlighting contrast and thus maximizing the saliency of markers as contextualization cues' or 'reducing the heavier cognitive load' inherent to processing the markers (Maschler and Schiffrin 2015: 200).

With relation to World Englishes, Methrie and Bhatt claim that:

> [t]hese discourse particles share more or less the same distributional properties across different varieties of English. However, there is some evidence of their relatively restricted use in New Englishes (cf. de Klerk 2004 on BlSAf Eng [Black South African English]). Furthermore, some discourse/pragmatic particles are variety specific. (Methrie and Bhatt 2008: 136)

The authors mention the use of *la* and *what* in colloquial Singaporean English and *only* in Indian English as such.

For Ugandan English, Nassenstein (2016: 414–15) discusses discourse markers in some detail, referring to them as 'modal particles' (2016: 414). As he explains, these markers express a speaker's personal stance towards the utterance they are preceding and thus 'decide how FTAs [face-threatening acts] are either preserved or avoided and whether face-loss is intended or not' (Nassenstein 2016: 414). Whilst *mbu* 'introduces clauses whose content information is less ascertained and has been perceived by the speaker as a rumour, possibly false information or through gossiping' (Nassenstein 2016: 414), *oba* indicates confusion and open choice, *nga* serves to criticise the hearer (interestingly, and importantly, it is frequently calqued into *now* with the same semantics), *ate* expresses astonishment, *nawe* expresses hope for the hearer's empathy, and *wama* (also *wamma*; compare Isingoma 2016) empathy and appeasement. To this list, Isingoma (2016) adds *anti* ('because, as a matter of fact'), *bambi* ('oh dear!, please'), *kale* ('okay'), *kyokka* ('but, however'), *mpozzi* ('apparently, maybe') and *naye* ('but'). As Isingoma (2016) notes, these are typically used in informal spoken discourse.

As Isingoma (2013: 28) points out, discourse markers also surface in the form of the calques, for example *nga* to *as*, as in *As you are brave!* expressing surprise (or at times even shock) on the side of the speaker. Another discourse marker in UgE is *also*, with rising intonation, which encodes disappointment at the referent's behaviour as in *Jane also does not understand!* Further, *OK please*, used where British and American English would use *OK* only, is calqued from the Bantu expression *kale bambi*; it emphasises agreement and goodwill and is 'intended to show a positive attitude of the speaker, that is, the speaker agrees fully with the addressee' (Isingoma 2016: 167).

As we report in Isingoma and Meierkord (2019: 315), in Web-UG '[o]f the three discourse markers *mbu*, *nga* and *nti*, only *mbu* occurs somewhat regularly, attested 40 times (30.77 pmw), whilst *nga* and *nti* are rather marginal with three (0.24 pmw) and one (0.08 pmw) occurrence respectively'.[9] Also, in Web-UG, *nti* only occurs in code-switched sequences produced in Luganda, but not as a borrowing in an English sentence. In addition to these three discourse markers, Web-UG has ten instances of *wama*, seven hits for *oba*, another seven of *bambi*, and five instances of *naye* and only one of *nawe*, while there are no uses of *kyokka*, *mpozzi* and *kale*. These results compare to the findings in ICE-UG [W200] and ICE-UG [S131] as summarised in Table 6.5.[10]

In ICE-UG [W200] and ICE-UG [S131], only few discourse markers were attested, but some of them with comparatively high frequencies, given the small size of the data. In ICE-UG [S131], *oba* occurs 15 times, *nga* four and *mbu* three times, which is rather different from the finding for Web-UG. Example 14 nicely illustrates how *oba* is also calqued into *what* and sometimes used in sequence with it.

(14) May be I had this thing of the movies I watched when I was young<,> those people<,> do they do <indig>oba</indig>

Table 6.5 Discourse markers in the three data sets

Item	Web-UG	ICE-UG [W200]	ICE-UG [S]
mbu	40	1	3
wama/wamma	10	0	0
oba	7	1	15
bambi	7	1	0
naye	5	2	0
nga	3	0	4
nti	1	1	0
ate	0	2	1
nawe	1	0	0

> genetic engineering <indig>oba</indig> what<,> those things where they come up with clones<,> what what<,>

Not surprisingly, the written ICE data have fewer L1 discourse markers in the English passages. There are two instances of *ate* and *naye* and one each for *mbu*, *oba*, *nti* and *bambi*.

6. CONCLUSION

The various results of our analyses of Ugandan English corpus data have shown that, in these data, writers and speakers of this variety express attitudes and values shared by and typical of Ugandan society and cultures. Whilst they are sensitive to the demands of their society by indicating social relations and power through careful choice of greetings and address terms (at times with a changed semantics and with a preference for formal items) as well as by framing their utterances through a number of discourse markers, only limited code-mixing or borrowing of indigenous material can be found in the data. Isingoma and Meierkord (2019) report similarly low attestations of L1 items for cultural objects and notions, that is, what would constitute nexus 1 in the sense of Schneider (this volume). They point out that even large corpora may not contain individual lexical items due to the genres captured and the topics discussed in the data that make up the corpus data. In Uganda, it is typically less formal genres where code-switching is found more often, and these are seldom captured in corpus data. At the same time, however, Ugandans tend not to use English in informal conversation all that frequently.

In the data discussed in this chapter, items borrowed from the speakers' L1s are mainly discourse markers, where speakers and authors seem to feel, more than with greetings and address forms, that the English words at their disposal do not fully express the semantics of the L1 markers. Thus, the borrowing seems to be caused by the lack of a sufficiently complex system of English discourse markers that would allow speakers to express stance, making the motivation behind the borrowing similar to what has been observed with borrowings for and calques of kinship terms in those varieties where precise reference is deemed necessary for reasons of politeness and/or deference (see Mesthrie and Bhatt 2008: 112–13 and Nihalani et al. 2004 for Indian English).

For greetings and addressing others, the data display a strong overall preference for English terms, which may be explained by three factors. Two relate to the acquisition trajectories of most Ugandans, who still predominantly acquire English through formal instruction in an exonormatively oriented school system, and to globalisation, as explained in Sections 1 and 3.

However, a further significant factor is the fact that English is used to communicate across cultures and Englishes, that is, as a lingua franca in interactions across Englishes in the sense of Meierkord (2012). As Meierkord (2012: 161–71) explains, lingua franca communication in English is (among many other things) characterised by a lexicon that 'presents itself as reduced and culturally largely neutral' (Meierkord 2012: 171). In the Ugandan context, when English serves as a lingua franca it is used across 65 cultures and 41 languages. Integrating borrowed items in Ugandan English, thus, is not as easily done as in a variety such as NZ English or Pakistani English, where the number of languages (traditionally and historically) used in the countries is considerably smaller. Employing an indigenous greeting or address term from one's L1 may fail to express the desired social relation or simply not be understood, if the addressee is not a member of the same culture as the writer or speaker and/or does not command the language.

In general, in uses of English as a lingua franca, unless participants are familiar with each other's mother tongues, the number of different cultures demands that speakers cope with unexpected uses and interpretations of individual words and phrases whilst at the same time having to deal with imperfect knowledge of and competence in their own and their interlocutors' L2 English(es) (Meierkord 2000). From this results a certain level of insecurity experienced by the participants, which has the effect of making them establish a unique set of rules for interaction.

This often includes the use of a limited range of vocabulary items that participants consider safe and which they assume their interlocutors are familiar with to avoid misunderstanding (see Meierkord 2002).

More research into post-protectorate Englishes as well as studies comparing lingua franca uses across a wide range of different L1 speakers with those where the L1s are fewer is required to substantiate whether and how post-protectorate status, exonormative L2 acquisition norms and lingua franca use and culture interact.

NOTES

1. However, schools typically still demand parents pay for, for example, teaching materials and stationery.
2. Relatedly, Igboin (2012) documents the use of *E ku* ('well done') in Yoruba.
3. Extracts from the individual corpora are presented here with any original (mis)spellings.
4. Note that the figures for ICE-UG [S131] here differ from the ones reported above for the interview starts, since not all of the starts are included in the transcriptions.
5. Address terms are here distinguished from reference terms, following Braun (1988: 11).
6. One example of such a system, reflecting societal roles, some gendered, others not, is the Zulu system of hlonipha as discussed in de Kadt (1998).
7. MLEN stands for Multilingual Language Education Network.
8. Discourse markers further function to produce coherent discourse, either at the textual level or to convey meaning across individual sentences.
9. pmw = per million words.
10. Discourse markers which are not attested in any of the three data sets are not included.

REFERENCES

Agyekum, K. (2008). The pragmatics of Akan greetings. *Discourse Studies, 10*(4), 493–516.

Akindele, D. F. (2007). Lumela/Lumela: A socio-pragmatic analysis of Sesotho greetings. *Nordic Journal of African Studies, 16*(1), 1–17.

Anchimbe, E. (2011). On not calling people by their names: Pragmatic undertones of sociocultural relationships in a postcolony. *Journal of Pragmatics, 43*(6), 1472–83.

Ariel, M. (1998). Discourse markers and form-function correlations. In A. Jucker and Y. Ziv (Eds.), *Discourse markers: Descriptions and theory* (pp. 223–60). John Benjamins.

Awonusi, V. O. (1990). Coming of age: English in Nigeria. *English Today, 6*(2), 31–5.

Bamgbose, A. (1992). Standard Nigerian English: Issues of identification. In B. B. Kachru (Ed.), *The other tongue: English across cultures* (pp. 148–61). University of Illinois Press.

Blum-Kulka, S., House, J. and Kasper, G. (Eds.). (1989). *Cross-cultural pragmatics: Requests and apologies*. Ablex.

Braun, F. (1988). *Terms of address: Problems of patterns and usage in various languages and cultures*. Mouton de Gruyter.

de Kadt, E. (1998). The concept of face and its applicability to the Zulu language. *Journal of Pragmatics, 29*(2), 173–91.

de Klerk, V. (2004). Expressing levels of intensity in Xhosa English. *English World-Wide, 26*(1), 77–96.

Duranti, A. (1997). Universal and culture-specific properties of greetings. *Journal of Linguistic Anthropology, 7*(1), 63–97.

Eberhard, D. M., Simons, G. F. and Fennig, C. D. (Eds.). (2019). Ethnologue: Languages of the world (22nd ed.). SIL International. <http://www.ethnologue.com> (last accessed 7 January 2021).

Edmondson, W. and House, J. (1981). *Let's talk and talk about it*. Urban & Schwarzenberg.

Gough, D. (1996). Black English in South Africa. In V. de Klerk (Ed.), *Focus on South Africa* (pp. 53–77). John Benjamins.

Hymes, D. (1974). Ways of speaking. In R. Bauman and J. Sherzer (Eds.), *Explorations in the ethnography of speaking* (pp. 433–51). Cambridge University Press.

Igboin, B. O. (2012). The semiotic of greetings in Yoruba culture. *Culture: International Journal of Philosophy of Culture and Axiology, 9*(2), 123–42.

Isingoma, B. (2013). Innovative pragmatic codes in Ugandan English: A relevance-theoretic account. *Argumentum, 9*, 19–31.

Isingoma, B. (2014a). Empaako 'praise names': an historical, sociolinguistic, and pragmatic analysis. *African Study Monographs, 35*(2), 85–98.

Isingoma, B. (2014b). Lexical and grammatical features of Ugandan English. *English Today, 30*(2), 51–6.

Isingoma, B. (2016). Lexical borrowings and calques in Ugandan English. In C. Meierkord, B. Isingoma and S. Namyalo (Eds.), *Ugandan English: Its sociolinguistics, structure and uses in a globalising post-protectorate* (pp. 149–72). John Benjamins.

Isingoma, B. and Meierkord, C. (2019). Capturing the lexicon of Ugandan English: ICE-Uganda, its limitations, and effective complements. In A. U. Esimaje, U. Gut and E. B. Antia (Eds.), *Corpus linguistics and African Englishes* (pp. 293–328). John Benjamins.

Kachru, B. B. (1977). New Englishes and old models. *English Language Forum, 15*(3), 29–35.

Kachru, Y. (1991). Speech acts in World Englishes: Toward a framework for research. *World Englishes, 10*(3), 299–306.

Kachru, Y. (1992). Speech acts in the other tongue: An integrated approach to cross-cultural research. *World Englishes, 11*(2–3), 235–40.

Kilgarriff, A., Baisa, V., Bušta, J., Jakubíček, M., Kovvář, V., Michelfeit, J., Rychlý, P. and Suchomel, V. (2014). The Sketch Engine: Ten years on. *Lexicography, 1*(1), 7–36.

Lüpke, F. and Storch, A. (2013). *Repertoires and choices in African languages.* De Gruyter Mouton.

Maschler, Y. and Schiffrin, D. (2015). Discourse markers: Language, meaning and context. In D. Tannen, H. E. Hamilton and D. Schiffrin (Eds.), *The handbook of discourse analysis* (pp. 189–221). Wiley.

Meierkord, C. (2000). Interpreting successful lingua-franca interaction: An analysis of non-native-/non-native small talk conversation in English. *Linguistik Online, 5*(1). <https://doi.org/10.13092/lo.5.1013> (last accessed 7 January 2021).

Meierkord, C. (2002). 'Language stripped bare' or 'linguistic masala'? Culture in lingua franca communication. In K. Knapp and C. Meierkord (Eds.), *Lingua franca communication* (pp. 109–33). Peter Lang.

Meierkord, C. (2012). *Interactions across Englishes: Linguistic choices in local and international contact situations.* Cambridge University Press.

Meierkord, C. (2016). A social history of English in Uganda. In C. Meierkord, B. Isingoma and S. Namyalo (Eds.), *Ugandan English: Its sociolinguistics, structure and uses in a globalising post-protectorate* (pp. 51–71). John Benjamins.

Meierkord, C., Isingoma, B. and Namyalo, S. (Eds.). (2016). *Ugandan English: Its sociolinguistics, structure and uses in a globalising post-protectorate.* John Benjamins.

Mesthrie, R. and Bhatt, R. M. (2008). *World Englishes: The study of new linguistic varieties*. Cambridge University Press.
Namyalo, S., Isingoma, B. and Meierkord, C. (2016). Towards assessing the space of English in Uganda's linguistic ecology: Facts and issues. In C. Meierkord, B. Isingoma and S. Namyalo (Eds.), *Ugandan English: Its sociolinguistics, structure and uses in a globalising post-protectorate* (pp. 19–49). John Benjamins.
Nassenstein, N. (2016). A preliminary description of Ugandan English. *World Englishes*, 35(3), 396–420.
Nelson, G. (1996). The design of the corpus. In S. Greenbaum (Ed.), *Comparing English worldwide: The International Corpus of English* (pp. 27–35). Clarendon Press.
Nihalani, P., Tongue, R. K. and Hosali, P. (2004). *Indian and British English: A handbook of usage and pronunciation* (2nd ed.). Oxford University Press.
Odebunmi, A. (2013). Greetings and politeness in doctor–client encounters in Southwestern Nigeria. *Iranian Journal of Society, Culture & Language*, 1(1), 101–17.
Oumarou, C. E. (1997). Context and meaning: A semiotic interpretation of greetings in Hausa. *Folklore Forum, 28*(2), 31–40.
Oyetade, S. O. (1995). A sociolinguistic analysis of address forms in Yoruba. *Language in Society, 24*(4), 515–35.
Rossari, C. (1996). Considérations sur la méthodologie contrastive français-italien: À propos de locutions adverbiales fonctionnant comme connecteurs. In M. B. Hansen and G. Skytte (Eds.), *Le discours: Cohérence et connexion, Etudes Romanes, 35* (pp. 55–68). Museum Tusculanum Press.
Schmied, J. (2008). East African English (Kenya, Uganda, Tanzania): Morphology and syntax. In R. Mesthrie (Ed.), *Varieties of English: Africa, South and Southeast Asia* (pp. 451–71). De Gruyter.
Schneider, E. W. (2007). *Postcolonial English: Varieties around the world*. Cambridge University Press.
Searle, J. (1976). A classification of illocutionary acts. *Language in Society, 5*, 1–23.
Simons, G. F. and Fennig, C. D. (eds) (2017). *Ethnologue: Languages of the world* (20th ed.) SIL International. <http://www.ethnologue.com> (last accessed 7 January 2021).
Ssempuuma, J. (2018). *Morphological and syntactic feature analysis of Ugandan English: Influence from Luganda, Runyankole-Rukiga, and Acholi-Lango*. Peter Lang.

Uganda Bureau of Statistics. (2016). *The National Population and Housing Census 2014 – Main Report*.

Wolf, H. and Polzenhagen, F. (2009). *World Englishes: A cognitive sociolinguistic approach*. Mouton de Gruyter.

CHAPTER 7

Cultural Relations? Kinship Terminology in Three Islands in the Northern Pacific

Sara Lynch, Eva Kuske and Dominique B. Hess

1. INTRODUCTION

In many smaller island communities of the Northern Pacific, the relationships and interdependence between family members remain fundamental to social structure. Here we explore three Pacific cultures[1] – namely, Guam, Kosrae and Saipan – which are each undergoing social and economic transformation but are at different stages. We conduct a comparable exploratory analysis using the theme of kinship based on the parallels and divergences of the concept in each community. Schneider (2018: 114) states that kinship terminology is 'a mainstay of signaling culture-specific social relations' and finds that results can show evidence of Western or non-Western practices regarding kin and community. Kinship ties construct their own individual 'cultural schema' (Sharifian 2015) and influence these Micronesian communities in terms of evolving cultural practices, entangled economic systems, and even shared and competing ideologies. Kinship is one of the foundational themes in the field of anthropology (Malinowski 1922, 1927; Radcliffe-Brown 1922; Lévi-Strauss [1949] 1969; Murdock 1949); however, the relationship between language and the 'conceptualisation' of kinship has generally been overlooked in English sociolinguistics until recently (Kronenfeld 2009). Rather than providing an exhaustive terminological analysis, this chapter is intended as a means of preliminary experiment where we explore the applicability of a newly formulated methodology as originally set out in *The Interface between Cultures and Corpora: Tracing Reflections and Manifestations* (Schneider 2018; this volume). We use our own Micronesian English corpora obtained from ethnographic sociolinguistic interviews to investigate the manifestations of 'cultural key words' (Hua 2013; Schneider 2018) under the category of kinship. We seek to verify that by employing corpus-based analysis methods (lexical quantification), we can find alternative routes for analysing culture in linguistic data.

The three post-colonial islands are particularly suited to this study based on their shared geographical area and political histories and alliances to varying degrees. Each community could be placed at different stages along a continuum of Western acculturation, diverging in terms of its exposure to societal internal and external stimuli. At one end of this scale, Guam is considered to have moved closest to US culture due to the historical oppression of the indigenous Chamorro. Kosrae lies on the other end of the scale with local language and cultural identity (Lawson 1996) consciously performed in all aspects of daily life and many local customs remaining organically routine. Saipan sits at the centre, because of its many ethnicities; focus is given here to the Saipan Carolinians (originally from the Caroline Islands which are part of the Federated States of Micronesia (FSM) today) and Chamorros, as these two groups make up the indigenous population.

Firstly, Guam has advanced furthest along the path of Westernised linguistic and social change (Topping 2003) in some ways similar to Hawai'i and NZ. It is an official territory of the US, which grants the inhabitants of Guam American citizenship with limited voting rights. The island's long-standing involvement with the US as a colonial power that persisted in 'Americanising' the indigenous population has resulted in generations who 'share American ideals and aspire to an American life style' (Barusch and Spaulding 1989: 61). Secondly, Saipan is generally considered to be undergoing the process of globalisation as ties are strengthening between the island and the US with regard to the federalisation of the minimum wage in 2018 (Perez 2018) and the federalisation of the immigration law until 2029 (US Citizenship and Immigration Services 2018). However, overall large-scale immigration remains a strong characteristic of the island. Finally, Kosrae, one of four FSM, remains tentatively more isolated and less directly affected by globalisation. However, the religiously conservative island is suffering massive emigration, facilitated by a freedom of movement agreement with the US. A cultural revolution occurred in the 1960s across Micronesia and this transformation has spread much further than the observable traditional practices of Micronesians, such as canoe building and local dance; it also affects concepts of the 'island family and the way that the family operates' (Hezel 2008).

Regarding these current Pacific social changes, we imagine Guam, Saipan and Kosrae as archetypally sitting at three different phases along a spectrum of (what can be described best as) Westernisation. Our hypothesis assumed that Kosrae, as the most traditionally ideological of the three, would prove to be consistently more family oriented and that Guam, deemed the Westernised nation state, would prove less family focused or nuclear-only focused. This logical hypothesis is supported by Schneider's finding that in Great Britain, kinship terms are significantly less likely to appear in speech than in Singapore and Hong Kong, which he states may 'reflect the reduced importance of family bonds in western cultures' (2018: 114–15). Hence, we seek to determine the degrees and complexities of the social and cultural transitions on these three island communities through comparative frequency analyses of lexis associated with kinship.

2. OVERVIEW OF THE ISLAND COMMUNITIES IN TERMS OF KINSHIP

In the following subsections, each island is discussed in terms of its socio-historical background with emphasis given to the significance of family and kinship in each culture. These descriptions help in determining the different familial relationships and cultural schema on the islands in order to interpret the results at a later stage.

2.1 Guam

The earliest inhabitants of Guam were the Chamorros, descendants of Austronesian people. Their first contact with the Western world was with Spain as a colonial power, followed by an American colonial period briefly interrupted during World War II when Japan occupied the island between 1941 and 1944. Since 1944, Guam has been back under American rule and is now considered a territory of the US. The close contact with the US had an influence on the use of the indigenous language as early as the first years of colonial contact. Chamorro was forbidden in schools and English was enforced and widely promoted (Rogers 1995). However, the use of Chamorro remained active in the islanders' homes until the return of the US prior to the end of World War II. Due to the economic changes happening in early post-war times, Chamorros started viewing English as the language of economic success and a majority decided to raise their children in English. This caused the use of Chamorro to decline rapidly to a point where it has now become endangered. Efforts to revitalise the indigenous language have been taken, such as making Chamorro a mandatory subject in public schools. Many islanders have a basic knowledge of the language but only the older generations still speak it fluently, while a majority of the younger speakers remain monolingual English speakers (Kuper 2014). Nevertheless, Chamorro enjoys high status in the island community as it is viewed as a carrier of cultural traditions. Santos-Bamba (2013) evaluates language attitudes towards Chamorro and English in three generations of women. She finds that attitudes towards Chamorro are more similar in the grandmother and daughter generations who have positive associations with the language. The generation in between, however, was the one that put little value on the indigenous language and spoke to the children only in English as it was considered the vehicle of success in entering the workforce. The main access route that younger generations have to learn the language of their ancestors is therefore the generation of their grandmothers.

2.1.1 Family and kinship terms in the traditional Guam Chamorro culture

Family (Chamorro *i-familia*, Spanish borrowing) remains an essential part of the Chamorro culture. Free time is often spent with the nuclear as well as the extended family – that is, aunties and uncles, cousins and the in-laws. The family usually takes care of the sick or elders who likely live in the same house with them or are visited frequently (Barusch and Spaulding 1989). The older Chamorro family structure remains to the extent that elders were and still are the ones responsible for decision making (Cunningham 1992).

Some Chamorro kinship terms are used regularly in the English language, even by Chamorros who do not speak their indigenous language fluently anymore. *Neni* is the Chamorro term for baby and is often used by elders to address younger loved ones regardless of their age. Younger Chamorros are likely to be called *neni* by their grandmothers, even when they are well into their 30s. *Che'lu* is the Chamorro word for brother and is often used not only for a sibling but also for close friends, similar to the English term 'bro'. Along the same lines is the use of the term *primu*, occasionally abbreviated to *prim*, which translates to 'cousin' but is also used in a wider sense to address a male friend. The Chamorro terms for grandparents are *nanan biha* 'grandmother' and *tatan bihu* 'grandfather'.

The terms *guella* and *guello* also mean grandmother and grandfather and are additionally used to refer to ancestors. A Chamorro custom that is still practiced on the island is to ask the ancestors for permission before entering the jungle:

Guella yan Guello, dispensa ham låo Kåo siña ham manmaloffan yan manmanbisita gi tano miyu sa' yanggen un bisita i tano'må mi faloffan-ha' sin un famaisin.
Grandmother and grandfather, excuse us. May we walk through and visit your land and when you come to our land we will welcome you to do the same. (Bevacqua 2018)

Grandparents enjoy a high status in the Chamorro culture on Guam. Though many of the indigenous traditions were lost due to colonial influence, the respect for the elders and their high position when it comes to decision making remains today. Grandparents are viewed as the carriers of knowledge and are especially valued for their fluency in Chamorro. In regard to the potential loss of the indigenous language, great responsibility is ascribed to the elders, who have the power to pass down the language to the youngest generations.

2.2 Saipan

Saipan is the political capital of the Commonwealth of the Northern Mariana Islands (CNMI), which comprises 14 islands in the Northern Pacific Ocean. The Commonwealth came into existence in 1978 and has had a long colonial history: Saipan was first colonised by Spain in the 17th century, by Germany at the beginning of the 20th century, by Japan between 1914 and 1944, and finally, by the US. The Chamorros and Carolinians are the indigenous people of Saipan. Islanders from the Central Carolines (south of the CNMI) settled on Saipan during the Spanish Administration (1668–1899). The Spanish permitted the Carolinians to stay because of a devastating typhoon on their home island in 1815. The newly arrived Carolinians started to live alongside local Chamorros. The Chamorros and Carolinians have shared the same physical environment for approximately 150 years and have experienced the same historical events and impacts on the islands but the two ethnic groups remained culturally distinct during the initial contact with the US: the Chamorros allowed a greater modern and Western influence, whereas the Carolinians were still much closer to their traditional culture

(Joseph and Murray 1951: 80). A major consequence seems to have been the loss of the Chamorro language and the emergence of English as a first language for the Chamorros (McPhetres 1992: 263), whereas the Carolinians have continued to practice the Carolinian lifestyle and retained both their culture and language (Spoehr 1954: 26) to a considerable extent even now. The groups remain individual in many respects but due to such a lengthy coexistence, friendships and marriages, they unite as the indigenous island community of Saipan and are thus treated as one local community in this paper.

2.2.1 Family and kinship terms in Saipan Chamorro and Saipan Carolinian

A Saipan Chamorro kinship system is particularly important in crisis rites rather than in day-to-day living and on the whole is of a fluctuating type (Spoehr 1954).[2] The culture of the Saipan Chamorros shows a greater global influence than the culture of Saipan Carolinians due to Saipan's long period of colonial contact with other cultures. Upon marriage, Chamorros acquire a new status and when a child is born, they have established their own family as is known in the Western culture. Nevertheless, the family is still strongly bonded to the father, mother and siblings via consanguinity and puts more emphasis on the nuclear family than Western societies do.

Carolinian kinship is characterised by the extension of kinship that is particularly important in 'day-to-day life and in routine co-operative activities' (Spoehr 1954: 332). Saipan Carolinians distinguish between two types of matrilineal kin group, that of the clan and that of the lineage. Considering the maternal clan, it is a group of individuals, including both sexes, 'who count descent through the maternal line and believe they are all related, though an actual genealogical relationship usually cannot be demonstrated' (Spoehr 1954: 333). On the other hand, maternal lineage is a group of individuals who 'trace descent in the maternal line from a known ancestor by virtue of a known genealogical relationship' (Spoehr 1954: 335).

The kinship terminology of the Saipan Chamorros and that of the Saipan Carolinians are distinct, even though most of the Carolinians also know most of the kinship terms in Chamorro culture. In contrast to the relationships outside the nuclear family in Chamorro culture, Saipan Carolinians' immediate family 'is not so sharply marked off within the network of extended kinship relations' (Spoehr 1954: 350) and is manifested by a greater extent of sharing labour and food, and more adoption of children by relatives without asking for anything in return, which is more common in the Chamorro culture. Moreover, visits among kinfolk are much more common among Carolinians, whereby individuals may stay at a relative's house for a few days (Spoehr 1954: 350). Sibling behaviour, as in the brother–sister respect behaviour, is extended towards cousins as well. Even though kinship and other major facets of the Saipan Carolinians are still highly important in their social organisation, they have 'gradually become more like the Chamorros' over time (Spoehr 1954: 370) and together represent Saipan's indigenous community in this study.

2.3 Kosrae

The smallest of the three island communities, with fewer than 7,000 inhabitants, Kosrae underwent a similar colonial history, seeing Spanish and German (and much later, Japanese) administrations leaving their respective marks to varying degrees. The Protestant missionaries arriving in the 1800s were much more impactful guests. The diseases brought by whalers had decimated the population, but with the medical provisions of the missionaries population numbers were somewhat restored and religion has been a Kosraean cultural marker since. English survived as the primary language of education via the missionaries until the Japanese administration. Following World War II, American military personnel and experts were sent to the islands in an effort to reconstruct the communities. English was taught in schools and training centres and the US visitors were warmly received on Kosrae. By 1986, a political-economic agreement was enacted: the Compact of Free Association. This secures a level of financial sustenance from the US, alongside an exchange agreement concerning territorial access for security. In return, residents of the FSM are free to live and work in the US, gain access to US medical care and join the US military.[3] English is the official language of the FSM and is primarily used for government and commerce and as a lingua franca, though not usually used in day-to-day Kosraean domestic activities.

2.3.1 Family and kinship terms in Kosrae

Since the arrival of the missionaries, Christian practices have been incorporated into Kosraean culture and many older Pacific traditions and knowledge are reported to have disappeared.[4] Christian practices were introduced, clanships and a hierarchal system with kings and chiefs operated and a well-developed respect vocabulary was in use (Cordy 1993), potentially similar to that of present-day neighbouring Pohnpei (see Keating 2001). Though formally these institutions ceased to exist, respect and honour and an awareness of unofficial clanship are still apparent, as is expected in small, secluded communities.

Family members are expected to participate in daily communal tasks, and all members of the extended family are expected to attend and help provide food for important ritual ceremonies such as weddings and funerals. The practice of adoption within the immediate family is also embedded in Kosraean society with the older siblings or parents of the mother frequently raising children in their home. Adoption is often due to practical decisions, such as limited space in a house, or as an act of reciprocity, maybe to a sister who has no children of her own. Hezel (1992) adds that the purpose of adoption is 'to strengthen ties between kin, and to keep precious commodities such as land'. A current additional motivator for adoption appears to be the large-scale Micronesian emigration to Hawai'i and other economic centres. Younger Kosraeans often leave to earn money while the grandparents look after the children in the meantime, temporarily or more permanently. This allows the parents to both work and send stipends home to the family, and the children can grow up in the family home surrounded by Kosraean culture.

The small community is tight-knit and adults are well-versed on the histories of local families. Debates have ensued over an intrusion of the individualist mentality of the US and efforts are made, for example in schools, to preserve the traditional collectivist ideology which forms part of the local identity. According to Hezel (2001: 8–32), the modern 'cash economy' is the root of the cause of this change in interpersonal dynamics. He claims that the structure has been altered due to a shift in power dynamics based on resource access and pressure to provide for the entire family. This is causing a revision of boundaries of the word *family*.

Respect has historically been a powerful indicator of Kosraean identity. Indeed, early visitors noted that the 'homage shown to the ruler and high chiefs on Kosrae was the most extreme that they had seen' (Cordy 1993: 96). Respect encompasses familial dependence and intimacy and connects local understandings of honour, shame and religious devotion.

3. METHODOLOGY

As Schneider's (2018: 97) initial study was designed as 'exploratory and exemplary', we set out to examine the applicability of this method to other cultures and other types of data collections and separately as a way to examine our own data through a new lens.

We used the data obtained on our respective fieldwork trips between 2015 and 2017 when the authors lived in the communities for a minimum of three months. The data consist of a combination of ethnographic data and semi-structured informal interviews that were conducted with a stratified sample of the local community (based on gender, age, ethnicity, education, mobility and occupation). The individual and group interviews varied between 25 minutes and more than two hours in length. These separate corpora compiled during and after our trips were transcribed, prepared and coded as part of a larger project. The corpora collectively comprises 939,402 words. The smallest corpus obtained from 96 speakers in Kosrae contains 188,093 words of Kosraean English. For the Saipanese corpus, 384,905 words of Saipanese English from 95 speakers were collected and the Guam corpus contains 366,404 of 89 informants' words. We used each corpus in its entirety but excluded any obviously non-semantically related words, for example, *engaged* used for *busy* rather than *having formally agreed to marry*.

Based on a triangulation of methods, a thorough analysis of the literature and data together with ethnographic insights into the informants and cultures led the authors to their informed understandings of the local forms and conceptualisations of kinship. In the steps of Schneider (2018; this volume), we isolated a range of lexical items which we deemed relevant to the themes of kinship and family.

Frequencies were then compared, and differences interpreted in terms of previous literature available on systems of kinship in the communities and based on our informants' narratives and our own ethnographic records. We decided to focus our analysis on the tokens listed in Table 7.1.

This list is a condensed version of the various words we actually analysed. We considered all morphological variations of the lemma (for example, *marrying*, *engagement*) and noted them separately in the initial stages to gain an accurate impression of the data. We also counted plurals and possessives and grouped them with the word (for example, *sisters*, *sister's*). We excluded ambiguities which were few and only related to recording clarity, hesitations or repetitions, and alternative meanings (for example, *mother tongue*). Next, we counted the raw numbers of each

Table 7.1 Selected kinship terms

mother	*father*
colloquial variant of *mother* – for example, *mom*[a]	colloquial variant of *father* – for example, *dad*
daughter	*son*
parent	*child*
baby	*kid*
aunt/aunty	*uncle*
niece	*nephew*
grandmother	*grandfather*
grandparent	*grandchild*
granddaughter	*grandson*
sister	*brother*
sibling	*cousin*
wife	*husband*
girlfriend	*boyfriend*
engaged	*marry/married*
adopt/s/ed/ adoption	*family*
local word for older woman – for example, *nena*, Kosrae *ma'am*[b]	local word for the elderly – for example, *manamko*, Chamorro, Guam and Saipan

[a] We took only the colloquial variant of parents as a means of testing a pattern of formality as to do so with each individual lexical variable would have skewed results, due to lack of frequencies and semantic ambiguity.
[b] Unlisted antonyms did not appear in the data, for example *sir*.

lexical occurrence in each of the three datasets using a combination of the annotation tool ELAN (2017) and the concordance program AntConc (Anthony 2017) and then coded each occurrence with the associated lemma. The numbers of each token (for each of the three islands) were relativised by dividing the number of the kinship lexifiers into the total of the combined informants' words in each corresponding corpus and then calculated to a percentage of one decimal place. We created a series of descriptive bar plots and compared data results and evaluated the varying frequencies. At this point, we merged the correlating variants of each lexical variable (except for the more conversant words for parents – that is, *mom*, *mam*, *ma*, and so on – kept apart for further analysis). Upon calculating the totals of all tokens and plotting the final numbers, we could easily compare themes across varieties in order to discern the narrative.

Finally, we focused on six kinship term groupings that showed interesting distributions and a sound observable pattern. We used a triangulation of methods, quantitatively comparing frequencies and qualitatively positioning these in terms of the previous relevant studies and conversations on-island.

4. RESULTS AND ANALYSIS

The quantitative analysis provided us with promising results which point to clear cultural differences suggested through the lexical usage frequencies.

4.1 The Extended Family

As discussed previously, Saipanese speakers use kinship terms to include non-family (blood relative) members. The results show that Saipanese are more likely to use the terms *brother*, *sister* or *sibling* than Kosraeans, who in turn used the terms more than the Guam speakers. Table 7.2 shows the breakdown of the percentages of these categories in terms of total usage of the indexifier. We infer that the use of sibling terminology (and potentially reference to cousins too) in fact establishes its own indexical field (Eckert 2008) which conveys the unique local boundaries to which such referential meanings pertain; that is, these words have a 'local social meaning' and constitute a 'field of potential meanings' (Eckert 2008: 453).

Table 7.2 Percentage of tokens for cousin- and sibling-related terms

% of all instances	*Kosrae %*	*Saipan %*	*Guam %*
Total *cousin(s)*	34.7	**42.2**	23.1
Total *brother(s)*	32.8	**37.5**	29.7
Total *sister(s)*	32.7	**37.8**	29.5
Total *sibling(s)*	0.0	**55.9**	44.1

It is not considered unusual for friends, neighbours and even strangers to be addressed using kin terms all over the world, as in Indian, East Asian and African languages (Evans-Pritchard 1948; Kachru and Smith 2008). In some cases, African American Vernacular English speakers may refer to someone with the term *brother* or *sister* (Mufwene 1998a,

1998b). Reference terms, *bro/brah*, are associated with some Northern American social groups, for example gym talk (Krupnick 2016). In Spanish, the term for an uncle or aunt, *tío* or *tía*, can be used referring to a friend, acquaintance or stranger, especially with younger speakers (Jørgensen 2008). In Saipan Carolinian culture, *cousin* and *brother/sister* may be used similarly as a broader term of reference.

Lino Olopai, a respected elder of the Saipan Carolinians, explains that on an abstract level all Carolinians are related to each other to some extent because of their traditional clan system:

> If your mother, her sister, brother are a member of the Rebwel clan (Ailangil rebwel), all their children are clans of the Rebwel and they will address each other as *bwii* 'my brother or sister' or as *bwibwi* 'we are brothers or sisters' from the Bwel clan. We do not have a cousin in our language. Let alon[e] ... first cousin, second cousin, third cousin, and so on. (L. Olopai, personal communication, March 2019)

Many Saipan Carolinians used the term *brother/sister* in interviews referring to a cousin. They explained proudly that they call their cousins 'brothers' or 'sisters'. As Saipan Carolinians do not have an equivalent word for *cousin*, the English lexeme becomes more flexible.

4.2 The Role of Grandparents

The grandparent- and grandchild-related terms are strikingly more likely to arise in conversations on Guam than on Kosrae or Saipan respectively (see Table 7.3).

Table 7.3 Percentage of tokens for grandparent- and grandchild-related terms

% of all instances	Kosrae %	Saipan %	Guam %
Total *grandchild(ren)/kid(s)*	26.3	12.9	60.8
Total *grandson(s)*	0.0	13.7	86.3
Total *granddaughter(s)*	0.0	45.8	54.2
Total *grandmother/ma(s)*	10.1	39.2	50.7
Total *grandfather/pa(s)*	32.6	18.0	49.3

As mentioned, in Guam, elders hold an especially high position of admiration and respect within the Chamorro community and generally live in the house with the family. While this is quite normal in many other communities, the extent of the Westernisation of Guam may point to these features as becoming somewhat idiosyncratic:

> her grandmother taught her Chamorro so she wanted us to to grow up in the same way you know with with the language I mean mostly partly we she she's more passionate about it now about bringing the language back but when we were born it wasn't about that it was about just she wanted to give us something. (Speaker Gu31f22, Guam Chamorro female, aged 22)

This informant is reflecting on the passing down of the indigenous culture and language, which nowadays is considered a precious gift that younger generations generally have access to only through contact with their grandmothers.

4.3 Respect

The islands in the FSM are built on respect, and Kosrae in particular, though this is more of a deferential respect. Here, the conservative form as opposed to casual form of address for *mother* shows us the different ideologies on the islands.[5] While Saipanese informants rarely used the lexifier *mother*, in Kosrae preference is given to *mother* over the less formal variants, for example, *mom*. This occurrence is in sharp contrast to the linguistic behaviour of this feature in Saipanese English as we can see in Table 7.4. Guam uses both terms quite equally.

Table 7.4 Percentage of tokens for *mom* and *mother*

% all tokens	Kosrae %	Saipan %	Guam %
Total *mom(s)*	17.9	40.9	41.2
Total *mother(s)*	45.0	13.3	41.7

This respect behaviour on Kosrae has been a defining feature of the Kosraean community since early reports in the 1850s when 'merely passing a chief, they content themselves by stooping low and passing at a respectful distance' (Appleton 1934, in Cordy 1993: 106). This practice is still especially observed by older conservative women to men. These results correspond to what we would expect with regard to the reverential respect pattern associated with elder relatives in Kosrae, which is reportedly less salient in Saipanese culture but is similar to the filial piety described by Ho (1996) in China. Spoehr (1954: 344) states that, in Saipan, '[p]ersonal names rather than kinship terms are used extensively in a referential context, particularly for persons outside the elementary family', which lends itself to the idea that a more relaxed, informal approach is taken to family referentials. He later affirms this notion by stating that '[w]ithin the nuclear family, husband–wife relationships are informal and easy. Spouses call each other by their personal names and do not use respect forms of address' (Spoehr 1954: 346).

4.4 Romantic Partnerships

Lexemes related to marriage, husband and wife are most likely to appear in Kosraean conversation, while the mention of boyfriends is consistently avoided. Romantic relationships in Kosraean culture are approached with conservatism and ceremony. Schneider (2018: 44; this volume) explores these cultural key terms in the scope of socio-sexuality, citing displays of courtship, attitudes to monogamy and promiscuity, and romantic intimacy as salient features specific to a community.

Table 7.5 Percentage of tokens for courtship-related terms

% of all tokens	Kosrae %	Saipan %	Guam %
Total *boyfriend(s)*	1.5	30.0	68.5
Total *girlfriend(s)*	19.4	60.6	19.9

The disparity between the tokens in Kosraean English in Table 7.5 is striking. The token *boyfriend(s)* appeared only once in the data, while *girlfriend(s)* was much more frequent. Kosraeans are proud of their conservative, Christian values and men are the proactive initiators. Family is involved in courtship and stay present during 'dates', though these reportedly still occur without parents' knowledge and can be sexual in nature (though this is extremely taboo). Table 7.5 also shows a noticeable difference in the use of *boyfriend* and *girlfriend* for Guam versus Saipan and would be an interesting investigation for further study.

The courtship findings are mirrored in the results for matrimonial terms in Table 7.6; Guam and Saipanese speakers statistically mention *husband*, *wife* or being *married* less often than Kosraean speakers. This could of course be related to demographics, but it would still be evidence of societal contrasts.

Table 7.6 Percentage of tokens for marriage-related terms

% of all tokens	Kosrae %	Saipan %	Guam %
Total *married*	41.2	19.2	39.6
Total *husband(s)*	55.0	16.0	29.0
Total *wife/wives*	57.9	20.8	21.3

4.5 Adoption Practices

Adoption is frequently mentioned in conversation with Kosraeans, more so than in the other islands' corpora, and this was a predicted result. Although adoption is a cultural practice throughout many Pacific islands, including Guam and Saipan, Kosrae remains the least urbanised of the three and, as discussed, these traditional practices are more intact. The following excerpt details a local's interpretation of the practice on Kosrae:

> [. . .] if my daughters have a baby before they're married and because [. . .] giving birth to a baby before especially girls before you're getting married is it's like a [. . .] offensive thing to your parents right and so do these parents would adopt the [. . .] child [. . .] from their daughter to raise them so it would be a l- a little bit legitimate on that on their side but it's like they're [. . .] because they would know the [. . .] new husband of the girl [. . .] they wouldn't know if he will treat the baby well [. . .] so they would keep the baby to themself [. . .] but [. . .] I've seen a lot of parents that adopt their daughter's or they're kid's err babies their first-born babies because I think that's what they used to do [. . .]. (Speaker KO1M40, Kosraean male, aged 40)

As we can see in Table 7.7, Kosrae presents a much larger approximated share of the tokens related to adoption; however, Saipan is far below Guam in occurrence frequencies. Spoehr (1954: 356) notes that 'adoption is recognized by the Carolinians as one of their own long-established institutions, and a point of contrast with the Chamorros, among whom it is much less common'.

Table 7.7 Percentage of tokens for adoption-related terms

% of all tokens	Kosrae %	Saipan %	Guam %
Total *adopt(s)(ed)(ion)(s)*	55.9	9.9	34.3

In the interim, adoption rates may have decreased on Saipan as the numbers suggest, though a more thorough analysis is required. Adoption continues on Kosrae in large numbers due to the aforementioned high level of emigration coupled with the cultural demand on sharing and reciprocity in all areas. As Hezel (2001: 2) says, 'what one family member owns should be shared with other family members' and, in certain cases, this may also apply to offspring.

4.6 The Significance of Family

Finally, when we measured the relativised number of tokens for family in the three corpora, we obtained the results shown in Table 7.8.

Table 7.8 Percentage of tokens for *family*

% all tokens	Kosrae %	Saipan %	Guam %
Total *family/families*	18.2	12.5	16.1

These figures curiously do not coincide with our expectations when setting out on this investigation. The results should have demonstrated parallel decline in the production of cultural key terms within a community according to the significance of the cultural practice in daily life. As expected, the self-reportedly less acculturated Kosraean speaker will mention family considerably more than a Saipanese speaker will. This appears to coincide with Schneider's findings and also mirrors the explicit desire for Kosraeans to remain more collectively than individually oriented. However, logic suggests that speakers from Guam would then produce fewer of these tokens based on their move towards Americanisation or a more capitalist urban interpretation of Pacific identity. Yet, just as with the other data results, Guam speakers act unpredictably and are closer to the Kosraeans than their Mariana Island neighbours are. It is worth noting that *family* in Australian Aboriginal English 'refers to a much wider set of categories than it does in British English' (Kirkpatrick 2010: 443) and we must also consider that the word has further significance beyond the scope of our interpretation.

5. DISCUSSION

With regard to tracing culture in corpora, the methodology proved successful. We found results which contradicted our initial hypothesis but this gave us the opportunity to think about our data from a new angle. Rather than the results showing the islands dotted along a clear spectrum, the study actually brought to light the individual local attributes which make the processes of social change interesting to each case.

The spread of English does not necessarily reflect a spread of English-speaking cultures and vice versa. While recordings of young Guam speakers may be nearly indistinguishable from certain mainland US varieties, the Chamorro history remains alive on Guam and while it may not permeate day-to-day activities, it rests below the surface of society, traversing lifestyle. Pacific islanders in fact often speak of the entire Pacific community being a family of sorts. This is foreseeable for such an expansive part of the world which is made up of relatively smaller and more isolated populations than the rest of the global community.

Considering that we ultimately found ourselves identifying kinship terms with respect levels, formality and informality, and perceived social distance/intimacy, another option to analyse our data may have been to look into indicator terms as Schneider (2018) did, for example, with high status differences, and this would be a suitable adjunct study.

5.1 Methodological Application

As the corpora are yielded from sociolinguistic interviews, and each community was interviewed solely by the researcher assigned to that society, inconsistencies in data collection are assumed, not to mention the large number of norm violations which are inevitable in an unnatural, reasonably unspontaneous interview (cf. Briggs 1986). Corpus linguistics is usually regarded as 'the study of language based on examples of real life language use' (McEnery and Wilson 1996: 1) and with large anonymous corpora such as the International Corpus of English (ICE), the data are unselective and random. However, due to the nature of these fieldwork corpora, the authenticity or consistency of the content becomes less certain. For example, if at some point *siblings* were referred to during an interview, then perhaps the word *sibling* would have later arisen in the data due to either response or reduplication (more than *brother* or *sister*). At this level, it is difficult to account for such priming.

Another issue we faced is that we consider the communities' Englishes to lie at different stages of Schneider's dynamic model (2007). While for those on Guam, English is the first language, in Kosrae it behaves as a lingua franca for most. In the case of Saipan, this is generally dependant on the ethnicity of the informant and sometimes their language choices may depend on certain practices such as their occupation (Hess forthcoming). These issues may also result in different sizes of lexicons being available to the informant, and relatively rarer words such as *sibling* may be heard somewhat less often in Kosrae than in Guam.

A third issue with regard to our application of the methodology is that, unfortunately, the cultural schema and categorisation (Sharifian 2015) of several terms and relationships are ultimately potentially indiscernible. Take, for example, the term *aunt*: there is no indication as to whether this is on the side of the mother or father or is a symbolic aunt figure to the individual, the family or even the community. We may not understand all the social rights and obligations attached to the concept. We can only take the word on its most basic lexical value without adequate ethnography. Equally, the kin terms are ambiguous when we are discussing three individual cultures. As we have seen, the semantic properties of *cousin* in Guam do not necessarily correlate with those of Saipan. While this adds to the nuance of such a study, it also hinders true comparative studies of kinship relations, instead necessitating emphasis on the qualitative side of the analysis.

6. CONCLUSION

Following the lead of Sharifian (2015) in his enquiry into anthropological matters from a cognitive linguistic perspective, we see in observations such as those of Franz Boas (1911, 1940, 1945) that language reflects manifestations of mental life and cultural phenomena. Without leaning too much on the Whorfian concepts of language effect on cognition and culture, it is fair to say discursive objects contribute to 'practices which systematically form the objects of which they speak' (Foucault 1972: 49). As claimed by Schneider (2018: 118), cultural dimensions in cross-cultural anthropology 'do show manifestations and substantial traces in corpora and language forms, defined as sets of indicator terms', yet as with his foundational paper (this volume), we have also found inconsistencies and outliers. Schneider called for further study to explore the potential for this new way of analysis. We have found here that in the case of dealing with interview data (that is, smaller/fewer corpora, but more familiarity with data), conclusions can be drawn but with caution. In sum, we can verify that we found that 'differences between cultures find systematic manifestations in language forms' (Schneider 2018: 97) and specifically in sociolinguistic interviews. Using a corpus linguistic methodology, we were able to confront predesigned lines of inquiry using an innovative approach and compare and connect findings under a compelling schematic approach.

NOTES

1. For an explanation of the definition of *culture* in this article, refer to Schneider (2018: 98).
2. The following sections rely heavily on Spoehr (1954).
3. The terms of the compact were under renegotiation at the time of writing.
4. According to interviews with many locals.
5. Though Kosraean speakers often lean towards less idiomatic language, the preference for such formalities is certainly not the norm. Commonly accepted 'general' English colloquialisms are the norm.

REFERENCES

Anthony, L. (2017). AntConc (Version 3.5.0) [Computer software]. Waseda University. <http://www.antlab.sci.waseda.ac.jp/> (last accessed 7 January 2021).

Barusch, A. and Spaulding, M. (1989). The impact of Americanization on intergenerational relations: An exploratory study on the US territory of Guam. *Journal of Sociology & Social Welfare, 16*(3), 61–79.

Bevacqua, M. L. (2018). *Taotaomo'na*. Guampedia. <https://www.guampedia.com/taotaomona-taotaomona/> (last accessed 7 January 2021).

Boas, F. (1911). *The mind of primitive man*. Macmillan.

Boas, F. (1940). *Race, language and culture*. Macmillan.

Boas, F. (1945). *Race and democratic society*. Augustin.

Briggs, C. L. (1986). *Learning how to ask: A sociolinguistic appraisal of the role of the interview in social science research*. Cambridge University Press.

Cordy, R. (1993). *The Lelu stone ruins*. University of Hawai'i Press.
Cunningham, L. (1992). *Ancient Chamorro society*. Bess Press.
Eckert, P. (2008). Variation in the indexical field. *Journal of Sociolinguistics*, *12*(4), 453–76.
ELAN. (2017). (Version 5.1) [Computer software]. Max Planck Institute for Psycholinguistics, The Language Archive. <https://archive.mpi.nl/tla/elan> (last accessed 7 January 2021).
Evans-Pritchard, E. E. (1948). *The divine kingship of the Shilluk of the Nilotic Sudan*. Cambridge University Press.
Foucault, M. (1972). *The archaeology of knowledge and the discourse on language*. Pantheon Books.
Hess, D. B. (forthcoming). *Saipanese English: Local and global sociolinguistic trends*. John Benjamins.
Hezel, F. X. (1992). Changes in the Pohnpeian family: 1950–1990. *Micronesian Seminar*. <http://micronesianseminar.org/media/pubs/articles/famchange/frames/chngpnifr.htm> (last accessed 8 February 2021).
Hezel, F. X. (2001). *The new shape of old island cultures: A half century of social change in Micronesia*. University of Hawai'i Press.
Hezel, F. X. (2008). The cultural revolution of the '60s. *Micronesian Counselor*, *73*, 22 September. <https://micronesianseminar.org/micronesian-counselo/cultural-revolution-of-the-60s/> (last accessed 7 January 2021).
Ho, D. Y. F. (1996). Filial piety and its psychological consequences. In M. H. Bond (Ed.), *The handbook of Chinese psychology* (pp. 155–65). Oxford University Press.
Hua, Z. (2013). *Exploring intercultural communication: Language in action*. Routledge.
Jørgensen, A. M. (2008). Tío y tía como marcadores en el lenguaje juvenil de Madrid. In I. Olza Moreno and R. Casado Velarde (Eds.), *Actas del XXXVII Simposio Internacional de la Sociedad Española de Lingüística (SEL)* (pp. 387–96). Servicio de Publicaciones de la Universidad de Navarra.
Joseph, A. and Murray, V. F. (1951). *Chamorros and Carolinians of Saipan: Personality studies*. Harvard University Press.
Kachru, Y. and Smith, L. E. (2008). *Cultures, contexts and World Englishes*. Routledge.
Keating, E. (2001). Language, identity, and the production of authority in new discursive contests in Pohnpei, Micronesia. *Journal de la Société des Océanistes*, *112*, 73–80.

Kirkpatrick, A. (2010). World English and local cultures. In F. Sharifian (Ed.), *The Routledge handbook of language and culture* (pp. 460–70). Routledge.

Kronenfeld, D. (2009). *Fanti kinship and the analysis of kinship terminologies*. University of Illinois Press.

Krupnick, J. C. (2016). *I go, you go: Searching for strength and self in the American gym* [Doctoral dissertation, Harvard University]. FAS Theses and Dissertations. (4795). <http://nrs.harvard.edu/urn-3:HUL.InstRepos:33493523> (last accessed 7 January 2021).

Kuper, K. (2014). *Na'la'la' i hila'-ta, na'matatnga i taotao-ta: Chamorro language as liberation from colonization* [Master's thesis, University of Hawai'i at Manoa]. ScholarSpace. <https://scholarspace.manoa.hawaii.edu/handle/10125/100554> (last accessed 7 January 2021).

Lawson, S. (1996). Cultural relativism and democracy: Political myths about 'Asia' and 'the West'. In R. Robison (Ed.), *Pathways to Asia: The politics of engagement* (pp. 108–28). Allen & Unwin.

Lévi-Strauss, C. (1969). *The elementary structures of kinship*. Beacon Press. (Original work published 1949).

McEnery, T. and Wilson, A. (1996). *Corpus linguistics*. Edinburgh University Press.

McPhetres, S. F. (1992). Elements of social change in the contemporary Northern Mariana Islands. In A. B. Robillard (Ed.), *Social change in the Pacific Islands* (pp. 241–63). Kegan Paul International.

Malinowski, B. (1922). *Argonauts of the Western Pacific: An account of native enterprise and adventure in the archipelagoes of Melanesian New Guinea*. Dutton.

Malinowski, B. (1927). *The father in primitive psychology*. W. W. Norton.

Mufwene, S. S. (1998a). The structure of the noun phrase in African-American vernacular English. In G. Bailey, J. Baugh, S. S. Mufwene and J. R. Rickford (Eds.), *African-American English* (pp. 69–81). Routledge.

Mufwene, S. S. (1998b). What research on creole genesis can contribute to historical linguistics. In M. Schmid, J. Austin and D. Stein (Eds.), *Historical linguistics 1997* (pp. 315–38). John Benjamins.

Murdock, G. P. (1949). *Social structure*. Macmillan.

Perez, J. (2018). Effective yesterday 7.25 USD per hour: CNMI minimum wage reaches federal level. *Saipan Tribune*, 1 October. <https://www.saipantribune.com/index.php/7-25-per-hour/> (last accessed 7 January 2021).

Radcliffe-Brown, A. R. (1922). *The Andaman islanders: A study in social anthropology*. The University Press.
Rogers, R. (1995). *Destiny's landfall: A history of Guam*. University of Hawai'i Press.
Santos-Bamba, S. (2013). The languages of three generations of Chamorro women. *Pacific Asia Inquiry*, 4(1), 84–93.
Schneider, E. W. (2007). *Postcolonial English: Varieties around the world*. Cambridge University Press.
Schneider, E. W. (2018). The interface between cultures and corpora: Tracing reflections and manifestations. *ICAME Journal*, 42(1), 97–132. <https://doi.org/10.1515/icame-2018-0006> (last accessed 4 January 2021).
Sharifian, F. (2015). Language and culture: Overview. In F. Sharifian (Ed.), *The Routledge handbook of language and culture* (pp. 3–17). Routledge.
Spoehr, A. (1954). *Saipan: The ethnology of a war-devastated island*. Chicago Natural History Museum.
Topping, D. (2003). Saviors of languages: Who will be the real Messiah? *Oceanic Linguistics*, 42(2), 522–7.
US Citizenship and Immigration Services. (2018). New law extends CNMI CW-1 program, mandates new fraud fee, and will require e-verify participation. <https://www.uscis.gov/news/alerts/new-law-extends-cnmi-cw-1-program-mandates-new-fraud-fee-and-will-require-e-verify-participation> (last accessed 7 January 2021).
Wolf, H. and Polzenhagen, F. (2009). *World Englishes: A cognitive sociolinguistic approach*. Mouton de Gruyter.

CHAPTER 8

Somewhere between Australia and Malaysia and 'I' and 'we': Verbalising Culture on the Cocos (Keeling) Islands

Hannah Hedegard

1. INTRODUCTION

All post-colonial nations, including those discussed in this volume, are by definition based on a blend of two or more cultures. In the process of colonisation, the settlers absorb, adapt or deny aspects of the indigenous peoples' practices, philosophies and politics. The fusional nature of the resulting society can be readily observed in its language, as Schneider demonstrated in his culture-in-corpora research (2018), where cultural values were manifest on multiple linguistic levels in post-colonial English varieties such as those spoken in Hong Kong, Singapore and India. In the second nexus of the study, Schneider provided evidence for the existence of a perceptible linguistic spectrum amongst his selected Englishes in relation to Hofstede's ([1980] 2001) notion of 'dimensions of culture'. In an initial disclaimer, however, he recognises that the idea of drawing conclusions from correlations between cultural characteristics and distributional analysis of linguistic corpora is problematic, due principally to the 'fuzzy' nature of the concept of culture, but also to the low representativeness of the speech and text samples included and the implied assumption that nations are homogenous entities with little internal cultural diversity (Schneider 2018). The validity of the correlations detected between culture and language in the English varieties Schneider examines is somewhat tainted then. The community in focus in this chapter presents an interesting opportunity to apply Schneider's framework without the latter two caveats, as it is both highly culturally homogenous and very small; the corpus of speech data collected from the population that forms the basis for the analysis has a representation rate of over 20 per cent.

The Cocos (Keeling) Islands (CKI) are a small, remote atoll in the south Indian Ocean, home to approximately 500 islanders, the majority of whom identify as belonging to the distinct ethnic group of Cocos Malay. As a result of its recent colonial narrative involving a drastic political shift into the dominion of Australia, the island community's cultural identity is currently in a state of flux, as they grapple with balancing their Malay cultural heritage with their new Australian status. Whilst the same recency of established nationhood can be said for Singapore and Hong Kong, both their narratives prior to political and cultural independence involved prolonged ethnic contact and mixing, a degree of political independence and inter-group variety in terms of cultural identity. In the case of the CKI, the islanders were entirely socially and physically isolated until being handed over to Australia in 1984, as one collective group. Their introduction to Western culture has been abrupt, all-encompassing and not necessarily on their own terms.

In earlier research on this community, I described how the Cocos Malay are in the early stages of developing a distinct new and localised variety of English (Hedegard 2020). Variationist sociolinguistic analysis of two phonetic variables, high rising terminals (HRTs) and the NEAR vowel, alongside a general linguistic description, revealed the stratification of English use and character across the generations, reflecting the sudden bilingualism of Cocos Malay and Australian English on the islands. Whilst those socialised before Australian integration are either monolingual Cocos Malay or second-language (L2) speakers of Australian English (AusE), all Cocos Malay under the age of 50 (that is, those brought up post-integration) are bilingual. Interestingly, the complex societal and cultural dynamic with Australia was discernible in quantitative analysis of HRTs in particular, where empirical evidence suggested intonation was employed by the community in its pragmatic function as a politeness marker (Britain 1992) to mitigate face-threatening speech acts in Cocos Malay culture. Further, through third-wave qualitative analysis of HRTs, I showed how some Cocos Malay also invoked ironic caricatures of Australian-ness in their speech, presenting themselves as proficient in sociolinguistic practices in AusE but culturally distinct from the mainland. It is clear that the Cocos Malay express their sociopsychological and cultural identity through their variety of English, at least on a phonetic/pragmatic level. This prompted the question of whether their cultural values, both Cocos Malay and Australian to unknown degrees, are also manifesting in their English at a lexical level, in a similar form to other World Englishes. In this chapter, therefore, I explore the insight to be gained from a culture-in-corpora analysis of the English spoken by the CKI community, in light of their relationships with Malaysia and Australia, small size, homogeneity and fraught recent political and social history.

2. CULTURAL DIMENSIONS AND THE COCOS (KEELING) ISLANDS

The central idea behind Schneider's (2018) cultural dimensions framework is that culture is structurally apparent in language, the empirical testing of which he identified as a research gap in the field of cultural linguistics. Schneider tested for the existence of linguistic effects of culture across three nexuses: (1) use of words for particular cultural items, (2) use of indicator terms as expressions of psycho-sociological and cultural traits, and (3) use of grammatical constructions as reflections of cultural tendencies and attitudes. He showed that visibility of cultural characteristics is inversely correlated with the abstractness of the analysis: frequencies of words for cultural items correlated predictably with the countries where they originate, drawing correlations from indicator terms was also viable but trickier, and grammatical constructions, the most fine-grained structural analysis, produced the most ambiguous results. Since this chapter focuses on the second nexus, discussion of the first and third will be precluded for reasons of space.

The second nexus of the cultural dimensions paradigm relates to the degree to which nations are, amongst others, collectivism or individualism oriented, long-term or short-term oriented, and conservative or open in terms of (verbal) expression of emotion (Hofstede [1980] 2001). Hofstede and subsequent scholars established that several of the dimensions together neatly distinguish the West (mostly based on data from northern Europe, the US and the Antipodean countries of Australia and NZ) from the East (principally South and East Asian countries). Eastern countries tend to place a greater cultural value on familial ties, the group rather than the individual, as well as hierarchical social structures, for example. Investigating post-colonial varieties of English in terms of cultural dimensions presents an interesting premise, therefore, because their speakers have been socialised in cultures that often share aspects of both Western and Eastern countries, such as Indian and Hong Kong English.

Just as Hofstede was criticised for lack of nuance, Schneider's approach suggests that within a nation state, its people are culturally homogenous. This is presumably partly a result of the preliminary and macro-level nature of the study in that it was meant to only paint the larger picture of international cultural differences discernible in various World Englishes, but also a result of methodological constraints: identifying demographic information of speakers and writers in large corpora is often not possible, as in the case of the International Corpus of English (ICE). I see the next stage in testing the applicability and fruitfulness of the framework as examining variation within varieties of World Englishes. This could be undertaken on language data from new contact varieties of English whose speakers belong to different ethnic groups, for example looking at inter-ethnic differences in Singaporean English. Another option, though, is to test Schneider's framework on a newly formed contact English that has speakers socialised on either side of the moment of contact between the indigenous and settler languages (and therefore between Western and Eastern cultures). This allows a close look at how the co-occurrence of language and cultural shift in a community presents itself in the resulting English variety. I aim to answer the following question: can we detect variation in the linguistic manifestation of cultural traits in young English-speaking communities that capture the apex of cultural shift? Clearly Schneider's results provide strong evidence for Eastern cultural values remaining noticeable in contact varieties of English, but we do not know whether the degree to which they occur changes over time and in line with the cultural circumstances of the community.

Setting out why CKI English is a suitable variety for this study requires an overview of the history of the islands. The Cocos (Keeling) Islands, Australia's most remote external territory, are a tropical atoll of just $14km^2$ in the south-east Indian Ocean (Figure 8.1). The atoll's current population count sits at 596 (Australian Bureau of Statistics 2016), divided between two of the 26 islands in the chain. Approximately 100 predominantly short-term contract worker Anglo-Australians and their families live on West Island, by far the larger and more infrastructurally dominant island. The majority of the population, around 500, live on the smaller Home Island, a 20-minute ferry ride away across the lagoon (Figure 8.2). This community almost categorically identifies as Cocos Malay, an ethnic group that developed out of the slavery system instituted by the islands' founder at the end of the first quarter of the 19th century.

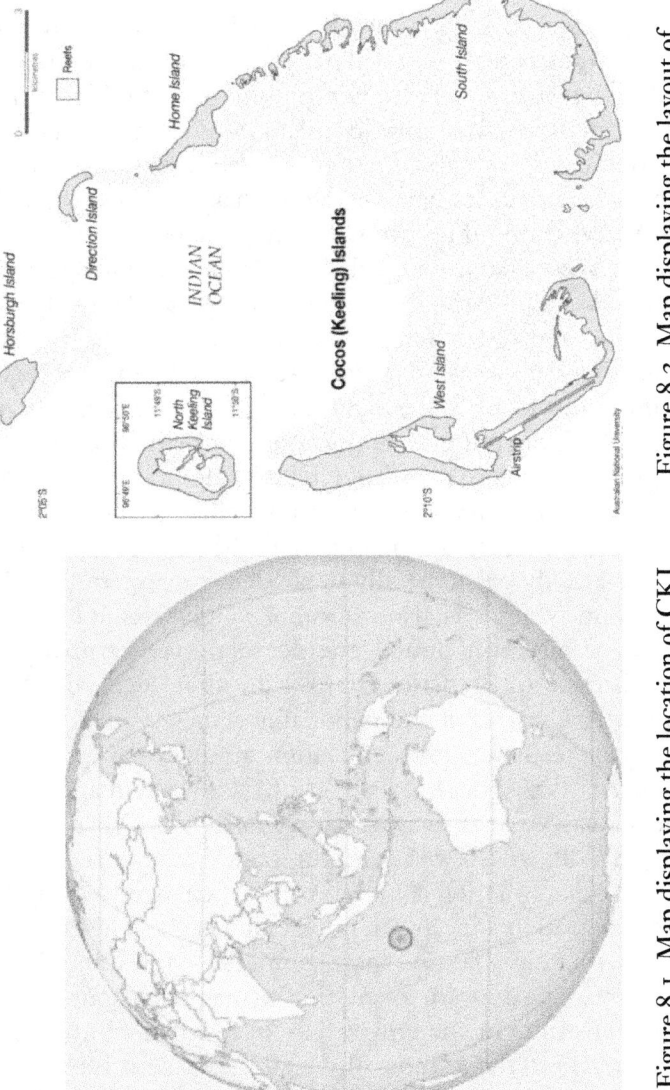

Figure 8.1 Map displaying the location of CKI in the world

Figure 8.2 Map displaying the layout of the islands

In 1827, a Scottish merchant named John Clunies-Ross established a fiefdom on the islands, bringing over 120 slaves from Borneo and Java, who went on to form a distinct ethnic group and create their own language variety, both named 'Cocos Malay'. The dominion, ruled in relative social isolation by the Clunies-Ross family for the next 150 years, came to an abrupt but bloodless end in 1984, when, after United Nations intervention, the Cocos Malay voted to become part of Australia. Since their integration with Australia in 1984, the Cocos (Keeling) Islands have been politically administered by the state of Western Australia (WA). Home Island, as its name suggests, has remained the domain of the Cocos Malay community, though many live on, or commute across the lagoon to, West Island for work. The Australian Government owns and monitors the housing on the island, renting the identical 100 houses to the locals, a point of contention for the Cocos Malay, who see this a continuation of the dominance put in place by the Clunies-Ross dynasty. Home Island is just $1km^2$ in area, and further construction is limited and tightly controlled, resulting in a one-in-one-out situation, and multiple houses having in excess of 12 people living under one roof.

After the coconut harvesting industry came to an end in the late 1800s, the islands struggled to maintain a reliable source of income and they are now heavily economically dependent on government funding. Unemployment, which has always been a weighty issue for the islanders, now sits at just over double the national average of 6.9 per cent (Australian Bureau of Statistics 2016). Education levels on the islands are significantly lower than the national averages, with the percentage of university or tertiary higher education graduates amounting to just 9.7 per cent compared with 22 per cent on the mainland (Australian Bureau of Statistics 2016). Despite this, most Cocos Malay families are financially well-off, with few expenditures and broadly well-paying jobs.

The linguistic situation of the islands changed abruptly upon Australian integration in 1984. Under Clunies-Ross law, English was largely kept to the ruling family, apart from a select few Cocos Malay, who were taught the language for plantation management purposes. Those that left for Australia in the emigration waves of the 1950s and 1970s and then returned to the islands, of which there are at least 20, brought with them at least a conversational level of English. The older generation on the islands now, however, generally has little to no English, as a result of the lack of education on the islands until integration. Instead, they speak Cocos Malay, a dialect of Malay (or Indonesian; it remains to be typologically defined) with influence from Dutch, English, as well as Papua New Guinean and South African languages (Ansaldo 2009). Those younger than six or seven years old in 1984 or born after that have received Australian standard education at schools based on Home and West Island by teaching staff brought in from Western Australia. Cocos Malay very much remains the home language, however. This has resulted in a clear diglossia, with most Cocos Malay below the age of 50 bilingual, in the layperson's sense. There is no scope here for discussion regarding the phonological, morphosyntactic and discourse marker inventories that characterise Cocos Malay or CKI English; these can be found in other publications from the author on this community.

So why is this community suited to a study of culture in corpora? As noted above, the Cocos Malay community has strong affiliations with two distinct cultural regions: the East Indies, that is, what is now Malaysia and Indonesia, and Australia. Unlike other contact varieties, where its speakers have formed their own nation, with their own localised and independent identity and culture, CKI English is spoken by a small minority community that has been subsumed by a comparatively mammoth nation state: the Cocos Malay community is now deeply entrenched in the Australian way of life. To the uninitiated visitor to the islands, the community is patently Malay in culture. Due to historical physical and social isolation the Cocos Malay people are extremely tight-knit and local community-focused. Marriage with non-Cocos Malay is still relatively limited, with marriage between neighbours and long-standing family friends remaining the preferred option. The islanders' maintenance of their Malay ethnicity and culture is also salient in their cultural practices and attitudes, particularly through their total adherence to the Islamic religion. The Islamic faith, brought with them from the Malay peninsula, plays an integral role on Home Island, dictating not only cultural practices, dress and diet, but also island routine, signalled via the call to prayer audible from anywhere on the island. The Cocos Malay people have cultivated stronger ties with Malaysia in the past few decades for reasons relating initially to the waves of emigration to Sabah in the 1970s and their reconnection with relatives via social media, but also latterly an intensification of the Islamic faith that they share with Malaysia.

Nevertheless, the Cocos Malay community has also embraced their new Australian cultural and national identity. Self-identifying first and foremost as Australian, most young Cocos Malay interviewed very much see themselves as part of Australian society, receiving an Australian education and partaking in most key cultural practices. Australia Day and Anzac Day are major events on the islands and several Cocos Malay identified the relaxed lifestyle and informal communication style on the islands as reflective of the Australian way of life rather than Cocos Malay. The CKI thereby present a unique context for recent contact between, and potential blend of, an Eastern and Western culture: Cocos Malay (in essence Malaysian) and Australian.

3. METHODOLOGY

As in Schneider's study, the methodology of this study is based on identifying correlations between cultural orientations and linguistic form, specifically indicator terms relating to Hofstede's cultural dimensions work. It is not comparative, in that I have focused on a single corpus from one speech community; however, familiarity with the speakers allows for a closer look at intra-community variation in the use of indicator terms, a form of analysis not possible in Schneider's research.

The data used in this study were taken from a corpus of 55 hours (321,892 words) of English speech collected by the author on the Cocos (Keeling) islands in 2016 during a two-month period of fieldwork spent living in the Cocos Malay community. A supplementary section of the corpus was collected from the Cocos Malay diaspora community living in Perth and Katanning in Western Australia in the two weeks following the island fieldwork. Sociolinguistic interviews were carried out with a total of 60 Cocos Malay people and lasted on average around 50 minutes. In so far as possible in the given population and sociolinguistic fieldwork in general, the corpus is balanced in terms of age and sex (Table 8.1).

Table 8.1 Demographic summary for the Cocos (Keeling) Islands Spoken English

Social/Demographic factor	Number of speakers
Age	
18–30	23
30–50	21
50–80	16
Sex	
Male	31
Female	29

Schneider's data was a mix of both relatively old and recent speech and text from the ICE project, the incompatibility of which arguably weakens the analytical value of the results. Here the data is speech only, collected by the same researcher over a short period of time from 20 per cent of the community in question, ensuring it is a highly representative sample of the linguistic patterns of a community at a specific point in their existence. Distributional analysis of indicator terms in the corpus was undertaken in the transcription software ELAN (2016) and the statistical program R was used for subsequent ANOVA testing. In order to broaden the possible scope for detection of cultural traits, I analysed the frequencies of Schneider's lexical items (*take care of, protect, loyal, harmony, concerned about, sensitive*) as well as other indicator terms identified as typical of collectivism by Grossmann and Varnum (2015): *community, help, give, look after, share, together*. For kinship terms, I looked at only those from Schneider's analysis: *uncle, aunt, brother, cousin*. I lemmatised the search terms, such that inflected and derivational forms and cognates from different word classes were included in cases where the same semantic concept was invoked – that is, *help (n), helping, helps, helped* were all counted in the analysis. Lexical items indexing meaning unrelated to the cultural value were excluded – for example, *give* when relating to any meaning other than 'supplying or gifting someone with something' was not included.

Included in this study are two types of linguistic manifestations, categorised by Schneider based on research by Hofstede ([1980] 2001), Minkov (2013) and Schmitt (2005): (1) individualism v collectivism and (2) kinship. Other dimensions evaluated in the ICE corpus by Schneider, such as high and low context (Hall and Hall 1990; Hua 2013), long-term orientation, and power distance (Hofstede [1908] 2001; House et al. 2004), were not investigated for reasons of low frequency or irrelevance (sociolinguistic interviews are not a setting that would naturally encourage the use of respect pronouns such as *madame, miss*, and so on).

4. RESULTS

4.1 Individualism vs Collectivism

Following Schneider (2018), Uz (2014) and Yu et al. (2016), the frequency and overall proportions of first-person singular and plural pronouns were calculated. There were 1,245 instances of *I* and 508 instances of *we* in the CKI English data. When the proportion of first-person singular forms are compared with the equivalent values in Schneider's study (Table 8.2), it is evident that the Cocos Malay community sits between Singapore and India in regard to this cultural dimension, expressing a relatively collectivist orientation in their lexis.

Table 8.2 Proportion of total pronoun frequencies that are first-person singular across Schneider's five nations (2018: 8–9) and CKI

	GB	Hong Kong	NZ	Singapore	CKI	India
% 1st SG out of total	76.90%	76.10%	73.80%	72.10%	71%	66.30%

Closer inspection of CKI English in light of sociolinguistic factors reveals cross-generational variation, however. The older generation, that is, those Cocos Malay aged 50 and over, produced on average almost twice as many first-person plural pronouns as the youngest generation (aged 30 and under) (Figure 8.3). At 60 per cent singular forms, the older speakers of CKI English are more collectivist in terms

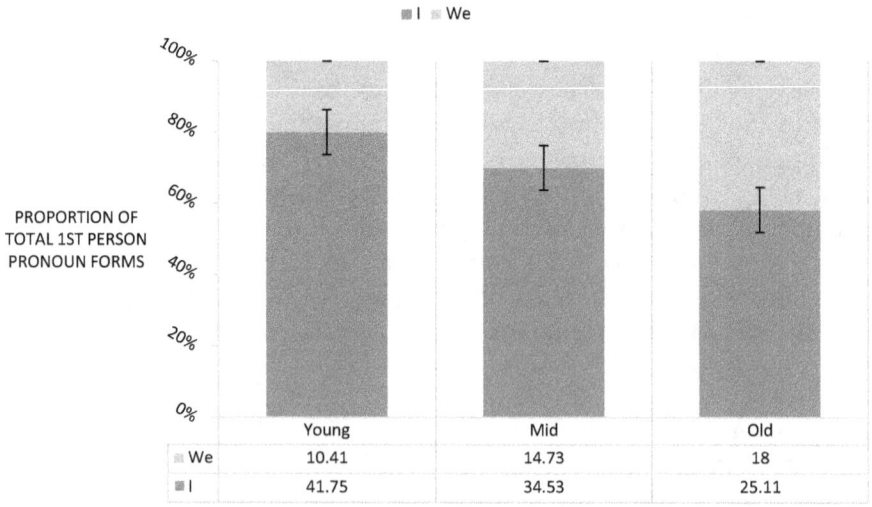

Figure 8.3 Proportions of first-person singular and plural pronoun forms across three age groups in the CKI data (bar plot), and the average frequency of both forms for each group (table beneath). Standard deviations for age groups are young = 11.329, mid = 7.292 and older = 7.739

of language use than any of Schneider's five nations included in his study. The 'middle' age group, meanwhile, were closest to the overall community average of 71 per cent first-person singular. One-way ANOVA confirmed the (albeit weak) statistical significance of the age group effect (F = 4.003, p = .022). The values were adjusted to take into account differences in total word count between speakers during statistical modelling. The younger generation is, in fact, presenting proportions of singular and plural pronouns (80 per cent singular) that more closely mirror that of Great Britain and Hong Kong, at the individualistic end of the spectrum.

An overall total of 172 collectivist indicator terms were identified in the CKI English data. Interestingly, indicator terms with the highest frequencies differed from those in Schneider's study; indeed, *protect*, *take care of*, *harmony*, *loyal*, *sensitive* and *concerned about* did not feature at all. Instead, terms excluded by Schneider such as *community*, *give* and *help* proved to be the most commonly used (Table 8.3).

Table 8.3 Frequency distributions for collectivist indicator terms in the CKI English data

Word	*Frequency*
community	32
give	54
help	30
look after	19
share	14
together	23
Total	172

The cross-generational stratification apparent in the *I* vs *we* analysis was also visible in the distribution of indicator terms relating to collectivism (Figure 8.4). Once again, ANOVA yielded a statistically significant result for the age group effect (F = 5.882, p = .004).

We can summarise at this point that the general pattern for the collectivist vs individualist dimension in CKI English is for the older speakers to produce a greater number of collectivist linguistic forms than the younger generations, particularly the Cocos Malay under 30 years old.

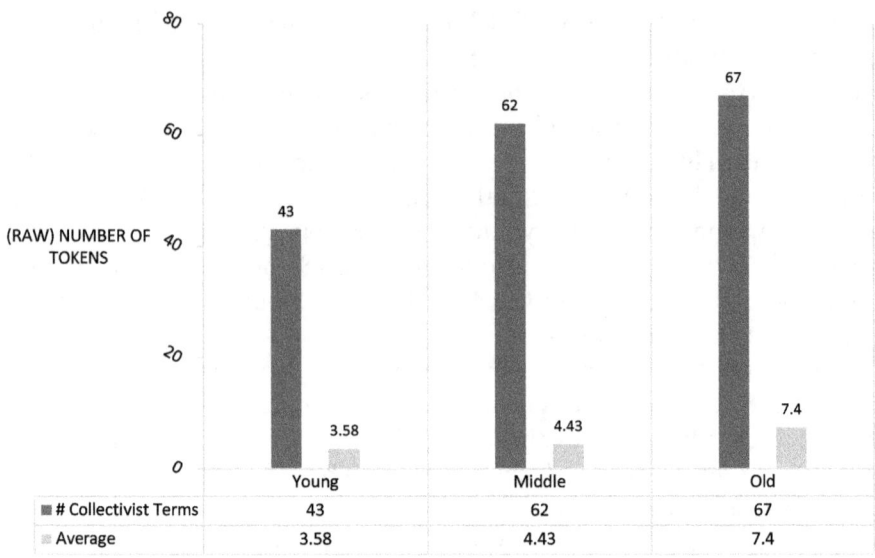

Figure 8.4 Frequencies of collectivist indicator terms across three age groups in the CKI English data (dark grey) and the average frequency per speaker for each group (light grey). Standard deviations for age groups are young = 3.315, mid = 3.817 and older = 3.643

4.2 Kinship

Analysis of kinship indicator terms in CKI English, presented in Table 8.4, reveals an extremely high frequency rate, especially when we bear in mind that the CKI data is approximately five times smaller than the corpora employed by Schneider. Despite the large discrepancy in size

Table 8.4 Distributional frequencies for four kinship terms in six varieties of English

	GB	NZ	Hong Kong	Singapore	India	CKI
uncle	13	30	39	53	14	12
aunt/ie	31	41	76	42	26	20
brother/s	59	148	195	121	152	53
cousin/s	35	36	39	21	60	40
Total	138	255	349	237	252	125

Source: data for GB, NZ, Hong Kong, Singapore and India taken from Schneider 2018.

between the two corpora, the total number of kinship indicator terms for CKI is approaching that of Great Britain. The word *family*, though not formally included in the study, was mentioned 52 times by the Cocos Malay.

If we compare ratios of collectivist and kinship indicator terms for the GB, NZ, Hong Kong, Singapore, India and CKI data, we can see that the Cocos Malay favour family-related linguistic forms over collectivist vocabulary far more than speakers of other varieties (Figure 8.5).

Furthermore, the high frequency in use of kinship terms does not appear to vary across generations, as comparative analysis showed little difference between the age groups in this regard. In this case, however, there was some minor variation between the sexes in the Cocos Malay community, with the average Cocos Malay woman producing four more kinship terms than her male counterpart (Figure 8.6). ANOVA revealed the effect to be only approaching statistical significance, however ($F = 3.711, p = .059$).

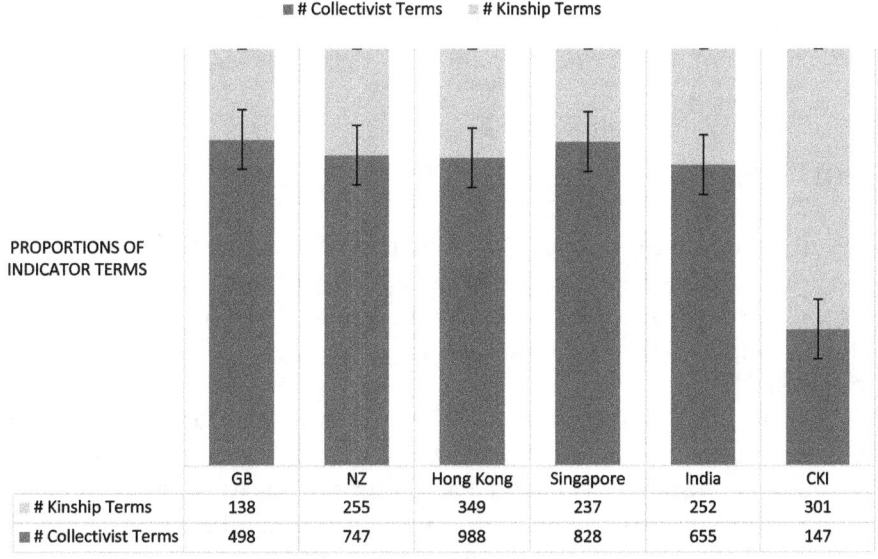

Figure 8.5 Proportions of collectivist and kinship indicator terms for six English varieties with the raw frequencies for each beneath
Source: data for GB, NZ, Hong Kong, Singapore and India taken from Schneider 2018.

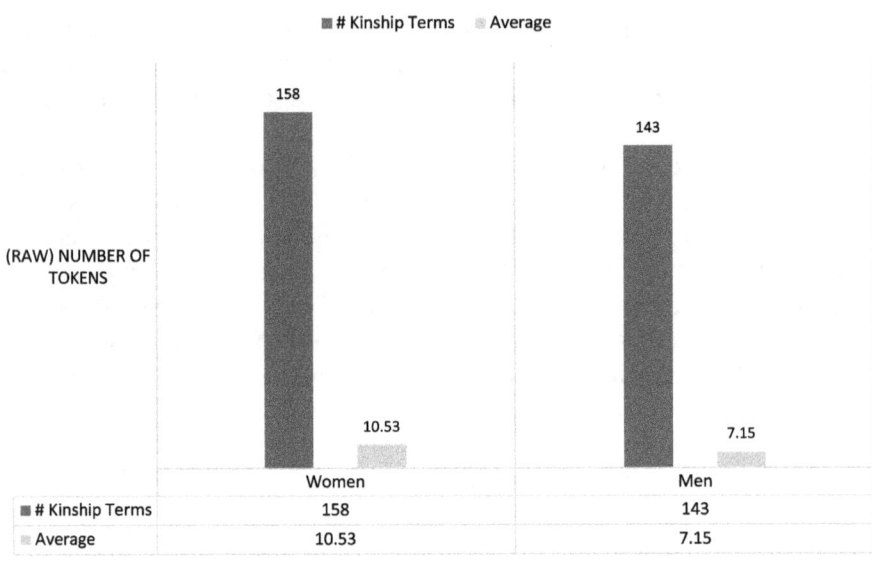

Figure 8.6 Frequencies of kinship indicator terms across the sexes in the CKI data (dark grey) and the average frequency per speaker for each group (light grey). Standard deviation values for the two sexes were: women = 7.867, men = 5.604

5. DISCUSSION

Broadly speaking, the results here suggest that the application of cultural dimensions theory to the CKIE speech corpus using Schneider's second nexus (that is, indicator terms) is not only viable, but also rather illuminating. There are several findings of note, each of which I address in turn here.

Despite the size limitations of the speech data relative to the ICE corpora, analyses of both collectivist and kinship terminology yielded a considerable number of tokens. Particularly in regard to pronoun use, where proportions of singular and plural forms can be compared with Schneider's findings, it is clear that CKI English, and by extension the Cocos Malay as an ethnic group, can be positioned towards the collectivist end of Hofstede's spectrum ([1980] 2001), alongside Asian countries such as India, Singapore and Hong Kong. This collectivist character is perhaps unsurprising given the insularity and solidarity amongst the community as well as retention of Malay cultural values. The exceedingly high rates of kinship terms also support the positioning of CKI

English as a variety with lexical manifestations of values from Asia, where familial values take a more central role than in the West. Again, this is to be expected in a dense community with multiplex ties such as this, where everyone is closely related by blood and lives and works in close proximity. Thus this study has shown that though there is no direct comparison for this data in terms of corpus size, type and time, and the variety is very much still in a fledgling state with only two generations of speakers, it is still possible to extract meaningful conclusions regarding the community's cultural orientation expressed in their language.

Exploring intra-community variation revealed particularly thought-provoking patterns. In terms of both pronoun use and indicator vocabulary, the older generation were found to use more collectivist forms than the younger Cocos Malay. Without more data it is of course difficult to confirm this as a robust pattern; however, I tentatively argue that this apparent age stratification is a reflection of the CKI's recent political and societal narrative. Speakers in the older age category were raised, and lived most of their adult life, in Cocos Malay society, where, like in their cultural homeland of Malaysia, a 'collectivist community orientation prevails' (Fang 2012: 28). Those in the younger age categories, especially those under the age of 30, were socialised on post-Australian integration CKI, received an Australian education, and may have lived for long periods of time on the mainland and/or interacted on a daily basis with non-Cocos Malay on West Island. They are exposed in multiple domains to the cultural temperament of Australia, including a heightened orientation towards individualism than Malaysia or other Asian cultures. I propose, then, that the younger generation of Cocos Malay may likely use fewer collectivist lexical items than their grandparents and parents as a result of the shift in cultural influence from purely Cocos Malay to a mix of both Australian and Cocos Malay values; the stratified results in the CKI corpus across age groups reflects the radical cultural changes the community has undergone – a form of acculturation (Berry and Sam 1997; Stephenson 2000). Additionally, research has shown that communities living in a state of poverty and threat are more likely to be collectivistic, since they rely on each other to survive (Zuckerman 2000). With relative affluence in the community today, the average Cocos Malay is no longer reliant on other community members for economic survival, lessening the importance of a collectivist outlook.

We must also acknowledge the effects of globalisation and technology on the social psyche of today's youth: collectivist cultures are increasingly shifting towards a more individualistic position on the spectrum as a result of intercultural connectivity (Oyserman et al. 2002) and Cocos Malay youth are avid internet consumers and social media users. It is difficult to estimate the visceral impact of this type of media exposure on the culture of the Cocos Malay youth, but it would be naïve to exclude it as a potential factor in the creation and expression of their modern-day community identity.

There may well be other factors involved in the pattern here, however, that are unrelated to the collectivist/individualist dimension, such as a general age effect. Social psychological research has demonstrated that group vs individual attitudes and orientations are not consistent across one's lifetime; until full physical and psycho-emotional maturity is reached, young people are constantly processing and learning collectivistic/individualistic behaviours from their experiences, suggesting that co-dependent and independent attitudes grow over time (Wang et al. 2020). It may be the case that these results reflect this maturity discrepancy rather than any cultural characteristic or, alternatively, the factors are working in combination. This would help to explain the unexpectedly high frequency of singular personal pronouns in the CKI, such that the Cocos Malay use *I* more than British speakers, for example, at the individualist end of the spectrum.

Whilst the collectivist dimension showed intra-community variation in terms of age, kinship indicator term frequencies were more sensitive to the social factor of sex. Women were marginally more likely to use lexical items relating to family than men. This may be, in part, due to the traditional gender roles maintained in Cocos Malay society, where women are more engaged in managing household and family matters, looking after children and elderly parents whilst their husbands, sons and fathers are working; they are more inclined to talk about family than male Cocos Malay. Methodological effects could also have inadvertently caused an increase in talk surrounding family amongst the women. Since I am a woman, the female Cocos Malay may have been more inclined to discuss personal topics about their family than the men, who generally maintained a more reserved attitude in conversation.

It is worth highlighting that though Schneider's framework appeared to elicit linguistic structures reflecting cultural characteristics of the Cocos Malay, this was made possible only through a widening of indicator terms utilised in the analysis beyond Schneider's original roster. Most of the collectivist terms found to have high frequencies in the CKI data were not present in the ICE study, whilst the most commonly found lexical items in the ICE study barely featured at all in the CKI corpus. This does not necessarily imply that one methodology is superior over the other, but rather, I believe, that the variation between data types necessitates localisation and adaptation of methods to ensure validity across all World English varieties. Words such as *harmony*, *concerned about* and *loyal* (Schneider 2018), which are much more likely to appear in formal contexts, are suitable in analyses involving written texts and speech in educational, entertainment or news-related domains such as television and radio shows, but are less relevant and appropriate for natural speech. This is particularly pertinent for contact varieties that have L2 speakers, where unusual vocabulary is unlikely to occur, even if the semantic concepts they represent are important to the community in question. This raises the question regarding the potential data lost as a result of a narrow selection of indicator terms that show a feature bias towards particular varieties over others: perhaps the rates of collectivism would have been significantly different had the vocabulary inventory included synonyms of key concepts tailored to each variety. Frequencies of each lexical item would not be comparable; however, overall collectivism scores would be more reflective.

6. CONCLUSION

In conclusion, this study of cultural dimensions in the lexicon of CKI English demonstrated the successful extension of Schneider's nexus of culture framework to include intra-community sociolinguistic variation, illustrating how a recent major cultural shift in the community may be visible in the cross-generational use of certain cultural indicator terms. The individualising effect of globalisation was also discussed as a possible cause for the variation in expressions of culture amongst the Cocos Malay. The impact of globalisation is increasingly discouraging the dichotomous, mutually exclusive characterisation of the collectivist/ individualist paradigm around the world, and instead demonstrating that single people and single communities can be constituent of both individualistic and collectivistic aspects. As Wang et al. (2020: 7) note, this modern-day co-existence of both ends of the spectrum may be resulting in 'an autonomous-related sense of self that . . . enable[s] youth to strike a balance between, on the one hand, meeting family responsibilities and staying psychologically close to their parents and, on the other hand, becoming self-directed and self-actualized'. The variation across generations in the CKI community in terms of collectivist cultural expression, but lack thereof in terms of kinship expression, would certainly corroborate this perspective.

Finally, this study also serves to point out how considerable caution must be employed when applying theoretical frameworks to vastly differing linguistic data, even if they all fall under the umbrella term of 'World Englishes'.

REFERENCES

Ansaldo, U. (2009). *Contact languages: Ecology and evolution in Asia.* Cambridge University Press.

Australian Bureau of Statistics. (2016). 2016 Census QuickStats. <http://quickstats.censusdata.abs.gov.au/census_services/getproduct/census/2016/quickstat/90102?opendocument> (last accessed 7 January 2021).

Berry, J. W. and Sam, D. (1997). Acculturation and adaptation. In J. W. Berry, M. H. Segall and C. Kagitçibasi (Eds.), *Handbook of cross-cultural psychology. Volume 3: Social behavior and applications* (2nd ed.; pp. 291–326). Allyn and Bacon.

Britain, D. (1992). Linguistic change in intonation: The use of high rising terminals in New Zealand English. *Language Variation and Change, 4*(1), 77–104.

ELAN. (2016). (Version 4.9.4) [Computer software]. The Language Archive, Max Planck Institute for Psycholinguistics. <https://archive.mpi.nl/tla/elan> (last accessed 7 January 2021).

Fang, T. (2012). Yin Yang: A new perspective on culture. *Management and Organization Review, 8*(1), 25–50.

Grossmann, I. and Varnum, M. E. W. (2015). Social structure, infectious diseases, disasters, secularism, and cultural change in America. *Psychological Science, 26*(3), 311–24.

Hall, E. T. and Hall, M. R. (1990). *Understanding cultural differences.* Intercultural Press.

Hedegard, H. (2020). *The emergence and development of Cocos (Keeling) Islands English: A new NEAR-Australian variety?* [Doctoral dissertation, University of Bern].

Hofstede, G. (2001). *Culture's consequences: Comparing values, behaviors, institutions and organizations across nations* (2nd ed.). Sage. (Original work published 1980).

House, R. J., Hanges, P. J., Javidan, M., Dorfman, P. W. and Gupta, V. (Eds.) (2004). *Culture, leadership, and organizations: The GLOBE study of 62 societies.* Sage Publications.

Hua, Z. (2013). *Exploring intercultural communication: Language in action.* Routledge.

Minkov, M. (2013). *Cross-cultural analysis: The science and art of comparing the world's modern societies and their cultures.* Sage.

Oyserman, D., Coon, H. M. and Kemmelmeier, M. (2002). Rethinking individualism and collectivism: Evaluation of theoretical assumptions and meta-analyses. *Psychological Bulletin, 128*(1), 3–72.

Schmitt, D. P. (2005). Sociosexuality from Argentina to Zimbabwe: A 48-nation study of sex, culture, and strategies of human mating. *Behavioral and Brain Sciences, 28*(2), 247–75.

Schneider, E. W. (2018). The interface between cultures and corpora: Tracing reflections and manifestations. *ICAME Journal, 42*(1), 97–132. <https://doi.org/10.1515/icame-2018-0006> (last accessed 4 January 2021).

Stephenson, M. (2000). Development and validation of the Stephenson Multigroup Acculturation Scale (SMAS). *Psychological Assessment, 12*(1), 77–88.

Uz, I. (2014). Individualism and first-person pronoun use in written texts across languages. *Journal of Cross-Cultural Psychology, 45*(10), 1671–8.

Wang, Q., Qu, Y. and Ding, R. (2020). Adolescence in collectivistic cultures. In S. Hupp and J. Jewell (Eds.), *The encyclopedia of child and adolescent development* (pp. 1–13). John Wiley & Sons.

Yu, F., Peng, T., Peng, K., Tang, S., Chen, C. S., Qian, X., Sun, P., Han, T. and Chai, F. (2016). Cultural value shifting in pronoun use. *Journal of Cross-Cultural Psychology, 47*(2), 310–16.

Zuckerman, D. M. (2000). Welfare reform in America: A clash of politics and research. *Journal of Social Issues, 56*(4), 587–600.

CHAPTER 9

Expressing Concepts Metaphorically in English Editorials in the Sinosphere

Kathleen Ahrens and Winnie Huiheng Zeng

1. INTRODUCTION

Conceptual Metaphor Theory postulates that metaphors are a cognitive phenomenon (Lakoff and Johnson [1980] 2003; Lakoff 1993), one that is instantiated in language, but with conceptual underpinnings. Conceptual metaphors link two conceptual domains: a source domain and a target domain, where a conceptual domain is a set of entities, qualities and functions that are semantically linked (Ahrens 2010). The source domain usually consists of a concrete concept, such as MONEY, while the target domain involves an abstract concept, such as TIME.[1] For example, if people want to talk about TIME, they can use the source domain of MONEY to do so (that is, TIME IS MONEY), as in the example, 'He didn't want to spend any more time on his math homework'. In this case, 'spending' is mapped from the source domain of MONEY to the target domain of TIME. A set of mappings between a given source and target domain (as in the case of 'spend', 'waste', 'cost', which can occur in both conceptual domains) indicate that these two domains are conceptually linked in the language.[2]

A number of studies have examined cross-linguistic differences in metaphor usage, arguing that conceptual metaphors are not only cognitively, but also culturally motivated (Kövecses 2010; Yu 1995, 2000, 2004). For example, Kövecses (2003) used the conceptual metaphor LOVE IS A JOURNEY as an example to demonstrate that two languages may share a conceptual metaphor and the conceptual metaphor may be instantiated by largely overlapping expressions in both languages. In addition, languages may also differ in how they prioritise the use of a source domain. Simó (2011), for example, noted that the metaphorical use of 'blood' in English and Hungarian shows large differences in frequency, connotation and usage patterns, which suggests that experiential and cultural background play a large role in metaphoric production. Bas (2019) has also argued that Turkish and American English have different preferences for conceptualising DEMOCRACY, with Turkish prioritising democracy as a DESTINATION and American English using WAR as the prototypical source domain for democracy. With these cross-linguistic differences in mind, we turn next to exploring Schneider's (2018: 98) idea that 'corpora can be employed for searching for traces of culture, that is, search terms and strategies' and moreover, that these differences can be found within the same language across different cultures.

Schneider's proposal involves three methods: the first method searches for lexemes that reference cultural terms and objects, which are often manifested in cultural keywords (Mukherjee and Bernaisch 2015). The second method is to look at 'indicator terms', which are 'words or phrases assumed to indicate, reflect or be associated with the cultural domain or issue in question' (Schneider 2018: 101), such as honorifics or kinship terms. The third category looks at the potential contribution of syntactic constructions that are 'motivated by culturally-based' principles (Schneider 2018: 120), such as verb complementation patterns in British English and Indian English (Olavarría de Ersson and Shaw 2003). In this chapter we seek to extend Schneider's proposal by looking for evidence that mappings between source and target domains in conceptual metaphors are different for different varieties of English. We propose this metaphor-based approach within the lexical-conceptual dimension of cross-cultural analysis as an additional way to analyse aspects of culture within a given language.

2. VARIETIES OF ENGLISH IN THE SINOSPHERE

Schneider (2018) looks at varieties of English from different cultural orientations, with Hong Kong, Singapore and India representing Asian cultures with an associated Asian 'collectivist orientation' and furthermore, with Hong Kong and Singapore representing 'two Chinese-dominated, Buddhist-influenced cultures, which have undergone varying degrees of modernization and westernization' (2018: 101). Both Hong Kong and Singapore also represent what Kachru (1992) calls 'outer circle Englishes' which came about due to Great Britain's colonialism in these two regions. After Hong Kong's handover to China as a Special Administrative Region of China in 1997, the Hong Kong government promoted a policy of 'trilingualism and biliteracy' whereby students are taught to speak Putonghua, Cantonese and English and taught to read and write in Chinese and English.

In contrast to the situation in Hong Kong, where English is taught and used as a second official language, English is taught as a foreign language throughout China and Taiwan and is used primarily as a medium of international communication. Their official languages are two varieties of Mandarin Chinese (Lin et al. 2019) that anchor the inner circle of 'World Chineses'. The official language of the Republic of China (Taiwan) is called *Guoyu*, and *Putonghua* is the official language of the People's Republic of China (China). The relations between them are somewhat analogous to American and British Englishes, with subtle grammatical differences that are overshadowed by apparent orthographic divergence.[3] Thus, in Kachru's (1992) 'three circles' model of English, China and Taiwan are considered to be part of the 'Expanding Circle' of English.[4]

The major cities have had newspapers published in English for at least 30 years, with Beijing having two papers, Hong Kong having three papers and Taipei having two papers during the period we examine in our corpus. In addition, all the newspapers have editorials, or commentaries, or op-eds. These types of articles are intended to influence the reader to a particular point of view. In doing so, it is a genre that strives to communicate the values, cultural beliefs and ideologies of the writer or the editorial board and, in general, reflects the opinions of the owners of the newspaper. In this study, we aim to examine the differences in conceptual metaphor use related to the idea of 'democracy' in these editorials/commentaries in the contemporary English language newspapers in Beijing, Hong Kong and Taipei. Given that Taiwan holds elections on a regular cycle and elects the president by direct vote (Fell 2011), Hong Kong holds elections on a regular cycle but does not elect its Chief Executive by direct vote (Fong 2019), and China holds some very local elections (Saich 2015) and also does not elect its leadership by direct vote, we expect to see the metaphors related to democracy to vary across these three political systems. We propose four research questions to test the above hypothesis:

1. Is there a difference in how often topics related to democracy are discussed among English editorials published by news organisations in Beijing, Hong Kong and Taipei?

2. Is there a difference in how often topics related to democracy are metaphorised among the English editorials in Beijing, Hong Kong and Taipei?
3. Is there a different pattern of source domain usage for the target domain of DEMOCRACY among the English editorials in Beijing, Hong Kong and Taipei?
4. Do the countries/regions being referenced when using keywords related to DEMOCRACY vary among the Beijing, Hong Kong and Taipei editorials?

3. CORPUS CREATION

This paper examines the differences in conceptual metaphor use related to the idea of 'democracy' in editorials in contemporary English language newspapers in Hong Kong, Beijing and Taipei during a six-week period – one month before and two weeks after the 2016 US presidential election held on 2 November 2016 in which Donald Trump (Republican) unexpectedly beat Hillary Clinton (Democrat). We undertook this task by independently compiling an English corpus of editorials from two newspapers published in Beijing (*China Daily* and *Global Times*), three newspapers published in Hong Kong (*South China Morning Post*, *The Standard* and *Hong Kong Free Press*) and two newspapers published in Taipei (*The China Post* and *Taipei Times*). The *Hong Kong Free Press* is the only crowd-funded newspaper and the only one that is available exclusively online. The other two newspapers in Hong Kong – the *South China Morning Post* and *The Standard* – are published by companies that are perceived as supporters of the government in Beijing.[5] The two papers published in Beijing are overseen by the Chinese government. The private companies that publish the newspapers in Taipei have different political alignments: *The China Post* publisher is more pro-Kuomintang, which recognises the One-China Principle (Wang 2009), and the publisher of the *Taipei Times* is more pro-Democratic Progressive Party which has not officially recognised the One-China Principle (Guo 2012).[6] Table 9.1 provides information about the titles used for the category of opinion-type articles that were extracted, the article count and the word count.

To construct the corpus, we searched for all articles in the category name listed for that newspaper during the time period 1 October to 15 November 2016, as follows: for *Global Times*, *The Standard*, *Hong*

Table 9.1 English editorials in the Sinosphere Corpus

City	Newspaper titles	Categories of articles	Number of articles	Word count	
Beijing	China Daily	Opinions/editorials/op-ed contributors	37	19,887	37,556
	Global Times	Opinion/editorials/op-eds	36	17,669	
Hong Kong	South China Morning Post	Comment/opinion	31	21,730	51,807
	The Standard	Editorial	27	14,029	
	Hong Kong Free Press	Opinion	15	16,048	
Taipei	The China Post	Op-eds	23	13,669	41,478
	Taipei Times	Editorials	45	27,809	
Total				130,841	

Kong Free Press and *Taipei Times*, the search function on the newspaper website was used to retrieve articles under the categories listed in Table 9.1. For *China Daily* and *South China Morning Post*, the Google search function was used as the search function as both newspaper websites did not allow searches under specific newspaper sections within their archive records.[7] For *The China Post*, articles were extracted from the WiseNews Database (a database available to Hong Kong Universities) in late 2016 for the period 8 October to 15 November 2016.[8]

4. METHODS

Following the Metaphor Pattern Analysis approach (Stefanowitsch 2006), keywords related to the target domain of DEMOCRACY were searched in the corpus using the key-word-in-context search function in WordSmith 6 (Scott 2012). We included lemmas under the keywords of 'democracy', 'elect', 'vote' and 'campaign'.[9] Table 9.2 lists all the lemmas of the four keywords searched for DEMOCRACY.

The obtained concordances were sorted into an Excel file for further analysis of metaphorical tokens and types.

Table 9.2 List of lemmas searched for the target domain of DEMOCRACY

Keyword	Lemmas				
DEMOCRACY	democracy	democracies			
ELECT	elect	elects	elected	electing	election elections
VOTE	vote	votes	voted	voting	
CAMPAIGN	campaign	campaigns	campaigned	campaigning	

5. RESULTS AND DISCUSSION

5.1 Differences in the Topics Related to Democracy

The first research question dealt with the differences in how often topics related to democracy are discussed among Beijing, Hong Kong and Taipei editorial corpora. We extracted all instances of the lemmas related to the target concept of DEMOCRACY in the corpus, which yielded 401 cases. We excluded the uses of the lemmas in titles (6 cases; for example, 'Tsai's policy coordination meetings threaten democracy') and hyphenated lexemes (52 cases; for example, 'pro-democracy activists'), and the uses of the lemmas as proper nouns (3 cases; for example, 'Election Committee'). This left us with 340 cases for analysis. Table 9.3 presents the total numbers and normalised ratios (NR) for each keyword in the three corpora.

Table 9.3 Frequencies of the topics related to DEMOCRACY in Beijing, Hong Kong and Taipei editorial corpora

	DEMOCRACY	ELECT	VOTE	CAMPAIGN	Total	NR
Beijing	10	43	4	36	93	24.76
Hong Kong	11	85	31	18	145	27.99
Taipei	23	52	8	19	102	24.59
Total	**44**	**180**	**43**	**73**	**340**	**25.99**

Table 9.3 shows a total frequency of 24.76 per 10,000 words (NR = 24.76) for keywords related to the target domain of DEMOCRACY in the Beijing corpus, compared with 27.99 in the Hong Kong corpus and 24.59 in the Taipei corpus. We further used a log-likelihood test to compare the significance of the differences in the frequencies between cities.[10] The results show that there are no significant differences between the Beijing and Hong Kong corpora (NR = 24.76 vs 27.99; LL = -0.86),

Beijing and Taipei corpora (NR = 24.76 vs 24.59; LL = +0.00), and also Hong Kong and Taipei corpora (NR = 27.99 vs 24.59; LL = +1.01).

These indicate that newspapers in the three cities overall touched upon issues related to democracy with similar frequencies. The results are surprising given that there are no direct elections or campaigns of senior government officials in China and that the Communist Party of China strongly supports one-party rule, and also given that Taiwan does hold direct elections and people in Hong Kong would like to hold direct elections; this linguistic finding does not align with the geopolitical situation we see on the ground. However, given that the time period covered was directly before and after the United States election, it may be the case that the discussion of democracy had to do with that particular election. We will return to this question in Section 5.4.

5.2 Differences in the Metaphorisation of Democracy

Next, let us look at the second research question, which asks how often topics related to democracy are metaphorised among Beijing, Hong Kong and Taipei editorial corpora. Two linguists trained in metaphor identification completed the coding of metaphorical and literal use of 'democracy' cases. We followed the general metaphor identification approaches of Metaphor Identification Procedure – MIP (Pragglejaz Group 2007) and Metaphor Identification Procedure VU Amsterdam – MIPVU (Steen et al. 2010), and source domain verification (Ahrens and Jiang 2020). The two coders received pre-coding training to familiarise themselves with the approach and the corpus. Following Wimmer and Dominick (2013: 175), we calculated the inter-coder reliability in a subset of 10–25 per cent of the data. The result shows the reliability is 'substantial' (qualification from Landis and Koch 1977, Cohen's kappa = 0.765) for coding metaphors. Ambiguous cases were discussed and resolved based on opinions from a third metaphor expert.[11] The frequencies of metaphorical and literal 'democracy' instances in the three corpora are presented in Figure 9.1.

We found there is significant association between cities and metaphorisations of DEMOCRACY based on chi-square results χ^2 (2, N = 340) = 10.570, p = .005.[12] The table in Appendix 9.1 is the cross-tabulation with cell counts, expected counts, adjusted residuals and chi-square results.[13] The results of the significant residuals (residual > 2 or < -2) on a tinted background in Appendix 9.1 show that Beijing editorials used more

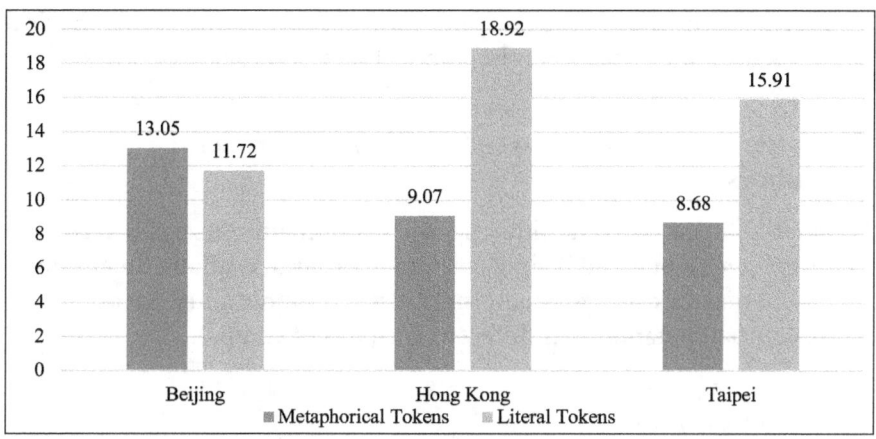

Figure 9.1 Normalised ratios of metaphorical and literal tokens related to DEMOCRACY in Beijing, Hong Kong and Taipei editorial corpora. A colour copy of this figure is available on the EUP website: edinburghuniversitypress.com/EcologiesofWorldEnglishes

metaphors and fewer literal instances than expected by chance when using keywords related to the concept of DEMOCRACY.[14] For example, in (1), 'campaign' is conceptualised as a PHYSICAL OBJECT that can be pushed in the editorial from *Global Times*.

(1) The newly released recording of a lewd conversation in 2005 is *pushing* Donald Trump's **campaign** to a knife edge. (*Global Times*, 10 September 2016)

Hong Kong opinion writers instead used more literal instances and fewer metaphorical instances for keywords related to DEMOCRACY than expected by chance. Example (2) provides an example of a literal use of 'democracy' in the Hong Kong corpus.

(2) the government committed to upholding five core values of Hong Kong: freedom, human rights, **democracy**, the rule of law and clean governance. (*South China Morning Post*, 11 July 2016)

Thus, so far, we have seen that during this time period immediately before and after the US presidential election in 2016, Beijing was more likely to metaphorise keywords related to DEMOCRACY, while Hong Kong was less likely to do so. We now turn to the third research question, which looks at whether the source domains used to express these metaphorical concepts differ or not among the publications in these three cities.

5.3 Differences in the Source Domains of Democracy Metaphors

In what follows, we examine the source domains' usage patterns in Beijing, Hong Kong and Taipei corpora in order to evaluate the proposal that there may be different mappings between source and target domains in conceptual metaphors in different varieties of English.

5.3.1 Source domain verification

The source domain of a metaphor is typically a more concrete conceptual domain which is used to understand a more abstract target domain (Lakoff and Johnson [1980] 2003), that is, in 'Taiwan's *road* to democracy', the abstract target domain of DEMOCRACY is described with the concrete source domain of JOURNEY. We follow the previous approaches to source domain verification (Ahrens and Jiang 2020; Zeng et al. 2020; Ahrens and Zeng 2017) and the two coders were trained to familiarise with these steps before they coded the data independently. Results of the reliability tests show reliability is 'substantial' for coding the five most frequently used source domains (with an NR more than 1): LIVING BEING (Cohen's kappa = 0.819), PHYSICAL OBJECT (Cohen's kappa = 0.716), COMPETITION (Cohen's kappa = 0.796), BUILDING (Cohen's kappa = 0.891) and JOURNEY (Cohen's kappa = 0.836).[15]

5.3.2 Source domain analysis results

We found opinion writers for Beijing, Hong Kong and Taipei newspapers primarily rely on the source domains of LIVING BEING, PHYSICAL OBJECT, COMPETITION, BUILDING and JOURNEY when using keywords related to the target domain of DEMOCRACY. Figure 9.2 compares the frequencies of the top five frequent source domains associated with the target domain of DEMOCRACY in Beijing, Hong Kong and Taipei corpora.

Chi-square results χ^2 (8, N = 119) = 18.060, p = .021 indicate significant differences in the use of the five source domains among the editorial corpora in Beijing, Hong Kong and Taipei corpora. The results of the significant residuals (residual > 2 or < -2) on a tinted background in the table in Appendix 9.2 show that, when conceptualising the target

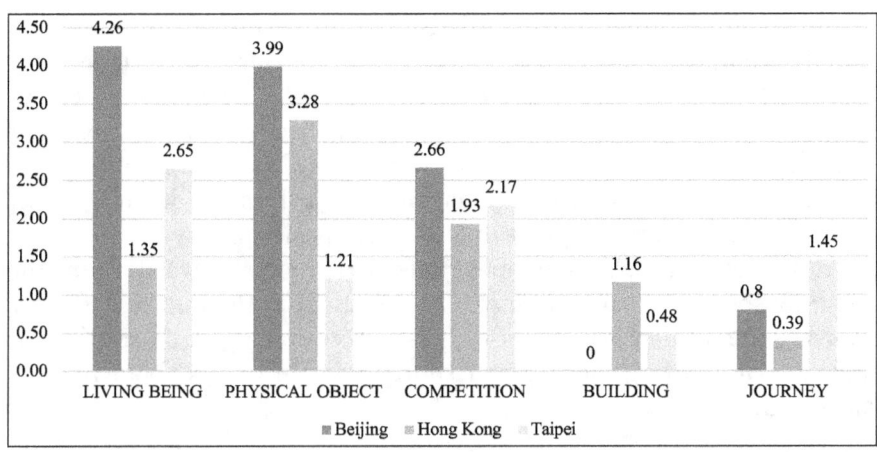

Figure 9.2 Normalised ratios of the top five frequent source domains associated with the target domain of DEMOCRACY in Beijing, Hong Kong and Taipei editorial corpora. A colour copy of this figure is available on the EUP website: edinburghuniversitypress.com/EcologiesofWorldEnglishes

domain of DEMOCRACY, Beijing editorials used fewer keywords from the BUILDING source domain than expected by chance. In contrast, Hong Kong editorials used more keywords from the BUILDING source domain and fewer keywords from the LIVING BEING source domain than expected by chance. Taipei editorials used more keywords from the JOURNEY source domain and fewer keywords from the PHYSICAL OBJECT source domain than expected by chance. Examples (3) and (4) are illustrative for the use of the BUILDING source domain in the conceptualisation of DEMOCRACY in the Hong Kong corpus.

(3) <u>*Consolidating*</u> the **election platforms** of the 35 elected legislators from the five geographical constituencies . . . (*South China Morning Post*, 7 November 2016)

(4) Those self-proclaimed attributes are clearly the political philosophy that he will <u>*base*</u> his **campaign** on. (*The Standard*, 1 November 2016)

The ELECTION PLATFORMS in example (3) were described as A BUILDING that can be 'consolidated'. In example (4), the CHIEF EXECUTIVE CAMPAIGN was conceptualised as A BUILDING that was 'based on' the political philosophy of the candidate. Hong Kong editorial writers used keywords (for example, *consolidate*, *base*) related to the process of constructing a building, emphasising that campaigning and elections are difficult work that takes time. In contrast, the zero occurrences of BUILDING source domain in the Beijing corpus suggests that the editorial writers for Beijing newspapers either avoid or do not need to use this concept, as the current political election system in China does not include direct elections for the large majority of leadership positions.

In Taipei editorials, opinion writers used more keywords from the JOURNEY source domain and fewer keywords from the PHYSICAL OBJECT source domain than expected by chance. Example (5) is illustrative for Taipei writers using the JOURNEY source domain to talk about DEMOCRACY issues.

(5) Hopefully, the grand justice nominees can affect real change . . . or at least help initiate a new round of talks about issues that have been a _hurdle_ on Taiwan's _road_ to **democracy**. (*Taipei Times*, 21 October 2016)

In example (5), DEMOCRACY in Taiwan was conceptualised as a destination on a journey. Example (5) talked about the 'hurdle' on the 'road' to this destination. JOURNEY source domains have been widely used in public discourse to present goodwill and appeal to solidarity from the public (Charteris-Black [2005] 2011). The use of the JOURNEY source domain here emphasises the future goal of 'moving toward a more progressive democracy in Taiwan', reflecting that the democratic system in Taiwan has been established while it needs further improvement by advancing towards an ultimate goal.

The above discussion shows the variations of source–target domain mappings in corpora of three regions with different cultural contexts. The findings suggest that patterns of mappings between a target domain and possible source domains in conceptual metaphors may be an additional way to distinguish between varieties of English within Schneider's lexical-conceptual dimension of cross-cultural analysis.

5.4 Differences in Democracy Metaphor References

In Section 5.1, we found that there was no difference in keyword usages (literal and metaphorical) related to DEMOCRACY. We hypothesised that this might have to do with the fact that during the time period under analysis, the United States election took place and thus the democratic process in America would be widely discussed in Beijing, Hong Kong

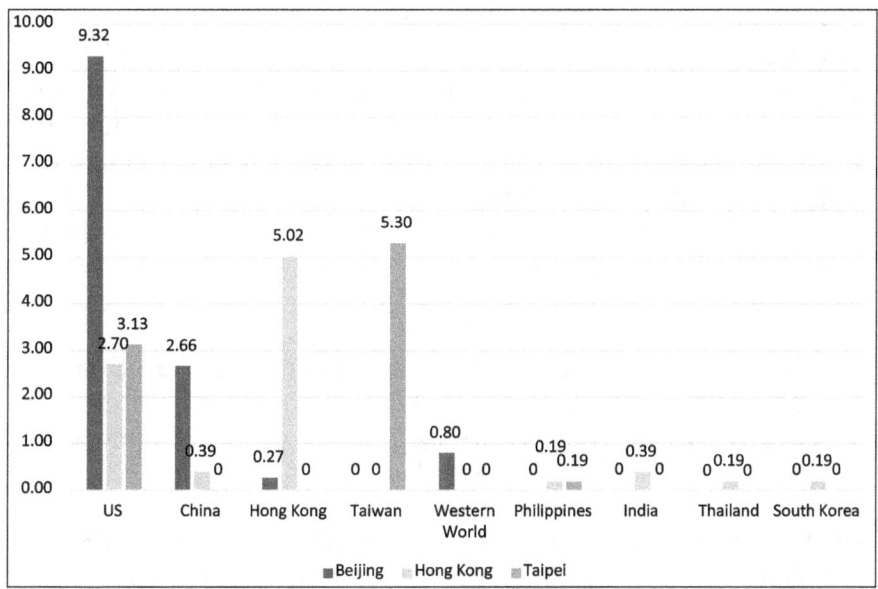

Figure 9.3 Normalised ratios of metaphor references to particular countries in Beijing, Hong Kong and Taipei editorial corpora. A colour copy of this figure is available on the EUP website:
edinburghuniversitypress.com/EcologiesofWorldEnglishes

and Taipei editorials given the importance of the United States as a world power. In this section, we look at which countries or regions are referenced when keywords related to the DEMOCRACY metaphor are used. Figure 9.3 presents the frequencies of the DEMOCRACY metaphor references in Beijing, Hong Kong and Taipei corpora.

Beijing editorials used keywords in metaphorical expressions related to the target domain of DEMOCRACY when talking about the United States more frequently than Hong Kong editorials (NR = 9.32 vs 2.70; LL = +17.32) or Taipei editorials (NR = 9.32 vs 3.13; LL = +12.77).[16] This contrasts with the other two significant differences that we see, where Hong Kong editorials use keywords related to DEMOCRACY to refer to the situation in Hong Kong more often than Beijing (NR = 5.02 vs 0.27; LL = +21.53) and Taipei (NR = 5.02 vs 0.00; LL = +30.58) editorials did, with a similar pattern for Taipei editorials, that is, keywords related to DEMOCRACY were used to signal the situation in Taiwan more often than Beijing (NR = 5.30 vs 0.00; LL = +28.37) and Hong Kong (NR = 5.30 vs 0.00; LL = +35.66). Also, for the Beijing corpora, keywords related to DEMOCRACY were used to talk about the situation in China more often than Hong Kong (NR = 2.66 vs 0.39; LL = +8.70) and Taipei (NR = 2.66 vs 0.00; LL = +14.88). It is understandable that editorials in these cities would focus on the situation in their regions; what is interesting is that neither Hong Kong nor Taipei editorials spent as much time weighing in on the United States election as China did, perhaps because it is a global power seeking to influence the outcome via its soft power, as seen in (6), where the *China Daily* insinuates that Trump may lose the election.

(6) But whether Democrat Hillary Clinton or Republican Donald Trump wins the election, one thing is certain – that the presidential election **campaign** *has widened the rift* in American society. (*China Daily*, 7 November 2016)

Another point is that in the 10 examples where keywords were used metaphorically in Beijing editorials to refer to China, only one example had to do with democratic elections in China and this example was to argue against it; instead, editorial writers focused on initiatives led by the government, particularly those related to rooting out corruption. In addition, it is interesting to note that when Beijing editorials discuss elections and democracy in the United States, the metaphors used occur within a negative (vs neutral) context 30 out of 35 times. However, an analysis of the examples used indicates that this is not necessarily due to an aversion on the part of the editorial writers to the democratic process, although some examples could certainly be read that way. A possible alternative interpretation has to do with the fact that the 2016 US presidential election was particularly rancorous and the negative context surrounding the metaphor usage is limited to the negativity in the election itself.

In sum, the data above show that Beijing editorials referred to the US democracy most often, while Hong Kong and Taipei editorial writers primarily referred to the democracy of their own countries. Both Hong Kong and Taipei editorial writers secondarily talked about US democracy. This is not surprising considering the time frame of the corpus is one month before and two weeks after the 2016 US presidential election. In addition, the Beijing editorials also mentioned the Western world, for example the democracy in European countries; however, Hong Kong and Taipei corpora have no references to European politics. Hong Kong and Taipei instead talked about the democracy in the Philippines,

Thailand, South Korea or India, which Beijing does not mention during this time period.

6. CONCLUSION

This chapter has examined the differences in how abstract concepts are conceptualised in editorials in English-language newspapers published in Hong Kong, Beijing and Taipei. Using three independently compiled English corpora of editorials from these three cities within a parallel time frame, we argued that the pattern of source domain usage found for an abstract target domain has provided insight into the lexical-conceptual dimension proposed by Schneider (this volume) as a second layer of cross-cultural analysis given that we found similarities and differences in DEMOCRACY metaphors which reflect the socio-political contexts for each city.

Regarding attention to the general topic of democracy, editorials in Beijing, Hong Kong and Taipei discussed the topics of democracy with similar frequencies during this time period. Furthermore, we found evidence that Beijing editorials referred to US democracy more often compared with Hong Kong and Taipei editorials. This explains why the three regions have similar frequencies on the subject of democracy even though currently there is no direct election system in China (Saich 2015).

Moreover, in terms of conceptual metaphor use, we found significant variations in the metaphorisation of 'democracy' in editorials in Beijing, Hong Kong and Taipei. Beijing editorial writers used more metaphors and fewer literal expressions, while Hong Kong editorial writers used more literal than metaphorical expressions than expected by chance when addressing the 'democracy' issue.

In addition, in terms of source domain use, the editorial writers in Beijing, Hong Kong and Taipei primarily rely on metaphorical uses of keywords from the five source domains of LIVING BEING, PHYSICAL OBJECT, COMPETITION, BUILDING and JOURNEY. We observed variations on the source domains' use among the three regions and hypothesised that these variations reflect the differences found in the current political situations in the three regions. Zero occurrence of the BUILDING source domain in Beijing editorial writing may reflect the fact that China does not have a direct electoral system. The more frequent use of keywords related to 'building construction' under the BUILDING source domain in

Hong Kong, on the other hand, reflects the discussion surrounding the election system in Hong Kong (for example, the elections of the Chief Executives and Legislative members). Taipei editorial writers applied more keywords referring to 'future goals' under the JOURNEY source domain, indicating a well-established democratic system in Taiwan, with a clear future focus. We thus found evidence of source–target domain mapping variations in corpora with different cultural contexts, which we suggest is an additional way to distinguish between varieties of English within Schneider's lexical-conceptual dimension of cross-cultural analysis.

Lastly, contrasts were also found regarding what country or region was being referenced when DEMOCRACY metaphors were used. Beijing editorials referred to US democracy most often while Hong Kong editorials and Taipei editorial writers primarily made reference to their own situations and only secondarily talked about US democracy. Given that the time period selected was directly before and after the US presidential election of 2016, the focus of the Beijing editorials on the election is understandable as the editorial writers may have hoped to influence readers' opinions about the democratic process in the United States.

Of course, given the limited size of the corpus under study, these findings should be considered preliminary. Future work is needed to expand the time period under study so as to gain more insight into each paper's views on democracy at different points in time. In addition, we want to be careful not to take a simplistic view of metaphor as a straightforward reflection of culture at a given point in time. As Deignan (2003) points out, metaphoric expressions may result from subtle, diachronic differences in the cultural-ideological background in which a conceptual metaphor functions. We suggest that future work that examines which source domains are used for a given target domain (that is, Mapping Principles, Ahrens 2010) on larger corpora will assist in noting these subtle changes. Moreover, we suggest that examining the keywords used metaphorically within a given source domain may also serve as indicator terms that may be useful in distinguishing between varieties of English (Schneider 2018: 101).

Appendix 9.1 Cross-tabulation of cities and metaphor/literal DEMOCRACY

Cities		Metaphor	Literal	Total	Statistics
Beijing	Count	49	44	93	χ^2 (2, N = 340) =
	Expected count	36.1	56.9	93.0	10.570, p = .005
	Adjusted residual	3.2	−3.2		
Hong Kong	Count	47	98	145	
	Expected count	56.3	88.7	145.0	
	Adjusted residual	−2.1	2.1		
Taipei	Count	36	66	102	
	Expected count	39.6	62.4	102.0	
	Adjusted residual	−.9	.9		
Total	Count	132	208	340	
	Expected count	132.0	208.0	340.0	

Cities * metaphorical/literal democracy cross-tabulation[a]

[a] * represents the association or effect between the variables 'cities' and 'metaphorical/literal democracy'.

Appendix 9.2 Cross-tabulation of cities and source domains

Cities * source domains cross-tabulation[a]

			Source domains					
			LIVING BEING	PHYSICAL OBJECT	COMPETITION	BUILDING	JOURNEY	Total	Statistics
Cities	Beijing	Count	16	15	10	0	3	44	χ^2 (8, N = 119) = 18.060, p = .021
		Expected count	12.6	13.7	10.7	3	4.1	44	
		Adjusted residual	1.4	0.5	−0.3	−2.2	−0.7		
	Hong Kong	Count	7	17	10	6	2	42	
		Expected count	12	13.1	10.2	2.8	3.9	42	
		Adjusted residual	−2.1	1.6	−0.1	2.4	−1.2		
	Taipei	Count	11	5	9	2	6	33	
		Expected count	9.4	10.3	8	2.2	3.1	33	
		Adjusted residual	0.7	−2.3	0.5	−0.2	2.1		
Total		Count	34	37	29	8	11	119	
		Expected count	34	37	29	8	11	119	

[a] * represents the association or effect between the variables 'cities' and 'metaphorical/literal democracy'.

ACKNOWLEDGEMENTS

Both authors would like to acknowledge the support of the Research Center for Professional Communication in English at The Hong Kong Polytechnic University and the first author would also like to acknowledge the support of a research grant (#12600317) from the General Research Fund of the Hong Kong University Grants Council. The authors also would like to thank Mandy Lee for initiating the corpus and Serina Cheung for developing and finalising the corpus.

NOTES

1. By convention, conceptual metaphors are written in small capitals in the form of X IS (A) Y, where X stands for the target domain and Y stands for the source domain.
2. There has been a great deal of discussion in the literature as to what extent these mappings are active in online processing (Gibbs 2006, 2011; Steen 2011); however, for the purposes of this paper, what is crucial is the assumption that these mappings do indicate a systematic cognitive patterning between the two conceptual domains.
3. See Huang et al. (2019) for further information about how children in Hong Kong, China and Taiwan are taught to read and write in Chinese.
4. China considers Taiwan to be part of China, and in 1992 China and Taiwan agreed that there was 'one China' and that they could each hold different viewpoints regarding who represented China (Xu 2001).
5. The Alibaba group, which publishes *South China Morning Post*, holds a position aligned closely with the Beijing government (Barboza 2015). *The Standard* is owned by the Sing Tao News Corporation, which supported the British colonial government before the 1997 reunification of Hong Kong with China and then claimed to be a staunch supporter of the Beijing government after 1997 (Yu 2014).
6. The One-China Principle states that 'Taiwan is an inalienable part of China' and the Central People's Government is 'the sole legitimate government representing the People's Republic of China' (PRC White Paper 2000).

7. The Google search function allows you to search for the occurrence of a specific word within a customised date range on a website. An example of a Google search is 'editorials site: chinadaily.com.cn'.
8. On 15 May 2017, the newspaper ceased its print edition, and the website discontinued in October 2017. The website for the digital newspaper currently belongs to NOWnews Group. All the articles extracted for our corpus using WiseNews Database are from the old website, which is no longer accessible. However, the links that were saved in the corpus file are still valid. The original articles can be viewed using these links: <https://www.taiwannews.com.tw/en/news/3161858>, <https://en.wikipedia.org/wiki/The_China_Post> and <https://www.linkedin.com/company/the-china-post-nownews> (all last accessed 8 January 2021).
9. 'Ballot', 'poll', and 'referendum' were also searched for originally but together made up less than 10 per cent of the total instances found and were not included in subsequent analyses.
10. Log-likelihood was calculated using the online Log-likelihood and Effect Size calculator at <http://ucrel.lancs.ac.uk/llwizard.html> (last accessed 8 January 2021). According to the scale for the significance of log-likelihood values provided on the website, items with a log-likelihood value over 3.84 (positive or negative) are significantly overused (+) or underused (-) in the corpus at the level of $p < 0.05$. We used an alpha level of .05 for all statistical tests.
11. See all the data and analyses on the Open Science Framework, available at at <https://cutt.ly/metaphor_sinosphere> (last accessed 8 January 2021).
12. Both chi-square and log-likelihood test can be used in comparing unbalanced sized corpora (Rayson et al. 2004).
13. Adjusted residual is the standardised residual divided by the standard deviation of all residuals. It reflects the degree of deviation of the observed frequencies from the expected frequencies and thus the significance in each cell. Unlike the standardised residual, the adjusted residual takes into account the overall size of the sample to ensure a fairer indication of the significance of the differences between the observed count and the expected count.
14. A significant association is one where the observed frequencies deviate far from the expected frequencies. In a normal distribution, 95 per cent of the values are within the mean plus/minus two standard deviations. If the value of the adjusted residual is more than +2

or less than -2, the probability of observing this value by chance will be less than 5 per cent; thus, the residual is significant.
15. All the data and analyses can be found on the Open Science Framework at <https://cutt.ly/metaphor_sinosphere> (last accessed 8 January 2021).
16. We used log-likelihood here as the chi-square approximation is appropriate only if 'no more than 20% of the expected counts are less than 5 and all individual expected counts are 1 or greater' (Yates et al. 1999: 734).

REFERENCES

Ahrens, K. (2010). Mapping principles for conceptual metaphors. In G. Low, Z. Todd, A. Deignan and L. Cameron (Eds.), *Researching and applying metaphor in the real world* (pp. 185–207). John Benjamins.

Ahrens, K. and Jiang, M. (2020). Source domain verification using corpus-based tools. *Metaphor and Symbol, 35*(1), 43–55.

Ahrens, K. and Zeng, H. (2017). Conceptualizing EDUCATION in Hong Kong and China. In *Proceedings of the 31st Pacific Asia Conference on Language, Information and Computation (PACLIC 31)* (pp. 303–11). University of the Philippines Cebu. <https://www.aclweb.org/anthology/Y17-1041.pdf> (last accessed 8 January 2021).

Barboza, D. (2015). Alibaba buying South China Morning Post, aiming to influence media. *The New York Times*, 11 December. <https://www.nytimes.com/2015/12/12/business/dealbook/alibaba-scmp-south-china-morning-post.html> (last accessed 8 January 2021).

Bas, M. (2019). A crosslinguistic and corpus based critical metaphor analysis of democracy [Paper presentation]. Metaphor Festival, 28–31 August, University of Amsterdam, Netherlands.

Charteris-Black, J. (2011). *Politicians and rhetoric: The persuasive power of metaphor*. Palgrave Macmillan. (Original work published 2005).

Deignan, A. (2003). Metaphorical expressions and culture: An indirect link. *Metaphor and Symbol, 18*(4), 255–71.

Fell, D. (2011). *Government and politics in Taiwan*. Routledge.

Fong, B. C. (2019). *Hong Kong politics: In search of autonomy, democracy and governance*. Springer.

Gibbs Jr, R. W. (2006). Metaphor interpretation as embodied simulation. *Mind and Language, 21*(3), 434–58.

Gibbs Jr, R. W. (2011). Evaluating conceptual metaphor theory. *Discourse Processes, 48*(8), 529–62.

Guo, S. H. (2012). Yuyan yu yishi xingtai: Taiwan meiti lunshu fenxi [Language and ideology: An analysis of Taiwan media discourse]. National Tsing Hua University Institutional Repository. <http://archive.ph/20120712171100/http://nthur.lib.nthu.edu.tw/bitstream/987654321/10698/1/912411H007023.pdf> (last accessed 1 February 2021).

Huang, C.-R., Ahrens, K., Becker, T., Llamas, R., Tam, K. F. and Meisterernst, B. (2019). The role of language and linguistic devices in literary and artistic expressions. In C.-R. Huang, Z. Jing-Schmidt and B. Meisterernst (Eds.), *The Routledge handbook of Chinese applied linguistics* (pp. 237–55). Routledge.

Kachru, B. (Ed.). (1992). *The other tongue: English across cultures*. University of Illinois Press.

Kövecses, Z. (2003). Language, figurative thought, and cross-cultural comparison. *Metaphor and symbol, 18*(4), 311–20.

Kövecses, Z. (2010). Metaphor and culture. *Acta Universitatis Sapientiae, Philologica, 2*(2), 197–220.

Lakoff, G. (1993). The contemporary theory of metaphor. In A. Ortony (Ed.), *Metaphor and thought* (2nd ed.; pp. 202–50). Cambridge University Press.

Lakoff, G. and Johnson, M. (2003). *Metaphors we live by*. University of Chicago Press. (Original work published 1980).

Landis, J. R. and Koch, G. G. (1977). The measurement of observer agreement for categorical data. *Biometric, 33*(1), 159–74.

Lin, J., Shi, D., Jiang, M. and Huang, C.-R. (2019). Variations in World Chineses. In C.-R. Huang, Z. Jing-Schmidt and B. Meisterernst (Eds.), *The Routledge handbook of Chinese applied linguistics*. Routledge.

Mukherjee, J. and Bernaisch, T. (2015). Cultural keywords in context: A pilot study of linguistic acculturation in South Asian Englishes. In P. Collins (Ed.), *Grammatical change in English world-wide* (pp. 411–35). Benjamins.

Olavarría de Ersson, E. O. and Shaw, P. (2003). Verb complementation patterns in Indian standard English. *English World-Wide, 24*(2), 137–61.

Pragglejaz Group. (2007). MIP: A method for identifying metaphorically used words in discourse. *Metaphor and Symbol, 22*(1), 1–39.

PRC White Paper. (2000). The One-China Principle and the Taiwan Issue. The Taiwan Affairs Office and the Information Office of the State Council, 21 February 2000. *China Report, 36*(2), 277–92. <https://doi.org/10.1177/000944550003600211> (last accessed 8 January 2021).

Rayson, P., Berridge, D. and Francis, B. (2004). Extending the Cochran rule for the comparison of word frequencies between corpora. In G. Purnelle, C. Fairon and A. Dister (Eds.), *Le poids des mots: Proceedings of the 7th International Conference on Statistical Analysis of Textual Data (JADT 2004)* (Vol. II; pp. 926–36). Presses universitaires de Louvain.

Saich, T. (2015). *Governance and politics of China*. Palgrave Macmillan.

Schneider, E. W. (2018). The interface between cultures and corpora: Tracing reflections and manifestations. *ICAME Journal, 42*(1), 97–132.

Scott, M. (2012). WordSmith Tools (Version 6) [Computer software]. Lexical Analysis Software.

Simó, J. (2011). Metaphors of blood in American English and Hungarian: A cross-linguistic corpus investigation. *Journal of Pragmatics, 43*(12), 2897–910.

Steen, G. (2011). Metaphor, language, and discourse processes. *Discourse Processes, 48*(8), 585–91.

Steen, G., Dorst, A. G., Herrmann, J. B., Kaal, A., Krennmayr, T. and Pasma, T. (2010). *A method for linguistic metaphor identification: From MIP to MIPVU* (Vol. 14). John Benjamins.

Stefanowitsch, A. (2006). Corpus-based approaches to metaphor and metonymy. In A. Stefanowitsch and S. T. Gries (Eds.), *Corpus-based approaches to metaphor and metonymy* (pp. 1–16). Mouton de Gruyter.

Wang, H. (2009). Divergent news representations of Lien Chan's visit to China: A corpus-based lexical comparison between the *China Post* and the *China Daily*. *Journal of Asian Pacific Communication, 19*(2), 179–98.

Wimmer, R. D. and Dominick, J. R. (2013). *Mass media research: An introduction* (10th ed.). Wadsworth Cengage Learning.

Xu, S. (2001). The 1992 consensus: A review and assessment of consultations between the association for relations across the Taiwan strait and the straits exchange foundation. *American Foreign Policy Interest, 23*(3), 121–40.

Yates, D., Moore, D. and McCabe, G. (1999). *The practice of statistics*. W. H. Freeman.

Yu, J. M. (2014). Hong Kong newspapers, pro- and anti-Beijing, weigh in on protest. *The New York Times*, 6 October. <https://sinosphere.

blogs.nytimes.com/2014/10/06/hong-kong-newspapers-pro-and-anti-beijing-weigh-in-on-protests/> (last accessed 8 January 2021).

Yu, N. (1995). Metaphorical expressions of anger and happiness in English and Chinese. *Metaphor and Symbolic Activity*, *10*(2), 59–92.

Yu, N. (2000). Figurative uses of finger and palm in Chinese and English. *Metaphor and Symbol*, *15*(3), 159–75.

Yu, N. (2004). The eyes for sight and mind. *Journal of Pragmatics*, *36*(4), 663–86.

Zeng, H., Tay, D. and Ahrens, K. (2020). A multifactorial analysis of metaphors in political discourse: Gendered influence in Hong Kong political speeches. *Metaphor and the Social World*, *10*(1), 139–66.

CHAPTER 10

L1 Singapore English: The Influence of Ethnicity and Input

Sarah Buschfeld

1. INTRODUCTION

Singapore English (SingE) is one of the most extensively researched postcolonial varieties of English. Many contributions have approached and described it as one of the most important and furthest developed second-language (L2) varieties of English. However, it has experienced important changes in status and usage conditions throughout the last decades. Most importantly – and unprecedentedly in postcolonial contexts – it has developed from a second-language (L2) variety to first language (L1) status. Even though this change has often and long been noted in the World Englishes literature (for example, Bolton and Ng 2014; Gupta 1994; Lim 2007; Tan 2014), it has never been investigated in a comprehensive empirical fashion until recently. Buschfeld (2020a) is the first large-scale study that offers (1) a detailed account of the usage conditions, namely, the children's acquisitional background and the use of English in various domains of their daily lives; (2) a feature screening of characteristics found in the child data collected by the author; and (3) quantitative analyses of the acquisition and realisation of two morpho-syntactic features (that is, subject pronouns (zero vs realised)) and past tense marking (marked vs unmarked) and a set of phonological features (vowel quality and length in the lexical sets KIT and FLEECE and FOOT and GOOSE (Wells 1982)).

The present paper draws on a selection of the findings from this original study and shows how Singaporean children combine linguistic elements drawn from the different input varieties available in the sociolinguistic ecology of Singapore (most prominently colloquial and standard varieties of L2 SingE, but also British and American English). In addition, the paper illustrates how both inter- as well as intra-speaker variation guide the acquisition and use of L1 SingE. I highlight the role of the children's ethnicity as well as of the linguistic input (provided by parents, caretakers and so on) they receive in explaining this variation and discuss what the findings suggest about the development and status of L1 SingE.

I first give a brief introduction to the historical context and the development of English in Singapore (Section 2) as well as to the methodology (Section 3). In the main part of this chapter (Sections 3.1 and 3.2), I present and discuss results illustrating the linguistic variability in L1 SingE pertaining to the influence of the children's ethnicity. I further discuss which impact can be attributed to cross-linguistic transfer from the children's other L1, to the input provided by the parents and caretakers in the children's home environment and, for the older children, also via the school system, and to further socio-psychological factors such as language attitudes. I finally address the socio-cultural impact on these linguistic forms in light of the three nexuses, that is, 'intrinsic connections between language forms and cultures' discussed by Schneider (this volume).

2. ENGLISH IN SINGAPORE: SOME FACTS AND FIGURES

Singapore is a densely populated, sovereign city-state in Southeast Asia, located between Malaysia and Indonesia, with a total of 709.2km^2 of land area and approximately 5,866,139 inhabitants (estimates as of July 2021; CIA 2020). It has experienced a comparatively short but intense history of changing hands and immigration, which has led to a high ethnic and linguistic diversity. According to 2018 estimates, the majority of Singapore's inhabitants are of Chinese ethnic origin (74.3 per cent); 13.4 per cent are of Malay and 9 per cent of Indian descent; and then there is a group commonly summarised as being of 'other' ethnic origin (3.2 per cent). As the result of British foundation and colonisation (1819–1965), English is one of the four official languages of the country, spoken alongside a variety of other mostly Chinese and Indian languages and dialects. However, due to Singapore's unique language policy of 'English-based bilingualism' (Tickoo 1996: 438, in Schneider 2007: 153), the ethnic neutrality of English, and then, in more recent times, forces of ever-increasing globalisation (see also, for example, Coupland

2010; Blommaert 2010), English has become deeply entrenched in Singapore, which, in the last three to four decades, has led to a gradual increase in first language speakers of SingE. In fact, as of 2015 estimates, English is now the most widespread language in Singaporean homes, spoken by about 36.9 per cent of the population. In this function, it has even overtaken Mandarin, which is spoken by about 34.9 per cent of the population. Other Chinese dialects (including Hokkien, Cantonese, Teochew and Hakka) are spoken by 12.2 per cent, Malay by 10.7 per cent, Tamil by 3.3 per cent, and a group of minority languages classified as 'other' is spoken by 2 per cent of the population (CIA 2020). Further census data report an increase in use of English as a home language for five- to nine-year-olds from 34.1 per cent in 2000 to 51.5 per cent in 2010 (Census of Population 2000, 2010) and we can safely assume that the 2020 report will reveal even higher numbers.

The linguistic situation of English is often described as diglossic (in particular in earlier accounts, most prominently Gupta 1994) though it has been argued it is better characterised as a lectal continuum or as the use of more or less basilectal features (thus colloquial SingE/Singlish), chosen according to speaker and situation (for example, Buschfeld 2020a: ch. 2.3.2; Leimgruber 2013: 20–1; Alsagoff 2007). Conceptualising the spectrum of SingE might constitute a still 'unresolved debate' (Wee 2004: 1022–3) though most of these recent approaches convincingly point towards the weak spots of the strictly diglossic approach. However one approaches this question, it seems quite uncontroversial that the linguistic ecology of Singapore is characterised not only by the coexistence of different languages and dialects of the Chinese and Indian languages, but also by a variety of 'versions' of the English language. On the one hand, British English (BrE) is strongly represented and in many ways extra-normatively admired and propagated in Singapore as the historical input variety and 'proper English'. It has long been the model of norm orientation to which the standard forms of SingE (often conceptualised as Singapore Standard English) are highly similar. American English (AmE), on the other hand, has become the variety currently exerting major influence on the sociolinguistic situation in many parts of the world and this has also had linguistic repercussions on SingE linguistic repertoires (for example, Brown et al. 2000; Deterding 2007; Tan 2016). Together with the existence of more or less colloquial realisations and variants of SingE (for example, the simultaneous existence of realised subject pronouns and zero variants or the overt marking of past tense contexts vs local forms or zero marking on verbs) this creates a highly variable input for the children acquiring English as L1 in Singapore these days.[1] The following sections will illustrate how that surfaces in the linguistic productions by Singaporean children, which are characterised by strong inter- but even intra-speaker variability between BrE and AmE on the one hand and more or less formal realisations of SingE on the other.

3. THE ACQUISITION OF ENGLISH AS A FIRST LANGUAGE IN SINGAPORE: THE INFLUENCE OF ETHNICITY AND CROSS-LINGUISTIC INFLUENCE

The following sections present data and results relating to the acquisition, usage conditions and linguistic characteristics of L1 SingE. The features analysed quantitatively, namely, the acquisition and realisation of subject pronouns, past tense marking, and vowel contrasts between KIT and FLEECE and FOOT and GOOSE, were chosen according to different criteria, most importantly the existence of a local variant of the feature in the adult input the children receive (here: zero subject pronouns, missing or other local past tense marking strategies, merger of KIT–FLEECE and FOOT–GOOSE).

The data were collected in August 2014 and come from 30 bi- or multilingual Singaporean children aged 2;5 to 12;1, 20 of Chinese ethnicity, 9 of Indian descent, and one of mixed ancestry (Malaysian-Turkish).[2] The data were elicited systematically in video-recorded task-directed dialogue between researcher and child, consisting of several parts: the past tense probe of the Rice/Wexler Test of Early Grammatical Impairment (Rice and Wexler 2001), a story retelling task, elicited narratives, and free interaction. In the following, I present a selection of qualitative as well as quantitative findings illustrating that much of the children's production shows a high degree of intra- as well as inter-speaker variation, the latter in particular motivated by the children's ethnicity.

3.1 Intra- and Inter-speaker Variability in L1 Child SingE

3.1.1 Examples from the phonological domain

The first set of examples (examples (1)–(13)) illustrate intra- and inter-speaker variability in the phonological domain. In general, L1 child SingE is largely similar to BrE in pronunciation. This basically corresponds to what has been reported for the adult L2 variety, especially at the more acrolectal end of the spectrum (for example, Brown 1988; Tay 1982). However, as reported earlier, AmE is clearly making inroads and constitutes one of many input varieties feeding into the feature pool from which the children apparently 'pick and mix'. Most children, indeed, do not show consistent pronunciation patterns, which is why pronunciation varies between and within individual children. Paru,[3] for example, shows a clear orientation towards a BrE pronunciation most of the time, but sometimes also produces AmE patterns. Compare the following examples:

(1) Paru (12;1, female, Indian): The boy has painted ['peɪntəd].
(2) Paru (12;1, female, Indian): She ice-skated ['aɪsskeɪtɪd].

Rosie, too, shows variable pronunciation, clearly AmE rhotic in example (3):

(3) Rosie (6;3, female, Indian): Door [dɔːʳ][4]! A door [doːr]? [=!laughs]

Variation even shows in immediately successive utterances of the very same kind by the same child, as the following example illustrates:

(4) Love (2;8, female, Chinese): Frog. # He can jumping in the water ['wɔːtə].
Sarah: [=!laughs]
Love (2;8, female, Chinese): [/] can jumping in the water ['wɔːtə].

The following examples illustrate that this is an overarching phenomenon, not restricted to a limited set of features or a few of the children only:

(5) Rosie (6;3, female, Indian): Socks [sɒks]!
(6) Rosie (6;3, female, Indian): Oh my God [gɑːd]!
(7) Lisa (8;6, female, Chinese): She might not [nɒt] have time to play [. . .]
(8) Maggie (4;11, female, Chinese): You watch [wɑːtʃ], we play.
(9) Qi (5;8, female, Chinese): Also got [gɒt] spider and a mouse.
(10) Stella (6;9, female, Chinese): [. . .] then we dance [dɑːns] and play, right?

(11) Stella (6;9, female, Chinese): We are going to dance [dæns], okay?
(12) Pinky Pie (5;6, female, Chinese): [. . .] until I ask [ɑːs] him the last [lɑːs] time [. . .]
(13) Pinky Pie (5;6, female, Chinese): She plant [plænt] all the flowers.

In a similar vein, Table 10.1 illustrates both intra- as well as interspeaker variability in the realisation of vowel length differences between the lexical sets KIT and FLEECE and FOOT and GOOSE. The four vowels were elicited by a picture naming task and vowel length was subsequently measured in Praat (Boersma and Weenink 2018) in milliseconds. Finally, the average length differences between KIT and FLEECE and FOOT and GOOSE were calculated for each child.

As Table 10.1 shows, the average differences between FLEECE and KIT in the individual children range from 4ms (Xu) to 199ms (Isla and Pinky Pie); differences between GOOSE and FOOT range from -1ms difference (Mechelle) to 152ms (Ana). This translates to a difference of 195ms and 153ms between the children with the lowest mean differences and the two children with the highest and attests a quite strong variation between the children. The other children distribute across the whole continuum, but Xu is the only child that does not clearly differentiate long and short FLEECE and KIT and GOOSE and FOOT; Manikandan and Mechelle do not employ the GOOSE–FOOT split. This was measured against a yardstick of 50ms as suggested by Labov and Baranowski (2006: 223) as a minimum benchmark that 'can effectively preserve a phonemic distinction'. The results therefore suggest that L1 child SingE is not characterised by a merger of the respective two sets, except for the few cases reported above – even though the merger is often reported for L2 SingE (for example, Deterding 2007: 25–7; Lim 2004: 20–2; Wee 2004: 1024–6).

Table 10.1 further illustrates that in the case of vowel length the heterogeneity found between the children does not seem to be governed by one of the two major sociolinguistic variables under observation, namely, ethnicity or MLU/age.[5] Thus – even though variationist sociolinguists ever since the early days of William Labov (for example, Labov 1972) have shown that variation is never fully random but constrained by both linguistic and non-linguistic factors – differences in average vowel length appear rather eclectic in the present data. What is more, vowel length is by no means consistent within the individual child; that is, children seldom strictly follow one or the other pattern of realisa-

Table 10.1 A comparison of average length differences between KIT–FLEECE and FOOT–GOOSE

Child	Length difference KIT–FLEECE (ms)	Length difference FOOT–GOOSE (ms)
Xu (7;1/f/C)[a]	4	41
Ben (8;0/m/C)	53	67
Ana (3;8/f/I)	54	152
Paru (12;1/f/I)	62	146
Lisa (8;6/f/C)	68	85
Stella (6;9/f/C)	69	72
Rosie (6;3/f/I)	72	132
Manikandan (7;11/m/I)	74	41
GorGor (8;0/m/C)	86	119
Jun (5;0/m/C)	95	124
Kabs (5;4/m/I)	99	134
Mechelle (7;0/f/I)	108	−1
JieJie (5;0/f/C)	116	103
Nithin (8;9/m/I)	121	98
Maggie (4;11/f/C)	124	73
Qi (5;8/f/C)	136	94
Pinky Pie (5;6/f/C)	199	133
Isla (5;2/f/C)	199	98

[a] Ages are given in the format years;months; f = female, m = male; C = Chinese ethnicity, I = Indian ethnicity.

tion, associated with the standard or non-standard variants (the latter being characterised by reduced vowel length as discussed earlier in the section).

3.1.2 Examples from the morphosyntactic domain

Looking into a set of selected examples from the quantitative analysis of the acquisition and realisation of subject pronouns and past tense marking reveals a similar degree of heterogeneity between the children. Before presenting the quantitative results, I provide a brief overview of the features under investigation.

In general, L1 child SingE is characterised by the variable use of overt and zero subject pronouns of different types: referential *I*, *you*, *he*, *she* and so on and different types of *it* (expletive, referential, contextual referential).[6] Consider the following examples:

(14) Sarah: [. . .] And this guy is picking some flowers for his mummy # and h&+/.
Isla: Now Ø [HE] is done picking the flower.
(15) Stella: Oh, Enen, Ø [IT] is your turn. [. . .]

In a similar vein, L1 child SingE is characterised by variable past tense marking, displaying a comparatively high rate of unmarked forms. The following examples illustrate this:

(16) Jun: Then he **wanted** to climb a ladder to a chimney. Then the big bad wolf **is** in the pot. Then all the water **splash** and the carrot and the onion.
(17) Kabs: but he couldn't. And then he **took** a ladder and **climb** up the [/] the chimeney [=chimney].
(18) Xu: He **do** a bird house and then he # [/] and then he # **build finish** for the birds.

Example (18) is particularly interesting since it illustrates a very specific SingE past tense marking strategy (though one also found in Pacific English contact varieties). As the result of cross-linguistic influence from Chinese and also to be found in the linguistic input the children receive from their parents and caretakers and so on (cf. Bao 2005: 248–9; Leimgruber 2013: 80), past tense is sometimes marked by *finish*. Chinese employs a very similar strategy, namely, V+*wán-(le)*, with *wán* translating to *finish* and *le* being the prototypical Chinese particle indicating completeness of an action. Consider example (19) and its gloss:

(19) wǒ xǐ-wán-(le)   shǒu   cái   chī   dōngxi.
     I wash-finish-(asp) hand only eat things
     'I only eat after I have washed my hands'
     (example from Bao 2005: 48)

As Figures 10.1 and 10.2 illustrate, both the results for subject pronoun realisation and the past tense marking results once more show important differences between the individual children. The use of zero subjects ranges from 0 per cent to 50 per cent and the use of SingE past tense marking strategies even from 0 per cent to 100 per cent. The frequencies of the variants under observation (that is, the use of zero subject pronouns and SingE bare verbs and the LEXV+*finish* strategy) were calculated manually and were measured against the use of the 'standard' English variants (that is, overt subjects and past tense marking via the regular English ending -*ed* or via one of the irregular strategies).

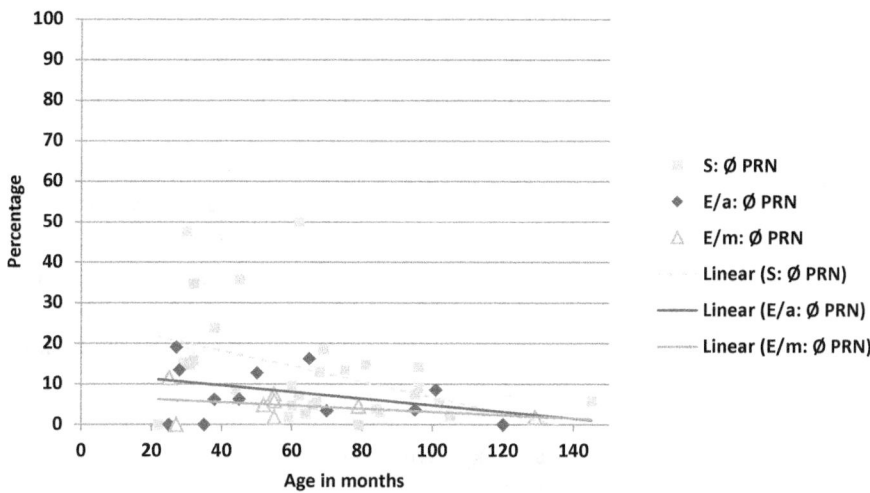

Figure 10.1 Zero subjects by individual participant (Singaporean, English–ancestral, English–migrant/mixed). A colour copy of this figure is available on the EUP website: edinburghuniversitypress.com/EcologiesofWorldEnglishes

The Singapore children's data (S) was compared with data collected from monolingual and bi-/multilingual control groups from England (E) to account for the specific characteristics of L1 SingE and to highlight its unique, local and independent character.[7]

The two E groups are labelled 'ancestral' (abbreviated to E/a) and 'migrant/mixed' (abbreviated to E/m). The children in the first group are growing up in families where both parents were born and raised in England and where English is spoken as the only home language; the children in the second group are growing up in families of mixed parentage, that is, at least one of the parents is of non-English descent and the families are bi- or even multilingual.

When comparing the results for the three groups, a general decline in the use of zero pronouns (Figure 10.1) and 'non-standard' past tense realisations (Figure 10.2) can be observed for all three (compare the linear trendlines). However, there are important differences in the acquisitional 'outcomes', that is, in the realisation of subject pronouns and past tense marking in the older children. For the children growing up in England, zero subject rates and bare verbs drop to zero, which is in line with the research literature on the acquisition of BrE and AmE (for example, Valian 2016; Wexler 1994). What is more, the results clearly

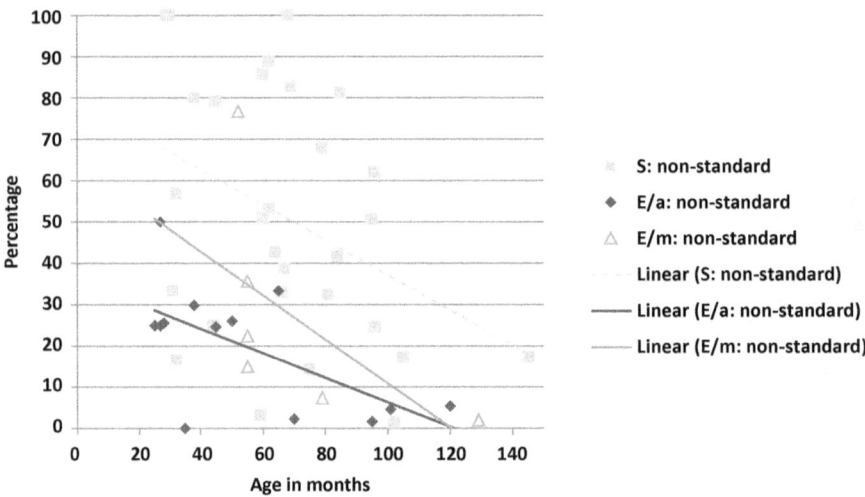

Figure 10.2 Non-standard realisations past tense marking (all types) by individual participant. A colour copy of this figure is available on the EUP website: edinburghuniversitypress.com/EcologiesofWorldEnglishes

show that individual variation in Singapore is much higher than in the two groups of children from England.

However, the variability observed is indeed not as random as it appears at first sight. The following findings (Figures 10.3 and 10.4) illustrate how the use of linguistic variants in L1 child SingE is constrained by ethnicity. Figure 10.3 illustrates the results for the use of zero vs realised referential *it* of all three types, namely, referential *it*, expletive *it*, and contextual referential *it*. The three uses are conflated here since earlier investigations of the influence of pronoun type on the realisation of subject pronouns have shown that all three types are dropped at similar rates.

As was found for the whole range of pronoun types investigated, the results for *it* illustrate that the Indian group produces much lower rates of zero subject pronouns than the Chinese group.[8] Statistical testing by means of mixed-effects models, random forests and conditional inference trees has confirmed that ethnicity is a significant predictor for the realisation of subject pronouns, namely, significant differences exist between the two groups. However, there is no straightforward explanation in terms of cross-linguistic differences and influence for this finding since the languages in the children's linguistic repertoires (Chinese and Indian) are all languages that allow for zero subjects, even if licensed by different semantic and syntactic principles. Whether and

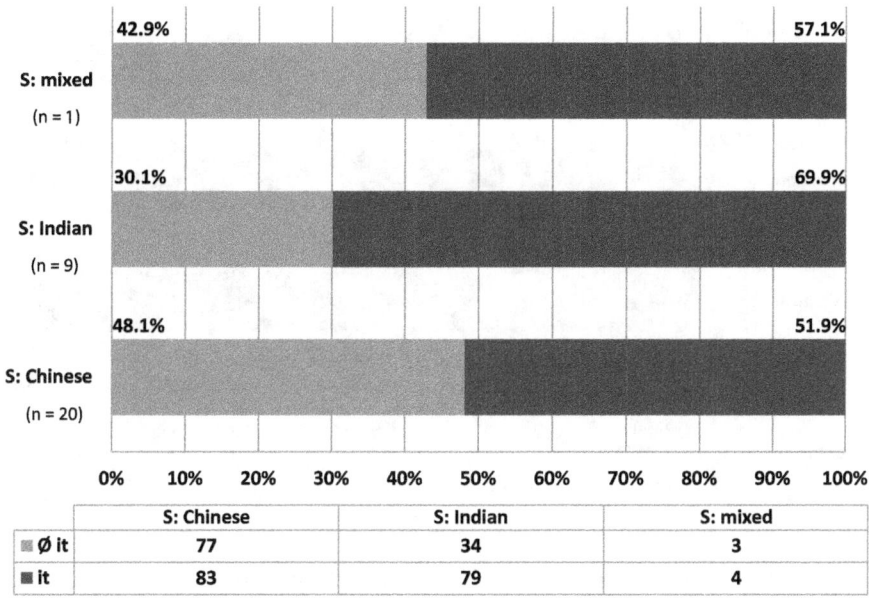

Figure 10.3 Realisation of subject *it* (all types) by ethnicity. A colour copy of this figure is available on the EUP website: edinburghuniversitypress.com/EcologiesofWorldEnglishes

what particular effects these differences might have on the results here cannot be accounted for within the framework of this study; in any case, the general principle of leaving out subject pronouns should be known to all of the children.

The results discussed for the realisation of past tense marking on regular verbs (Figure 10.4) point towards an interesting finding related to the question addressed above, namely, that cross-linguistic influence is not always the most important factor when it comes to feature realisation in principle. Still, it seems to condition the quantitative differences found between the groups.

Similar to the results for subject pronoun realisation, the Chinese group shows a higher percentage of the local variant, namely, unmarked verbs (52.7 per cent) than the children of Indian descent (29.3 per cent of unmarked verbs). Still, the variant is clearly present in the Indian children too. This time, the quantitative difference between the two groups in whether they mark the verbs for past tense can be easily explained on the basis of L1 transfer effects. In contrast to the Chinese languages/ dialects, which are all isolating languages, the three languages spoken by

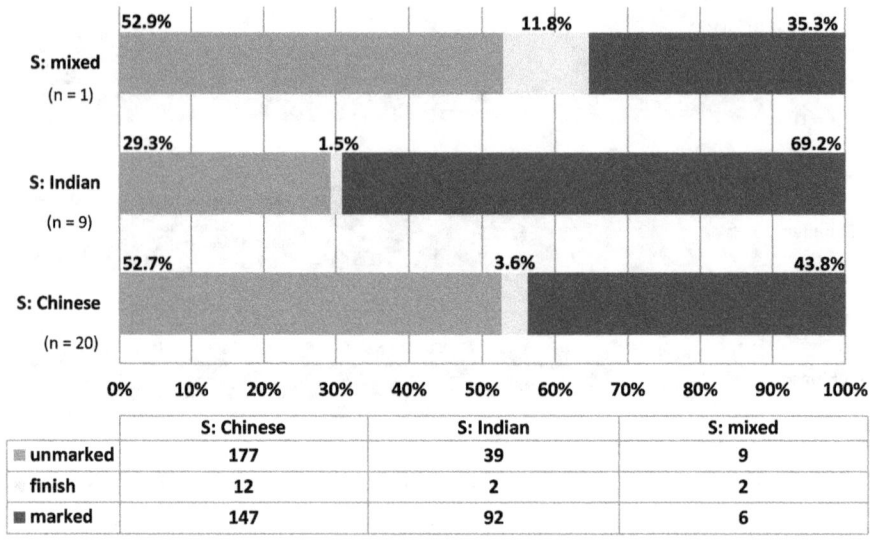

Figure 10.4 Past tense marking with regular verbs by ethnicity. A colour copy of this figure is available on the EUP website: edinburghuniversitypress.com/EcologiesofWorldEnglishes

the Indian children inflect verbs for past tense (for example, Dhongde and Wali 2009: 74, 78–9, 83; Kachru 2006: 79; Krishnamurti 2003: 291–301). The synthetic strategy of inflectional past tense marking is therefore known to the Indian children. This, of course, raises the question of why these children produce such a high number of unmarked verb forms at all. I suppose the answer lies in the historical, demographic and sociolinguistic development and current background of Singapore, in which the Chinese languages/dialects have always had a very prominent influence on the development of SingE. The results therefore suggest that linguistic strategies employed by the Chinese group on the basis of cross-linguistic influence (here: missing past tense marking) have started to spread into the Indian group as well.

Even more interesting in this respect and clearly corroborating this argument are the results for the use of the LEXV+*finish* structure, briefly discussed above. Even though the Indian children do not have any evidence for this variant in their other first languages (and this strategy is, other than the use of bare verb forms, not a characteristic of early child language), they still make use of the structure. The difference between the two groups when it comes to the proportions of use is very similar to the differences between the groups in their use of bare verb forms (that is, 1.5–3.6 per cent and 29.3–52.7 per cent). I interpret these findings as indicative of homogenisation tendencies in SingE (further discussed in Buschfeld 2020b).

3.2 The Current State of Singapore English: The Influence of Ethnicity, Linguistic Input and Language Attitudes

As the previous sections have shown, L1 SingE appears to be characterised by two major trends, that is, heterogeneity between speaker groups and between and within individual speakers on the one hand and homogenisation tendencies on the other. Focusing on the first aspect, I will now discuss what the findings reveal about the current status of L1 SingE, in particular with recourse to the role linguistic input from parents, caretakers and so on and language attitudes have played in its more recent development.

The variability found in the data suggests a certain degree of 'instability' (not meant in a pejorative way) since not all variation can be easily pinned down to the influence of an intra- or extralinguistic source. This could, admittedly, be due to limitations in corpus size and thus lack true representativeness; maybe a larger data set would reveal further and more detailed patterns that finally would explain the data's variability in all its details. However, the inexplicable, apparently unguided part of the variability could also point towards the status of L1 SingE as a system 'still in the making', in which different realisations (variants) of a linguistic variable still have to scramble to become the default choice.

The clear patterns of variation observed along ethnic lines suggest that cross-linguistic influence from the children's other L1s may play a role. The results presented in Section 3.1, however, also show that transfer cannot be the only explanation. An excursion into language attitudes and the role of input in language acquisition may allow for further interesting insights when explaining the patterns of variation found in the data.

Coming from a language acquisitional perspective, linguistic heterogeneity between children is a common observation especially in bi-/multilingual acquisitional contexts and can be explained in terms of the variability in bi-/multilingual children's linguistic experiences. This, in turn, has been ascribed to a variety of factors, in particular social ones. Some children in dual- (or multiple-)language environments experience a fairly balanced amount and quality of exposure; other children receive much more exposure and experience in one language than in the other

(De Houwer 2009; Paradis 2007: 17; compare the notion of balanced vs unbalanced bilingualism). Language dominance is one important result of variable experience and input, and is often related to not only the quantity but also the quality/type of input a child receives (for example, De Houwer 1995: 221; Grüter and Paradis 2014). Though long neglected in language acquisition research, and in particular by formal approaches, both quantity and quality of input have repeatedly been shown to have an important influence on the acquisition and development of language (for example, De Houwer 1995: 223–7; Paradis 2017; Place and Hoff 2011; Unsworth 2013: 30), especially on bi-/multilingual language acquisition. Quantity of input and its relevance for language dominance and frequency of exposure is a matter of simple arithmetic. Since English is the strongest/dominant language for all children in this study and the language most frequently used in all but four of the 30 families, quantity of input can be safely excluded as a factor influencing the variation found between the children.

In terms of input quality, the richness of the input has been reported and discussed as a relevant factor. This is a complex notion in itself, which encompasses a variety factors and is guided by several mechanisms (for example, listed in Unsworth 2013: 38; for a similar list, see Paradis 2017: 28). These cannot be listed and explained in full detail here. Relevant in the context of the present discussion are:

1. the input variety in terms of different sources of input (for example, family, friends, reading, television; classroom input vs community exposure; and so on; cf. Jia and Fuse 2007; for the latter pair, see Mougeon and Rehner 2017); and
2. socio-psychological factors (see, for example, Carroll 2017; De Houwer 2017; Maneva 2004: 115, 119–20), in particular issues of language attitudes and identity.

It has, for example, been shown that even for young children, language use might depend on their attitudes towards the users of a particular language and 'the values that we associate with the labels we name it [the language] with' (Carroll 2017: 12). When considering the social dimensions of language choice, it has been shown that speakers, even small children, take into account a wide range of factors (for example, Lanza 1997; Taeschner 1983; see Clark 2016: 399 for a brief overview). The Singapore Government still strongly propagates the use of Standard English, and Indians, in general, tend to strive for higher education levels and academic professions more than other ethnic groups (for example, Schneider 2007: 147). Educational status in Singapore is often associated with standard language use (for example, Alsagoff 2007: 39). Therefore, the differences between the Chinese and Indian groups may simply indicate that the Indian Singaporeans show a stronger orientation towards standard language use and that, in turn, the linguistic input the children receive as well as the attitudes conveyed by the parents may be more standard. On the other hand, it can certainly be argued that children pay less attention to governmental norms – why should they? – and that the kind of linguistic exploitation (namely, the deliberate choice of one linguistic variant over the other) as, for example, envisaged by Leimgruber (2013: 20–1; see also Alsagoff 2007) presupposes too strong a metalinguistic competence on the side of children. What is more, the language input for Singaporean children is very diverse, and we cannot assume that they get input only from members of their own ethnic groups (see factor 1 listed above). In this respect, it has been shown that '[i]n high-contact polyglossic scenarios, a target language with reference norms is not available, and children pick and mix features from the caregivers' speech and may later develop innovations during adolescence' (Schreier 2014: 232).

Another interesting factor listed by Unsworth (2013: 38) taps into an even more important question for the present study, namely, the concept of the native speaker and the potential influence of L2 speaker input on child language acquisition. SingE clearly originates in an L2 acquisition context. However, the majority of studies investigating bi-/multilingual children focus on contexts where each parent speaks their native language to the child (Paradis 2007: 15). To my knowledge, only very few studies have investigated the influence of non-native input on the ultimate success of bi-/multilingual child language acquisition (for example, Cornips and Hulk 2008; Place and Hoff 2011; Paradis and Navarro 2003). In sum, all these studies show that, of course, 'non-native' – and what is meant here is non-British or non-American – input makes a difference: not surprisingly, the children's productions reflect the input they receive from their parents and therefore the L2 features the parents produce. Hauser-Grüdl et al. (2010: 2639) offer yet another possible explanation for the strong heterogeneity in the data presented. Their study clearly shows that 'the extent to which a bilingual is affected by cross-linguistic effects is child-dependent' (2010: 2645). Taking this into consideration, it might well be that the linguistic heterogeneity found in the Singapore data is not a sign of instability of the L1 variety but the result of the bi-/multilingual acquisitional context.

Taking into consideration the three nexuses between language and culture introduced by Schneider (this volume), the results partly lend themselves to such an interpretation. One can certainly speculate that the use of zero subject pronouns can be interpreted in the light of individualist- vs collectivist-oriented societies, namely, that omitting pronouns and thus deemphasising the weight of the individual expresses the collectivist nature of the Singaporean society. As found by the overall study (Buschfeld 2020a: 165–7), *it* is the most frequently dropped subject pronoun, followed by zero *I*, and at quite some distance *he* and *she*; zero forms of *they* and *we* are considerably less frequent. I interpreted these findings as mostly the result of pronominal reference, that is, what is easiest to be inferred from the context (see also Bloom 1970; Hyams 1989: 222). However, the cultural considerations brought forth by Schneider might, of course, play a role here too.

4. CONCLUSION

As the present chapter has shown, L1 SingE is characterised by strong intra- as well as inter-speaker variability between not only BrE and AmE variants but, even more interestingly, between more or less colloquial realisations of SingE, as can be, for example, seen in the variable use of overt and zero subjects, 'standard' vs bare verb endings and the use of the LEXV+*finish* strategy, as well as variable vowel length realisations. The realisations of these forms are strongly, but not exclusively, determined by the children's ethnicity. I have suggested that the strong heterogeneity can be interpreted as indicative of the fact that L1 SingE is a variety still 'in the making'. However, acquisition-based explanations, attributing differences in cross-linguistic influence to the individual child, are also conceivable. As the discussion has shown, explaining the heterogeneity found in the data is a complex issue which is influenced by a variety of different social and linguistic factors. The most prominent ones that were identified and discussed in the present chapter are ethnicity, diversity of input, language attitudes and, of course, cross-linguistic influence. As the results presented and discussed in Section 3.1 have shown, homogenisation appears to develop in favour of the variants of Chinese language origin (the largest ethnic group in Singapore).

Beyond the pervasive language–culture nexuses discussed by Schneider (this volume), this research shows how demographic factors play out in the Singapore acquisitional context – and in the evolution of

Singapore English. The study highlights the importance of social variables (such as ethnicity) in identifying the relationship between language and culture.

ACKNOWLEDGEMENTS

I am grateful to the reviewers for their helpful comments and suggestions. Any remaining shortcomings are, of course, my own responsibility.

NOTES

1. It has to be noted here that these are only the major varieties contributing to the feature pool (see Mufwene 2001) the children choose from. The story is even more complex and further interesting adstrate varieties (Schneider 2007) are spoken by, for example, the children's nannies who often come from surrounding Southeast Asian countries like the Philippines or Myanmar.
2. The third major section of the population, Malay children, is, unfortunately, not represented in the study. I could not recruit any Malay families for this project for a variety of practical reasons (see Buschfeld 2020a: ch. 4.4). Ages are given in the format '2;5' for years and months.
3. All examples presented here, and in the following, come from the child participants in Buschfeld's (2020a: ch. 2.4) study; names provided are all pseudonyms.
4. The superscript *r* here indicates that pronunciation is rhotic though less prominently than in the second example.
5. Measuring MLU (mean length of utterance) is a long-established procedure in child language acquisition and development research to measure grammatical complexity and to determine the exact stage of acquisition in young children. When comparing the linguistic performance of different children, MLU values have been shown to be much more reliable than age alone (Brown 1973) even if a strong correlation between MLU and age has often been reported (for example, Miller and Chapman 1981; Parker and Brorson 2005). The results for MLU/age are not discussed in the present paper. This would bring in the psycholinguistic issue of acquisitional stages children go through, which is not relevant for the present discussion.

6. The latter type corresponds to what Halliday and Hasan (1976: 52–3) call 'extended reference' or 'text reference', which shows stronger referentiality than expletive *it* but weaker referentiality than referential *it*.
7. The approach was by no means prescriptive in orientation and the author is fully aware of the fact that a comparison of bi-/multilingual children and monolingual children is long outdated in the language acquisition paradigm due to the normative implications these comparisons have carried in the early days of language acquisition research. In a similar manner, the terms 'standard' and 'non-standard' are merely employed as terminological means to measure and describe the unique and local character of SingE.
8. I exclude the mixed ancestry child here and from the following discussion since she is not representative of any specific group. I focus on a comparison of the two larger groups.

REFERENCES

Alsagoff, L. (2007). Singlish: Negotiating culture, capital and identity. In V. Vaish, S. Gopinathan and Y. Liu (Eds.), *Language, capital, culture: Critical studies and education in Singapore* (pp. 25–46). Sense Publishers.

Bao, Z. (2005). The aspectual system of Singapore English and the systemic substratist explanation. *Journal of Linguistics, 41*(2), 237–67.

Blommaert, J. (2010). *The sociolinguistics of globalization.* Cambridge University Press.

Boersma, P. and Weenink, D. (2018). Praat: Doing phonetics by computer (Version 6.0.37) [Computer software]. <http://www.praat.org> (last accessed 8 January 2021).

Bolton, K. and Ng, B. C. (2014). The dynamics of multilingualism in contemporary Singapore. *World Englishes, 33*(3), 307–18.

Bloom, L. (1970). *Development: Form and function in emerging grammars.* MIT Press.

Brown, A. (1988). Vowel differences between Received Pronunciation and the English of Malaysia and Singapore: Which ones really matter? In J. A. Foley (Ed.), *New Englishes: The case of Singapore* (pp. 129–47). Singapore University Press.

Brown, A., Deterding, D. and Low, E. L. (2000). *The English language in Singapore: Research on pronunciation.* Singapore Association for Applied Linguistics.

Brown, R. (1973). *A first language: The early stages*. George Allen & Unwin.
Buschfeld, S. (2020a). *Children's English in Singapore: Acquisition, properties, and use*. Routledge.
Buschfeld, S. (2020b). Multilingual language acquisition in Singapore: Heterogeneity and homogenization tendencies in the emergence of a new first language variety of English. In J. Leimgruber and P. Siemund (Eds.), *Multilingual global cities: Singapore, Hong Kong, Dubai* (pp. 205–28). Routledge.
Carroll, S. E. (2017). Exposure and input in bilingual development. *Bilingualism: Language and Cognition, 20*(1), 3–16.
Census of Population. (2000). Statistical Release 2. <http://www.singstat.gov.sg/publications/publications_and_papers/cop2000/cop2000r2.html>.
Census of Population. (2010). Statistical Release 1. <http://www.singstat.gov.sg/publications/publications_and_papers/cop2010/census10_stat_release1.html>.
Central Intelligence Agency. (2020). The World Factbook: Singapore. <https://www.cia.gov/the-world-factbook/countries/singapore/> (last accessed 8 January 2021).
Clark, E. V. (2016). *First language acquisition* (3rd ed.). Cambridge University Press.
Cornips, L. and Hulk, A. (2008). Factors of success and failure in the acquisition of grammatical gender in Dutch. *Second Language Research, 24*(3), 267–95.
Coupland, N. (Ed.) (2010). *The handbook of language and globalization*. Wiley-Blackwell.
De Houwer, A. (1995). Bilingual language acquisition. In P. Fletcher and B. MacWhinney (Eds.), *The handbook of child language* (pp. 219–50). Basil Blackwell.
De Houwer, A. (2009). *Bilingual first language acquisition*. Multilingual Matters.
De Houwer, A. (2017). Bilingual language input environments, intake, maturity and practice. *Bilingualism: Language and Cognition, 20*(1), 19–20.
Deterding, D. (2007). *Singapore English*. Edinburgh University Press.
Dhongde, R. V. and Wali, K. (2009). *Marathi*. John Benjamins.
Grüter, T. and Paradis, J. (2014). *Input and experience in bilingual development*. John Benjamins.

Gupta, A. F. (1994). *The step-tongue: Children's English in Singapore*. Multilingual Matters.
Halliday, M. A. K. and Hasan, R. (1976). *Cohesion in English*. Longman.
Hauser-Grüdl, N., Guerra, L. A., Witzmann, F., Leray, E. and Müller, N. (2010). Cross-linguistic influence in bilingual children: Can input frequency account for it? *Lingua, 120*(11), 2638–50.
Hyams, N. M. (1989). The null subject parameter in language acquisition. In O. Jaeggli and K. J. Safir (Eds.), *The null subject parameter* (pp. 215–38). Kluwer Academic Publishers.
Jia, G. and Fuse, A. (2007). Acquisition of English grammatical morphology by native Mandarin speaking children and adolescents: Age-related differences. *Journal of Speech, Language and Hearing Research, 50*(5), 1280–99.
Kachru, Y. (2006). *Hindi*. John Benjamins.
Krishnamurti, B. (2003). *The Dravidian languages*. Cambridge University Press.
Labov, W. (1972). *Sociolinguistic patterns*. University of Pennsylvania Press.
Labov, W. and Baranowski, M. (2006). 50 msec. *Language Variation and Change, 18*(3), 223–40.
Lanza, E. (1997). *Language mixing in infant bilingualism: A sociolinguistic perspective*. Oxford University Press.
Leimgruber, J. R. E. (2013). *Singapore English: Structure, variation, and usage*. Cambridge University Press.
Lim, L. (2004). Sounding Singaporean. In L. Lim (Ed.), *Singapore English: A grammatical description* (pp. 19–56). John Benjamins.
Lim, L. (2007). Mergers and acquisitions: On the ages and origins of Singapore English particles. *World Englishes, 26*(4), 446–73.
Maneva, B. (2004). 'Maman, je suis polyglotte!': A case study of multilingual language acquisition from 0 to 5 years. *International Journal of Multilingualism, 1*(2), 109–22.
Miller, J. F. and Chapman, R. S. (1981). The relation between age and mean length of utterance in morphemes. *Journal of Speech, Language, and Hearing Research, 24*(2), 154–61.
Mougeon, R. and Rehner, K. (2017). The influence of classroom input and community exposure on the learning of variable grammar. *Bilingualism: Language and Cognition, 20*(1), 21–2.
Mufwene, S. S. (2001). *The ecology of language evolution*. Cambridge University Press.

Paradis, J. (2007). Early bilingual and multilingual acquisition. In P. Auer and L. Wie (Eds.), *Handbook of multilingualism and multilingual communication* (pp. 15–44). Mouton de Gruyter.

Paradis, J. (2017). Parent report data on input and experience reliably predict bilingual development and this is not trivial. *Bilingualism: Language and Cognition, 20*(1), 27–8.

Paradis, J. and Navarro, S. (2003). Subject realization and crosslinguistic interference in the bilingual acquisition of Spanish and English: What is the role of the input? *Journal of Child Language, 30*(2), 371–93.

Parker, M. D. and Brorson, K. (2005). A comparative study between mean length of utterance in morphemes (MLUm) and mean length of utterance in words (MLUw). *First Language, 25*(3), 365–76.

Place, S. and Hoff, E. (2011). Properties of dual language exposure that influence two-year-olds' bilingual proficiency. *Child Development, 82*(6), 1834–49.

Rice, M. L. and Wexler, K. (2001). *Rice/Wexler Test of Early Grammatical Impairment: Examiner's manual*. Psychological Corporation.

Schneider, E. W. (2007). *Postcolonial English: Varieties around the world*. Cambridge University Press.

Schreier, D. (2014). On cafeterias and new dialects: The role of primary transmitters. In S. Buschfeld, T. Hoffmann, M. Huber and A. Kautzsch (Eds.), *The evolution of Englishes: The dynamic model and beyond* (pp. 231–48). John Benjamins.

Taeschner, T. (1983). *The sun is feminine*. Springer.

Tan, Y.-Y. (2014). English as a 'mother tongue' in Singapore. *World Englishes, 33*(3), 319–39.

Tan, Y.-Y. (2016). The Americanization of the phonology of Asian Englishes: Evidence from Singapore. In G. Leitner, A. Hashim and H.-G. Wolf (Eds.), *Communicating with Asia: The future of English as a global language* (pp. 120–34). Cambridge University Press.

Tay, M. W. J. (1982). The phonology of Educated Singapore English. *English World-Wide, 3*(2), 135–45.

Tickoo, M. L. (1996). Fifty years of English in Singapore: All gains, (a) few losses? In J. A. Fishman, A. W. Conrad and A. Rubal-Lopez (Eds.), *Post-imperial English: Status change in former British and American colonies, 1940–1990* (pp. 431–55). Mouton de Gruyter.

Unsworth, S. (2013). Current issues in multilingual first language acquisition. *Annual Review of Applied Linguistics, 33*, 21–50.

Valian, V. (2016). Null subjects. In J. Lidz, W. Snyder and J. Pater (Eds.), *The Oxford handbook of developmental linguistics* (pp. 386–413). Oxford University Press.

Wee, L. (2004). Singapore English: Phonology. In E. W. Schneider, K. Burridge, B. Kortmann, R. Mesthrie and C. Upton (Eds.), *A handbook of varieties of English* (Vol. 1; pp. 1017–33). Mouton de Gruyter.

Wells, J. C. (1982). *Accents of English*. Cambridge University Press.

Wexler, K. (1994). Optional infinitives, head movement and the economy of derivations. In D. Lightfoot and N. Hornstein (Eds.), *Verb movement* (pp. 305–50). Cambridge University Press.

CHAPTER 11

Across Three Kachruvian Circles with Two Parts-of-speech: Nouns and Verbs in ENL, ESL and EFL Varieties

Tobias Bernaisch and Sandra Götz

1. INTRODUCTION: ESL AND/VS EFL: BRIDGING THE 'PARADIGM GAP'

1.1 EFL and/vs ESL: Same, Same or Different?

Kachru's (1985) distinction between English as a native language (ENL), English as a second language (ESL) and English as a foreign language (EFL) has had an enormous influence on the modelling of Englishes worldwide, triggering a wealth of lexical and grammatical descriptions of varieties in all three Kachruvian circles. In research studies following this paradigm, institutionalised ESL varieties (for example, Indian English or Singapore English) and EFL variants (for example, French or German Interlanguage) have been treated fundamentally differently on the basis of these different paradigms alone. For example, ESL varieties are characterised as norm-developing, so that all kinds of emerging innovative linguistic features are described and evaluated as signs of 'nativization' (Schneider 2007: 5) in dialect formation. Accordingly, in ESL, innovative features are considered essential for the 'identity construction' (Schneider 2007: 6) of the speakers of a new variety. In more advanced ESL speech communities, ENL norms are consequently not propagated by language politicians, as they would be perceived as '"foreign" – unnatural and affected' (Nihalani et al. 2004: 203) in comparison with the more naturally and locally evolved linguistic models.

EFL speech communities, on the other hand, are typically described as being norm-dependent, so that all emerging linguistic features deviant from ENL are considered 'misuses', 'errors' or 'non-attested forms' (see

Deshors et al. 2016a). Consequently, in EFL speech communities, we typically find a strict adherence to native speaker models in ELT and the EFL speakers themselves often aim for ENL norms (Mukherjee and Rohrbach 2006; Krenz 2015). Despite this stark contrast in their perceptions and evaluations in EFL as opposed to ESL contexts, a closer look at the actual linguistic features reveals them as often very similar or even identical, such as the use of discourse markers transferred from speakers' L1, that is, their first language (see Deshors et al. 2016a).

Following a recent trend to bridge this still existing 'paradigm gap' (Sridhar and Sridhar 1986) between EFL and ESL approaches to World Englishes, we witness an increased number of corpus-linguistic studies comparing EFL and ESL contrastively. This happens either by drawing parallels between the two types of varieties (for example, Nesselhauf 2009; Gilquin 2011; Davydova 2012; Götz and Schilk 2011; Laporte 2012; Deshors and Gries 2015; Edwards 2015), or by showing that EFL users share linguistic features with ESL speakers (Edwards and Laporte 2015; Gilquin 2015; Deshors et al. 2016a). Theoretically, there is also an increased number of researchers questioning the suitability of theoretical frameworks based on historical and geographical legacy to accommodate discussions on language varieties (Bruthiaux 2003; Mukherjee and Hundt 2011; Li and Mahboob 2012; Deshors et al. 2016b).

The complex linguistic reality in (often multilingual) postcolonial speech communities makes it even more difficult to uphold this distinction, as we often find all three types of English represented in what might be referred to as three Kachruvian circles in miniature (compare, for example, Meyler 2007: x–xi; Mukherjee et al. 2010: 65). This issue is even put more sharply by Mendis and Rambukwella (2010), who criticise that in research on Sri Lankan English (SLE), this linguistic complexity:

> is often ignored or not clearly understood in descriptions that label SLE as a second-language variety – i.e. that English is used and spoken both as a first language and as a second/third language in Sri Lanka. In order to be both accurate and valid, any description of SLE as a regional variety must acknowledge and address the complexities arising from this contextual situation. (Mendis and Rambukwella 2010: 181)

Previous corpus-based research in this vein, however, has not yet been able to meet the challenge to capture the linguistic complexity/reality in

ESL/EFL research, including research into multilingual speech communities. So far, due to data sparsity, corpus-based research on ESL and/vs EFL has mainly compared EFL data from (European) learner corpora with postcolonial second-language varieties from different L1 backgrounds. However, investigating data usually compiled according to different standards from such different speech communities can lead to infelicitous interpretations of findings, as L1-specific influences can either go unnoticed or be over-interpreted because the linguistic complexity of countries with a colonial past is often not acknowledged, including – but not limited to – cultural conventions.

With the present exploratory study, we offer a first attempt at testing if it is possible to capture the linguistic complexity in South-East Asia by investigating ESL and EFL speakers who live in the same cultural regions. In doing so, we explore data from three different speech communities at different evolutionary stages (namely, Hong Kong, the Philippines and Singapore). We want to test if we can trace general trends for a possible cline from EFL to ESL (as suggested by Gilquin and Granger 2011) across the speech communities or if we rather see similarities in the local discourse cultures, regardless of the speakers' proficiency levels. Also, we compare these data with British English inner-circle language data (GB), in order to test if there are differences compared with an ENL type of English.

1.2 Stylistic Variation in ENL, ESL and EFL as a Sign of Culture?

Previous studies on stylistic variation have mainly been conducted within the ENL paradigm. Most notably, Biber's (1988) multi-dimensional studies of register variation have uncovered the fundamentally different discourse styles between the spoken and the written register in ENL. While the written register has been shown to be more 'nominal' in nature, that is, relying heavily on the use of nouns, attributive adjectives and prepositional phrases, the spoken register is, in turn, more 'verbal', especially due to a high use of present tense and stative verbs, extensive clausal embedding and a frequent use of pronouns and elliptical structures. Earlier, partly non-empirical accounts of ESL and EFL varieties have suggested that the respective spoken variants feature what would be stylistic indicators of writing in ENL varieties. In this light, Kachru (1983: 42) and Mesthrie and Bhatt (2008: 114–16) profile spoken postcolonial Englishes as having a more 'bookish flavour' in the sense that written norms may be adopted in spoken discourse. Similarly, EFL users compared with ENL users have been shown to lack a native-like 'text-type sensitivity' (Lorenz 1999: 64) and a 'register-awareness' (Gilquin and Paquot 2008), leading EFL users to employ many typically written features in their speech, but also typically spoken features in their writing. However, systematic stylistic comparisons across all the three Kachruvian circles have not yet been undertaken.

In the light of the overall theme of the present volume, we would like to explore whether we can identify cultural differences between varieties of English which are reflected in formal differences in local discourse styles. For example, one culture might be more written/nominal while another is more oral or verbal (Biber and Finegan 1992) in different types of Englishes, as used by EFL vs ESL speakers in the same region. By investigating ESL and EFL speakers from Singapore, Hong Kong and the Philippines, we would like to test whether preferences for specific linguistic patterns might be motivated by different 'discourse cultures' between the regional speech communities we investigate or if they are rather motivated by the type of English spoken by the speakers under scrutiny (that is, ESL or EFL). If culture is reflected through language in the corpus data, we would hypothesise finding some tendency for ESL and EFL speakers within the same speech communities to show similar stylistic preferences in using a more written or more oral style of speaking (that is, showing signs of belonging to the same 'discourse cultures') regardless of the type of English they speak. If this is not the case, we would expect the EFL variants and the ESL variants to show more similarities between speaker types, rather than within speech communities. We would also like to explore if it is possible to take Schneider's (2018) cultural findings on lexical, lexicogrammatical and pragmatic levels to the even more coarse-grained level of discourse and test if we can identify formal representations of 'culture' in the speakers' systematic expression of different 'discourse cultures' across speaker types.

Against this background, we study spoken and written texts produced by acrolectal ESL users from Hong Kong, Singapore and the Philippines in contrast to texts produced by EFL users from the same territories. Using the method suggested by Mair et al. (2002) for tracing diachronic style shifts, we would like to present a first feasibility study to analyse speaker styles on the basis of differences in their part-of-speech (POS) frequencies alone, despite the obvious limitations of this approach. The aims of our study thus are:

1. to document the use of local discourse cultures in using rather written/nominal or oral/verbal styles in speech and writing of ESL and/vs EFL users living in the same territories;
2. to test if cultural differences are reflected in abstract formal manifestations of local discourse cultures in different types of English (namely EFL vs ESL) by speakers living in the same/different territories; and
3. to compare these findings with ENL users in order to check whether the conceptualisation of the relation between EFL, ESL and ENL as a continuum applies to stylistics in World Englishes.

2. METHODOLOGY

The data stem from the International Corpus of English (ICE; Greenbaum and Nelson 1996) and the International Corpus Network of Asian Learners of English (ICNALE; Ishikawa 2013), both of which feature data from the three South-East Asian regions of interest. The salient difference between the two corpus environments is that ICE represents 'acrolectal language use by competent English speakers' (Mukherjee et al. 2010: 66) in outer-circle territories clearly characterising the texts as ESL products, while ICNALE sampled EFL material 'from leaners [sic] in ten countries and areas in Asia' (Ishikawa 2014: 66–7). While both spoken and written texts are available in ICNALE and ICE, only one genre was sampled per medium in the former corpus. In ICNALE, the written texts are relatively short argumentative essays on either of two topics, that is, the importance of a part-time job for college students or whether smoking should be banned completely from all restaurants in the country, and the same topics were adopted for the spoken data where informants were asked to elaborate on the set topic for approximately one minute as a relatively spontaneous exercise since each speaker was only given 20 seconds for preparation (Ishikawa 2014: 68–9). As the ICNALE data under scrutiny are supposed to reflect EFL use, informants in ICNALE were allowed to have a maximum proficiency level of B1 as measured via the Common European Framework of Reference for Languages: Learning, Teaching, Assessment (CEFR; Council of Europe 2017) for their texts to be included in the present study. In order to eliminate genre as a potential source of variation for the frequencies of nouns and verbs across ICE and ICNALE, we chose monologic unscripted speeches and student writing as matching subsections of the regional components of ICE.

As suggested by Mair (2002), we analysed the POS-tagged versions of these corpora and compared the numbers of nouns and verbs. More specifically, we considered all the forms that were POS-tagged with _N* as nouns and all the words with a _V* tag as verbs, taking the relative frequencies of nouns and verbs to be indicative of local written and spoken discourse cultures respectively. Rather than using a more fine-grained word class categorisation that could have probably distinguished, for example, modal verbs from lexical verbs, we preferred to work with more general analyses of nominal and verbal frequencies in the different communicative settings.

After part-of-speech tagging the relevant corpus texts with the CLAWS C7 tagset, we established separate relative frequencies for nouns (mean ≈, 21.53, sd ≈ 4.59) and verbs (mean ≈ 21.62, sd ≈ 3.46) in relation to the total number of words for each of the 1,876 texts analysed.[1] Other than the dependent variables just described, we considered a number of independent variables potentially exerting an influence on the frequencies of nouns and verbs:

- VARIETYSTATUS: was the text produced by an ENL (13.49 per cent), ESL (13.17 per cent) or EFL user (73.35 per cent)?
- REGION: did the text come from Great Britain (GB; 13.49 per cent), Hong Kong (HK; 18.5 per cent), the Philippines (PHL; 43.12 per cent) or Singapore (SIN; 24.89 per cent)?
- MEDIUM: is the text spoken (45.26 per cent) or written (54.74 per cent)?
- TTR: what is the type-token ratio of the text (mean ≈ 51.49, sd ≈ 10.01)?
- FREQOTHER: when investigating nouns, what is the frequency of verbs and vice versa?

The statistical modelling of the data relies on two complementary methods, that is, conditional inference trees and linear regression modelling. Conditional inference trees as implemented in the package PARTYKIT for R (Hothorn et al. 2006; Hothorn and Zeileis 2015; R Development Core Team 2016) calculate predictions for the dependent variable – in our case the relative frequencies of nouns and verbs – based on several binary splits of the data. This recursive partitioning ends when the next binary split no longer sufficiently increases the predictive accuracy of the model, which is by default represented in the form of a hierarchical tree with the most important splits at the top and the less important ones at the bottom. As conditional inference trees do not make distributional assumptions about the data to be analysed, they are well suited for the modelling of most corpus-linguistic data. Yet classification trees do not always account adequately for significant interactions between individual predictors (Bernaisch et al. 2014: 14), which is why we decided to complement conditional inference trees with two linear regression models – one for nouns and one for verbs – where each interaction making the overall model significantly better was included and the danger of overlooking important interactions thus considered in a forward model selection process.

3. ANALYSIS

Section 3.1 describes the results of the conditional inference trees for nouns and verbs across the varieties studied, and Section 3.2 focuses on linear regression models for the two objects of investigation.

3.1 Conditional Inference Trees for Nouns and Verbs across Three Kachruvian Circles

The conditional inference tree shown in Figure 11.1 models the relative frequencies of nouns with the help of the independent variables described in Section 2. The model formula used was:

NOUN ~ VARIETYSTATUS + REGION + MEDIUM + TTR + VERB

and the tree that emerged from the data has a predictive accuracy of 0.5057. While prediction accuracies of conditional inference trees can generally be higher, we are modelling a numeric and not a binary dependent variable, and particularly high scores for goodness of fit tend to occur with the latter and not with the former, which is why we consider the tree to be reliable enough for interpretation.

The reading and interpretation of a conditional inference tree always starts at the top node (node 1), and at each node there is a binary choice in that proceeding to the next node to the left (here node 2) or right (here node 15) means accepting that the predictor depicted in the node assumes the values placed on the line connecting the node from which the reader departs to the next one. This procedure is repeated down to the terminal nodes at the bottom of Figure 11.1 (for example, node 4). The terminal nodes provide (a) the number of the node; (b) the number of texts (out of the total of 1,876) that match the configurations of the predictors from node 1 to the terminal node concerned (for example, node 4 captures 111 texts); and (c) the frequencies of (the levels of) the dependent variable, in this case the relative frequencies of nouns depicted in the form of a box plot.

With a focus on local discourse cultures, the factor combinations including REGION and/or VARIETYSTATUS in Figure 11.1 are of particular relevance. Nodes 12 to 14 show that Hong Kong users employ more nouns than users from the other territories when the frequency of verbs ranges between 17.355 and 21.017 in the written medium, which is indicative of a more strongly written discourse culture with Hong Kong writers. This trend is also visible in nodes 26 to 33 since – ceteris paribus – British writers use fewer nouns than writers from the Philippines or Singapore, who, in turn, use fewer nouns than Hong Kong writers. It is to be noted that these tendencies hold uniformly across speaker groups in the same territory since VARIETYSTATUS did not emerge as a significant predictor in the conditional inference tree for nouns.

The conditional inference tree for verbs is provided in Figure 11.2. The model formula was:

VERB ~ VARIETYSTATUS + REGION + MEDIUM + TTR + NOUN

and each predictor is also part of the resulting model for VERB, which marks a difference to the noun model where VARIETYSTATUS was not a significant factor. The predictive accuracy of the model for VERB is 0.4537 and also acceptable for a numeric dependent variable to proceed with the interpretation of the model.

With the intention of uncovering various degrees of localised oral discourse cultures, it is noteworthy that – independent of VARIETYSTATUS – Philippine users employ more verbs than users from other territories when nouns range between 12.048 and 16.446 (nodes 6 and 7). With the frequency of nouns between 16.446 and 22.764, Philippine EFL users (nodes 18 and 19) also employ more verbs than – on average – users of English from Hong Kong or Singapore (nodes 11, 13, 15, 19). Yet, it is worth mentioning that this regional differentiation

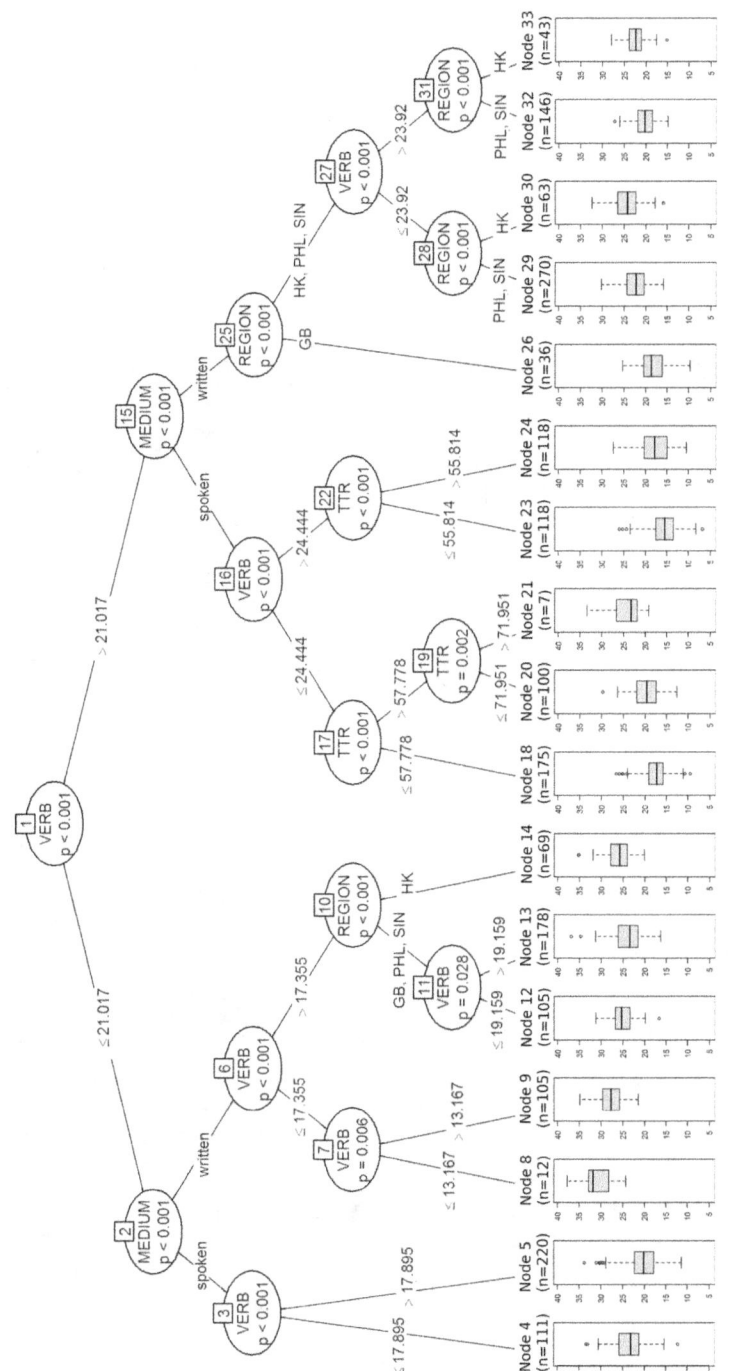

Figure 11.1 Conditional inference tree for nouns

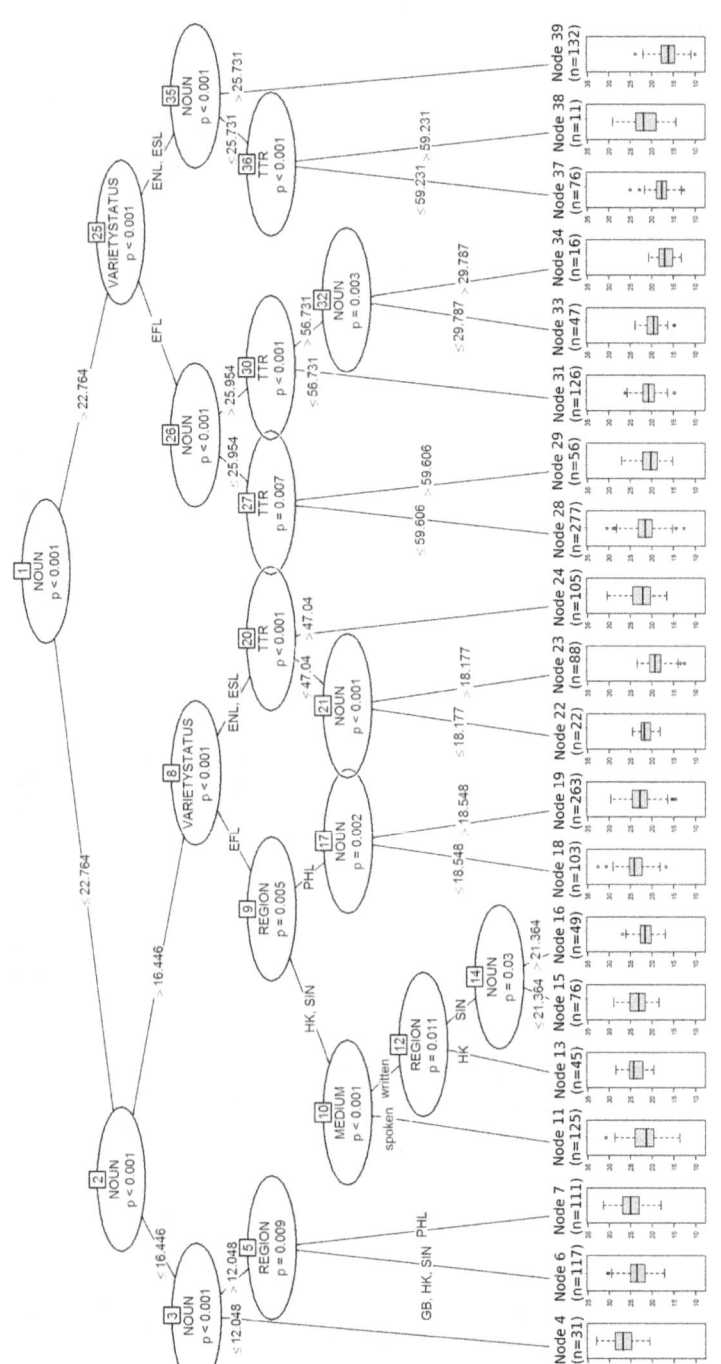

Figure 11.2 Conditional inference tree for verbs

only applies to the EFL (not the ESL) users from these territories, with the ESL users employing fewer verbs. When the frequency of nouns is larger than 22.764, EFL (nodes 28, 29, 31, 33, 34) users can also be shown to use more verbs than ENL or ESL users (nodes 37, 38, 39) except when ENL/ESL users have a relatively high TTR (node 38). Consequently, it appears that patterns indicative of oral discourse cultures are prominent with EFL speaker groups and most prominent with learners from the Philippines.

3.2 Linear Regression Models for Nouns and Verbs across Three Kachruvian Circles

The predictors for the conditional inference trees were also used for the linear regression models but the predictors VARIETYSTATUS (for example, ESL as one level) and REGION (for example, SIN as one level) were combined into one predictor STATUSREGION (for example, ESL|SIN as one level) since not all levels of VARIETYSTATUS have values for all levels of REGION (for example, there are understandably no data for ESL or EFL from GB).

The final model for nouns has the structure:

NOUN ~ VERB + MEDIUM + VERB * MEDIUM + STATUSREGION + STATUSREGION * MEDIUM + STATUSREGION * VERB + TTR + TTR * MEDIUM + TTR * STATUSREGION

The model with an $R^2_{multiple}$ of 0.5282 and an $R^2_{adjusted}$ of 0.5208 is highly significantly better than the intercept model ($p < .001$). Model diagnostics covering standardised residuals, independence of errors and non-multicollinearity suggest that this model is statistically robust. In the light of the overall research questions, we restrict ourselves to the description and interpretation of a selection of interactions featuring STATUSREGION as a predictor, which provides a more general perspective on how the frequency of nouns is affected by different speaker groups.

The effect plot of MEDIUM*STATUSREGION depicted in Figure 11.3 highlights clear-cut differences between outer-circle (ESL) as opposed to the inner-circle (ENL) and expanding-circle (EFL) varieties. With second-language speakers in Hong Kong, the Philippines and Singapore, there are only minute differences in nominal frequencies in speech compared with writing, while the learners of English in the respective territories use markedly more nouns in writing than in speech. The markedly written discourse culture with Hong Kong writers identified in the conditional inference tree in Figure 11.1 is also evident in Figure 11.3 since (a) EFL users in Hong Kong use nouns the most in their written texts and show the largest difference in nominal frequencies across modes with nouns occurring notably more often in writing than in speech; and (b) ESL users in Hong Kong employ the largest amount of nouns in their writing compared with other ESL writers.

More generally, this difference in medium-dependent nominal frequency of South-East Asian learners is more pronounced than with British English native speakers, who also quantitatively mark differences between speech and writing in their noun usage, but to a lower degree. The opposite tendency, language featuring a particularly low frequency of nouns, that is, 6.73 per cent of the total number of words, was produced by a 17-year-old male biology major from the Philippines. An excerpt from the spoken text he produced is shown in example (1), in which nouns identified by the POS-tagger are underlined.

(1) Okay, so what I can say about this is that the people around you what will they say if you smoke in the restaurant. Actually I am 50:50 about this argument, because if it is an open restaurant, then you can do so, but if it is not, then it is prohibited, of course. All I can say is that you just have to be conscious about the people around you. You should be disciplined in that. [. . .] (ICNALE_S_PHL_SMK1_028_B1_2)[2]

In example (1), verbs (25 per cent) constitute the largest part of words used followed by pronouns (17.31 per cent) and adverbs (12.5 per cent). This distribution across the parts-of-speech mentioned can be indicative of interactive, communicatively immediate text types as opposed to the characteristic written text where interlocutors are spatially and temporally removed from one another and thus need, for example, more complex heavily modified noun phrases to make themselves understood. A written text with a particularly high nominal frequency of 36.86 per cent was put together by a 20-year-old Singaporean female learner of English majoring in environmental studies. A short sample of her writing is provided in (2).

(2) Students can learn life skills such as management, communication and people skills while as well as get a sense of the working

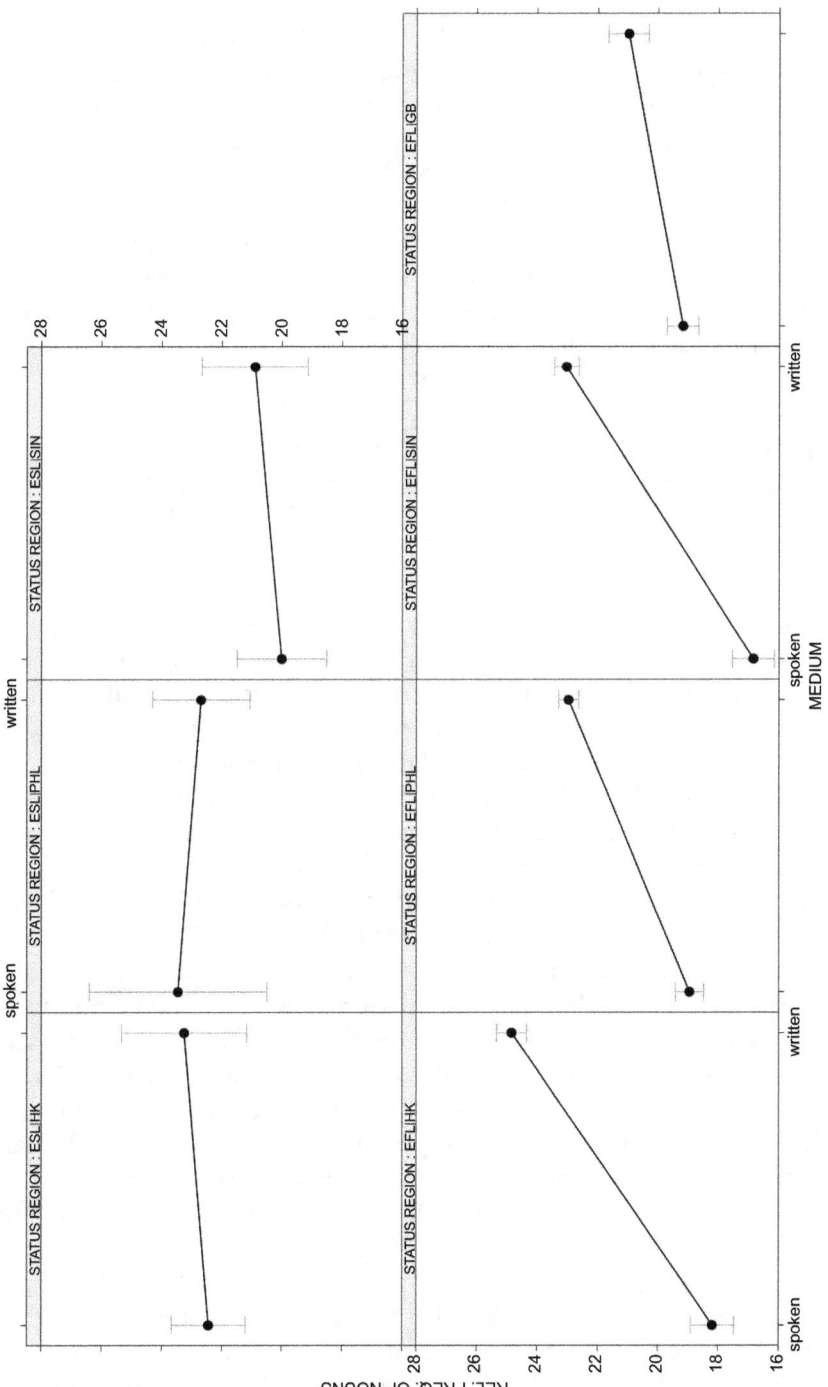

Figure 11.3 Effect plot for the interaction between MEDIUM and STATUSREGION for nouns

environment and life. Working broadens students' social circle and provides important networking opportunities. Part time jobs also boost student portfolios and can provide onsite learning experiences relevant to the student's course of study. [...] (ICNALE_W_SIN_PTJo_178_B1_2)

In her writing, verbs (20.34 per cent) also figure prominently. Still, it is noteworthy that prepositions (associated with noun phrases) rank third in terms of their frequency of use (11.44 per cent) and pronouns are almost absent with a relative frequency of 1.69 per cent.

The final model formula for verbs is:

VERB ~ NOUN + STATUSREGION + NOUN * STATUSREGION + MEDIUM + MEDIUM * STATUSREGION + TTR + TTR * STATUSREGION + TTR * MEDIUM ($R^2_{multiple}$ = 0.458 and $R^2_{adjusted}$ = 0.4498)

The resulting model is highly significantly better than the intercept model ($p < .001$). Also, the model for verbs is statistically robust based on standardised residuals, independence of errors and non-multicollinearity. As with the nominal model, we restrict ourselves to the analysis of interactions involving STATUSREGION as a predictor.

The interaction STATUSREGION*MEDIUM in the verbal model – unlike their interaction in the nominal model – hardly shows any clearcut tendencies for the individual Kachruvian circles as evident from Figure 11.4, which is compatible with the findings in the conditional inference tree in Figure 11.2, where MEDIUM plays a more marginal role than for nouns. Another parallel to the earlier conditional inference tree findings is that verbal frequencies are relatively high for Philippine users independent of MEDIUM. For the ENL and ESL variety users as well as the EFL users from the Philippines, precise medium differentiation in terms of verbal use is absent; one might deduce a slight common tendency of the respective users to produce more verbs in speech than in writing. For learners in Hong Kong and Singapore, the frequency of verbs somewhat depends on the medium in that they use more verbs in writing than in speech.

Example (3) depicts a monologue from a 22-year-old Hong Konger with an academic degree in English. The text is remarkable in that comparatively few verbs (13.64 per cent) are featured in this spoken text and nouns (18.18 per cent) are not used noticeably more often either,

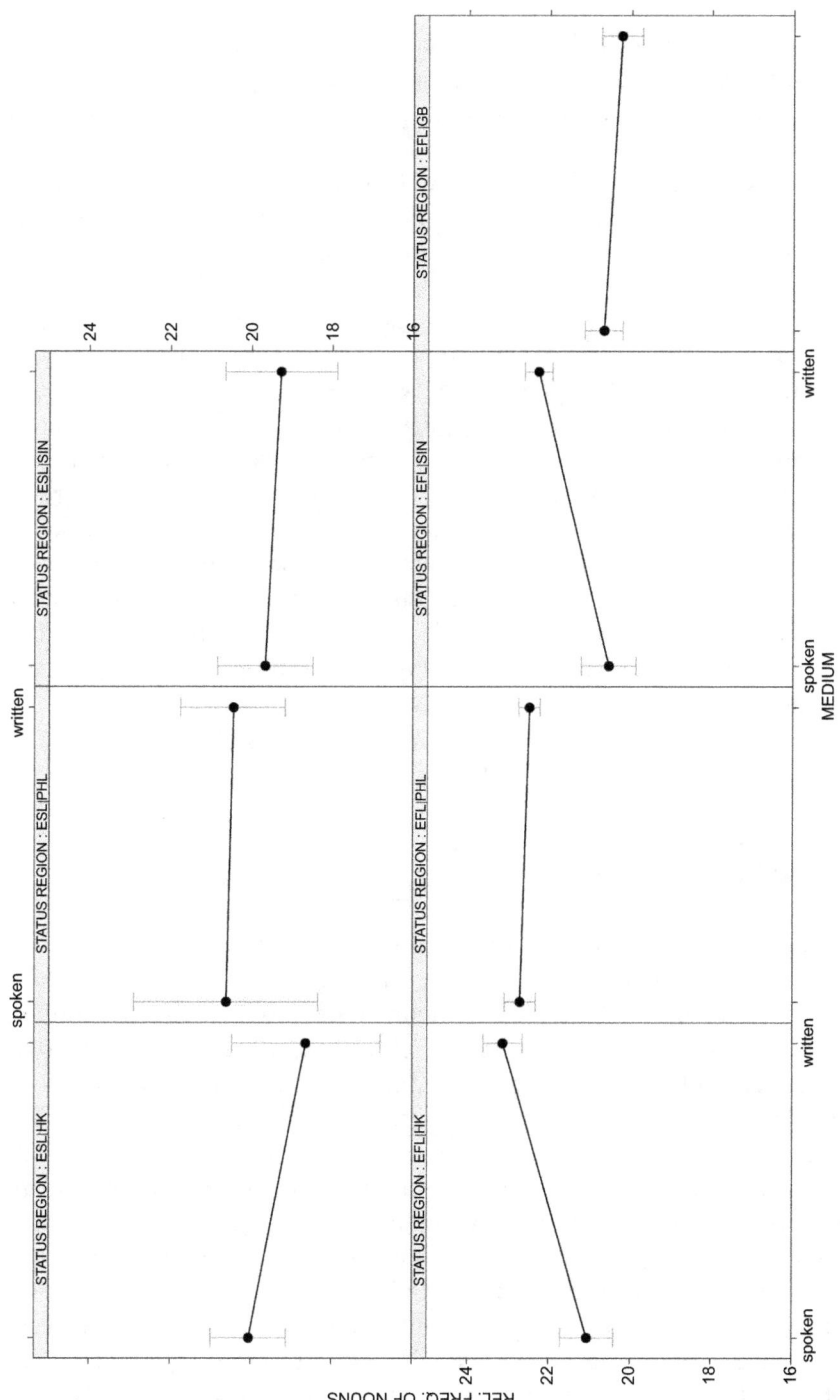

Figure 11.4 Effect plot for the interaction between STATUSREGION and MEDIUM for verbs

but – alongside adverbs (11.36 per cent) – determiners (10.61 per cent) and conjunctions (10.61 per cent) figure relatively prominently. The usage of definite articles with general nominal heads has been described as a characteristic of ESL speakers of Hong Kong English (Hung 2012: 127), but also seems to be prevalent at least with some learners in Hong Kong as illustrated here (for example, *the part-time job*, *the personal development*, *the academic knowledge*, and so on).

(3) Well, I think that the students should have the part-time job, not because mainly, not mainly because of the nature or money but because of the personal development. Well, personally, it is so important for one to acquire the academic knowledge and both the personal development, the social experience in the society. This is because the in class role and lecture, they are only academic and knowledge and they may be involved in the academic environment, but they need some personal development which is outside the classroom and exists in society. And in society through participating in part-time of course they earn some money, but most importantly, they have the opportunity to learn these things in the society. For example, when they take part in a company, then they know how to [. . .] (ICNALE_S_HKG_PTJ1_019_B1_2)

4. SUMMARY AND DISCUSSION

This paper set out to model noun and verb frequencies of speakers and writers in different Kachruvian circles and regions in the light of their TTRs and other word class frequencies to explore possible differences in the respective discourse cultures. Generally, it became obvious that the frequency of the other word class (that is, verbs in the nominal model and nouns in the verbal model) is a central predictor. It appears that nouns and verbs balance each other out at least to a certain extent in that, for example, low verbal frequencies in a set of texts have a tendency to go hand-in-hand with comparatively high nominal frequencies in the same texts. As for the role of the medium, it can be observed that nouns occur with higher frequencies in written than in spoken texts, although verbs – as shown for learners in Hong Kong and Singapore – do not exclusively occur more often in spoken contexts. The geographical region served to profile high frequencies of nouns in Hong Kong, especially in writing, and high frequencies of verbs in the Philippines – particularly with the local learners of English – relatively independent of medium. These findings profile Hong Kong writers as approximating the characteristics of a written discourse culture most notably, in comparison with writers from other regions, and independent of whether they are first-, second- or foreign-language users since the factor VARIETYSTATUS was not a significant predictor for nominal use. Still, VARIETYSTATUS profiled unambiguous differences between EFL as opposed to ENL and ESL users, in that foreign-language users employ verbs more often – a tendency particularly prominent with Philippine learners, indicating their more typically oral discourse culture across mediums.

For nouns, the data indeed yield indications of the bookishness of spoken South-East Asian second-language varieties (compare, for example, Kachru 1983: 42) as well as a 'transfer of register' (Gilquin and Paquot 2008) in the writing of South-East Asian learners. Especially regarding the use of verbs, we hardly see a mode differentiation for the ESL speakers. It seems that the 'exonormative power' (in our case the medium distinction that is clearly evident from the British English native speaker data) applies more consistently to learners than to ESL users in South-East Asia. Our findings are, however, not uniform 'across methods': while in the regression models, the distinction between second-language users and learners holds uniformly across the three South-East Asian Englishes, suggesting that user status may be a more important diagnostic than regional provenance; the VARIETYSTATUS does not even figure in the conditional inference tree for nouns. Adding to the complexity, the ESL speakers behave more similarly to the ENL speakers in the conditional inference tree on nouns, while this is not as evident in the regression models. Due to these diverse findings, our study does not show a first-second-foreign-language cline.

5. CONCLUSION AND OUTLOOK

With the present study, we have presented a first exploration of stylistic variation in ENL, ESL and EFL from – where possible – the same territories by using POS-tagged corpora and sophisticated statistical techniques. As could be seen, this approach comes with a number of caveats and rather diverse findings, and we can thus only reveal some first overall trends in the data, rather than definite findings. Future studies differentiating between the different types of nouns and verbs as well as different levels of stylistic variation (Biber 1988) will certainly arrive at more fine-grained results.

Being aware of the limitations the POS-tag-based approach we took entails, we would now like to reassess our research questions. A cultural motivation behind specific linguistic patterns diverging across varieties can only be partly confirmed by our findings. While the conditional inference tree on nouns, for example, does not include the variety type as an important predictor, we do find significant splits between different regions. This finding suggests that a closer investigation of nouns is worthwhile in order to trace different discourse cultures by using corpora, as represented in a similar preference of using a more verbal/nominal style regardless of the proficiency of a speaker. However, we must acknowledge that, by conducting POS-tag analyses, we naturally arrive at a level of abstraction that makes it rather difficult to draw any definite conclusions to connect language and culture as proposed by Schneider (2018), who investigates constructions as the most abstract category of analysis. This being said, we do find different 'medium cultures' between the varieties we investigated, so that the present study might serve to complement Schneider's (2018) structural profiles of linguistic features that represent culture in corpus data. Since nouns seem to be particularly apt candidates to represent the 'cultural identity' of a region, we hope our findings might inspire follow-up studies that investigate the 'cultural keywords' (compare, for example, Mukherjee and Bernaisch 2015) of these regions more thoroughly in order to put this hypothesis to the test.

Revisiting our second research question, that is, questioning whether ESL and EFL varieties should be modelled as two discrete categories or permeable groups on a continuum (Gilquin and Granger 2011), we actually found ESL and EFL to behave differently from each other regarding their styles, with EFL showing more similarities to the ENL speakers than to the ESL speakers (see also Edwards and Laporte 2015). If future studies on different linguistic levels arrive at similar findings, we might argue that EFL speakers of English – even in postcolonial habitats – at the beginning stages still adhere more rigidly to ENL norms before they reach a certain threshold, become ESL speakers of English and use the language more creatively and innovatively, thus starting to create their own discourse styles as they progress. Concerning investigations of 'culture' in corpora, however, we must conclude that EFL speakers might not be the ideal speaker group with which to conduct such investigations, as they are probably still too norm-dependent (that is, focused on the ENL target norm) and thus do not reflect their own culture to the same extent as an ESL speaker would when speaking English.

With the present study, we were able to present only a first feasibility study. Future research comparing EFL and ESL variants of English in the same speech communities at different linguistic levels of description can be extended on many descriptive levels. Here, especially the levels of phonology, lexis and lexicogrammar suggest themselves to be worthwhile candidates to generate interesting findings to bridge the paradigm gap even further.

ACKNOWLEDGEMENTS

We are extremely grateful to a number of people who have supported us in the course of this research project. We would like to express our sincerest thanks to Joybrato Mukherjee for the initial idea for the investigation, Stefan Th. Gries and Christoph B. Wolk for their statistical recommendations and guidance, and the ICAME 36 delegates for sharing their valuable views when we presented the first results of the present study. We are also thankful to Jasmin Ruckelshaussen for her support in POS-tagging that data. Any shortcomings in this paper remain, of course, our own.

NOTES

1. For the extraction of the part-of-speech frequencies, we used Stefan Th. Gries's R script exact.matches and thank him for making the script available to us.
2. The identification code of an ICNALE corpus file represents medium (speech vs writing), country, topic and trial, the participant identification code and the participant's CEFR level (for non-native speakers only).

REFERENCES

Bernaisch, T., Gries, S. T. and Mukherjee, J. (2014). The dative alternation in South Asian Englishes: Modelling predictors and predicting prototypes. *English World-Wide*, 35(1), 7–31.

Biber, D. (1988). *Variation across speech and writing*. Cambridge University Press.

Biber, D. and Finegan, E. (1992). The linguistic evolution of five written and speech-based English genres from the 17th to the 20th centuries. In M. Rissanen, O. Ihalainen, T. Nevalainen and I. Taavitsainen (Eds.), *History of Englishes: New methods and interpretations in historical linguistics* (pp. 688–704). Mouton de Gruyter.

Bruthiaux, P. (2003). Squaring the circles: Issues in modeling English worldwide. *International Journal of Applied Linguistics, 13*(2), 159–78.

Council of Europe. (2017). *Common European Framework of Reference for Languages: Learning, Teaching, Assessment: Companion volume with new descriptors.* <https://rm.coe.int/cefr-companion-volume-with-new-descriptors-2018/1680787989> (last accessed 11 January 2021).

Davydova, J. (2012). Englishes in the outer and expanding circles: A comparative study. *World Englishes, 31*(3), 366–85.

Deshors, S. C., Götz, S. and Laporte, S. (2016a). Linguistic innovations in EFL and ESL: Rethinking the linguistic creativity of non-native English speakers. *International Journal of Learner Corpus Research, 2*(2), 131–50.

Deshors, S. C., Götz, S. and Laporte, S. (Eds.). (2016b). Corpus-linguistic perspectives on linguistic innovations in non-native Englishes [Special issue]. *International Journal of Learner Corpus Research, 2*(2).

Deshors, S. C. and Gries, S. T. (2015). EFL and/vs. ESL? A multi-level regression modeling perspective on bridging the paradigm gap. *International Journal of Learner Corpus Research, 1*(1), 130–59.

Edwards, A. (2015). *English in the Netherlands: Functions, forms and attitudes*. John Benjamins.

Edwards, A. and Laporte, S. (2015). Outer and expanding circle Englishes: The competing roles of norm orientation and proficiency levels. *English World-Wide, 36*(2), 135–69.

Gilquin, G. (2011). Corpus linguistics to bridge the gap between World Englishes and Learner Englishes. In L. Ruiz Miyares and M. R. Álvarez Silva (Eds.), *Comunicación en el siglo XXI* (Vol. II; 638–42). Centro de Lingüística Aplicada.

Gilquin, G. (2015). At the interface of contact linguistics and second language acquisition research: New Englishes and Learner Englishes compared. *English World-Wide, 36*(1), 91–124.

Gilquin, G. and Granger, S. (2011). From EFL to ESL: Evidence from the International Corpus of Learner English. In J. Mukherjee and

M. Hundt (Eds.), *Exploring second-language varieties of English and Learner Englishes: Bridging a paradigm gap* (pp. 55–78). John Benjamins.

Gilquin, G. and Paquot, M. (2008). Too chatty: Learner academic writing and register variation. *English Text Construction, 1*(1), 41–61.

Götz, S. and Schilk, M. (2011). Formulaic sequences in spoken ENL, ESL and EFL: Focus on British English, Indian English and Learner English. In J. Mukherjee and M. Hundt (Eds.), *Exploring second-language varieties of English and Learner Englishes: Bridging a paradigm gap* (pp. 79–100). John Benjamins.

Greenbaum, S. and Nelson, G. (1996). The International Corpus of English (ICE) project. *World Englishes, 15*(1), 3–15.

Hothorn, T., Hornik, K. and Zeileis, A. (2006). Unbiased recursive partitioning: A conditional inference framework. *Journal of Computational and Graphical Statistics, 15*(3), 651–74.

Hothorn, T. and Zeileis, A. (2015). partykit: A modular toolkit for recursive partytioning in R. Journal of Machine Learning Research, *16*, 3905–9.

Hung, T. T. H. (2012). Hong Kong English. In E. L. Low and A. Hashim (Eds.), *English in Southeast Asia: Features, policy and language in use* (pp. 113–33). John Benjamins.

Ishikawa, S. (2013). The ICNALE and sophisticated contrastive interlanguage analysis of Asian learners of English. In S. Ishikawa (Ed.), *Learner corpus studies in Asia and the world* (Vol. 1; pp. 91–118). Kobe University.

Ishikawa, S. (2014). Design of the ICNALE Spoken: A new database for multi-modal contrastive interlanguage analysis. In S. Ishikawa (Ed.), *Learner corpus studies in Asia and the world* (Vol. 2; pp. 63–76). Kobe University.

Kachru, B. B. (1983). *The Indianization of English: The English language in India*. Oxford University Press.

Kachru, B. B. (1985). Standards, codification and sociolinguistic realism: The English language in the outer circle. In R. Quirk and H. G. Widdowson (Eds.), *English in the world: Teaching and learning the language and literatures* (pp. 11–30). Cambridge University Press.

Krenz, J. (2015). *Attitudes of German university students towards varieties of English: An empirical study* [Undergraduate thesis, University of Giessen].

Laporte, S. (2012). Mind the gap! Bridge between World Englishes and Learner Englishes in the making. *English Text Construction, 5*(2), 265–92.

Li, E. and Mahboob, A. (2012). *English today: Forms, functions, and uses*. Pearson Education.

Lorenz, G. (1999). *Adjective intensification. Learners versus native speakers: A corpus study of argumentative writing*. Rodopi.

Mair, C. (2002). Tagged corpora as a new resource in the study of linguistic change in progress: Nominal and verbal styles in English. In G. Fischer, G. Tottie and H. M. Lehmann (Eds.), *Text types and corpora: Studies in honour of Udo Fries* (pp. 177–89). Narr.

Mair, C., Hundt, M., Leech, G. and Smith, N. (2002). Short-term diachronic shifts in part-of-speech frequencies: A comparison of the tagged LOB and F-LOB corpora. *International Journal of Corpus Linguistics, 7*(2), 245–64.

Mendis, D. and Rambukwella, H. (2010). Englishes in Sri Lanka. In A. Kirkpatrick (Ed.), *The Routledge handbook of World Englishes* (pp. 181–96). Routledge.

Mesthrie, R. and Bhatt, R. M. (2008). *World Englishes: The study of new linguistic varieties*. Cambridge University Press.

Meyler, M. (2007). *A dictionary of Sri Lankan English*. Mirisgala.

Mukherjee, J. and Bernaisch, T. (2015). Cultural keywords in context: A pilot study of linguistic acculturation in South Asian Englishes. In P. Collins (Ed.), *Grammatical change in English world-wide* (pp. 411–35). John Benjamins.

Mukherjee, J. and Hundt, M. (Eds.). (2011). *Exploring second-language varieties of English and Learner Englishes: Bridging a paradigm gap*. John Benjamins.

Mukherjee, J. and Rohrbach, J. (2006). Rethinking applied corpus linguistics from a language-pedagogical perspective: New departures in learner corpus research. In B. Kettemann and G. Marko (Eds.), *Planing, gluing and painting corpora: Inside the applied corpus linguist's workshop* (pp. 205–32). Peter Lang.

Mukherjee, J., Schilk, M. and Bernaisch, T. (2010). Compiling the Sri Lankan component of ICE: Principles, problems, prospects. *ICAME Journal, 34*, 64–77.

Nesselhauf, N. (2009). Co-selection phenomena across New Englishes: Parallels (and differences) to foreign learner varieties. *English World-Wide, 30*(1), 1–26.

Nihalani, P., Tongue, R. K., Hosali, P. and Crowther, J. (2004). *Indian and British English: A handbook of usage and pronunciation* (2nd ed.). Oxford University Press.

R Development Core Team. (2016). *R: A language and environment for statistical computing.* R Foundation for Statistical Computing. <https://www.R-project.org> (last accessed 11 January 2021).

Schneider, E. W. (2007). *Postcolonial English: Varieties around the world.* Cambridge University Press.

Schneider, E. W. (2018). The interface between cultures and corpora: Tracing reflections and manifestations. *ICAME Journal*, 42(1), 97–132. <https://doi.org/10.1515/icame-2018-0006> (last accessed 4 January 2021).

Sridhar, K. K. and Sridhar, S. N. (1986). Bridging the paradigm gap: Second language acquisition research and indigenized varieties of English. *World Englishes*, 5(1), 3–14.

CHAPTER 12

Modality, Rhetoric and Regionality in English Editorials in the Sinosphere

Pam Peters, Tobias Bernaisch and Kathleen Ahrens

1. INTRODUCTION

English modal verbs have been the focus of much recent research, because of continuing shifts in the dynamic system they form and the range of verbal and interpersonal meanings they express. Their interaction with different mediums, genres and text-types and their usage in different varieties of English are also under continual investigation. The research indicates the wide range of intrinsic and extrinsic factors relevant to their use and the value of bringing multifactorial analysis to bear on their usage. Modal verb data also need to be fully contextualised in their communicative situation if we are to appreciate their sociolinguistic importance within a given speech community.

Drawing on this range of research, this paper focuses on 21st century use of modal and quasi-modal verbs in editorials published in major English-language newspapers in Hong Kong, Beijing and Taipei. While recent corpus-based research on modal usage in Hong Kong (Noël and van der Auwera 2015; Loureiro-Porto 2016) provides useful benchmarks on the relative frequencies of the modals and quasi-modals, there has been no comparable study of their frequencies in data from other regions in the Sinosphere. This invites further research, given the different histories of English in each region, as a foreign language in mainland China and Taiwan (that is, 'expanding-circle' English regions), and as previously a second 'outer-circle' English in Hong Kong (Kachru and Nelson 2006). Although these distinctions are no longer categorical, the functions of English within each region (more and less extensive) may affect the relative frequencies of modals and quasi-modals in the more hybrid forms of regional English in the 21st century, as well as their degree of grammaticalisation (Loureiro-Porto 2016).

The aim of this study is to see how those variables play out in a given text-type, that is, English newspaper editorials published in Beijing, Hong Kong and Taipei. What are the baseline similarities and differences in the repertoires of modals and quasi-modals used in the three regions? How do they contribute to the rhetorical styles communicated through the editorial column? Does the use of modals/quasi-modals seem to express the newspaper's political stance and/or reflect the sociocultural climate of its region of the Sinosphere? The data analysed may thus contribute to identifying a more or less abstract nexus between varieties of English in their respective regional contexts.

2. RESEARCH FRONTIERS: PARAMETERS OF VARIATION IN THE USE OF MODALS

2.1 Changing Trends in Modal Usage World-wide: Forms and Linguistic Functions

Millennial research on the frequencies of English modals in contemporary standard corpora has pointed to the changing relationship between the two subcategories – modals and quasi-modals[1] – with the steadily increasing frequency of the latter and relative decline of the former (Mair and Leech 2006: 328; Collins 2009a). At the same time, additional quasi-modals such as *had better*, *supposed to*, *want to* are emerging through grammaticalisation and semantic shifts. These trends are borne out in research based on multigeneric corpora such as the International Corpus of English (ICE) set (Collins 2009b) but not in large monogeneric corpora of *Time Magazine* (Millar 2009) or major US and UK newspapers (Noël and van der Auwera 2015). It suggests that genre is an important factor in the use and distribution of modals. Apart from these studies focusing on the distribution of the modals as verbal forms, others have noted the polysemy of usage attached to modal verbs and their quasi-modal counterparts and their distinctive functions. Modals vary in the illocutionary force they express – strong, medium, weak (Halliday and Matthiessen 1994: 619; Huddleston and Pullum 2002: 176–7), and in the types of force (logical, general, internal, external) that they express (Loureiro-Porto 2016: 150–1). Individual modals within the broad categories of intrinsic and extrinsic meaning (Biber et al. 1999: 485), and epistemic and dynamic modality (Collins 2009b), can take on the function of another category. For example, deontic modals of necessity (for example, *must* – intrinsic) can express epistemic (extrinsic) meaning. Their polysemy is an ongoing issue for pedagogy (Zhang 2015),[2] and for larger scale modal research – though helped by including contextual factors in the framework for analysing modal usage.

The meanings/functions of modals vary to some extent with clausal syntax. There are differences according to the grammatical person of the subject (Biber et al. 1999: 485; Huddleston and Pullum 2002: 183). Compare the functions of *may* in the following examples:

(1) I/we/they may come on Tuesday. (extrinsic possibility)
(2) You may come whenever you're back in town. (intrinsic permission)

Modal verbs with contrasting present and past tense forms (*can>could, may>might, shall>should, will>would*) can be subject to 'backshifting' in the selection of tensed verbs from the main to dependent (subordinate) clause.[3]

(3) The government will not consider using atomic methods for generating electricity.
(4) Officials said the government would not proceed with atomic energy.

The backshifting of verb forms in subordinate clauses is often associated with reported speech. It is also found in complex sentences that spell out mental concepts (Huddleston and Pullum 2002: 154–5) and their inherent modality (Halliday and Matthiessen 1994: 463, 613–14). This use of past tense forms in subordinate clauses was mandated by prescriptive English grammarians from Fowler (1926) to Gowers (1965) as the proper 'sequence of tenses', on the basis of Latin grammar. It remains a stylistic option in formal rather than everyday writing and speech.

2.2 Variable Usage of Modals Relative to Regional Varieties and Their Evolutionary Status

The availability of ICE corpora from the 1990s on, and other regional databases of text, has supported much research into regional differences in the use of modals and quasi-modals. Quantifiable differences in their relative frequencies have been found in inner-circle and outer-circle varieties, for example by Mair and Leech (2006), Collins (2009b) and Leech (2003). But the findings differ considerably according to the datasets used. In Collins's research, the modal and quasi-modal frequencies in millennial data from the Hong Kong ICE corpus (including samples of written and spoken discourse) were far greater than those in ICE corpora from Singapore, the Philippines or the UK. By contrast, a big data study by Noël and van der Auwera (2015) of the use of modals and quasi-modals in Hong Kong's *South China Morning Post* (1990–2010) showed levels of usage much like those of the British *The Times* and *The Guardian*. While the second study suggested Hong Kong's continuing (exonormative) alignment with British English before and after 1997, the first study found uniquely intense and diverse use of modality in Hong Kong English, as of an endonormative[4] variety of English. Clearly the types of data used affected the findings.

The current evolutionary status of regional varieties is a variable in more recent studies of the English modals (Collins 2013; Loureiro-Porto 2016), especially the reversion of some former outer-circle regions like Hong Kong and Sri Lanka to expanding-circle status. This affects the functions of English within those countries and circumscribes its regular use in line with changes in official language policies. In mainland China, there is ongoing emphasis on English in the education system (Wang and Fang 2019: 4) and some online discussion of the standard of English used as a lingua franca. But it is far from evolving as a regional standard. English is not generally used in informal social encounters and then only among the younger generation. The putative continuum from EFL to ESL is no longer predictable, either for ex-colonial English-using speech communities or for those which were never British colonies (Buschfeld and Kautzsch 2017). While English is developing its profile in mainland China and Taiwan as a supplementary language (Burridge and Peters 2020), primarily in metropolitan areas such as Beijing and Taipei, the official and educational contexts for English are changing in Hong Kong. It is therefore of interest to see how far the modals/quasi-modals as a structural system reflect different cultural contexts; and whether it is evolving along the same or different lines (that is, nexus 3; see Schneider's paper, this volume).

2.3 Distribution of Modals and Quasi-modals Relative to Medium and Text-type

The use of modal verbs and quasi-modals varies considerably across written and spoken language, as found in Biber's pioneering research

(1988). As a set they are deployed more often in spoken than written language, but differentially represented according to their functions. So those expressing ability (especially *can*) and volition/prediction (*will*, *would*) are more frequently used in conversation than any written text-type (Biber et al. 1999: 489), whereas those relating to obligation are evenly represented across speech and writing.

Finer-grained analysis using multidimensional methods (Biber 1988) showed the association of particular types of modals with different discourse dimensions. The modals expressing possibility (*can*, *could*, *may*, *might*) correlated positively with Biber's 'involved dimension' (Factor 1), where ideas are being negotiated with the other party, that is, in speech and the more interactive forms of writing. All three types of modal – possibility, necessity (*must*, *ought*, *should*) and prediction (*shall*, *will*, *would*) – were found characteristic of the 'persuasive dimension' (Factor 4) because of the stances and attitudes they express. Press editorials (both institutional and personal) rate especially high on the persuasive scale (Biber 1988: 149). Some of them are more characteristic of formal writing – for example, *may*, *ought*, *shall* – and their decreasing use in Australian Hansard records contributes to the increasingly colloquial style of the parliamentary records through the last century (Kruger and Smith 2018: 315).

Quasi-modals are far more frequent in speech – approximately twice as common in conversation as in news writing (Biber et al. 1999: 486). This helps to explain their association with more informal colloquial discourse among native-speaker users of English (Mair and Leech 2006: 336; Millar 2009; Collins 2013). They are thus a symptom of the 'informalisation' and democratisation of public discourse, imbuing it with a more colloquial tone and modifying the tenor so as to reduce the communicative distance between speaker/writer and audience.

2.4 Modal Verbs: Politeness and Politics

Politeness conventions with some English modal verbs are centuries old, for example the complementation between *will* and *shall* dating back to the 17th century grammarian John Wallis, who prescribed *will* for use in statements with first- or second-person subjects and *shall* for the third person (Fries 1925). These patterns were notionally reversed in questions such as *Shall we begin with . . .?* which have become idiomatic. In ordinary usage, it might be *Will we wait for her?*. English politeness conventions of the 20th century preferred *May I?* to *Can I?* when formulating requests, on the strict understanding that *may* expressed permission and *can* ability (*Webster's Dictionary of English Usage*, ed. Gilman 1989: 218)[5] – thus *may* was more polite in conceding the discretionary right to the other party. Likewise, *could, might, should, would* were preferable to *can, may, shall, will* because the built-in past tense of the first group gives them a certain remoteness that seems to make them less assertive (Biber et al. 1999: 485). The tentative tone they lend to statements is valued as a form of negative politeness. They could thus be regarded as indicator terms of polite discourse (Schneider's nexus 2, this volume) shared by British-infused cultures. How such polite or tactful uses of selected modals in private conversation play out in the public arena, and in written text-types such as newspaper editorials, is a further question.

Modal verbs have been shown to be significant in public discourse and political rhetoric, as in Rayson's (2008) research on the 'keywords' in the manifestos of two political parties in connection with a British election. Rayson (2008: 533–5) demonstrated the 'keyness' of modal *would* by the opposition party (Liberal Democrats), flagging the new agenda they were proposing and their readiness to negotiate it. The equivalent keyword for the governing Labour Party was the first-person plural possessive *our*. Both suggest significant connections between structural elements of the English language and the sociopolitical context and the text-type in which they are used (nexus 3).

Function words and especially the English modal verb system can reflect facets of the culture and society in the discourse in which they are used. Let us proceed to analyse the usage of modals and quasi-modals in English newspaper editorials published in the Sinosphere to identify elements of persuasion and politeness in their texts and the extent to which they reflect the characteristics of their respective cultural contexts.

3. METHODOLOGY

A customised corpus the English editorials in the Sinosphere Corpus was compiled by Ahrens and Zeng in 2016 from editorials/commentaries in English-language newspapers published in Hong Kong, Beijing and Taipei.[6] It was designed to include comparable data on English from the three regions in terms of medium (written) text-type (newspaper opinion pieces), almost entirely early 21st century material (Table 12.1).

The corpus frequency data were extracted from each corpus by AntConc (Anthony 2019) and normalised for the different sizes of the

Table 12.1 Sources for the English editorials in the Sinosphere Corpus

Region/period	Total words	Newspaper mastheads
Beijing (BJ) 2011–16	61,904	China Daily (CD) Global Times (GT)
Hong Kong (HK) 2012–16	51,216	South China Morning Post (SCMP) The Standard (SD) Hong Kong Free Press (HKFP)
Taipei (TP) 1999–2016	33,761	The China Post (CP) Taipei Times (TT)

three corpora in Figures 12.1–12.3 below. In classifying examples of the modals extracted from the three data sets, we used the three broad categories of Biber et al. (1999), including designated subtypes as shown in Table 12.2.

Table 12.2 Categorisation of modals used in this research

Modal group label	Subcategories/subtypes	Individual modals included
possibility	probability, ability, permission	can, could, may, might
obligation	necessity	must, ought, should
prediction	volition, inclination	shall, will, would

The categorisation of the subtypes in Table 12.2 shows how they relate to Biber et al.'s (1999) three major categories, though they vary in individual research studies. The examples given categorise individual modals by their core usage, rather than whether their function in context is epistemic, deontic or dynamic. The coding categories for the modals *may* and *can* used by Deshors and Gries (2014) informed both the descriptive statistics in Section 4.3 as well as the multifactorial conditional inference tree in Section 4.4.

4. FINDINGS AND DISCUSSION

4.1 Distribution of Modals in the Editorials from Beijing, Hong Kong and Taipei

Because modals embed distinct attitudes and orientations of the writer/speaker to the content of their discourse, they are a critical component in its rhetoric. They imbue individual clauses/sentences with an authorial stance, which may be reinforced by repeated use of the same type of modal (for example, obligation) or varied with other types that complement it within the discourse. Baseline comparisons between the editorial texts in the three regional corpora is provided in their overall use of core modal verbs. The data include both high frequency modals and two very low frequency ones for comparative purposes. Figure 12.1 depicts the relative frequencies of the individual modals in a given corpus in relation to all modals in that corpus. For instance, *will* occurs with an absolute frequency of 409 in the Beijing corpus, which features a total of 1,050 modals, resulting in a relative frequency of 38.95 per cent for *will* in the Beijing corpus. A chi-square test ignoring *shall* due to its non-occurrence in the Taipei data profiles statistically highly significant differences between the modal frequencies in the three data sets ($p < .001$, df = 16, $\chi^2 = 206.76$, Cramer's V = 0.212).

The three regional corpora are alike in their very low usage of *ought to* and *shall*, coinciding with their declining use everywhere in the world (Mair and Leech 2006; Noël and van der Auwera 2015). Elsewhere the data sets for the other modals are a mixed bag with the Hong Kong and Taipei data often patterning similarly, with one or the other showing higher frequency. The most remarkable feature of Figure 12.1 is how far the data from the Beijing editorials far outstrips the others in its use of *will* (strong prediction) and *should* (moderately strong obligation). The Beijing corpora frequencies for both modals are way above those of the other varieties and the intense usage of the two modals taken together suggests that maintaining a strong stance is a priority in the rhetoric of editorial writing in the English newspapers published in Beijing.

(5) We **will** get nowhere if we simply cater to Western opinion. (Beijing_GT_20160919_45.txt)[7]
(6) He **should** first weigh the consequences of China's countermeasures. (Beijing_GT_20161109_04.txt)

The frequency in the Beijing corpora for the often tentative *would* is far lower than in the other two regional corpora, as is its usage of the other two tentative modals: *could*, *might*. Expressing certainty is a sign of strength in Chinese culture, and hedging a sign of weakness (Yang 2018: 128), as is evident in greater use of the more assertive modals in

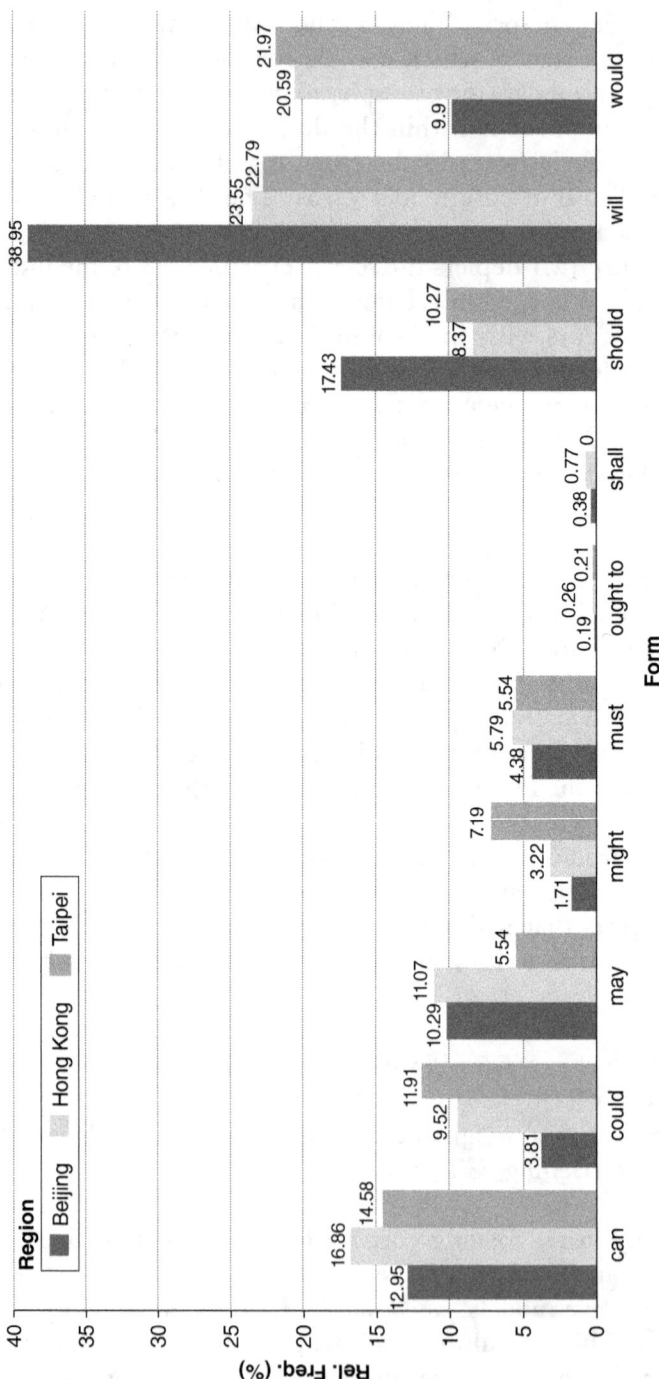

Figure 12.1 Relative frequencies of 10 modal verbs in corpora for Beijing, Hong Kong and Taipei

their L2 (second-language) English writing (Yang 2018: 126). Research on argumentative writing by Chinese learners of English has shown that their tone is more assertive than that of (first-language) English writers (Milton and Hyland 1999), a trait which could persist in their professional writing if they lack contact with English in social interactions.

The frequencies for *will* and *would* are quite similar in the Hong Kong and Taipei corpora: *will* is followed closely by *would* in Hong Kong and the other way around in Taipei. The parity in their use of these modals suggests that their editorial persuasive style has a more dynamic power relation between the writers and readers than in the style of editorial writers in Beijing, as both Hong Kong and Taipei editorials both allow for negotiation with the more tentative *would* built into conditional statements.

(7) If Woo is elected we **would** have a judge as the SAR leader. (Hong Kong_SD_20161027_13.txt)
(8) Withdrawal **would** also undermine relations with China. (Taipei TT 20161115_06.txt)

None of the top four modals in the Hong Kong or Taipei data expresses obligation. Their rhetoric is more exploratory, discussing possibilities in their respective regions rather than pre-empting discussion. Where they differ slightly it is that the Taipei corpora make more use of *could, might, should, would* with their somewhat remote aspect, whereas in the Hong Kong corpora it is *can, may, must, will*, the set with more direct semantics, that are used more. These differences are statistically significant ($p < .01$, df = 7, $\chi^2 = 24.261$, Cramer's $V = 0.139$).

4.2 Distribution of Quasi-modals in the Editorials from Beijing, Hong Kong and Taipei

Quasi-modals are associated with spoken English (Section 2.3), so their frequency reflects more interactive use of the language. Those studied in this research match those researched in most previous studies, including the relatively recent addition to the set of *want to* (Collins 2009a; Noël van der Auwera 2015). It emerged in American English during the 1990s and has since been far more frequent there than in British English (Mair and Leech 2006: 328; Collins 2009b: 290–1). *Want to* often projects volition, especially in first-person statements, and is included among the modals for that reason, and this is its regular use in all three subcorpora.

There are, however, a few instances of its use to express prediction and obligation in carefully modulated statements (one example in the Beijing data and three in the Hong Kong) as in:

(9) With that in mind, Washington may **want to** seriously rethink its approach. (Beijing_CD_20160711_84.txt)
(10) Come Tuesday ... you might **want to** pause at the historic moment of that announcement. (Hong Kong_HKFP_20161106_01.txt)

Figure 12.2 shows the relative frequencies of the nine quasi-modals in relation to the total number of quasi-modals in the editorials from the Beijing, Hong Kong and Taipei corpora. The frequencies of quasi-modal use among the three data sets all diverge and their differences – when *got to* and *had better* are discarded due to their low frequencies – are statistically highly significant ($p < .001$, df = 12, $\chi^2 = 33.307$, Cramer's $V = 0.239$).

The Beijing data profile stands out in Figure 12.2 with its restricted use of the quasi-modal range, apart from *have to, need to, want to*. The first two express obligation, complementing and diversifying the solid use of *should* and slight use of *must* among the core modals shown for the Beijing data in Figure 12.1. The very frequent use of *want to* (volition/obligation) in Figure 12.2 would reflect the Beijing commentators' strong interest in the actions of the United States in world affairs, and the remarkable rise of *want to* in American English. Limited use of other quasi-modals in the Beijing editorials would align with the fact that they often serve as the platform for announcing major national policies. The editor's voice reflects a top-down power relation and call for immediate adoption of whatever is announced. The use of quasi-modals may generally be considered stylistically inappropriate in official statements of policy. The very low frequency of *going to* in Beijing editorials is telling, given that it could offer a paraphrase for *will*. *Going to* is used very frequently in first-language English speakers' conversation (Biber et al. 1999: 487–8) – but is less likely to be encountered on a regular basis by editorial writers in the Sinosphere. It could also be that the literal meaning of *going* (= 'travelling') is still salient for Chinese second-language users.[8] These various factors in the use of quasi-modals suggest that the inputs to learning English in Beijing are less interactive than in Hong Kong or Taipei, as corpora from both these regions make more use of *going to* (rather than *will*) for prediction, as shown in Figure 12.2.

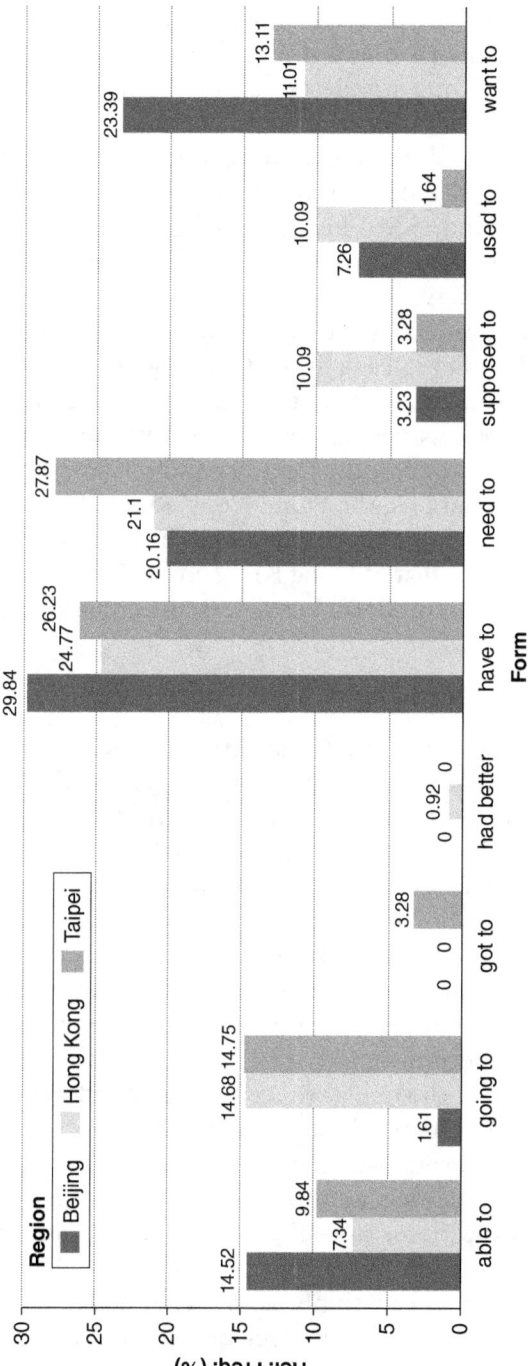

Figure 12.2 Relative frequencies for nine quasi-modals in corpora for Beijing, Hong Kong and Taipei

The Taipei profile for the quasi-modals includes more of the range than the Beijing profile (five out of the nine verbs in Figure 12.2), but less than the Hong Kong profile (seven of the nine). This difference may well reflect the fact that interactive English was in wider use in Hong Kong schools and other institutions up to 1997. Differences in the repertoires of quasi-modals in the Taipei and Hong Kong data thus seem to reflect their individual histories of English usage, that is, Hong Kong's 'outer-circle' colonial past and Taipei's consistent status as an 'expanding-circle' variety.

The profiles and frequency patterns of the modals and quasi-modals are significantly different in each of the three regional subcorpora. Their individual modal selections seem to reflect the different histories of English in each region as well as their respective political systems and outlook. While the rhetoric of the Beijing editorials is strong on political expectations and obligations, the Hong Kong editorials present issues in counterpoint, with attention to alternatives. The Taipei editorials' usage of modals approximates that of Hong Kong on the five commonest quasi-modals, while its overall profile is less diverse than that of Hong Kong.

4.3 Distribution of Modals with Interactive Pronoun Subjects

Let us now focus on some of the co-occurrence features associated with the use of modals that affect their meaning. As noted above (Section 2.1), the grammatical subject (first/second/third person) impacts on and fine-tunes the illocutionary force of modal verbs in different combinations. Their association with the first-person pronouns (*I/we*) and second person (*you*) contributes to the interactive dimension of communication (Biber 1988). The frequency of these interactive collocations with the core modals in regional editorials is shown in Figure 12.3. The relative frequencies stand for the proportions of the modal in question used with first- or second-person pronouns in relation to the overall absolute occurrence of the modal concerned. The differences across the varieties covered are statistically significant ($p < .01$).

In Figure 12.3, the very low rates of interactive pronoun usage with modal verbs in the Beijing editorials stand out from the other two corpora. Closer inspection shows that *you* is never used and *I* is used only once in a quotation. The Beijing corpora's instances of *we* with modals (total 11) are spread thinly across the modal verbs *can*, *must*, *should*, *will*, *would* and all found in declarative main clauses, apart from two with *can*.

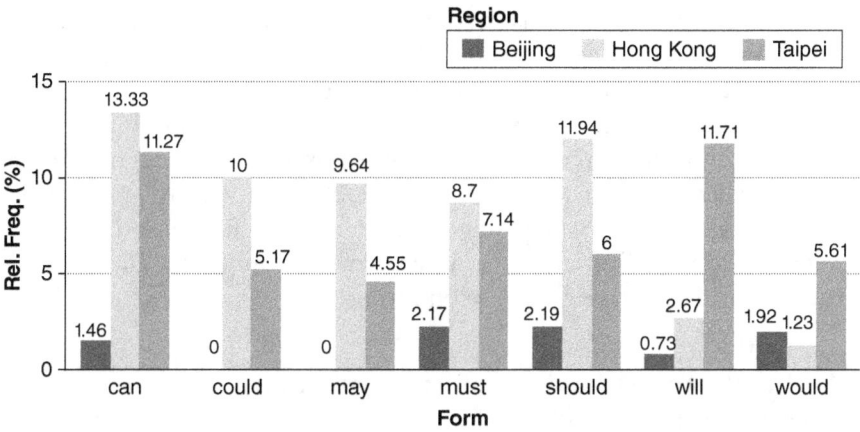

Figure 12.3 Frequencies of seven core modals with first- and second-person subjects in corpora for Beijing, Hong Kong and Taipei

(11) We **should** applaud and enjoy the achievements of all our sportsmen. (Beijing_CD_20160810_62.txt)
(12) There are some things we **can** learn from his previous talks and actions. (Beijing_GT_20160924_40.txt)

In addition, overall there is little use of *we* in the Beijing editorials as a collectivist strategy (Schneider 2018) or any appeal to shared values and interests. Figure 12.3 also shows that the interactive constructions using *we/you/I* with core modals occur far more in the Hong Kong editorials than in the other two data sets, except for *will* and *would*. The avoidance of *would* with first- or second-person pronouns can be explained in terms of the Hong Kong preference for exploratory discussion, seen above, and the use of *we* or *you* person with *will* projects a strong sense of commitment or direction rather than room for negotiation. A sensitivity to this again suggests greater familiarity with the illocutionary force of those constructions in face-to-face encounters – not shared by the editorial writers in Taipei. The outer-circle/expanding-circle difference in their evolutionary history is again evident.

Of the three personal pronouns, *you* is construed with modals much more frequently in the Hong Kong data than either of the others (Hong Kong 24: Taipei 5: Beijing 0), suggesting more articulation and accommodation of alternative perspectives in the Hong Kong editorial discourse. Hong Kong editorial writers also make most use of *we* (Hong Kong 23: Taipei 12: Beijing 11), which in English political rhetorical often serves to blur the distinction between inclusive and exclusive applications of *we* (Wales 1996: 62–3; Biber et al. 1999: 329). Its use in editorials blends the intrinsic voice of the newspaper with the extrinsic interests of the community it addresses, invoking support for its position. As a communicative strategy it is most used in Hong Kong editorials, balanced by greater use of *you*. In combination with the greater use of quasi-modals and a wider range of core modals, it makes the style of the Hong Kong editorials more interactive on the social and political issues they raise, inviting discussion rather than seeming to control it.

4.4 Multifactorial Analysis of Linguistic and Semantic Concomitants for *will/would*

To extend this research to other factors inherent in the linguistic context and the use of modals, we embraced a set including most of those discussed in Section 2. The coding categories used are based on eight of those used in Deshors and Gries (2014).

We used a conditional inference tree (compare Hothorn et al. 2006; Hothorn and Zeileis 2015) to profile how the language-external and language-internal factors shown in Table 12.3 influence modal choice. With a classification accuracy of 67.78 per cent, the conditional inference tree is significantly better ($p < .05$) than a baseline model always predicting the most frequent modal choice, that is, *will*.

Four of the eight independent variables, REGION, CLAUSE TYPE, VERB SEMANTICS and SUBJECT WORD CLASS – in decreasing order of importance – significantly influence the choice between *will* and

Table 12.3 Factors coded for *will* vs *would* for a multifactorial analysis of 1,080 corpus examples

FACTORS	and their levels
MODAL	*will, would*
REGION	Beijing, Hong Kong, Taipei
CLAUSE TYPE	co-ordinate, main, subordinate
VERB SEMANTICS	abstract, action, communication, copula, perception
SUBJECT ANIMACY	animate, inanimate
SUBJECT WORD CLASS	lexical, pronominal
SUBJECT NUMBER	singular, plural
NEGATION	yes, no
VOICE	active, passive

would. The most important split in the data is regional in that modal choice is modelled as different in Hong Kong and Taipei in comparison with Beijing, with the latter – on average – having a stronger tendency towards modal *will* than the other regions. In Hong Kong and Taipei editorials, *would* is more frequent (node 11) in subordinate than in main or co-ordinate clauses (node 10), which may to some extent reflect the traditional 'sequence of tenses' convention (Section 2.1). In Beijing editorials, *will* as a modal is most dominant in co-ordinated or main clauses with verbs denoting abstract processes, actions or communication (node 4 and example (13)).

(13) In so doing, farmers and food producers **will** also develop a greater awareness that antibiotics must not be overused. (Beijing_CD_20160829_49.txt)

When *would* is used by Beijing editors in main/co-ordinated clauses it tends to occur with copula verbs or verbs of perception, and with pronoun subjects; see nodes 6 and 7 and example (14). The greater use of *would* by Hong Kong and Taipei editors is not constrained by these syntactic factors, and much greater in subordinate clauses.

(14) Otherwise, we **would** have witnessed impressive headway toward both the FTA and RCEP. (Beijing_CD_20161031_10.txt)

The non-significance of ANIMACY as a factor in the overall model for selecting *will/would* probably reflects the low frequencies of interactive pronoun subjects (*I*, *we*, *you*) found with *will* and *would* in the Beijing editorials, discussed in Section 4.3 above. Other factors relating to noun phrase subjects – their grammatical word class and grammatical number – also proved non-significant. Among factors relating to the verb phrase, neither polarity nor voice construction proved significant.

The conditional inference tree for *will* and *would* (Figure 12.4) underscores the main finding of the preceding sections: there are significant regional differences in modal usage in Beijing editorials versus those used in Hong Kong and Taipei editorials. It identifies other key syntactic and semantic factors in the selection of *will* or *would*, that is, the association of *will* with main or subordinate clauses and their interconnection with the semantics of the accompanying lexical verb in the Beijing data. Finer-grained analysis of the subject-person pronouns and

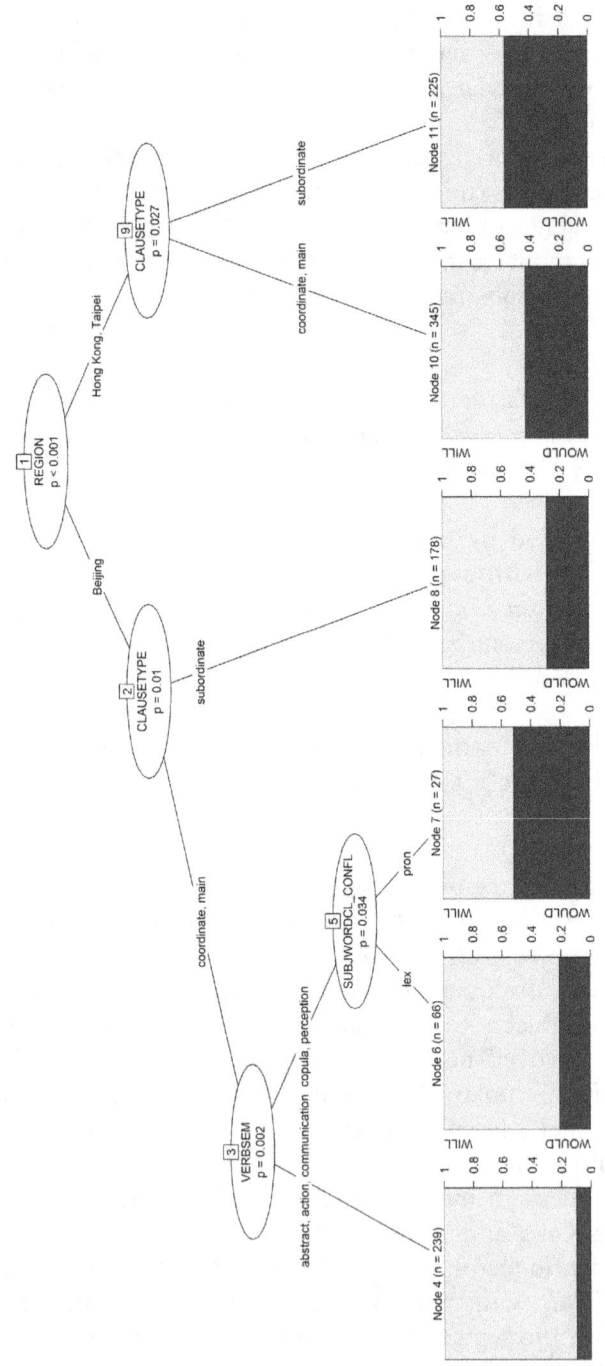

Figure 12.4 Conditional inference tree for modals *will/would* based on factors in Table 12.2

different noun types as subjects would be in order, to further explore the role of animacy in the selection of modals.

5. CONCLUSION

The association of different types of modals and quasi-modals with particular regions represented in the English editorials in the Sinosphere Corpus allows us to consider their communicative rhetoric in different regions. The frequent use of assertive modals such as *will* and *should* in Beijing editorials correlates with their clearly top-down political decision process and the government's dominance in sociopolitical policy and planning. This contrasts with the greater use of tentative modals such as *would* and in Hong Kong and Taipei editorials, suggesting more exploratory and interactive contexts for policy discussion with the community.

The data also illustrate the different styles of persuasion to be found in the same written text-type in newspaper discourse written by second-language users of English, even in closely related varieties in the expanding circle of English. How far they reflect the style of individual newspaper editors rather than the regional context of culture is a further question. Within each region we have used data from more than one newspaper to broaden the basis of evidence, but larger corpora of each regional newspaper would be needed to identify their individuality in communicating with their respective speech communities.

Other possible factors to consider are the subtle yet significant grammatical differences among varieties of Chinese (Lin et al. 2019), like those between varieties of English. Twenty-first century English variations in the Sinosphere may be compounded by the varieties of Chinese used by their speakers. Wang and Huang's (2018) study, using modal verbs as one of the key pieces of evidence, showed that the varieties of Mandarin in mainland China and Taiwan expressed power relations differently. This supports our current hypothesis. In other research, Hou and Huang (2020) showed that regional variations of Chinese are compounded by genre differences. Xu et al. (2020) showed significant differences between two different varieties of Chinese in their use of light verbs. Other variable elements of lexicogrammar such as modal verbs may show similar variations in different varieties of Chinese. Further research may shed light on whether the variations we observe may be attributed to the variations in L1.

The differing levels of interactive language we have found in English editorials examined here – reflected in the use of modals (with first-/second-person pronoun subjects) and of informal quasi-modals such as *going to* – may well be symptomatic of how much interactive use of English there is in the immediate speech community. These linguistic elements affect the degree of formality and closeness or distance constructed in the discourse (compare Nini 2014). Because the functionalities of English correlate with its evolutionary status within the region, the use of more informal constructions may be regarded as an indicator of the sociocultural context, that is, the third nexus in Schneider's terms (this volume). Meanwhile, the different proportions of modals of prediction and obligation such as *will* and *should* found in the three regions of the Sinosphere seem to construct different types of power relations in both social and political contexts with their respective readerships (that is, Schneider's second nexus).

NOTES

1. *Quasi-modal* is used in this paper for the category of periphrastic modals, in line with Huddleston and Pullum (2002) and Collins (2009a, 2009b), for the category otherwise known as *semi-modals* (Biber et al. 1999; Mair and Leech 2006) or *marginal modals* (Quirk et al. 1985).
2. See below, Table 12.2.
3. Dependent/subordinate clause is intended here to cover the projected clause (Halliday and Matthiessen 1994) and complement clause (Huddleston and Pullum 2002).
4. For the exonormative and endonormative phases in the evolution of varieties of English, see Schneider (2007).
5. The convention has always been challenged in actual usage, as in *Webster's Dictionary of Usage* (Gilman 1989) and the data from Biber et al. (1999: 489).
6. An earlier version of the corpus compiled by Ahrens and Zeng (this volume) was used for this study with dates slightly varying for each newspaper but starting no earlier than 4 July 2016 and ending no later than 15 November 2016.
7. In these identification codes, the initialism references the newspapers listed in Table 12.1, its publication date given in year/month/day order, and the sample number – its text (txt) number.

8. This is in keeping with the research findings of Müller (2005: 190) on L2 learners' use of spoken discourse markers: that German speakers use English discourse markers such as *you know* only in its more or less literal senses, and much less in the extended functions inherent in American students' uses of it.

REFERENCES

Anthony, L. (2019) AntConc (Version 3.5.8) [Computer software]. Waseda University. <https://www.laurenceanthony.net/software> (last accessed 4 January 2021).

Biber, D. (1988). Variation across speech and writing. Cambridge University Press.

Biber, D., Johansson, S., Leech, G., Conrad, S. and Finegan, E. (1999). Longman grammar of spoken and written English. Longman.

Burridge, K. and Peters, P. (2020). English in Australia – extraterritorial influences. In S. Buschfeld and A. Kautzsch (Eds.), *Modelling World Englishes: A joint approach to postcolonial and non-postcolonial Englishes* (pp. 202–27). Edinburgh University Press.

Buschfeld, S. and Kautzsch, A. (2017). Towards an integrated approach to postcolonial and non-postcolonial Englishes. World Englishes, 36(1), 104–22.

Collins, P. (2009a). *Modals and quasi-modals in English*. Rodopi.

Collins, P. (2009b). Modals and quasi-modals in World Englishes. *World Englishes, 28*(3), 281–92.

Collins, P. (2013). Grammatical variation in English worldwide: The role of colloquialisation. *Linguistics and Human Sciences, 8*(3), 289–306.

Deshors, S. C. and Gries, S. T. (2014). A case for the multifactorial assessment of learner language: The uses of *may* and *can* in French–English interlanguage. In D. Glynn and J. A. Robinson (Eds.), *Corpus methods for semantics: Quantitative studies in polysemy and synonymy* (pp. 179–204). John Benjamins.

Fowler, H. (1926). *A dictionary of modern English usage*. Clarendon Press.

Fries, C. (1925). The periphrastic future with *shall* and *will* in Modern English. *Publications of the Modern Language Association, 40*(4), 963–1024.

Gilman, W. (Ed.). (1989). *Webster's dictionary of English usage*. Merriam-Webster.

Gowers, E. (1965). *Fowler's dictionary of modern English usage*. Clarendon Press.

Halliday, M. and Matthiessen, C. (1994). *An introduction to functional grammar* (3rd ed.). Hodder Education.

Hothorn, T., Hornik, K. and Zeileis, A. (2006). Unbiased recursive partitioning: A conditional inference framework. *Journal of Computational and Graphical Statistics, 15*(3), 651–74.

Hothorn, T. and Zeileis, A. (2015). partykit: A modular toolkit for recursive partytioning in R. *Journal of Machine Learning Research, 16*, 3905–9.

Hou, R. and Huang, C. (2020). Classification of regional and genre varieties of Chinese: A correspondence analysis approach based on comparable balanced corpora. *Journal of Natural Language Engineering*. <https://doi.org/10.1017/S1351324920000121> (last accessed 11 January 2021).

Huddleston, R. and Pullum, G. (2002). *Cambridge grammar of the English language*. Cambridge University Press.

Kachru, Y. and Nelson, C. (2006). *World English in Asian contexts*. Hong Kong University Press.

Kruger, H. and Smith, A. (2018). Colloquialization versus densification in Australian English: A multidimensional analysis of the Australian Diachronic Hansard Corpus. *Australian Journal of Linguistics, 38*(3), 293–328.

Leech, G. (2003). Modality on the move: The English modal auxiliaries 1962–1992. In R. Facchinetti, M. Krug and F. Palmer (Eds.), *Modality in contemporary English* (pp. 223–40). De Gruyter.

Lin, J., Shi, D., Menghan, J. and Huang, C. (2019). Variations in World Chineses. In C.-R. Huang, Z. Jing-Schmidt and B. Meisterernst (Eds.), *The Routledge handbook of Chinese applied linguistics* (pp. 196–211). Routledge.

Loureiro-Porto, L. (2016). (Semi-)modals of necessity in Hong Kong and Indian Englishes. In E. Seoane and C. Suárez-Gómez (eds), *World Englishes: New theoretical and methodological considerations* (pp. 143–72). John Benjamins.

Mair, C. and Leech, G. (2006). Current changes in English syntax. In B. Aarts and A. McMahon (Eds.), *Handbook of English linguistics* (pp. 318–42). Blackwell.

Millar, N. (2009). Modal verbs in *TIME*. *International Journal of Corpus Linguistics, 14*(2), 191–220.

Milton, J. and Hyland, K. (1999). Assertions in students' academic essays: A comparison of L1 and L2 writers. In R. Berry, B. Asker, K. Hyland and M. Lam (Eds.), *Language analysis, description and pedagogy* (pp. 147–61). Hong Kong University of Science and Technology.

Müller, S. (2005). *Discourse markers in native- and non-native English discourse*. John Benjamins.

Nini, A. (2014). *Multidimensional Analysis Tagger 1.2 – manual*. <http://sites.google.com/site/multidimensionaltagger> (last accessed 11 January 2021).

Noël, D. and van der Auwera, J. (2015). Recent quantitative changes in the use of modals and quasi-modals in the Hong Kong, British and American printed press. In P. Collins (Ed.), *Grammatical change in English world-wide* (pp. 437–64). John Benjamins.

Quirk, R., Greenbaum, S., Leech, G. and Svartvik, J. (Eds.) (1985). *A comprehensive grammar of the English language*. Longman.

Rayson, P. (2008). From keywords to key semantic domains. *International Journal of Corpus Linguistics, 13*(4), 519–49.

Schneider, E. W. (2007). *Postcolonial English: Varieties around the world*. Cambridge University Press.

Schneider, E. W. (2018). The interface between cultures and corpora. *ICAME Journal, 42*(1), 97–132. <https://doi.org/10.1515/icame-2018-0006> (last accessed 4 January 2021).

Wales, K. (1996). *Personal pronouns in present-day English*. Cambridge University Press.

Wang, W. and Fang, F. (2019). Chinese netizens' reactions to the use of English as a lingua franca. *English Today, 35*(4), 3–12.

Wang, X. and Huang, C. (2018). From near synonyms to power relation variations in communication: A cross-strait comparison of 'guli' and 'mianli'. In J. Hong, Q. Su and J. Wu (Eds.), *Workshop on Chinese lexical semantics* (pp. 155–66). Springer.

Xu, H., Jiang, M., Lin, J. and Huang, C. (2020). Light verb variations and varieties of Mandarin Chinese: Comparable corpus driven approaches to grammatical variations. *Corpus Linguistics and Linguistic Theory*. <https://doi.org/10.1515/cllt-2019-0049> (last accessed 11 January 2021).

Yang, X. (2018). A corpus-based study of modal verbs in Chinese learners' academic writing. *English Language Teaching, 11*(2), 122–30.

Zhang, H. Y. (2015). Comparative analysis of modal auxiliary verbs in English and Chinese. *Sino-US English Teaching, 12*(2), 128–36.

CHAPTER 13

Where Grammar Meets Culture: Pronominal Systems in Australasia and the South Pacific Revisited

Kate Burridge and Carolin Biewer

1. INTRODUCTION

> The material and non-material conditions of a culture are reflected in the grammar of its language, which is not arbitrary; when these change, the language changes in response. The language thus optimises itself in relation to its environment. (Halliday [1990] 2003: 144)

In this paper, we explore the pronominal systems of some of the most significant Englishes currently spoken in Australasia and the South Pacific (AuSP). Our account includes representatives from the transplanted native varieties of English (L1 Englishes) and the English-based contact varieties of the area, in particular the second-language varieties of English (English as a second language – ESL).[1] In line with Kortmann's (2010) classification of recurring vernacular features around the anglophone world, a number of the widely attested AuSP features constitute (near) universals (or *angloversals*) of (non-standard) pronominal usage in English; for example, special second-person plural forms, levelled cases, null subjects. The focus here, however, is on unusual morphosyntactic features and practices (see Wagner 2012; Siegel 2013); for example, number contrasts (singular, dual (trial), plural), inclusive–exclusive distinctions (including the addressee or not) and null objects. The question is to what extent these features cluster according to geographical region (that is, as *areoversals*) or according to variety type (that is, as *varioversals*). Kortmann (2010: 410) argues that 'variety type outperforms geography as a predictor of the morphosyntactic profiles of Englishes around the world'. But why then do we find such strikingly different features in this region in contrast to others?

Clearly, there are substrate effects in play but it is only when we take account of the external ecology that we can explain why certain of these language habits are transferred. Many of these Pacific speech communities are small and closely integrated so people interact frequently with one other and share a large amount of common knowledge; often there are serious tensions between insiders and outsiders (historically and continuing to the present day). This paper revisits the impact of geography and explores how factors to do with the cultural and sociohistorical aspects of the linguistic setting have been involved in shaping some of the unusual pronominal patterns we find in this geographical area. We will be arguing here for the influence of social and cultural factors on grammar and the importance therefore of this sort of information in any account of areality.[2] We feel that our findings constitute what Schneider (this volume) discusses as the second nexus and third nexus between language forms and culture. In his paper, pronouns are presented as 'indicator terms', whose frequency (first versus second person) reveals specific cultural dimensions (an individualist versus collectivist orientation). Our account in Section 4 fits comfortably under this label 'individualism versus collectivism'. Here we align pronoun behaviour with the cultural perception of identity in the Pacific; forms *we*, *I*, *they* reflect 'ordered attitudes and values in a society', and thus constitute Schneider's second nexus (this volume). Our focus in Section 2, however, is on the actual grammatical properties of pronouns (for example, number and clusivity). We feel these linguistic distinctions are more like 'indicator structures' and better signify the more abstract third nexus. Pronouns have a borderline status within the linguistic system, showing characteristics of both lexical and functional categories, and it is entirely fitting that the cultural impact should involve both the lexical and structural levels.

2. CULTURE AND GRAMMAR

Grammars code best what speakers do most. (DuBois 1985: 363)

As Schneider describes (this volume), there have been a number of different approaches that investigate the relationship between language and its environment and highlight the importance of the extralinguistic environment in shaping the formation and use of grammatical structures

– how speakers interact with each other and with the world they live in; their attitudes, their cultural knowledge; the size of the speech community and so on.

Grammatical phenomena can come about because these cultural and social factors compel speakers to habitually include certain kinds of information in their conversations. Cultural preoccupations give rise to ways of thinking and ways of expressing that, spurred on by the usual linguistic processes of change, can then end up embodied in the grammar. Much like the kind of invisible-hand process in language change evoked by Keller (1994), the cumulative effect of many individuals' behaviour leads to useful purpose-built language structures – habitual conversational practices generate specialised constructions that then 'harden' into specific forms and constructions (see Goddard 2002).

English-speaking communities in Australasia and the Pacific Rim have common ancestries and hence there will be structural similarities between the native languages and local contact varieties. Similarities in the external ecology may be catalysts of areal features; in other words, shaping English usage will also be sociolinguistic, sociocultural and historical aspects of the setting in which the language is used and also factors such as social identity, language attitudes, language policies, immigration patterns and so on. Successful communication in English in Pacific communities requires a local form of English that is adequate to express the cultural needs of the community. Biewer (2015: 218) has shown, for instance, how the use of verbal past tense non-marking in South Pacific Englishes (such as *they start* for *they started*) is also related to local narrative techniques and culture-specific conceptualisations of time. Such cultural practices are having an influence beyond national borders, fashioning new Pacific forms of English usage.

3. PRONOUNS AND CULTURE

> Pronoun use is often cited, with good reason, as a domain in languages where grammatical usage can be highly sensitive to cultural attitudes and mores. (Pawley 2002: 111)

Pronouns can be thick with cultural meaning (to paraphrase Enfield 2002: 3); we need only to consider the current passionate debates around gender-neutrality in modern Standard English pronouns to see evidence of this. Pronouns encode culture-specific messages and ways of thinking; they 'carve up people space' (Mühlhäusler 2012: 110), expressing aspects of the social structure and identity to do with power, distance and solidarity, and, more recently, gender and sexuality. It is not surprising that Wagner in her account of pronominal features in World Englishes makes the point that '[p]ronominal systems are among those with the highest degree of variability in varieties of English' (2012: 379).

This variability can sometimes involve familiar pronoun forms having distinctive local functions. Take the second-person plural *youse* in Australian English (AusE), a ubiquitous pronominal feature in the English of this area, in fact a named angloversal of (non-standard) pronominal usage (Kortmann 2010). The interest lies not in *youse* itself but in what it does. Consider the following example where comedy character Michelle (Magda Szubanski) is giving a picture of life on the streets:

(1) 'Well, firsta all, if youse lag on someone, ya dob 'em in, ya become a dog,' Michelle says while the normally mute Ferret nods in agreement. (*TV Week* 1992: 14)

Here we see *youse* extending beyond the regular dialectal use and referring to a singular addressee. It is a type of hypercorrect behaviour, specifically a 'hyperdialectalism', where a local symbol expands to signal vernacular identity.[3] The 'incorrect' language of non-standard grammar falls outside what is good and proper and forms like *youse* help to define the gang. When it is important to indicate plurality, additional marking is usually applied: *all youse; youse all, youse guys, youse lot* and also *youses*.[4]

The expected pattern of change for plural pronouns is to extend to singular referents for the purpose of expressing distinctions to do with social status, politeness and social distance (Heine's 'honorification'; Heine and Song 2011: 601). Unusually, AusE *youse* has spread to singular referents for the purpose of expressing solidarity, vernacularity and membership. Australians have always regarded their colloquial idiom as a significant part of their cultural identity. True, the current climate of growing informality has seen a global increase of non-standard features but the penchant for informality does appear stronger in AusE compared with British and American English. Peters and Burridge (2012) and Collins and Yao (2018) point to the intensified use of colloquial features in the southern hemisphere – it has become a regional point of difference and one fostered by the historical and sociocultural context (see Burridge (2020) on the victory of the vernacular downunder; also Chapter 16, this volume).

3.1 'Societies of intimates': Contact-based Englishes in the AuSP

> If the phenomenon is rare cross-linguistically, then the explanation should not invoke universal characteristics, but use idiosyncratic reasons from the cultural or linguistic history of the language and its speakers. Only if a phenomenon is common cross-linguistically, general semantic, functional or structural explanations make sense. (Cysouw 2005: 101)

The most interesting variation will always involve features and practices that stand out as somehow abnormal or unexpected. As Cysouw suggests above, it is here we see cultural 'wild card' factors at work. In this spirit, we now go on to look at four of the more eccentric characteristics of pronominal usage in the Englishes of the AuSP area – 'insider–outsider' pronouns, null object pronouns, number contrasts and inclusive–exclusive distinctions. Space, alas, does not permit us to examine some of the other culturally motivated pronominal features such as resumptive pronouns and gender non-distinctions on pronouns and the role of the *fa'afafine* in Samoa. These we must leave for another day.

3.1.1 'Us and them' pronouns: Pitkern-Norf'k

> From the beginning, the Pitcairners emphasized differences between insiders and outsiders: the mutineers against the Tahitians, the old families against the 'interlopers' who arrived in the 1820s, the Pitcairners versus the 'English'. Norf'k has many words for outsiders . . . and the daily discussion is dominated by the tension between local Pitcairners and Australians and New Zealanders who dominate the economy. (Mühlhäusler 2012: 113–14)

Pitkern-Norf'k is the linguistic fall-out of the infamous mutiny on the *Bounty* that occurred in the South Pacific 28 April 1789 – it is also home to two of the most distinctive pronouns of the area, namely, first-person plural pronouns *auwa* and *uklan*. Mühlhäusler (2014) outlines the complex social and pragmatic conditions behind the use of these pronouns but a recurring theme in all of his examples is an 'insider–outsider' distinction – *auwa/uklan* 'we Norfolk Islanders' versus *dem* 'them'. The following is taken from a 2002 internet forum:

(2) *Sorry fer **ucklun** enn Norfolk cos we getten simmess d' mainland.*
Woe is **us** on Norfolk because we are getting like the mainlanders (Mühlhäusler 2014: 120)

'Insider–outsider' first-person pronouns are rare and some background is required to understand how these come about. Pitkern-Norf'k is a remarkable case of language contact because we know the number of English speakers who originally settled on Pitcairn in 1790, the origin of these speakers and even their names. In 1856, the entire population was relocated from Pitcairn to Norfolk Island (a small colony has since re-established itself on Pitcairn). Against enormous social tensions and division, and under constant threat of outsiders, the language evolved in this tiny remote community to become, as Mühlhäusler (2014: 106) describes, 'a symbol of non-identity with outsiders and a positive marker of a separate community'. It continues to provide the link with history and culture and is a central component of Islander identity. This speech community is the archetypal 'society of intimates' (Trudgill 2015) – all Norfolk Islanders know all other Norfolk Islanders (at least until recently) and small group communication is always more important than large group interaction. But more than this, Islander identity is, as Mühlhäusler emphasises, defined not by residence or birth but by bloodlines. In short, *auwa* and *uklan* are badges of identity for an in-group made up of *Bounty* mutineer descendants and early Pitcairn Island settlers – Pitcairn descendant Islanders with the 'correct' bloodlines.[5]

The origin of the *auwa* (*awwe*) is *all we* from 18th century St Kitts Creole; it reflects the influence of the mutineer Edward 'Ned' Young (Baker and Huber 2000: 835). The origin of *uklan* is less clear. All suggested sources, however, are nouns meaning 'person'/'people', a typical pathway for the development of first-person plural pronouns (Heine and Song 2011: 613). Of these nouns, the most likely source is *our clan* (from the mutineer Scotsman William McCoy; Klingel 1998). *Uklan* 'our clan' would have originated as a rhetorical strategy (a pragmatic marker) in face-to-face interaction to position islanders as part of the group, eventually grammaticalising into a pronoun via the usual processes of pragmatic unmarking. It is a clear illustration of grammar as the ossified retention of experience (Halliday [1990] 2003 and DuBois 1985): culture-specific patterns of usage freezing over time into morphosyntactic features. A comparable example is the genesis of the new pronoun *man* in inner city London English (Cheshire 2013) except that, in the case of Pitkern-Norf'k, sentiment goes beyond solidarity to more of an 'us–them' mentality.

3.1.2 Null object pronouns: South Pacific Englishes

> Listeners who are operating in a familiar environment in interaction with speakers whose language or dialect they are familiar with, with whom they are well acquainted, with whom they interact frequently and with whom they share a large fund of common knowledge, can make do with less phonetic and semantic information than listeners who are less familiar with the situation, the topic and other interlocutors. (Trudgill 1995: 144)[6]

Another concrete example of the culture–grammar relationship is the omission of pronouns in object position in acrolectal South Pacific English (SPE).[7] If the referent is recoverable, these L2 speakers tend to economise language production and extend zero anaphora to contexts beyond the ones acceptable in Standard English (Biewer 2015: 194).

(3)   but they can't use Māori . . . they can understand Ø but they can't speak Ø (CookE/BA.txt)

Null objects, as in example (3), are the fall-out of local practices of structuring discourse transferred from the mother tongue into a local use of English. Zero anaphora is a discursive device common in Pacific communities. As Mosel (1991: 297) describes for the Samoan language, 'whenever it is clear from the context which person, animal or object is involved in an action as the agent or patient, that participant does not need to be expressed'. These are small communities with high social density. Pacific Islanders will assume that everyone knows everyone and a lot of knowledge is shared and does not need to be spelled out.

3.1.3 Number and inclusive–exclusive contrasts: AuSP contact varieties

> In small language communities, value may be placed on whether someone is coming alone or with one other person or with a few or with many, shown by singular, dual, paucal, and plural pronouns. (Dixon 2012: 452)

The two most widespread features of the contact varieties in this region are the elaborate number contrasts and inclusive–exclusive distinctions (Wagner 2012; Filimonova 2012); indeed, both features have been listed as prime candidates for areality by Siegel (2013) and Kortmann (2010) for the region. The first-person pronouns of Pitkern-Norf'k, for example, show a complex grammatical number system (singular, dual, plural) and a clusivity contrast (inclusive versus exclusive of the addressee). Example (4) illustrates the dual inclusive pronoun *hemi/hemii*.

(4) *Orlrait,* **himii** *staat aut yena faiw aklok.*
All right, the two of us will go out there at five o'clock. (Buffet and Laycock 1988: 10)

The form derives in all likelihood from *thou* + *me* (via lenition to /h/) and is clearly calqued on the Tahitian model (Ross and Moverley 1964). Substratum influence, however, cannot be explained without reference to extralinguistic factors. As both Trudgill (2015) and Dixon (2012) point out, small-scale speech communities with high social density coincide with the most complex pronominal systems in the world's languages. Several number distinctions and inclusive–exclusive contrasts are a consequence of the importance placed on intimate dyadic interaction, communal obligations and classificatory relationships. In reference to Austronesian clusivity, for example, Lichtenberk (2005: 264) shows how by blurring the distinction between speaker and addressee, the integrative use of inclusive pronouns is 'indexical of solidarity, in-groupness, personal closeness'; in other words, it signals that the speaker and one addressee (or more) is in a relation of in-groupness.[8]

In this next section, we show how these contrasts, so important to the social life of speakers in the Pacific, can be maintained in their L2 Englishes by imbuing mainstream L1 pronouns with additional home-grown functions. Areality therefore can be a matter of function rather than structure, and the discussion attests to the need for more focus to be placed on local functions to understand pronoun usage and to uncover viable areal candidates.

4. INDIVIDUALITY AND COLLECTIVITY: PRONOUN COMPLEXITY IN THE SOUTH PACIFIC

I am not an individual; I am an integral part of the cosmos. I share divinity with my ancestors, the land, the seas and the skies. I am not an individual, because I share a 'tofi' (an inheritance) with my family, my village and my nation. I belong to my family and my family belongs to me. I belong to my village and my village belongs to me. I belong to my nation and my nation belongs to me. This is the essence of my sense of belonging. (Former Prime Minister of Samoa Tuiatua Tupua Tamasese Taisi Efi, in Henderson 2016: 316)

In this section, our attention shifts to pronominal usage in SPE in Fiji, Samoa and the Cook Islands. Polynesian languages and Polynesian culture have a noticeable effect on the grammar of Samoan and Cook Islands English (CookE); Fijian and Fijian cultural values and beliefs also have a vital influence on the grammar of Fiji English.[9] The data for this case study stem from Biewer's recordings of 24 Samoans, 24 Fijians and 24 Cook Islands Māori living in their home countries. The recordings, which add up to around 120,000 words, were made in 2007. The participants represent diverse age groups and both urban and rural backgrounds and speak mostly acrolectal SPE. Basilectal features occur rarely in the data set, though occasionally appear in commentary on features other speakers might use.

Remnants of the elaborate number and inclusive–exclusive contrasts just described for Pitkern-Norf'k are also found in SPE, albeit much more restricted. In basilectal Fiji English a three-fold distinction including a dual are observable (Tent and Mugler 2008: 549). Acrolectal SPE, however, follows L1 grammar more closely and, to capture such contrasts, it implements these structures by enriching the pronouns with local readings.

As far as the cultural perception of identity in the Pacific is concerned, Pacific Islanders have a sense of self that is relational – that is, the perception of the self is based on socio-spatial relationships within larger collectives. The *I* is considered inseparable from the community. Leo Tanoi, in his assessment of Samoan identity, comes to the conclusion that 'Samoan culture is . . . strict in a sense that you're very limited. You're the "we", you're not an individual' (Tanoi, in Drago 1998). In short, the *I* is part of the *we*. Added to that, there is also a strict separation between different island communities. Pacific identity means there is a strong identification with the family, the community and the nation. Identifying who 'we' is in the recordings is complex.

4.1 *We* versus *we all*

During the interviews, it was noticeable that when interviewees were asked about personal beliefs and opinions, they would answer in the first-person plural to identify with values, beliefs, actions and objects pertaining to the community. They would also display a fine-grained distinction between the use of *we* versus *we all*. While *we* referred to the family, the community, the nation or the congregation in its collectivity, *we all* designated everyone within the family, community and so on, the individuals in the group.[10] In example (5), every individual in the Aitutakian group that competed during Te Maeva Nui played a different instrument.[11] In (6), the speaker uses *we* to express that the family in its collectivity owns a pearl farm on Manhiki but *we all* to explain that all the individual members of the family bar the parents actually live on Rarotonga.[12]

(5) **we all** have a different uhm instrument (CookE/EL.txt)
(6) **we** have big farm in Manihiki . . . / my dad's looking after/ all of us is all here/ me my brother my sisters/ **we all**/ we all over here . . . (CookE/JN.txt)

In the CookE subcorpus, words that frequently co-occur with *our* are *language, homeland, own, culture, dancing, ancestors, forefathers, island* and *way*. To some extent, that is not surprising given the topics of these interviews (largely Pacific language and culture) but it shows a strong identification with the cultural background and interesting details about how speakers position themselves in terms of their identity. *We, our* often refers to the island community. The interviewees describe their own background in terms of what the community has and does and they describe themselves first and foremost as part of the island community. This sense of community is so strong that it transcends time, space and opposing views. In example (7), a community elder from Penrhyn talks about other Cook Islanders leaving for NZ. He previously stated that that would never be an option for him and yet he uses *we* and not *they* since he feels a strong bond with the community. He is part of this community just as they are. This still applies to those other community members who decided to live in a different place, NZ.

(7) all the people **we** go to NZ (CookE/AK.txt)

Equally striking is the use of *we* in (8). The same Penrhyn man talks about his ancestors who had been kidnapped by missionaries in the 1860s (a common procedure in the 19th century known as 'blackbirding'). Being asked whether people became suspicious of missionaries at the time, he starts talking about his ancestors first as *they* and then corrects himself, replacing *they* with *we*:

(8)   well the thing is **they**/ **we** didn't/ **we** didn't really knew (CookE/AK.txt)

As Tuiatua Tupua Tamasese Taisi Efi said, 'I share divinity with my ancestors'. There is the belief that 150 years later the ancestors are still around in some ways and still part of the community. It is a strong communal bond that survives time and place. Clearly, *we* refers to much more than Western scholars might believe.

4.2 *We* versus *they*

The pronouns of the first- and third-person plural are commonly used to distinguish between insiders and outsiders. Outsiders may be outsiders by cultural and/or ethnic distinctions. Pacific Islanders from different islands in the Cook Islands distinguish between these islands in terms of the cultural heritage and the ancestry of their inhabitants. Aitutakians – just as well as other island communities in the Cook Islands – would emphasise a different perspective from, say, the Manihikians or the Rarotongans. In a way, this is another means of expressing exclusivity when Cook Islanders use *we* to refer to their island community. It is a common theme of the recordings to compare cultural actions and beliefs of various island communities and discuss who is the better dancer and who stole dance movements from whom or forgot the traditional moves.

One such example can be found in (9) when a young Aitutakian woman compares the drumbeats of her home island with the drumbeats of other Cook Islands communities. It is noticeable that Cook Islanders, in particular, make a distinction between the culture and ethnicity of people from the Northern group and the Southern group. That explains the *us* vs *them* distinction that a young Cook Islander from the Northern group emphasises in (10) when talking about Cook Islanders from the Southern group.[13]

(9)   **we** got **our** own **our** own beat/ and the other outer islands got **their** own beat . . . tonight **we're** having **our** drum dance tonight (CookE/EL.txt)

(10) but the south island/ **they** like the north islands cultures (CookE/JN.txt)

(11) **we** always say 'kia orana'/ it means 'may you live on'/ . . . it's **our** way of greeting and welcoming people . . . (CookE/EL.txt)

In (11), however, *we* refers to the Cook Islanders in contrast to Westerners. In sum, *we* (versus *they*) is implemented to mark cultural and ethnic distinctions but at the same time to show strong community bondage – a very strong sense of community, which transcends space and time but also strongly divides.

4.3 *We* versus *I*

The recordings are not devoid of the first-person singular. *I* was used to recount personal experiences during the interviews (for example, to describe personal shortcoming or childhood memories).

(12) every time **I** do that/ **I** realize that **I**/ it's like **I**'m losing my mother language/ try to do some Maori/ and do some English (CookE/BA.txt)

In the Cook Island subcorpus *my* collocates with *brothers, sister, family, dad, friends, husband, children, parents*. The individual is emphasised when talking about his or her role within the nuclear family and his or her relationship with close friends – that is, those who surround them daily, to whom they feel a particularly close connection.[14]

On the other hand, experiences are often perceived as shared. In fact, to some extent the individual has to subvert their wishes to the collective; I am 'we', there is no real distinction. This leads to an interesting phrasing of a Fijian marriage proposal (mentioned in the recordings as part of a retelling of a story about a fruit bat who wanted to marry a Fijian girl):

(13) **we** love you/ can you be **my** wife? (Fiji/AT.txt)

In this case, the individual with his avowals of affection is a representative of the community. He asks for the hand of the girl in consent with his family, the community. Equally, the phrase 'we love you' uttered to a slightly puzzled Western linguist by a community member in the Cook Islands meant that this was a message from the clan chief representing the community and expressing closeness and the affection of the community. The phrasing *we love you* instead of *I love you* may not be appreciated by a Western girl who is waiting for an individual expression of affection and adoration of her boyfriend but it is actually a very serious and solemn avowal in the Pacific. So *I* may be used to share individual memories of a lifetime, but *we* to discuss habits, opinions, expertise, that belong to and are supported by the community.[15] So when looking at the first-person pronoun in SPE one has to be very careful in discerning who the referent is. What is the local function of 'we', 'I' in the community?

5. DISCUSSION

In Section 3, we looked at the rarities of pronominal usage found in the AuSP region. These rather unEnglish-looking features we attributed to the cultural preoccupations of the speakers in question. Of course, we are aware that establishing a culture–grammar relationship is risky; as Wierzbicka (1979: 313) states, '[i]t is commonplace to say that every language embodies in its very structure a certain world-view, a certain philosophy. To prove it in a rigorous and verifiable way, however, is quite a different matter'. We have tried to avoid any arbitrariness here by drawing our linguistic implications from well-established cultural descriptions (independent of the pronominal features). Section 3.1.2, for instance, attributed the implementation of null objects to well-recognised cultural ideas of structuring discourse.

In Section 4, we saw how special functions of *we*, *I*, *they* capture the relational perception of the self and the strong bond of the individual with the home island in the Pacific. On the structural surface, many pronoun uses may look similar to English as a native language (ENL) and that is not surprising (Anderson's 'Transfer to Somewhere Principle' states that every form of grammatical transfer from the substrate into ESL needs an ENL template). But once we look at the local functions of such structures, we can detect that regional differences are fostered by the local sociocultural context. Finding these local functions/motivations is how we detect areal features. As in the case of Tahitian influence on Pitkern-Norf'k, substrate influences tell only part of the story.

Looking at pronoun number and inclusivity–exclusivity, we can see the competition between variety type and areality – much like a cross-over, pidgin and creoles make areality more visible, while L2 has it in shades. We concluded this speaks to a model that shows L2 and pidgins and creole as belonging to a continuum rather than two different mutually exclusive types.

6. CONCLUDING REMARKS: W(H)ITHER THESE FEATURES?

> There is reason to suppose that many aspects of linguistic complexity developed in society of intimates. . . . It is therefore possible that with the gradual disappearance of society of intimates, we will also see the disappearance of complexifying linguistic changes. (Trudgill 2015: 145)

So where might these pronominal features be heading now? Societies like those in the AuSP region are not closed to innovation and they are of course not closed either to importing cultural and linguistic elements from outside. Of particular relevance here is the impact of Australian and NZ English, not just on account of geographical closeness but also because of political and economic clout.

The Pitkern-Norf'k pronominal forms earlier outlined are consistently found only in the traditional speech of older islanders; as Mühlhäusler (2014) describes, young speakers no longer distinguish all the forms and often use them in an idiosyncratic way. However, an important player in the pronoun story in Pitkern-Norf'k is Australian involvement in island affairs. On 12 May 2015, the Australian parliament made the bipartisan decision to abolish the Norfolk Island government. A *Guardian* article following this decision quotes Islander David Bigg:

> 'We're islanders, we're descendants from Tahiti and 17th-century Englishmen, we're not from Australia,' Bigg says. 'I don't feel connected to one other part of the planet the way I do to this place. It runs through my blood, and they can try as hard as they like, but they can't take out the blood that runs through our veins.' His friend, Timothy Pearson, 44, chimes in. 'It's not a matter of belonging to the larger nation,' he says. 'We belong to our own nation, five miles by three it may be.' (Davey 2015)

Self-government has always been a vital part of Islander identity and many see the intervention of the Australian government with its system of taxation and laws as a fresh round of colonial rule and punishment. Though critically endangered, the language remains a crucial barrier against the outside world – as do its pronouns that earmark the community of true Pitcairn descendants. Mühlhäusler's study of Norfolk Forum chat rooms (between 1999 and 2005) showed pronoun forms *wi*, *ucklan* and *auwa* as having high token frequency; even before

Australia's takeover, they were being used confrontationally to exclude outsiders and to challenge the authenticity of insiders who might not be of Pitcairn descent (2012: 217). Ironically, however, this will probably mean the loss of *auwa*. Many speakers shun it, seeing it as the English borrowing *our* (transcripts in Harrison 1986 show users of *auwa* being corrected; for example, *Yu tal 'aklan', 'auwa' es Inglish* 'Say "aklan". Auwa is English').

Trudgill (2015) predicts that morphosyntactic complexity disappears with the shift from a face-to-face society to a more mobile society (consider the loss in the complexity of mainstream English pronouns over time). Complicating factors here include the spread of new technologies, the demands of international communication, and the flourishing of novel creative and colloquial discourses online. And what will the influences of youth culture be on the young generation of speakers now so hooked to their smart devices? The etiology of innovation and change is never straightforward, with different physiological and linguistic pressures, working in concert with social and cultural pressures to coerce a language in a particular direction. As our brief foray into AuSP pronouns shows, linguistic structures do not exist outside these extralinguistic forces – and this makes change hard to predict.

NOTES

1. Here we are using 'contact variety' in a broad sense to refer to both the pidgin and creole languages and the L2 varieties of the area – both groups have been shaped through intensive language contact.
2. Note, we are using here a broader definition of 'areal' that also includes parallel developments within a given habitat without claiming any causal links (for a discussion of areoversals and how they can be identified, see Biewer and Burridge 2020).
3. Hernández-Campoy (2016: 180) describes *hyperdialectalisms* as 'the incorrect extension of vernacular features to linguistic contexts where they are not applicable' – the fall-out of either 'insufficient knowledge' or 'excessive effort in showing vernacular identity'.
4. A reported example cited in *The Sydney Morning Herald* (Column 8 2016): 'Recently my wife and I were waiting in a Newcastle fish shop for someone to emerge to take our order. We were joined by another couple when, a few minutes later, the attractive teenage shop assistant appeared from the kitchen, checked out the two

waiting couples, and politely and professionally asked, "Which of youses was first?"'.
5. A comparable example is the ultra-orthodox Haredi Jerusalemite Yiddish *mir* versus *undz*, described by Assouline (2010: 1) as reflecting 'the unique self-imposed seclusion that is the social reality of speakers of Haredi Yiddish' – 'us (Haredi Jews)' versus 'them (non-Haredi Jews)'.
6. Trudgill (1995) here relates rapid processes of grammaticalisation with the reduced need for elaboration (shared ground leads to phonological reduction, which in turn feeds the development of new grammatical structures).
7. South Pacific Englishes are second-language varieties of English used widely in postcolonial settings in the South Pacific. In the current paper, we are referring to ESL in Fiji, Samoa and the Cook Islands.
8. The closest Standard English comes to clusivity is the hortative *let's* construction (for example, in *Let's go!* the hearer is one of the goers).
9. See, for instance, Biewer (2009) on modal verbs in SPE and Biewer (2015) on verbal past tense non-marking in SPE.
10. This is reminiscent of the notional concord of collective nouns such as *team* in English as a native language (ENL). Speakers may choose singular verbs to indicate the collectivity of the group or plural verbs to depict the individuals within the group (Hundt 1998: 80).
11. Te Maeva Nui is an annual festival in the Cook Islands to celebrate the ratification of the Cook Islands Constitution. The different island communities take part in dancing and singing competitions to assess which community has the best dancers and singers.
12. The Cook Islands consist of 15 islands, 12 of which are inhabited. Cook Islanders further distinguish between a Northern group and a Southern group with '1000 km of empty sea' in between (Hunt and Keller 2003: 13). Aitutaki and Rarotonga belong to the Southern group, Manihiki and Penrhyn to the Northern group.
13. Example (10) also shows that there is a strong identification of the community with their homeland, which becomes visible in pronominal usage. The speaker uses *they* when talking about the Southern group of the Cook Islands as a reference to the inhabitants of the Southern group.
14. With words like *homeland* and *island*, however, the possessive pronoun *our* is used rather than *my* (this space belongs to everybody in the community).

15. The present discussion refers mostly to the Cook Islands subcorpus, but finds support in the Fijian data. In the Samoan data it was interesting to note that *they* can stand for other social groups in Samoa such as the *matai*, the *fa'afafine*, rather than other island communities. Here it depends more on the social hierarchies within the island nation and distinct gender roles, and not so much on ethnic distinctions. Most residents are full Samoan and see themselves as part of the same ethnic group.

REFERENCES

Assouline, D. (2010). The emergence of two first-person plural pronouns in Haredi Jerusalemite Yiddish. *Journal of Germanic Linguistics*, 22(1), 1–22.

Baker, P. and Huber, M. (2000). Constructing new pronominal systems from the Atlantic to the Pacific. *Linguistics*, 38(5), 833–66.

Biewer, C. (2009). Modals and semi-modals of obligation and necessity in South Pacific Englishes. *Anglistik*, 20(2), 41–55.

Biewer, C. (2015). *South Pacific Englishes: A sociolinguistic and morphosyntactic profile of Fiji English, Samoan English and Cook Islands English*. John Benjamins.

Biewer, C. and Burridge, K. (2020). World Englishes old and new: English in Australasia and the South Pacific. In D. Schreier, M. Hundt and E. Schneider (Eds.), *The Cambridge handbook of World Englishes* (pp. 282–308). Cambridge University Press.

Buffet, A. and Laycock, D. C. (1988). *Speak Norfolk today*. Himii.

Burridge, K. (2020). History of Australian English. In L. Willoughby and H. Manns (Eds.), *Australian English reimagined: Structure, features and developments* (pp. 175–92). Routledge.

Cheshire, J. (2013). Grammaticalisation in social context: The emergence of a new English pronoun. *Journal of Sociolinguistics*, 17(5), 608–33.

Collins, P. and Yao, X. (2018). Colloquialisation and the evolution of Australian English: A cross-varietal and cross-generic study of Australian, British, and American English from 1931 to 2006. *English World-Wide*, 39(3), 253–77.

Column 8. (2016). *The Sydney Morning Herald*, 21 January. <https://www.smh.com.au/national/nsw/column-8-20160121-gmatcj.html> (last accessed 11 January 2021).

Cysouw, M. (2005). Syncretisms involving clusivity. In E. Filimonova (Ed.), *Clusivity: Typology and case studies of inclusive–exclusive distinction* (pp. 73–112). John Benjamins.
Davey, M. (2015). 'We're not Australian': Norfolk Islanders adjust to shock of takeover by mainland. *The Guardian*, 21 May. <https://www.theguardian.com/australia-news/2015/may/21/were-not-australian-norfolk-islanders-adjust-to-shock-of-takeover-by-mainland> (last accessed 11 January 2021).
Dixon, R. M. W. (2012). *Basic linguistic theory: Further grammatical topics* (Vol. 3). Cambridge University Press.
Drago, C. (Director). (1998). *Island Style* [Documentary]. Video Education Australia.
DuBois, J. W. (1985). Competing motivations. In J. Haiman (Ed.), *Iconicity in syntax: Proceedings of a symposium on iconicity in syntax* (pp. 343–65). John Benjamins.
Enfield, N. J. (Ed.). (2002). *Ethnosyntax: Explorations in grammar and culture*. Oxford University Press.
Goddard, C. (2002). Ethnosyntax, ethnopragmatics, sign-functions, and culture. In N. J. Enfield (Ed.), *Ethnosyntax: Explorations in grammar and culture* (pp. 52–73). Oxford University Press.
Halliday, M. A. K. (2003). New ways of meaning: The challenges to applied linguistics. In J. Webster (Ed.), *On language and linguistics: Collected works of M.A.K. Halliday* (Vol. 3; pp. 139–74). Bloomsbury. (Original work published 1990).
Harrison, S. (1986). *Variation in present-day Norfolk speech* [Doctoral dissertation, Macquarie University].
Heine, B. and Song, A. (2011). On the grammaticalization of personal pronouns. *Journal of Linguistics*, 47(3), 587–630.
Henderson, A. K. (2016). Individuality, collectivity, and Samoan artistic responses to cultural change. *The Contemporary Pacific*, 28(2), 316–45.
Hernández-Campoy, J. M. (2016). *Sociolinguistic styles*. Wiley-Blackwell.
Hundt, M. (1998). *New Zealand English grammar: Fact or fiction?* John Benjamins.
Hunt, E. and Keller, N. (2003). *Rarotonga and the Cook Islands*. Lonely Planet.
Keller, R. (1994). *On language change: The invisible hand in language*. Routledge.
Klingel, M. (1998). A sociolinguistic attempt at explaining the dynamics of languages in contact: Pitkern ['Aklan] as a lexical act of identity. *The Creolist Archives Paper* online. Stockholms Universitet.

Kortmann, B. (2010). Variation across Englishes: Syntax. In A. Kirkpatrick (Ed.), *The Routledge handbook of World Englishes* (pp. 400–24). Routledge.

Lichtenberk, F. (2005). Inclusive–exclusive in Austronesian: An opposition of unequals. In E. Filimonova (Ed.), *Clusivity: Typology and case studies of the inclusive–exclusive distinction* (pp. 261–90). John Benjamins.

Mosel, U. (1991). The Samoan construction of reality. In R. Blust (Ed.), *The currents in Pacific linguistics: Papers on Austronesian languages and ethnolinguistics in honor of George Grace* (pp. 293–303). ANU Press.

Mühlhäusler, P. (2012). The complexity of the first person non-singular pronouns in Norf'k. In B. Kortmann and B. Szmrecsanyi (Eds.), *Linguistic complexity: Second language acquisition, indigenization, contact* (pp. 101–26). Walter de Gruyter.

Mühlhäusler, P. (2014). The pragmatics of first person non-singular pronouns in Norf'k. In T. Pavlidou (Ed.), *Constructing collectivity: 'We' across languages and contexts* (pp. 789–804). John Benjamins.

Pawley, A. (2002). Using *he* and *she* for inanimate referents in English: Questions of grammar and world view. In N. J. Enfield (Ed.), *Ethnosyntax: Explorations in grammar and culture* (pp. 110–37). Oxford University Press.

Peters, P. and Burridge, K. (2012). Areal linguistics in the South Pacific. In R. Hickey (Ed.), *Areal features of the anglophone world* (pp. 233–60). Mouton de Gruyter.

Ross, A. S. C. and Moverley, A. W. (1964). *The Pitcairnese language*. André Deutsch.

Siegel, J. (2013). Regional profile: Australia Pacific region. In B. Kortmann and K. Lunkenheimer (Eds.), *Mouton world atlas of variation in English* (pp. 765–82). Mouton de Gruyter.

Tent, J. and Mugler, F. (2008). Fiji English: Morphology and syntax. In K. Burridge and B. Kortmann (Eds.), *Varieties of English: The Pacific and Australasia* (pp. 546–67). Mouton de Gruyter.

Trudgill, P. (1995). Grammaticalisation and social structure: Non-standard conjunction-formation in East Anglian English. In F. R. Palmer (Ed.), *Grammar and meaning: Essays in honour of Sir John Lyons* (pp. 136–47). Cambridge University Press.

Trudgill, P. (2015). Society of intimates and linguistic complexity. In R. De Busser and R. J. LaPolla (Eds.), *Language structure and environment: Social, cultural, and natural factors* (pp. 133–48). John Benjamins.

TV Week. (1992). Melbourne: Southdown Press, 30 May. <https://televisionau.com/2012/05/1992-may-31-june-6.html> (last accessed 11 January 2021).

Wagner, S. (2012). Pronominal systems. In R. Hickey (Ed.), *Areal features of the anglophone world* (pp. 375–408). Mouton de Gruyter.

Wierzbicka, A. (1979). Ethno-syntax and the philosophy of grammar. *Studies in language, 3*(3), 313–83.

CHAPTER 14

Decolonisation and Neo-colonialism in Aboriginal Education

Ian G. Malcolm

1. ENGLISH AND THE AUSTRALIAN COLONIAL HERITAGE

The history of Australia is inescapably linked with colonialism. Many Australians have shown themselves to be increasingly uncomfortable with this, as shown in the ongoing unease with which the national day continues to be observed on the date corresponding to the arrival of the First Fleet. For many Indigenous Australians, life brings constant reminders of the negative consequences of the colonisation of the land with which they profoundly identify. Inherent in the colonial experience was the arrival of the English language and, in due course, the loss, for many, of their traditional languages. On the basis of experience on another colonised continent, it has been said that the English language has been 'the crucial instrument of colonization' (Ramanathan 2005: 23).

It could be said, however, that, just as the Indigenous cultures and their languages were colonised by the British, the victims of this experience may be seen in retrospect to have colonised – or, more properly, decolonised – the language brought by the British to make it their own. English in Australia, then, has been the instrument both of colonisation and of decolonisation, in that it has represented, on the one hand, an imposition on the Indigenous inhabitants of this land and, on the other, in the face of the loss of Indigenous languages, an agent of the maintenance of the culture it was expected to displace.

Australia may be compared with some other English-majority countries in that, following colonisation, English has been nativised separately by immigrant and Indigenous communities, leading to the existence of Australian English (AusE) and Aboriginal English (AbE) as distinctive dialects in their respective speech communities. In other countries, where other vernaculars have survived more strongly, a more unified form of postcolonial English may have survived (for example, Ramanathan 2005; Kamwangamalu 2012).

Reflecting the fact that the Indigenous inhabitants of Australia constitute a small proportion of the overall population, there has been an ongoing tension between the two varieties of English which have been nativised in Australia, and the dialect representing the majority prevails as the standard form used in service provision, including education and the law. It has been recognised relatively recently that the exclusion of the Indigenous dialect of English from the public sphere, in favour of the majority dialect, can be seen as a reassertion of colonial control, or 'neo-colonialism' (Eades 2013: 190). The way in which English has been used in response to competing social and political pressures in Australia may be seen as moving from colonisation by the initial immigrants to decolonisation by the Indigenous people who adopted and modified the language to neo-colonial reimposition by public policy under majority influence.

If English as taught in schools is to meet the needs of the contemporary Australian population and to be truly inclusive of Indigenous learners, it will not do so by means of neo-colonial reimposition. An attempt will be made here to look more closely at the processes of colonisation, decolonisation and neo-colonial reimposition with respect to English and to suggest a more inclusive – and realistic – way forward which might be labelled 'postcolonial biculturalism'.

2. COLONISATION AND LANGUAGE SUBSTITUTION

Prior to its colonisation by the British, Australia had had intermittent contact over some 300 years with Macassan fishermen from South-East Asia and more recently with European explorers from such countries as the Netherlands, Spain, France and England. The possibility of colonisation by Britain was enhanced by a pressing need to relocate convicts and by a positive report by James Cook after his first visit to Botany Bay in 1770 (Malcolm 2018a: 160).

The initial commission of the colonists under Governor Arthur Phillip was 'to live in amity and kindness' (Barton 1889: 129) with the Aboriginal occupants of the land, and the assumption was that it would be possible for the groups to interact with one another and reach understanding. To this end, Phillip himself was observed to have sought out opportunities to meet with Aboriginal people and talk with them about their customs (Barton 1889: 281). Early interactions, in the absence of a common language, involved the exchange of gifts and the use of sign language and drawings (Malcolm and Koscielecki 1997: 8, 10, 12). However, it seems that when language came into the picture, there was no reciprocity: the English-speakers, for the most part, expected English to prevail, even if employed cross-culturally as 'foreigner talk', and the Aboriginal people either kept to themselves – for as long as this was possible – or did their best, drawing on their existing cultural and linguistic resources, to use English as they reinterpreted it to exchange meanings.

Of course, the fact that the primary British motives for occupying the land were their imperial expansionist intentions, rather than their desire to befriend the Indigenous people, would not have taken long to become apparent. The conceptual context which they brought with them included the perception of Australia as owned by no one and therefore open to claim by another nation (*terra nullius*). There were pervasive views devaluing the 'primitive' in favour of the 'civilised' in keeping with the current social Darwinist philosophy, which also led to the view that the full-descent population would become extinct and be supplanted by one of mixed descent (Edwards 2004: 97). Despite the official rhetoric about having amicable relations with the Aboriginal people, the social objective was one of assimilation, where they would assent to the linguistic and cultural traditions of the majority (Beresford 2003b: 62, 68; McConnochie 1982a, 1982b).

It would be inevitable that colonisation, with these underlying views, would bring with it 'extreme social disruption' (Burridge and Kortmann 2008: 29). Many people would fall foul of practices of genocide (Partington 1998: 31) and of introduced diseases (McGregor 1994: xii; Edwards 2004: 6). People would be separated from the lands which they associated with their identity and their language; children would be forcibly removed from their families (Partington 1998: 45; Edwards 2004: 6; McConnochie 1982a: 23) and placed in dormitories (McGregor 1994: xiii). Rather than the law with which they were familiar, it would be British law to which Indigenous people would be subjected. Increasingly, Indigenous people would be made economically dependent on the colonists and would be expected to regard them as their colonial masters (Malcolm and Koscielecki 1997: 17).

With respect to language, as I have noted, the expectation was that the Indigenous people would acquire and use the language of the colonists but it soon became apparent that they were not choosing to intermingle with the white intruders. As a result, Phillip introduced a policy of 'abduction', whereby selected people would be involuntarily held within the colonial society to enable them to learn the language and culture, which might then enable them to act as 'go-betweens' between the two cultures. To some extent, this policy began to achieve its objectives, in that Arabanoo, a young man made captive in the governor's quarters, did learn English enough to serve as an interpreter, but, after a few months, he succumbed to smallpox and died. Another young man, Bennelong, showed exceptional language skills and spent time serving as a go-between in both colonial and Indigenous communities. He was subsequently taken on a trip to England to extend his understanding of civilisation, but he died not long after his return. Somewhat belatedly, the colonists began to provide schooling which would enable Aboriginal children to learn through the English language.

Colonisation, then, brought the English language to Indigenous people within a cultural framework of deprivation of their traditional sources of learning and reinforcement of the power inequality existing between Indigenous and introduced cultures. It broke the nexus between land and language and between the language of successive generations. It assumed a necessary link between language and civilisation. It presented English not as an option but as a civilised substitute for whatever language might have gone before.

3. DECOLONISATION AND LANGUAGE ADOPTION

The term 'decolonisation' has increasingly been used to refer to the reassertion of their identity by a people who have been colonised. It can be used with a political reference but here I wish to use it with a linguistic reference. As we have seen, colonisation meant for many Aboriginal Australians the substitution of a language and culture for those which had pre-existed. The majority of Indigenous Australians were not able to maintain their languages in the face of colonisation. However, this did not mean that the conceptualisations expressed by their languages were obliterated from their consciousness. I want to suggest that Indigenous Australians were already engaged in the process of decolonisation as soon as they were faced with the obligation to adopt English as a substitute language. They adopted English on their own terms, re-forming it as a unique dialect. Rather than allowing themselves to be anglicised, they caused English to be Aboriginalised. I have argued this in some detail elsewhere (Malcolm 2017). Part of what follows will draw on this discussion.

I am not suggesting that the processes I describe here are unique to Australian Aboriginal people. All formerly colonised societies have left their mark on the colonisers' language in adopting it and have had to re-evaluate its role and nature in setting their postcolonial directions. As Ramanathan (2005: vii) has put it, 'English in postcolonial communities is a splintered, hybrid English, being appropriated, nativized and adapted by local environments'. Where English has been used as a substitute for the language of a colonised people, many of these people may have been effectively silenced in some contexts, unless their conceptual reworking of their English has enabled them to recover their voice. Postcolonial studies, as seen by Ramanathan (2005: 3), may be seen 'to wrestle with issues of "voice", including finding voices by which to speak back to colonial powers'.

Reducing Aboriginal communication to one English, the English of the dominant group in society, is a double threat to Aboriginal 'voice'. As Aboriginal spokesperson Vic Forrest has put it, it has 'a damaging effect to the way Aborigines approach . . . both their own culture and also the dominant culture' (Forrest, in Eagleson et al. 1982: 245).

The adoption of English by Aboriginal speakers took place over an extended time period and in different parts of the country. The most influential bridge between the English of the colonists and the English which was to be widely adopted by Aboriginal people was New South Wales Pidgin, which developed in the early years of the colony and had consolidated by around 1820 (Troy 1994). This pidgin influenced the development of English-based communication among Indigenous people well beyond New South Wales (Malcolm 2018a: 164), as it was used in the course of further pastoral and exploratory development across the country. In some places the pidgin provided a direct pathway to English and in others, where it supplanted traditional languages, it influenced the development of varieties of creole which, in the course of time, in some locations, decreolised to become English. When AbE is compared, in terms of its variant features, with the variant features of the main varieties which prevailed in Australia while it was developing (English of Southeast England, Irish English, AusE, Australian Vernacular English, Roper River Creole [Kriol] and Torres Strait Creole), it is apparent that the influences of the creoles are more pervasive than those of the other varieties (Malcolm 2013). AbE is, then, appropriately seen as a post-creole variety and not as a variety of AusE.

It is important to recognise that the English which eventually emerged in Aboriginal and Torres Strait Islander speech communities was an English formed by those communities as they engaged with the varied English inputs they received to arrive at a variety which enabled the expression of the meanings which were important to them, and in the context of culturally authentic speech events. AbE is more than English decolonised: it is English which has been generated in the interactional life of Indigenous Australian communities and which has, over the course of time, stabilised (while remaining dynamic) to become a variety identified with by Indigenous speech communities across the country and claimed as their own. In order to gain this recognition, it was necessary for the variety to provide for its speakers an acceptable vehicle of cultural-conceptual expression, culturally appropriate social interaction and differentiation from non-Indigenous Australian speakers.

3.1 Conceptual Relevance

In order for the English used by Aboriginal speakers to have conceptual relevance to them, it needed to be modified – or 'reconceptualized' (Malcolm 2018b) – since it had been generated in speech communities with significantly different ways of approaching human life and the environment. When we examine AbE, we see that it represents a modification of English to make it a better vehicle for the expression of five elements which are essential to Aboriginal conceptualisation (see further Malcolm 2017). The following examples show the cultural impact on words/phrases (for example, kinship terms, pronoun choices) as well as morphosyntactic choices (for example, number, tense) and thus fall under Schneider's (this volume) second nexus ('indicator terms') and third nexus ('indicator structures').

3.1.1 Group orientation

Kinship terms have extended reference:

- *family* normally refers to the extended family, whereas in Standard Australian English (SAusE) it normally refers to the nuclear family
- *daddy* and *mummy* terms referring to the father and mother may be extended in AbE for use by parents as *little daddy*, *little mummy* referring to the children

- *auntie*, *uncle* have extended reference to cover niece, nephew and a respected elder person
- *granny* may be used reciprocally between grandparents and grandchildren
- *brother*, *brother boy*, *budda*, *bro* may refer to a brother or a male peer
- *sister*, *sister girl*, *sis* may refer to a sister or female peer
- *cousin*, *cuz* may refer to a cousin, distant relative or peer
- *cousin brother/sister* usually refers to a mother's sister's or father's brother's child (Arthur 1996: 74)
- *cross-cousin* denotes a mother's brother's, or father's sister's child (McGregor 1994: xv).

Group-consciousness is reinforced by:

- personal pronoun modification
    - plural *yous* is distinguished from singular *you*
    - dual forms (e.g. *me 'n 'im, you-two*) may be distinguished from plural *we, you-mob*
    - explicit inclusion/exclusion of addressee (e.g. *me 'n you*, 'we')
- a shared schema
    - demonstrative *that/dat* (*She nearly killed that snake*); *them/dem* (*one of them tea sets*);
    - indefinite extension (*me an my uncle an dat*)
    - inexplicit substitute (*They walked up to the thing*)
    - frequent tags (e.g. *unna, init, inti, ini, ina, na*) to invite confirmation (*They don't lay eggs here, inti?*); *you know, eh* to invite interaction (*It was so scary, you know*)
- discourse markers (e.g. *Choo! Nyorn!*) to express empathy (*E said, Choo, you better dress em up; Nyorn, poor thing, poor dog!*).

Default meanings assume the Aboriginal listener-context:

- *people* or *pepes* implies Aboriginal people
- *language* implies Aboriginal language
- *camping* implies staying overnight and *camping out* implies camping in the bush
- *a feed* implies what non-Aboriginal people would call a 'meal'
- *kangaroo* evokes a food source
- *a roast* implies eating outside, cooking on a fire.

The group's shared distinctive history is also connoted by the language:

- *gubba(h)*, the generalised term for European Australians in eastern Australia, identifies them with the 'government'
- officers of the law are referred to with terms (deliberately) not readily identified by speakers of AusE, such as: *gunjabal*, from 'constable', *bulliman*, from 'policeman' and *monarch*, from the Nyungar word for 'black cockatoo'
- the colonial past is echoed in the use of the term *boy* in a (mock-) demeaning way and in threats using the word *flog*
- the experience of the stolen generations remains in references to being *taken away* (by authorities) and *taken over* (by family).

3.1.2 Interconnectedness

Interconnectedness is a pervasive feature of the way Aboriginal people view themselves and the world they live in (Malcolm 2018a: 150). Everything in humanity, society and the natural world is seen to be interrelated. In many ways, the conceptualisations represented in SAusE favour the segmentation of reality. AbE shows resistance to such segmentation, as in the relaxation of the obligation to express the segmentation of time; hence, we find:

- inconsistent marking of verb tense (*We went to um Ellery Gorge. We get, um fish and we swim*; Harkins 1994: 204)
- reference to *old people* may refer to the present generation – as in SAusE – or to ancestors
- the past marker *ago* may not be maintained in the expressions *a long time* [ago] and *not long* [ago]
- experience may be recalled by event rather than time reference (*When we was down Geraldton . . .*).

The differentiation of genders in the pronoun system may not be observed, hence:

- *e* [he] *sleep ere* . . .
- *when e little girl* . . .
- *e nice country* . . .

Morphological differentiation of singular and plural number may not be observed, hence:

- *two window*
- *dey was out bush*
- *when he finish he go home.*

There may be reduced differentiation between human and non-human reference, as in:

- *He's a big man – very long, eh?*
- *They all cruel narrow* [referring to her sisters, who were very thin]
- *Me and Tony had a smash* 'Me and Tony had a fight'
- *the moon jumps up . . .*
- *Joe was jus hurtin it* 'Joe was making the vehicle go really fast'.

Meaning may be embodied (for example, by repetition or vowel elongation) rather than being expressed by more abstract means, as in:

- *The two men dug, dug, dug, got two goannas*
- *li–i–itle bit . . .*
- *bi–i–i–ges shark*
- *My heart was beating r-r-ee-al fast*
- *Hirrrim* 'Hit him!'

Embodiment may also be achieved by the suffixing of pronouns, adjectives, numbers and adverbs:

- *wefella, youfella, mintwofella*
- *That kid clever-one*
- *Twofella bin go . . .*
- *Come back afternoontime.*

3.1.3 Orientation to motion

Meaning may be expressed more dynamically, by means of verbs rather than by what may be seen to be more abstract forms; hence nouns, adjectives and prepositions may be converted to verbs:

- *instead of downing them . . .* 'instead of putting them down . . .'
- *I schooled in Derby* 'I went to school in Derby'
- *They cheek em* 'They give them cheek'
- *She blackeyed Amy* 'She gave Amy a black eye'.

The verb *to be* is avoided (which could be seen to be foregrounding existence rather than action):

- copula and auxiliary (*E big one* 'It's big'; *We workin* 'We are working')
- future with *go*, which, unlike *will*, embodies action (*We gonna work* 'We will work')
- passive (*E got smash* 'It was smashed')
- presentative *There is/are* (*E got lotta bird over dere* 'There are birds over there').

3.1.4 Orientation to observation

Observing what is going on and reporting what one has observed to the group is seen as an essential obligation in Aboriginal society. AbE is distinctive in the ways in which it accommodates to this.

The term *might be* (often in the form *might'e*), or alternatives such as *must be*, *must have*, will often be used in what has been called 'speculative reporting' (Eades 2013: 70), whereby, having reported an observation to the group, the observer (or an addressee) will proceed to explore the significance of what has been observed in case action is required:

- *The demons* [plain clothes detectives] *cruising round this wa; Aaay, they might'e lookin for Johnny an em, unna.*
- *Might be they fell by accident . . .*
- *Might be that emu bin kill them, finish them all off . . .*
- *Might be little rock get in the way and he fall over . . .*

The orientation to observation is also seen in the frequent replacement of the article by the demonstrative (already referred to):

- *They had big mob tucker at that barbecue*
- *We pulled up at this crossroads.*

It is also shown in deictic extension (often accompanied by gesture) at the end of an utterance:

- *Up in the hills there's a cave there*
- *So we always talk our own language in class here.*

Similarly, the observer perspective is shown with appended adverbs giving a time reference:

- *Well, dat fella bin take me now, walkin long footpath now* . . .
- *Then next day we ad a feed den.*

It is also not uncommon for right dislocation to function to enable further observed detail to be included:

- *We seen a clapper's egg. Green one*
- *We get five sheeps. Fat one.*

3.1.5 Awareness of the transcendent

A fifth strong influence apparent in the Aboriginal reschematisation of English is the recognition that frequently there are transcendent meanings in what, to non-Aboriginal users of English, might be seen to be purely physical entities. A few examples of this pervasive cultural conceptual feature are:

- *the dreaming* which is the time of creative spirit activity
- *country* which implies one's (or others') spiritual place of belonging
- *law* which is religious and cultural knowledge
- *man* which denotes an initiated man
- *ceremony* which denotes a cultural ritual
- *clever* which implies possessing spiritual powers
- *dangerous* which implies having possibly hazardous spiritual powers
- *fire*, *smoke* which are seen to offer protection from unwelcome spirits
- *little fellas* which are potentially tormenting spirit visitants
- *red eyes* which are evidence of spirit presence
- *singing* which may involve exercising spiritual control.

There are also transfers from Aboriginal languages which relate to spiritual entities, such as:

- *the wirlo bird* which is seen as a 'death bird'
- *min min lights* which may lead people astray at night
- *wudachis*, *balyits* which are troubling spirits

Research in Western Australia (Sharifian et al. 2012) has shown that the same stories may generate totally different reactions among Aboriginal and non-Aboriginal school children listening to them because the schemas relating to the transcendent are accessed only by the Aboriginal children.

3.2 Contextual Appropriateness

The decolonisation process which led to AbE was not only a matter of modifying the language linguistically and conceptually. The dialect co-exists in Australia with another English which is inevitably a part of the life experience of AbE speakers, and the AbE speech community has had to develop appropriate patterns of use of the two dialects.

An investigation among Aboriginal staff and students at Edith Cowan University (Malcolm 1997) showed that bidialectal Aboriginal people would choose to use AbE rather than AusE when

- the participants in the speech event were Aboriginal
- the setting was Aboriginal (in the bush or a camp)
- the domain was primarily Aboriginal (for example, the sacred)
- the tone of the interaction was personal or humorous
- an Aboriginal discourse form (for example, oral narrative) was being used.

Invited to give further comment, one participant observed with respect to the Aboriginal speech community: 'Aboriginal English is more persuasive and gets more respect than standard English' (Malcolm 1997: 78), while another, commenting on the wider speech community, wrote: 'We should be able to speak our own Aboriginal English and be understood and respected without feeling second class' (Malcolm 1997: 77). It is clear that, for these Aboriginal speakers, there was a sense of ownership of AbE and that this meant the dialect was the only appropriate mode of communication in Aboriginal contexts, while it demanded respect from speakers of other varieties.

Another participant who, being from the south-west of the country, identified as a Nyungar described his speech as 'the Nyungarisation or Aboriginalisation of Wedjela [non-Indigenous] speech' (Malcolm 1997: 77), thus showing how conscious he was of the fact that the language and the ways of using it represented what I have been calling a reschematisation of non-AbE. The word 'Koorified' is used with similar reference in Victoria (Adams 2014).

3.3 Participant-differentiated Identification

A third factor involved in the decolonisation of English by Aboriginal people is that it has introduced into the language ways of differentiating its speakers from speakers of SAusE. AbE is not simply a substitute for the Indigenous languages which earlier generations of its speakers spoke: it is a dialect of English for use in a culturally diverse English-speaking context. As such, it has extended the capacity of English to express the distinctiveness of an Aboriginal perspective in the context of a wider English-speaking society.

Prior to colonisation there was no need for a term for Aboriginal people in general, since groups differentiated themselves with localised expressions such as *Nyungar* or *Yindjibarndi*. Arthur (1996: 135) notes that the introduction of the term *blackfella*, probably copied from the British *blackfellow*, represented a 'change of perception' brought about by colonisation and paralleled by what happened among North American indigenous people following colonisation there. The term *whitefella*, exclusively used by the Indigenous people, would have developed around the same time. Other ways of referring to white people would have included *waibela*, *wetjala*, *balanda* (from *Hollander*) and later (as noted above) *gubba(h)* (from *government*).

AbE speakers, in more recent times, have also developed some humorous forms of self-reference by word play based on existing English expressions, such as *blackout*, referring to 'a lot of Aboriginal people in one place', and *flash black*, an 'Aboriginal person showy about money' (Adams 2014: 15, 10). It is possible also that the semantic reversal whereby such words as *deadly* and *cruel* have developed positive associations has developed similarly on the basis of a comic reaction to the English of majority speakers.

The distinctiveness of AbE is also seen in the way in which its speakers use tags which are not used in AusE, such as *sistagirl* 'sister or female peer', *brotherboy* 'brother or male peer', *sis* 'sister or female peer', *bro* 'brother or male peer', *cuz* 'cousin or peer', *-mob* 'family', *mum* 'mother's sister'.

Another way in which the Indigenous group reference of AbE is strengthened is in the maintenance of words which have been transferred from Aboriginal languages. Of course, many words which are common to SAusE (e.g. *kangaroo*, *boomerang* and so on) were originally transfers from Aboriginal languages, but there are many words specific to the locations of the speakers which support local identification, such as, for example, *jubby* 'lizard' in Mullewa, *yorga* 'female' in the southwest, *jarnkurna* 'emu' in Roebourne and many others.

4. NEO-COLONIALISM: THE MAINTENANCE OF COLONIAL DOMINATION

Ideally, the path towards a postcolonial existence might have continued to lead away from colonialism and to have built on the principle of the mutual recognition of cultures in the formerly colonised land. However, at least in some spheres, the ideal situation has not prevailed. Beresford (2003a: 28), citing the work of Anthony Welsh (1996), has argued that colonialism in Australia has given way to 'internal colonialism', which 'involves the subordination and continuing domination of a previously independent nation within the borders of another nation state'. This he applies particularly to education, in which, he argues, 'alienation is caused when the language of instruction is foreign to students and when their own language is not valued in the classroom. In other cases, problems of alienation arise when teachers denigrate Indigenous ways of using English' (Beresford 2003a: 34). This sense of alienation seems to be apparent in the following comment of an Aboriginal schoolgirl recorded in Sydney by Eagleson et al.:

> In schools Aborigines are not taught anything about our own culture. We're taught only white man's history and European ways of life . . . Aboriginal children always seem to end up in the lowest classes but this is not because of our ability but because as a group of people we have been neglected in education. We are not taught our own languages. All that we are appreciated for at school is because we are good at sports . . . (Eagleson et al. 1982: 240)

It is not that Australia has lacked language planning. The National Policy on Languages (Lo Bianco 1987) made Australia the first English-speaking country in the world with a policy on languages (Lo Bianco 1995) and it recognised the validity of AbE as well as Indigenous languages. It was succeeded by a report of the Aboriginal Education Task Force, which was supportive both of bilingual/bicultural programs and of the due recognition of AbE (Malcolm and Königsberg 2007: 272). Subsequently, the Council of Australian Governments set up a Ministerial Council on Education, Employment, Training and Youth Affairs (MCEETYA), which was to argue that the foundation for literacy development of Aboriginal and Torres Strait Islander students should be their home language, whether a traditional language, a creole or AbE (Malcolm and Königsberg 2007: 275). Further developments, however, have made such policies appear 'invisible' (Truscott and Malcolm 2010), and it has been argued that 'national educational authorities have been rather more concerned with monitoring the success of Aboriginal students in the achievement of outcomes common to the mainstream than in achieving outcomes relating to cultural affirmation and the maintenance of Aboriginal identity' (Malcolm and Königsberg 2007: 275–6).

In the 1990s, Australia moved from its inclusive National Policy on Languages (NPL) to an Australian Language and Literacy Policy, which, according to Lo Bianco (2000: 53), 'contradicted and sought to undermine the core multicultural and multilingual basis of the NPL' with its focus on SAusE literacy and foreign languages in the interests of the dominant group (Truscott and Malcolm 2010: 11).

The advocacy of diversity encompassing Aboriginal languages and AbE in the education system has been countered by a 'dominant culture' tradition which prioritises the induction of Aboriginal students into the culture of SAusE literacy and which encourages making SAusE cultural features explicit through direct instruction (Gray 1990; Rose et al. 1999). A survey of Western Australian Aboriginal child health reviewed by Sharifian (2008) found that low academic performance and school attendance among Indigenous students correlated with their use of AbE or an Aboriginal language and argued that these students needed explicit teaching of SAusE.

One of the arguments supporting the 'dominant culture' approach has been that it is equitable for Indigenous students to be given the same education as their non-Indigenous peers. However, as Partington (1998: 47) has argued, 'receiving the "same" education does not necessarily mean the education was entirely suitable for Indigenous students', and the failure of Indigenous students to succeed under such a system has led to lowered academic expectations of them on the part of authorities, rather than to questioning the validity of a system which is aimed at 'developing in Aboriginal children a set of skills, values and behavioural characteristics which approximate as closely as possible to those of their white peers' (McConnochie 1982a: 29).

Schools have been dominated by national SAusE testing which does not take into account the distinctive English of Aboriginal students, reflecting the 'hegemonic practices' which have been observed in other postcolonial contexts (Ramanathan 2005: 94). The effective undermining of inclusive language policy may be compared to 'the practice of agreeing with language policy publicly but subverting it privately' which has taken place in parts of Africa (Kamwangamalu 2012: 168).

Eades (2013: 190) has noted that despite the formal recognition of the equality of Indigenous with non-Indigenous Australians, such equality is in many ways 'a mere fiction' and the legacy of colonial dispossession remains. In particular, this is reflected in the criminal justice system, in overpolicing and overimprisonment. To this, Eades gives the label 'neo-colonial control'. It is not difficult to justify extending this descriptor to the ever-present trends in the education system to ignore the cultural and linguistic backgrounds of Indigenous students and expect them to succeed on the same cultural and linguistic terms as non-Indigenous students.

Although Australians seem reluctant to acknowledge their colonial past, we have seen that despite the significant resistance shown by Indigenous Australians in the development of a 'decolonised' English, there are still neo-colonial pressures from the wider society to redefine them culturally and linguistically through our educational and justice systems. Perhaps the wider society has not caught up with the Indigenous society, in that its 'decolonisation' has been in word rather than in action. Some implications of this need to be spelled out for educational practice.

5. POSTCOLONIAL BICULTURALISM IN EDUCATION

It is all too easy for members of the dominant culture to attribute colonialism to a past generation and to assume that it bears no continuing influence on contemporary practices which affect Indigenous Australians. The existence of what I have called 'neo-colonialism' obliges us to bring this assumption into question. In my view, we need to reconsider at least five key aspects of colonialism in terms of what it has meant to Indigenous Australians and to deliberately pursue policies and practices which will prevent their recurrence.

The first such aspect, as discussed by Edwards (2004), is oppression. Colonial control was imposed on Indigenous Australians without any consultation or invited input. Policies were pursued in education which initially restricted their access to education and, where access was allowed, which suppressed the use of the home language. Education on colonial terms was a part of colonial oppression. To ensure that oppression does not continue to occur in this or other ways, it is important that education involving Indigenous Australians should be based on affirmation, as demonstrated in community consultation and involvement.

A second – and related – aspect of colonialism is hegemonic cultural domination. Hegemony, as described by Ramanathan (2005: 37), entails social practices which privilege one group in society above another. Educational institutions founded in the dominant culture are liable to transmit it in a way which may extend its unequal economic and cultural control in the society. As such, they may serve the colonial purpose of 'Eurocentric diffusionism' (Kamwangamalu 2012: 182) and treat the local cultures as virtually invisible. In a postcolonial society, it is necessary to uphold and ensure the validity of more than one culture. Harris (1982) has argued for bicultural Aboriginal schools which teach two ways of life. The product of such a school would be a person who 'has the ability to shift into and operate in two cultures with relative ease and comfort, and is able to empathise with, the points of view of both cultures, without losing identity with the primary reference group' (Harris 1982: 127).

A third element of the experience of the colonised is de-voicing. Writing of the Indian context, Ramanathan (2005: 5) uses the term *de-voicing* 'to refer to ways in which Vernacular languages are relegated to subordinate positions and to ways in which English is seen to open social doors'. In Australian education, although there has been evidence (for example, Edwards 2004: 106) that students taught in their own language have been 'much more responsive' than students taught only in English, the dominance of SAusE remains. Bilingual education has struggled to gain acceptance and, although the existence of AbE gives evidence of its speakers needing to create a new dialect to give expression to conceptualisations not accommodated to by AusE, this dialect is often treated as educationally irrelevant. To overcome de-voicing of Indigenous Australians in school settings, it is essential to employ additive bilingual education where relevant, and in other cases to educate for bidialectalism.

The fourth element of the legacy of colonialism which needs to be recognised is the marginalisation experienced by Indigenous Australians. The profound implications of the severance of the link of Aboriginal and Torres Strait Islander people with their traditional lands often goes unrecognised. The connection was a significant part of their spiritual orientation, as well as essential to the maintenance of their languages. Another link colonisers paid scant regard to was that between generations, in that many children and parents were seriously traumatised by being forced apart. An important step towards overcoming the marginalisation of Indigenous Australians is provided by restoring Indigenous leadership by having Indigenous and non-Indigenous educators working together in the classroom (Malcolm and Königsberg 2007: 286).

Finally, it is necessary to recognise the humiliation brought to Aboriginal and Torres Strait Islander Australians by the colonial experience. The colonisers came to their land with assumptions which labelled them as primitive and which took it for granted that they would welcome civilisation. Rather than being recognised as equals, they were looked down upon. It is clear that some Aboriginal people today see this as a painful ongoing part of their experience. Education has not contributed as well as it might to bringing change, in that too often Aboriginal students have been judged on the basis of testing in SAusE, leading to poor performance and the assumption that they have low academic potential. Clearly, there needs to be a move towards mutual respect among Indigenous and non-Indigenous students and the development of appropriately and distinctively staged learning procedures to enable both to reach educational goals.

In short, it is possible and it is urgently necessary for neo-colonialism to be identified in and eliminated from educational practice but this requires a deliberate change not only in policy but in its implementation.

REFERENCES

Adams, K. (Ed.). (2014). *Koorified: Aboriginal communication and wellbeing*. La Trobe University and Victorian Aboriginal Community Controlled Health Organisation (VACCHO).

Arthur, J. M. (1996). *Aboriginal English: A cultural study*. Oxford University Press.

Barton, G. B. (1889). *Governor Phillip 1783–1789: History of NSW from the records* (Vol. 1). Charles Potter, Govt. Printer.

Beresford, Q. (2003a). The context of Aboriginal education. In Q. Beresford and G. Partington (Eds.), *Reform and resistance in Aboriginal education* (pp. 10–40). University of Western Australia Press.

Beresford, Q. (2003b). Separate and unequal: An outline of Aboriginal education 1900–1990s. In Q. Beresford and G. Partington (Eds.), *Reform and resistance in Aboriginal education* (pp. 41–68). University of Western Australia Press.

Burridge, K. and Kortmann, B. (2008). Introduction: Varieties of English in the Pacific and Australasia. In K. Burridge and B. Kortmann (Eds.), *Varieties of English: The Pacific and Australasia* (Vol. 3; pp. 23–36). Mouton de Gruyter.

Eades, D. (2013). *Aboriginal ways of using English*. Aboriginal Studies Press.

Eagleson, R. D., Kaldor, S. and Malcolm, I. G. (1982). *English and the Aboriginal child*. Curriculum Development Centre.

Edwards, V. (2004). *Multilingualism in the English-speaking world*. Blackwell.

Gray, B. (1990). Natural language learning in Aboriginal classrooms: Reflections on teaching and learning style for empowerment in English. In C. Walton and W. Eggington (Eds.), *Language: Maintenance, power and education in Australian Aboriginal contexts* (pp. 105–39). Northern Territory University Press.

Harkins, J. (1994). *Bridging two worlds: Aboriginal English and cross-cultural under- standing*. University of Queensland Press.

Harris, S. (1982). Traditional Aboriginal education strategies and their possible place in a modern, bicultural school. In J. Sherwood (Ed.), *Aboriginal education: Issues and innovations* (pp. 127–39). Creative Research.

Kamwangamalu, N. M. (2012). The medium-of-instruction conundrum and 'minority' language development in Africa. In A. Yiakoumetti (Ed.), *Harnessing linguistic variation to improve education* (pp. 167–88). Peter Lang.

Lo Bianco, J. (1987). *National policy on languages*. Commonwealth Department of Education. Australian Government Publishing Service.

Lo Bianco, J. (1995). Pluralist nations: Pluralist language policies? [Conference session]. Global Cultural Diversity Conference, 20–28 April, Darling Harbour, Sydney, Australia.

Lo Bianco, J. (2000). Making languages an object of public policy. *Agenda*, 7(1), 47–62.

McConnochie, K. R. (1982a). Aborigines and Australian education: Historical perspectives. In J. Sherwood (Ed.), *Aboriginal education: Issues and innovations* (pp. 17–32). Creative Research.

McConnochie, K. R. (1982b). Assimilation and Aboriginal education in the Northern Territory. In J. Sherwood (Ed.), *Aboriginal education: Issues and innovations* (pp. 67–80). Creative Research.

McGregor, W. (1994). Introduction. In N. Thieberger and W. McGregor

(Eds.), *Macquarie Aboriginal words* (pp. xi–xxxv). Macquarie University.
Malcolm, I. G. (1997). The pragmatics of bidialectal communication. In L. F. Bouton (Ed.), *Pragmatics and language learning* (Vol. 8; pp. 55–78). Division of English as an International Language Intensive English Institute, University of Illinois at Urbana-Champaign.
Malcolm, I. G. (2013). Aboriginal English: Some grammatical features and their implications. *Australian Review of Applied Linguistics, 36*(3), 267–84.
Malcolm, I. G. (2017). Terms of adoption: Cultural conceptual factors underlying the adoption of English for Aboriginal communication. In F. Sharifian (Ed.), *Advances in cultural linguistics* (pp. 625–59). Springer.
Malcolm, I. G. (2018a). *Australian Aboriginal English: Change and continuity in an adopted language.* De Gruyter Mouton.
Malcolm, I. G. (2018b). The Aboriginal reconceptualization of English in Australia: The spiritual dimension [Conference session]. 2nd International Conference on Cultural Linguistics, 23–26 July, University of Koblenz-Landau, Landau, Germany.
Malcolm, I. G. and Königsberg, P. (2007). Bridging the language gap in education. In G. Leitner and I. G. Malcolm (Eds.), *The habitat of Australia's Aboriginal languages* (pp. 267–97). Berlin: Mouton de Gruyter.
Malcolm, I. G. and Koscielecki, M. (1997). *Aboriginality and English: Report to the Australian Research Council.* Centre for Applied Language Research, Edith Cowan University.
Partington, G. (1998). 'In those days it was that rough': Aboriginal and Torres Strait Islander history and education. In G. Partington (Ed.), *Perspectives on Aboriginal and Torres Strait Islander education* (pp. 27–54). Social Science Press.
Ramanathan, V. (2005). *The English–vernacular divide: Postcolonial language politics and practice.* Multilingual Matters.
Rose, D., Gray, B. and Cowey, W. (1999). Scaffolding reading and writing for Indigenous children in school. In P. Wignell (Ed.), *Double power: English literacy and Indigenous education* (pp. 23–60). Language Australia.
Sharifian, F. (2008). Aboriginal English in the classroom: An asset or a liability? *Language Awareness, 17*(2), 131–38.
Sharifian, F., Truscott, A., Königsberg, P., Malcolm, I. G. and Collard, G. (2012). *'Understanding stories my way': Aboriginal-English speaking*

students' (mis)understanding of school literacy materials in Australian English*. Institute for Professional Learning, Department of Education, Western Australia.

Troy, J. F. (1994). *Melaleuka: A history and description of New South Wales Pidgin* [Doctoral dissertation, Australian National University]. Open Research. <https://openresearch-repository.anu.edu.au/handle/1885/112648> (last accessed 12 January 2021).

Truscott, A. and Malcolm, I. (2010). Closing the policy–practice gap: Making Indigenous language policy more than empty rhetoric. In J. Hobson, K. Lowe, S. Poetsch and M. Walsh (Eds.), *Re-awakening languages: Theory and practice in the revitalisation of Australia's Indigenous languages* (pp. 6–21). Sydney University Press.

Welsh, A. (1996). *Australian education: Reform or crisis?* Allen & Unwin.

CHAPTER 15

Modal and Semi-modal Verbs of Obligation in the Australian, New Zealand and British Hansards, 1901–2015

Adam Smith, Minna Korhonen, Haidee Kotze and Bertus van Rooy

1. INTRODUCTION

This chapter investigates changes in the use of (semi-)modal verbs in Australian, NZ and British parliamentary records (the Hansard), in the period 1901–2015. Parliamentary speeches and debates, as a form of political discourse, rely strongly on linguistic resources that allow speakers to express their stance in relation to a particular proposition, thereby attempting to influence the listeners' attitude towards that proposition. One linguistic resource to accomplish this is modal verbs (see Vukovic 2014). Modal verbs are subject to ongoing change (Mair 2006; Leech et al. 2009) that results in differences between varieties of English in terms of frequency but potentially also in terms of use (Collins 2009a, 2009b), and such differences have been attested between British, Australian and NZ English (Collins 2009c).

A range of possible reasons for these changes have been proposed. Through both colloquialisation and grammaticalisation, the increased use of semi-modals like *HAVE to* and *NEED to* over modals like *should* and *must* is favoured. Grammaticalisation results in the establishment of semi-modal forms which compete with the older modal auxiliaries for the expression of modal meanings (Krug 2000). Colloquialisation favours the use of more speech-like options in the written language and thus also favours the increased use of semi-modals in writing (Mair 2006; Collins 2009a, 2009b, 2009c; Leech et al. 2009). A trend towards democratisation (Myhill 1995; Mair 2006; Leech et al. 2009) is also identified as a driver of change for the modals of obligation. For example, the modal *must* that has a subjective source of modal force premised on hierarchical social obligations makes room for semi-modals that derive the source of modal obligation from objective circumstances and not the subjective authority of humans, such as *HAVE to* and *NEED to*.

Register is an important factor in the change of modals (see, for example, Mair and Leech 2006; Millar 2009; Collins 2009a; Bowie et al. 2013). Spoken registers change more quickly than written registers and among the written registers, the more formal registers change more slowly than the less formal ones. The register of parliamentary discourse is subject to change not only in terms of the factors that affect all registers, but also in terms of its own internal dynamics (Kruger and Smith 2018; Kruger et al. 2019). Bayley (2004) points out that parliamentary discourse varies across nations based on their history, cultural context and political culture. Kotze and van Rooy (2020) show how local changes such as new ruling parties and changes in the composition of parliamentary representation due to changes in franchise lead to very distinct local patterns of change in modal usage in the parliamentary discourse of South Africa. Rhetorical styles like consensus-seeking versus enhanced confrontation emerge as options that are more or less prominent at different times in the history of South African parliamentary discourse.

Kruger et al. (2019) identify an overall decrease in the frequency of necessity modals in the parliamentary discourse in Australia and Great Britain. They ascribe this to a decrease in overtly persuasive discourse over time, where parliamentarians engage one another less often in persuasive communication and address the general public 'out there' more often. They relate this change to the broadcasting of parliamentary discourse. However, their study relies on the multidimensional model of Biber (1988), and thus provides a broad-stroke quantification only, and excludes the frequencies of semi-modal auxiliaries that may also be involved in the formulation of persuasive language. This chapter aims to look more closely at the deployment of modals of obligation and necessity and includes the semi-modals alongside the modal auxiliaries.

The choice of modal in parliamentary discourse reflects power relations both between parliamentarians and between the parliamentarians and the general public as implied addressee, in terms of the strength of obligation/necessity imposed (from *must* to the much softer *should*). This dual (proximate and distal) audience (and parliamentarians' apparent increased attention to the latter) also opens up questions as to whether obligation/necessity is framed as a collective responsibility of society as a whole or a narrower responsibility of a political party or individual. These are among the examples of cultural and social dimensions of language use presented by Schneider (this volume). But they may also manifest in interestingly diverse ways when comparing data over time from the British parliament, with its long-standing practices, and the Australian and NZ parliaments that came into being in less hierarchical societies typical of colonial settlements. We will investigate these trends as manifested in (semi-)modal usage, looking beyond the determination of quantitative differences, with a closer examination of the co-occurrence of individual (semi-)modals with particular subjects to understand the rhetorical and possible sociocultural factors that motivate the selection of particular (semi-)modals to express obligation/necessity, across three different contexts and more than a century.

Section 2 briefly describes our corpus as well as the method used to extract the data for analysis. Section 3 presents our findings in two parts. We first investigate the frequency of four (semi-)modals of obligation/necessity (*must, HAVE to, NEED to, should*) in the three Hansards over the time period investigated, after which we consider the patterning of these forms with particular pronoun and noun subjects. Section 4 presents a summary of findings and some conclusions.

2. METHOD

A historical corpus of the Australian, British and NZ Hansard (the official record of parliamentary proceedings) was used for this study. The data were sampled from 1901, the year in which the Australian Commonwealth first established its parliament, and thereafter from 1935, 1965, 1995 and 2015. The last day of proceedings of each month in which the parliaments sat was included for these three countries – which resulted in rather an uneven distribution of data due to the irregular length of sittings (see Table 15.1). The electronic records were converted to txt files and proofread, with non-linguistic aspects such as tables removed.

The (semi-)modals included in the study are *must, HAVE to, NEED to* and *should*, which were extracted from the data using the concordance function of WordSmith 7 (Scott 2016).[1] All forms were first screened manually for inclusion (for example, removing cases where *have* or *need* were used as a main verb or *must* as a noun). The total number of valid instances of the four (semi-)modals was 34,108. These were subsequently coded for the syntactic subject of the verb phrase containing the modal, the tense, aspect and voice features of the verb phrase itself, and the main verb following the modal.

Table 15.1 Composition of the three Hansard corpora

Year	Australian Hansard (AusH)	New Zealand Hansard (NZH)	British Hansard (BrH)
1901	319,698	258,496	405,760
1935	155,642	150,499	553,596
1965	371,843	230,635	590,811
1995	869,339	624,250	653,648
2015	889,052	461,884	891,420
Total	2,605,574	1,725,764	3,095,235

For the analysis, two subclasses of subjects were selected. Overall, pronouns accounted for 57 per cent of all subjects (19,640/34,108), among which 52 per cent were first-person pronoun subjects, both plural (6,887) and singular (3,321), showing the prevalence of immediate face-to-face interaction in the clauses containing (semi-)modals of obligation and necessity. The first-person singular and plural pronouns were analysed further, with attention to the kinds of verbs that collocated with these pronoun–modal combinations.

Among the remaining subject types, common nouns (12,280) accounted for the most, alongside a smaller number of proper nouns (1,024). The remaining subjects were either the existential *there* (1,065) or non-nominal subjects like subject clauses, alongside infinitive clauses without overt subjects.

Three subclasses of nominal subjects were identified as particularly widespread and very particular to parliamentary discourse and were therefore analysed in more depth: noun phrases that referred to the GOVERNMENT, to MEMBERS of parliament and to the PUBLIC. These nouns can be regarded as representative of the three main sets of addressees of parliamentary proceedings – the government as a collective institution, the members of the house as individual institutional representatives and the people represented by the parliament, the collective public. In order to make these subclasses as inclusive as possible of the category identified, we manually examined the wordlist to identify other nouns that also belong to these categories. The following nouns were included in the three categories:

- GOVERNMENT: *administration(s), cabinet, chamber, commonwealth, Conservatives, government, house, Labo(u)r, Liberals, ministry, Nationals, office, opposition, parliament, party/ies, treasury* (1,165 tokens)

- MEMBERS: *chancellor* (and other titles), *colleague(s)*, *gentleman/men*, *lady*, *(deputy) leader*, *member(s)*, *minister(s)*, *MP(s)*, *speaker*, *spokesman/person*, names of individual parliamentarians (1,294 tokens)
- PUBLIC: *Australia(ns)*, *Britain*, *citizen(s)*, *constituent(s)*, *elector(s)*, *electorate(s)*, *England*, *individual(s)*, *nation*, *New Zealand(ers)*, *people*, *population*, *ratepayer(s)*, *society*, *taxpayer(s)*, *UK*, *United Kingdom* (585 tokens)

To keep these categories consistent with the audience each represented, external entities were excluded – for example, the government of France was not included in the GOVERNMENT category and the MEMBERS category included only members of that parliament. The PUBLIC category included only references to the public of the nation represented by that parliament as a whole, excluding particular groups within it such as 'young/old people'.[2]

3. RESULTS

In this section, we present the findings of the study starting with the overall distribution of the four (semi-)modals across time in the three parliamentary records (Hansards), followed by a closer look at their use with subject pronouns and subject nouns, as classified in Section 2. In the course of the discussion, we also consider the kinds of verbs that collocate with these modal forms and may thus contribute to the observed frequency changes in their use.

3.1 Overall Distribution

In all three Hansards, the overall distribution of *must*, HAVE *to* and *should* shows a declining trend towards the latest period, with NEED *to* showing a steady increase after 1965. The frequencies for each modal are presented in Figures 15.1–15.4, normalised per thousand words (ptw) according to corpus size.

Figure 15.1 shows a marked regional difference between the colonial parliamentary records and the British Hansard (BrH) for *must*, the modal with the strongest sense of obligation. Both the Australian (AusH) and NZ Hansard (NZH) decline in parallel (apart from a slight increase in 1965 for the NZH), from a slightly higher starting point than the BrH. The BrH, on the other hand, starts lower, but shows a sharp increase until 1965, with a decline in 2015 that cancels out the frequency rise

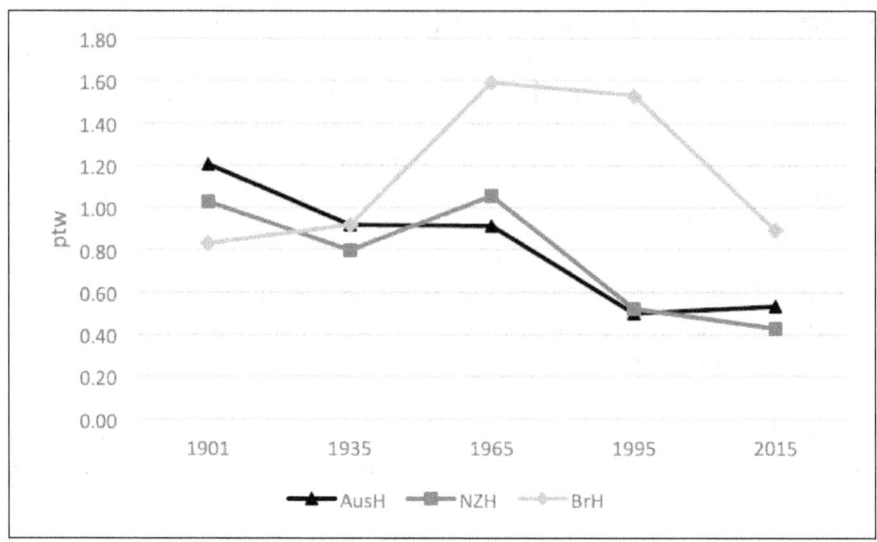

Figure 15.1 Distribution of *must* ptw in the three Hansards.

in the mid-20th century, although it ends slightly higher in 2015 than where it started in 1901. This demonstrates that the BrH is, in this register, lagging behind the general trend of a decline in the frequency of *must* (Smith 2003; Leech et al. 2009) and suggests a more strongly assertive expression of obligation/necessity in British parliamentary discourse than that of Australia or NZ.

For *HAVE to*, it is the BrH and NZH that track most closely over time, with almost identical starting and finishing points, just differing in the point at which they peak (Figure 15.2). The AusH has a noticeably high starting point with the highest usage rate present in 1901 (as is also the case, if to a lesser degree, with *must*). Frequencies in the AusH and NZH decline in the last period, whereas the frequency in the BrH stays steady and thus ends higher in 2015 than it started in 1901.

NEED to shows a very different pattern to the other (semi-)modals in all three Hansards with a clear emerging trend after 1935, as shown in Figure 15.3. The AusH and NZH adopt the incoming form earlier than the BrH, but in the latter the speed of change picks up from 1995 to surpass the other two Hansards in the use of this modal by 2015. It is also notable that the frequency of *NEED to* in each Hansard has surpassed the frequency of *must* and *HAVE to*.

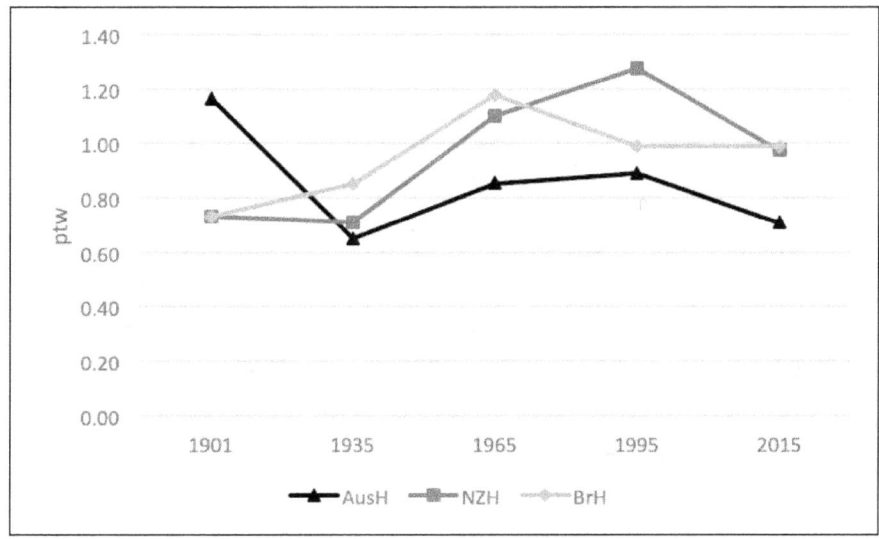

Figure 15.2 Distribution of *HAVE to* ptw in the three Hansards.

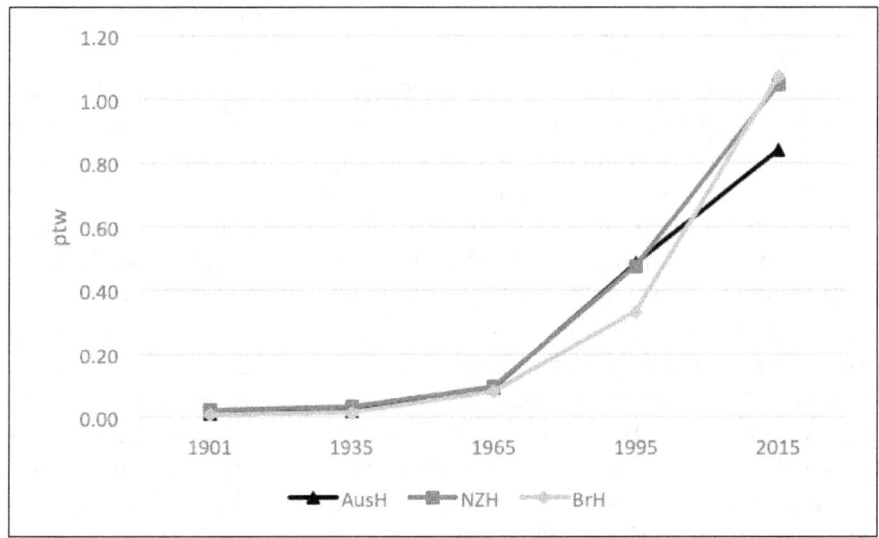

Figure 15.3 Distribution of *NEED to* ptw in the three Hansards.

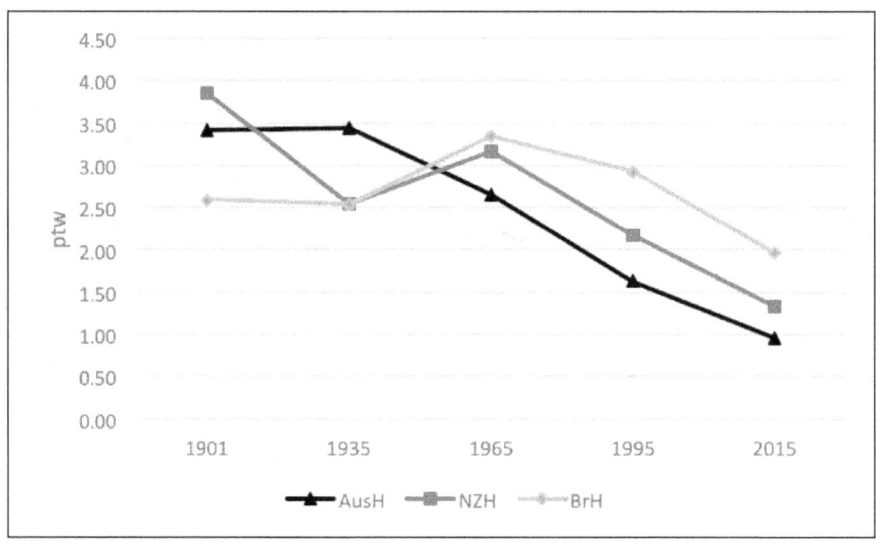

Figure 15.4 Distribution of *should* ptw in the three Hansards.

Figure 15.4 shows that in all three Hansards, *should* declines in frequency. The AusH and NZH started higher than the BrH in 1901, but from 1935 onwards, the NZH and BrH present a very similar pattern with an increase until 1965 and then a steady decline in the later periods. The decline started earlier in AusH. Despite the decline, *should* is still the most frequent modal of this set, although to a much lesser degree than at the start of the period under investigation.

To sum up the regional trends, the BrH shows a higher current frequency of usage for all the (semi-)modal forms investigated, particularly in the cases of *must* and *should*, having started from a lower point in each case. Effectively, the BrH has maintained or increased its use of these (semi-)modals of obligation/necessity over this period, except for *should*, but the decline in frequency of *should* is also considerably less than for the other two varieties. The AusH and NZH present similar trends for *must* and *NEED to*, but for *HAVE to* and *should*, there is not the same distinction with the BrH, with the AusH diverging from the similar patterns of the NZH and BrH.

In order to investigate this variability more closely, we consider evidence provided by different sets of subject categories and how they pattern with three of the four modals across the time period. *NEED to* has been excluded from this discussion because the very low number of occurrences before 1995 makes a diachronic analysis problematic. However, when considering changes in specific patterns over time, trade-offs between NEED to and the other forms are considered.

3.2 Subject–modal Combinations over Time

3.2.1 Must

Must is the modal that expresses the strongest sense of obligation/necessity and is also the one that shows the greatest variation in frequency across the three Hansards. Figure 15.5 shows the frequency of the combination of first-person pronouns with *must* for each region for each year, expressed as a percentage of the overall set of personal pronoun subjects.

The plural pronoun *we* makes up a higher proportion of uses of *must* except where the singular form *I* overtakes the plural in the NZH from 1995. The proportion of the plural form with *must* shows a steady increase in the BrH while the singular decreases, whereas the AusH and NZH present a more fluctuating pattern. The high proportion of *we* in Australian parliamentary discourse in 1901 appears to be related to a strong affirmation of collective responsibility for nation building at the start of federation,[3] as in example (1) and the statement of desiderata of what the new state needs, either in terms of the real-life conditions out there, shown in (2), or in terms of legislative desiderata, shown in (3).

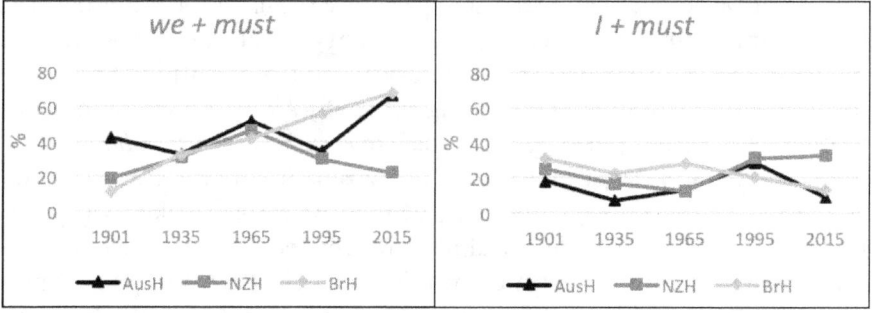

Figure 15.5 Proportional frequency of first-person pronoun subjects with *must*.

(1) We **must** preserve our shores inviolate against every swashbuckling foreigner who attempts to invade them. (AusH, 31 July 1901)
(2) We **must** not only grow produce for our people, but we **must** have places in which they can live and in which they can carry on their manufactures. (AusH, 31 October 1901)
(3) We are to have a uniform Tariff, and we **must** have uniform factory legislation. (AusH, 28 June 1901)

The peak at 1965 for both the AusH and NZH ties in with a period when both countries were challenged by Britain's application to join the European Economic Community (EEC) in 1961 (Rabel 2005), which led to a stronger expression of national identity in Australia (Collins and Yao 2018) and NZ (Bailey 1990: 85–6). The examples during this period reflect the sense, on both sides of the Tasman, of no longer being able to rely on Britain for security within their region, and the related necessity to develop international trade, as seen in examples (4) and (5).

(4) Despite these handicaps, we **must** develop an export market. This will call for specialisation and intensified effort in research and product development in which we **must** depart from the easier path of the copyist and become innovators. (AusH, 31 August 1965)
(5) ... that we can meet our commitment in Malaysia and at the same time send a force to South Vietnam. Let me deal with these four assumptions. The first is that this is a fight against communism and therefore we **must** be in it for the security of NZ. (NZH, 28 March 1965)

The BrH, unlike the others, shows a consistent proportional increase in the use of *we must* and an increase in absolute terms in the latter parts of the timeframe under investigation (1995–2015). The data show that this increase relates in particular to rhetorical strategies within the parliament, where the frequent collocating verbs of *we must*, absent or lower in frequency in earlier periods, are verbs like *ensure, recognise, address, deal, consider* and *remember*, as illustrated by example (6). These are often used as speech act verbs to encourage agreement with the speaker. In earlier periods, this particular rhetorical resource for seeking encouragement is less frequent. At the same time, the data show clear signs of polarisation in the debate, with Scottish independence and the relationship between Britain and the EU often occurring in the environment of things that *we must* decide on, as illustrated by example (7).

(6) We **must** remember that rationing is the denial of treatment that would benefit patients. (BrH, 31 January 1995)
(7) On the timing, some people want to have a quick referendum and I have already heard others saying that we **must** be willing to say yes to a reformed EU without knowing what that will look like. We **must** resist any attempt to bounce the British people into an early referendum. We can wait until we are ready. We **must** give our people a full explanation of the choices... (BrH, 28 May 2015)

The relative proportion for *I must*, conversely, shows a steady decline for the BrH, but a rise for the AusH and NZH that levels off in 1995 for the former, but has continued (albeit more slowly) for the latter. This can be explained as a particular use of the modal with the first-person singular that is not related to obligation, but in combination with communication or, occasionally, mental verbs used to introduce a proposition, and indicating something about the epistemic force of the proposition. The single most frequent main verb collocating with *I must* is *say*, which accounts for slightly more than 30 per cent of all main verbs combining with *I must* and can be regarded as a prefabricated chunk. In the NZH, a little more than half of all instances of *I must* combines with *say* (69/137) and slightly less than half (65/142) in the AusH, while the BrH shows more diversity, with other communication verbs like *ask*, *tell* and *apologise* occurring relatively frequently in the BrH but are all but absent from the Australian and NZ records. Nonetheless, *say* is still three times more frequent than the second most frequent collocating verb in the BrH as well.

This pattern should be considered alongside the collocation of *I HAVE to* and *say*, which is similarly dominant in Australia and NZ among all the collocates of *I HAVE to*, and similarly frequent in Britain to *I must say*. In all three countries' parliaments, these forms gained ascendancy in 1995 and maintained their proportional dominance in 2015, although the absolute frequencies are down in all three in 2015 compared with 1995. Such uses occur in lower frequencies in the UK parliament in 1965 and earlier, but are completely absent from Australia and NZ and then suddenly appear in 1995.[4] The dominant forms with *say* are illustrated in examples (8) and (9) for NZ and Australia, and while similar forms are also very frequent in Britain, the latter makes more use of lexical variants, such as illustrated by (10).

(8) However, I **must** say that perhaps the member for Nelson has not got it right ... (NZH, 30 March 1995)
(9) Of course, after voting time and time again to stop us abolishing the carbon tax, now Labor wants to bring back the carbon tax if they are elected. I **have to** say, this is something that is of great concern to businesses and residents in my electorate on the Central Coast. (AusH, 17 September 2015)
(10) I **must** tell the House that I shall be voting against the order tonight, and for two reasons ... (BrH, 28 February 1995)

Examining the context of expressions such as those exemplified by examples (8)–(10), it is usually the case that the speaker contributes a statement that is in strong disagreement with some proposal on the table or some statement by another speaker in a debate. Thus, the expressions *I must say*/*I HAVE to say* are disagreement markers. They flag overtly that the speaker is about to disagree, but the speaker selects a modal alongside the communication verb as if to show that this is unavoidable: they are compelled to disagree. The forms *I must* and *I HAVE to* have become specialised in this function and are otherwise rarely used. The verb *say* (and similarly *remember*) differs from most other verbs in the Hansards of 1995 and 2015 in that it does not show a strong increase in combination with *NEED to*, showing that these fixed collocations that manage interpersonal interaction across the parliamentary floors are more resistant to change under pressure from the incoming semi-modal *NEED to*.

Moving on to the subject–noun categories under investigation, Figure 15.6 shows the patterns of usage for each combined with *must*, expressed as percentages of the overall frequencies across the categories for each

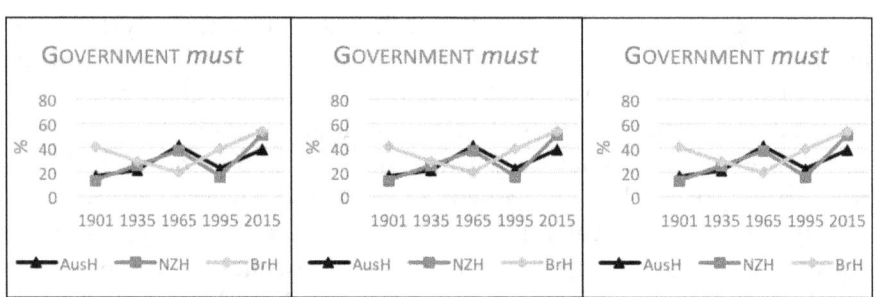

Figure 15.6 Proportional frequency of three categories of subjects with *must*.

region and time period.

There are rather similar patterns over time for the AusH and NZH, with *must* being applied strongly to the MEMBERS category at the start of the period, but decreasing in usage over time (with a fluctuation in 1995 for the NZH), to about the same level of use as for the GOVERNMENT category, which has fluctuated but is on the rise. In the early periods, *must* is used in expressions where the appropriate behaviour is not forthcoming (for example, *must know*, to mean 'is really supposed to know but clearly does not'), as illustrated in example (11), or the appropriate behaviour is directed, usually by the Speaker (*must withdraw*), as illustrated in (12). However, in later periods, especially in 2015, this function is taken over by *should*. This change is consistent with the democratisation trend that disfavours the expression of strong obligation through *must*.

(11) The right hon. Member **must** know, if he has read the Bill, that some completely uncertain sums are involved in its implementation. (BrH, 30 November 1965)

(12) Mr. DEPUTY-SPEAKER. - The honourable member **must** withdraw it. (NZH, 31 October 1901)

Later usage with *should* is exemplified by examples (13) and (15). In (13), early in the response of the speaker to another member, the assumption that the other member knows something is stated in an unmodalised fashion, but towards the end, the other member's presumed ignorance is sanctioned through the use of *should know*. By 2015, a very clear new pattern emerges with *know*, which is *we NEED to know* (example (14)), identifying an information gap that precludes the debate from progressing. It serves a similar function to 'the member must/should know', but phrased in a more polite and objective way than earlier. In (15), the more polite *should* is used in the place of the earlier *must*. However, as is clear from what follows, the effective force of the speaker's injunction is no less than what it would have been if *must* had been used.

(13) As I have already said to that member - and that member knows the Budget process - I cannot release that figure. What I can say is that since this Government took office, there are now 220 more doctors on the front line. There are now 433 more nurses on the front line in the Counties Manukau District Health Board, and there are now, in terms of orthopaedic surgery, more patients who are operated on in the Counties Manukau District

Health Board region, and that member **should** know all of this. (NZH, 26 February 2015)

(14) The Bill is still passing through the House, and we **need to** know how we will be working with agencies abroad and how the Home Office will be working with the Foreign and Commonwealth Office to ensure that . . . (BrH, 29 January 2015)

(15) The SPEAKER: To assist the House, the member **should** withdraw.
Mr Snowdon: I do not know what it is that I--
The SPEAKER: I would ask the member for Lingiari to withdraw if he used an unparliamentary term. (AusH, 26 February 2015)

The use of *must* with the PUBLIC category has stayed low and is in decline, such that it is completely absent from the NZH by 2015, and it is to be expected that a modal expressing obligation less firmly would be preferred for this category. The usage peak in 1995 in the AusH is interesting, but it is noticeable that most of the examples of *must* in this period are, in fact, not placing an obligation on the public, rather using the public as a means of putting pressure on a person/entity within parliament, as exemplified in example (16).

(16) I ask you, Prime Minister: how long **must** the Australian people wait until you finally deliver on the promises you have made about curing the fundamental problems of the Australian economy? (AusH, 30 March 1995)

The use of *must* with GOVERNMENT as subject fluctuates throughout time but is consistently less frequent than combinations with the modal *should* and semi-modal *HAVE to*. By 2015, though, the GOVERNMENT is the principal entity on which strong obligations with *must* are levelled, surpassing the MEMBERS and PUBLIC categories. This could represent members' desire to be more overtly assertive in obliging the government to take responsibility, as in example (17), which could be seen as a form of rhetorical grandstanding for a wider (public) audience.

(17) **The Government must demonstrate that will** and restore their credibility with the electorate (BrH, 19 July 1995)

Australia and NZ (more strikingly) show a similar rise in the use of *must* in this category, but only for the most recent period. It is possible that broadcasting could have had an influence here, with the televising of parliament starting in that period (Kruger et al. 2019).

When we compare these results with those for personal-pronoun usage, it seems possible that *must* is being used in the BrH more to place a strong obligation on the government, whereas in the NZH and particularly the AusH, it is more often used to frame collective responsibility. The peak in 1965 for both the AusH and NZH for both *we must* and GOVERNMENT *must* represents a point in time when collective responsibility and government responsibility converge to forge a stronger national identity. In Australia, the 1960s corresponds to what Collins and Yao (2018: 273) call an 'upsurge of nationalistic fervor' and the 'decline of Britishness', while Bailey (1990) points to a similar effect in NZ at this time, as noted earlier. The opposing trends in the NZH from 1995 to 2015, with *we must* decreasing while GOVERNMENT *must* increases, suggests a move away from collective responsibility to putting pressure on the government. Furthermore, the analysis of *must* points to its specialised uses in parliamentary rhetoric, such as the expression *I must say* that becomes very dominant by the final two periods under investigation.

3.2.2 HAVE to

The semi-modal *HAVE to* is used as a less subjective expression of obligation/responsibility than *must*. Figure 15.2 demonstrates that the usage of *HAVE to* has remained fairly consistent over time, unlike the other semi-modal, *NEED to*, which is clearly an incoming form. Its consistency of use may be connected to its flexibility – it can occur with other modals (for example, *will*, *shall*) whereas the other modals considered here cannot. Figure 15.7 shows the usage of the first-person pronouns + *HAVE to* in each Hansard, 1901–2015.

As shown in the overall frequency analysis in Figure 15.2, *HAVE to* is more frequent in the first period in Australia. Furthermore, *we + HAVE to*, like *we must*, is proportionally more frequent in 1901 as well, the first year of the parliament of the Australian Commonwealth, and similarly to *must* in Figure 15.5, the AusH starts at a higher level than the other varieties for *we + HAVE to*. A closer examination of the data reveals that a major reason for the selection of *HAVE to* with the pronoun *we* is the use of other modals, for instance *shall HAVE to* or *should HAVE to*. Overall, 39/110 cases of *we + HAVE to* in this period in Australia have modal combinations with *HAVE to*, far larger than the average

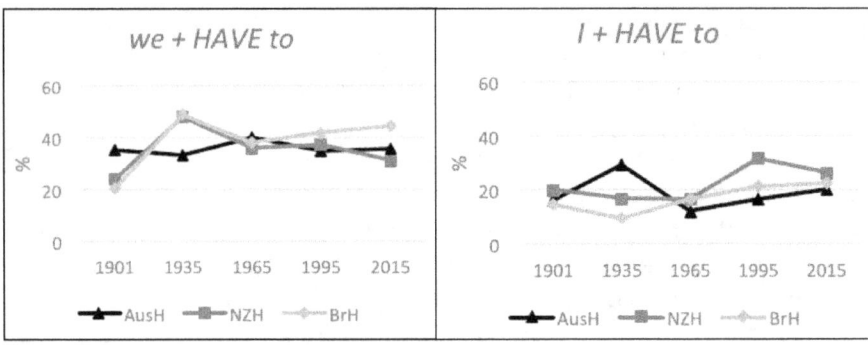

Figure 15.7 Proportional frequency of first-person pronoun subjects with *HAVE to*.

for the data. Moreover, the form *we shall HAVE to* accounts for just under half (18/39) of the instances of the modal combinations. There is a very strong prospective sense of the task that lies ahead which 'we shall have to deal' with, as illustrated by example (18). The verb *deal* is in fact the single most frequent verb collocating with *we + HAVE to* in 1901. Thereafter the pattern is quite consistent over time for the AusH, and indeed the other varieties – apart from a peak for the NZH and BrH in 1935 (although the token counts are quite low, so it is hard to draw a conclusion about this rise).

(18) This matter of closer settlement touches upon one of the most vital questions with which we shall **have to** deal in the future . . . (AusH, 30 August 1901)

The use of *I + HAVE to* has already been discussed in comparison with *I must*. It is mainly used with communication verbs as part of the rhetoric of defending one's own position or attacking the position of a political opponent. As was pointed out in Section 3.2.1, the form *I HAVE to say* is the most frequent modal+verb combination for *I HAVE to*, which manifests with especially high frequency in Australia and NZ from 1995, while its use in Britain starts earlier.

Figure 15.8 presents the comparison of the use of *HAVE to* across the three subject–noun categories. There is a much less distinct preference for *HAVE to* to be applied in one category compared with another than for *must*. The AusH data show a stronger early use in the GOVERNMENT category than the other two regions, parallel to the use of *we + HAVE to*, which suggests the need for collective responsibility and pressing future

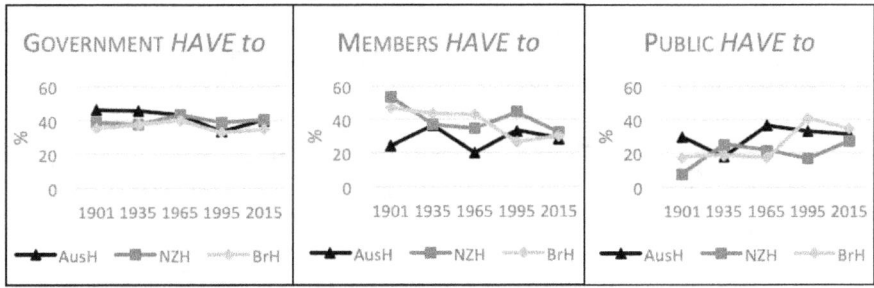

Figure 15.8 Proportional frequency of three categories of subjects with *HAVE to*.

needs in the early stages of federation, as illustrated in example (19), which shows the combination of *HAVE to* with another modal as well. This typical feature of the 1901 Australian Hansard data clearly relates to the important moment in the history of the new self-governing territory.

(19) ... in the future the Government will **have to** spend a great deal more money in the defence of the Commonwealth. (AusH, 1901)

There is no clear pattern of preference over time, but it is notable that the PUBLIC category displays the highest proportion of use at one point in the BrH data (1995), despite the lower number of items in this category overall. Many of the examples of usage in this category show recognition of obligation being placed, and are therefore sympathetic rather than authoritarian, as illustrated in example (20).

(20) Many people will **have to** travel long distances to find a new doctor. (BrH, 1995)

3.2.3 Should

Should is the weakest of the set in terms of modal strength and this may be reflected in its overall higher frequency compared with the other modals (see Figure 15.4) – its lack of assertiveness gives it a broader application. But there is an overall decrease in its use, which requires further explanation and clearly suggests that *should* does not take over the semantic space previously covered by *must* (and *HAVE to* to a lesser degree).

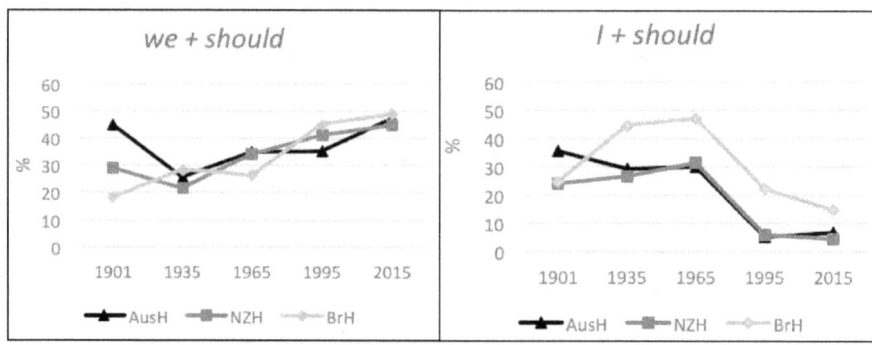

Figure 15.9 Frequency of first-person pronoun subjects with *should*.

As for the other modals, *we should* starts at the highest proportion in the AusH, reinforcing the interpretation of the importance of this specific moment in time already highlighted in reference to *we must* and *we HAVE to*. But from 1935, the pattern (Figure 15.9) shows a consistent increase in proportional usage across the varieties. *I should* does show a decrease from 1965, but only after a clear rise, particularly in the BrH. The reason for the frequent combination of *should* with *I* becomes clear when we look at the main verb following the modal verb.

Table 15.2 The most common verbs collocating with *I should*, raw frequency (N) and normalised frequency per 1,000 verbs (N/1,000 verbs)

	AU		NZ		BR	
	N	N/1,000 verbs	N	N/1,000 verbs	N	N/1,000 verbs
like	197	58	112	40	539	91
be	23	7	15	5	131	22
think	15	4	7	2	113	19
say	29	9	33	12	53	9

As Table 15.2 shows, *I should* is most commonly followed by *like*, indicating politeness rather than obligation, as in example (21).

(21) I confess that I have not made a study of the Clause, but I **should** like to ask the Minister two questions about it. (BrH, 31 May 1965)

This rather formal (and archaic) usage survives longer and at a higher rate in BrH, indicating a higher degree of conservatism and overt politeness in that variety. This use of *I should like* does not occur in the NZH after 1965 and only once in 1995 in the AusH but does occur up to the present time in the BrH. *Think* is most often used in the formulaic expression *I should have thought* (101/135 of *I should think*). However, as shown in the discussion of *I must* and *I HAVE to*, there are more assertive forms like *I must say* and *I HAVE to tell* that seem to replace the more polite *I should like to* and *I should have thought*, which disappear by 1995. Thus, perhaps counter to the expectations of a decrease in modal force over time raised by the general language change, the use of modals as epistemic hedges with the first-person singular subject moves in the opposite direction, with *must* and *HAVE to* taking on a stronger role than *should*.

Finally, consider the patterns for *should* with the subject–noun categories (Figure 15.10).

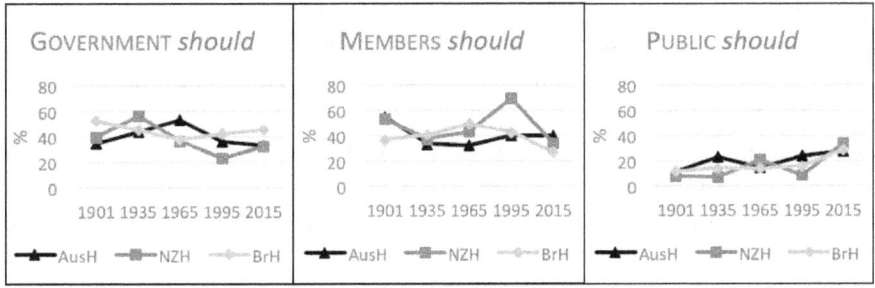

Figure 15.10 Proportional frequency of three categories of subjects with *should*.

For the GOVERNMENT category there is a similar trajectory for the BrH as for *must* (see Figure 15.6), but with less extreme fluctuations, compounding the rise in use of modals of obligation aimed at GOVERNMENT since 1965. The use of this modal for the MEMBERS category is fairly consistent, apart from the spike in 1995 for the NZH (also observed for *must*). The usage in the PUBLIC category, conversely, is on the rise, after some fluctuation, but at a lower level of frequency than for the other modals. In particular, the NZH has increased markedly since 1995. It is possible that broadcasting has had an effect on the increased use of modal obligation aimed at the public, with the choice of the weakest of the modals to temper the authoritative tone, as in example (22).

(22) That is why New Zealanders **should** continue to be worried. (NZH, 9 December 2015)

4. DISCUSSION

The results show that the parliamentary Hansards for all three countries participate in the large-scale changes in modal use: the decrease in frequency of *must* and modals generally, alongside the increase in frequency of the incoming semi-modal *NEED to*. The rate of change is different, with the AusH and NZH changing faster than the BrH. In other words, British parliamentary discourse seems to be more conservative than either the Australian or NZ, similar to the national varieties to which they belong (Collins 2009c).

Embedded within these overarching changes are local patterns of variation across time. A number of analyses point to a unique frequency peak in Australia, where the collective undertaking of a new self-governing territory is particularly important to a newly established parliament. This echoes the sense of collective responsibility that Kotze and van Rooy (2020) identify for the South African parliament of 1995, shortly after the franchise has been extended to all citizens. In the face of external threats, as in the mid-1960s, there are similar concerns in Australia and NZ to emphasise the collective responsibility for confronting those threats in a period when a growing sense of self-reliance appears to lead to stronger expression of national identity. Increased polarisation has been identified behind some of the uses of *we must* in the British parliament of more recent times.

Apart from external influences on the parliamentary language, changes in rhetoric within the parliaments have been identified as well. Strategies for disagreement have seen relatively fixed linguistic patterns such as *I must say* develop from 1995, while older patterns such as MEMBER *must know* have declined over time. These local changes and patterns are embedded within the larger changes, as shown by the partial replacement of MEMBER *must know* by the pattern *we NEED to know*, where *must* gives way to *NEED to*. Likewise, the obligations conveyed through *must* are replaced by expression through *should*, even if the modal force per se has not declined, only the surface expression used to encode it.

Broadcasting has been postulated as a contributing factor, with an awareness of an external audience possibly having an effect on the way that (semi-)modals are used by parliamentarians both in interacting with one another and as a rhetorical device to engage with the public. The current corpus covers too broad a span of dates to isolate this process effectively, with broadcasting coming in at different periods for the different parliaments.

Parliamentary discourse reveals itself to be receptive to long-term changes in the use of (semi-)modals that affect English in general. These changes are in part ascribed to cultural changes such as colloquialisation and democratisation, which are extralinguistic in the first instance, but with clear linguistic resonances. At the same time, the language of parliament is also responsive to local and time-bound changes in the political environment, sometimes placing more emphasis on collective undertakings. Moreover, as a register, the Hansard shows evidence of changes and the emergence of fixed expressions over time that are specific to the unique features of this register and under the influence of unique factors that impact on this register, such as broadcasting.

NOTES

1. *Have got to*, which is traditionally a member of this set, was excluded on the grounds of low frequency for this register.
2. It is interesting to note (but falls outside the scope of this chapter) that the PUBLIC category had less than half the number of tokens of the other two categories, demonstrating that the forms under investigation are much less likely to be applied to a notional external audience than the internal audience.
3. Collection of further data would be needed to discover if there is a similar effect for New Zealand, whose status changed from colony to independent dominion in 1907.
4. It may be that this change is related to a move towards a more verbatim style of parliamentary reporting (see also Kruger and Smith 2018; Kruger et al. 2019).

REFERENCES

Bailey, R. W. (1990). English at its twilight. In C. Ricks and L. Michaels (Eds.), *The state of the language* (pp. 83–94). University of California Press.

Bayley, P. (Ed.). (2004). *Cross-cultural perspectives on parliamentary discourse*. John Benjamins.

Biber, D. (1988). *Variation across speech and writing*. Cambridge University Press.

Bowie, J., Wallis, S. and Aarts, B. (2013). Contemporary change in modal usage in spoken British English: Mapping the impact of 'genre'. In J. I. Marín-Arrese, M. Carretero, J. Arús Hita and J. van der Auwera (Eds.), *English modality: Core, periphery and evidentiality* (pp. 57–94). De Gruyter.

Collins, P. (2009a). *Modals and quasi-modals in English*. Rodopi.

Collins, P. (2009b). Modals and quasi-modals in World Englishes. *World Englishes, 28*(3), 281–92.

Collins, P. (2009c). Modals and quasi-modals. In P. Peters, P. Collins and A. Smith (Eds.), *Comparative studies in Australian and New Zealand English: Grammar and beyond* (pp. 73–87). John Benjamins.

Collins, P. and Yao, X. (2018). Colloquialisation and the evolution of Australian English: A cross-varietal and cross-generic study of Australian, British and American English from 1931 to 2006. *English World-Wide, 39*(3), 253–77.

Kotze, H. and van Rooy, B. (2020). Democratisation in the South African parliamentary Hansard? A study of change in modal auxiliaries. *Language Sciences, 79*, 101264. <https://doi.org/10.1016/j.langsci.2019.101264> (last accessed 12 January 2021).

Krug, M. G. (2000). *Emerging English modals: A corpus-based study of grammaticalization*. De Gruyter.

Kruger, H. and Smith, A. (2018). Colloquialization versus densification in Australian English: A multidimensional analysis of the Australian Diachronic Hansard Corpus (ADHC). *Australian Journal of Linguistics, 38*(3), 293–328.

Kruger, H., van Rooy, B. and Smith, A. (2019). Register change in the British and Australian Hansard (1901–2015). *Journal of English Linguistics, 47*(3), 183–220.

Leech, G., Hundt, M., Mair, C. and Smith, N. (2009). *Change in contemporary English: A grammatical study*. Cambridge University Press.

Mair, C. (2006). *Twentieth-century English: History, variation and standardization*. Cambridge University Press.

Mair, C. and Leech, G. (2006). Current changes in English syntax. In B. Aarts and A. McMahon (Eds.), *Current changes in English syntax* (pp. 318–42). Blackwell.

Millar, N. (2009). Modal verbs in TIME: Frequency changes 1923–2006. *International Journal of Corpus Linguistics, 14*(2), 191–220.
Myhill, J. (1995). Change and continuity in the functions of the American English modals. *Linguistics, 33*(2), 157–211.
Rabel, R. (2005). *New Zealand and the Vietnam War: Politics and diplomacy*. Auckland University Press.
Scott, M. (2016). WordSmith Tools (Version 7) [Computer software]. Lexical Analysis Software.
Smith, N. (2003). Changes in the modals and semi-modals of strong obligation and epistemic necessity in recent British English. In R. Facchinetti, F. Palmer and M. Krug (Eds.), *Modality in contemporary English* (pp. 241–66). Mouton de Gruyter.
Vukovic, M. (2014). Strong epistemic modality in parliamentary discourse. *Open Linguistics, 1*, 37–52.

CHAPTER 16

Privileging Informality: Cultural Influences on the Structural Patterning of Australian English

Isabelle Burke and Kate Burridge

1. INTRODUCTION

> Ways of thinking which are widely shared in a society become enshrined in ways of speaking. Ways of speaking change as the underlying ways of thinking change. (Wierzbicka 2002: 1168)

The cultural values, beliefs and practices of speakers give rise to the linguistic habits of their daily discourse – and so it is that the cultural preoccupations of these speakers can work to sculpt the different aspects of their language, as well as their patterns of interaction. A prominent feature of Australian culture has always been its informality and its greater willingness to use colloquial styles of discourse. In this chapter, we consider the potential influence of this culture on structural choices in Australian English (AusE), examining corpus data to look for evidence that aspects of Australian conversational syntax go beyond the kinds of colloquialisation noted in other varieties. Our focus then is on Schneider's third nexus, specifically the construction involving what are known as negative polarity items (NPIs) – phrases usually used only within the scope of semantic negation of some kind.

Types of NPIs are many and varied but we will be concentrating on those usually called 'minimisers' or 'the minimal direct object class' (earlier 'the accusative of smallest measure'; Vennemann 1974: 378). Taboo items form a particularly interesting sub-class of these minimisers, especially for AusE. We identify two main types: under Type 1 are the constructions of indifference (the 'care/give a X' frame), involving negated verbs such as *care*, *give*, *matter* in combination with a taboo item (for example, *I don't give a damn/shit/fuck*); under Type 2 are constructions with a taboo item but the verb may or may not be negated; these involve straightforward mass nouns (the 'verb X' frame; for example, *I (don't) know shit/jack shit/diddly squat*) or they appear in combination with *all* (the 'X-all' frame; for example, *damn all/bugger all/fuck all*). It is these Type 2 constructions, particularly the 'X-all' frame, that hold most interest for the development of taboo negation down under.

2. BACKDROP: THE HISTORY OF ENGLISH NEGATION AND JESPERSEN'S CYCLE

For the historical background to our account, consider the most significant changes that have taken place in English negation over the years. We capture these changes with the following four sentences (these come from a range of early medico-magic and etiquette texts; see Burridge 2015). What these examples illustrate are clearly identifiable phases in the history of negation (the reality of course was not this neat, and there was considerable overlap between the stages):

(Old English) preverbal *ne*
(1) *Ne forlæt þu þæs blodes to fela* 'don't let too much of the blood'
(Middle English) embracing *ne-not*
(2) *Ne blow **not** on thy drynke* 'don't blow on your drink'
(Early Modern English) postverbal *not*
(3) *Drinke **not** above four times* 'don't drink more than four times'
(Modern English) *do*-support
(4) ***Don't** drink and drive* (Modern English)

As shown here, Old English negated by placing a negative particle *ne* before the finite verb. Often this was supported by one or more additional negative words and by Middle English multiple negation was common, with two (often more) postverbal negators present. During this period *noght/not* (< *ne-a-wiht* 'not-ever-anything') emerged as the favoured reinforcer and embracing negation (*ne . . . noght/not*) became the norm. With time, this element (the NPI) became bleached of its emphatic quality and was reanalysed as the negator proper (Modern English *not*). At this point, the original *ne* was dropped and the language was left with the new, reanalysed postverbal negator. In the course of the early Modern English period, the frequency of *do*-support in negative clauses rose considerably and by the 19th century it had stabilised as obligatory in all environments if no other auxiliary was present (*Drink not and drive*).

This kind of negator renewal is generally referred to as 'Jespersen's Cycle' – Jespersen (1914, 1917) saw this same pattern occurring again and again and in an astounding number and variety of languages (it is potentially even more widespread given that poorly documented examples of single negation could have evolved via precisely such a pattern of erosion and creation; see Horn 2001). In the case of English, we see the evolution of a negative quantifier into a general negator; but probably the most famous example of Jespersen's Cycle involves the French minimiser *pas* from the word meaning 'step' (for example, Latin *non vado passum* '(I) not go (a) step (or pace = two steps)' > Modern French *je (ne) vais pas*).

2.1 Taboo NPIs and Jespersen's Cycle

Taboo minimisers have been described as forming a mini-Jespersen's Cycle – the idea being that they appear in conjunction with other negators, allowing the original negator to then be dropped. Hoeksema, for example, explores these NPIs in American English:

(5a) He didn't tell me fuck all about the car
(b) He told me fuck all about the car
(6a) Fred doesn't know jack shit about the car
(b) Fred knows jack shit about the car (Hoeksema 2009: 20)

One unusual feature of the taboo items under Type 2 is that they are mass nouns – as Hoeksema (2009) has pointed out, NPIs of the minimising type are (not surprisingly) typically preceded by the indefinite article *a(n)* or *one* (compare *I didn't drink a drop*); usually, speakers are keen to emphasise the smallness of the amount to which they are referring and determiners are helpful in achieving this. The mass nature of these NPIs assists the grammaticalisation process – without all the trappings of nounhood, their reanalysis occurs more easily (Hopper and Traugott 2003).

The following example illustrates how this less respectable version of Jespersen's Cycle might work:

(7) He doesn't know **anything** → He doesn't know **jack shit/ fuck all** → He knows **jack shit/fuck all** → ??I've worked **jack shit/fuck all**

The final stage in this negation saga (*I've worked jack shit*) shows the extension of the taboo NPI from simple nominal quantifier (meaning 'nothing') to the more versatile negative adverb (meaning 'not'), available to other verb types. This stage has not yet been reported in any accounts of vulgar minimisers (though this literature admittedly is small and also confined to American English; Horn 2001; Postal 2004; Hoeksema 2009).

Focusing on the dismissive construction (our Type 1), Lawley describes the following American English sentences in the same way; rather than labelling it Jespersen's Cycle, however, he dubs the development 'negation by association'.

(8a) He couldn't care less/couldn't give a damn
(b) He could care less/could give a damn (Lawley 1974: 2)

While the existence of the (a) and (b) pairs here are certainly suggestive of a mini-Jespersen's Cycle, there are other ways of explaining the transition from *couldn't give a damn* to *could give a damn*. The sentiment of minimal direct objects (like *a damn/a pin/a farthing*) combined with verbs such as *care* and *matter* is dismissive regardless of whether the structure is negative or not (= 'I don't even care a pin' versus 'I care only a damn/a pin/a farthing'). There is also the possibility that positive versions like *I could care less* start life as a joke – the next generation of speakers misses the levity and learns *I could care less* as the general expression (see Bolinger 1975: 405 on the humour of *for free*). The complexity of the negator *not* combined with semantically negative *less* would assist *could care less* to slip in under the net (it is well established in the psycholinguistic literature that such combinations pose difficulties for cognitive processing; compare references in Danat 1980: 486).

3. TABOO NPIs IN AUSTRALIAN ENGLISH

> [Entry for bugger] The most versatile word in the Australian vernacular. Can be used as a noun to mean thing (e.g. 'Slippery little bugger') or nothing ('This grog cost bugger all'), as a verb to mean ruin ('You had one job and you buggered it up') or waste time ('I buggered around all arvo'), as an adjective to mean tired ('I'm buggered after work'), as an imperative to mean get lost ('Bugger off'), or as a mildly profane exclamation ('Bugger!'). (Smith 2018)

Our modern Australian data are based on Burke's (2017) exploration of the UWA Corpus of English in Australia. This corpus was collected by University of Western Australia (UWA) linguistics students in casual dialogue with friends and family in Perth between 2012 and 2015; it consists of 1,144,980 words transcribed by the linguistics students themselves. Audio is available for nearly all transcripts. At the stage of the investigation, the corpus was untagged, so whole-word searches centred on the lexicon were required.

The UWA corpus showed plenty of evidence of taboo words interacting with negation in different ways; some appear more pertinent to Jespersen's Cycle than others. We will consider only the two types of constructions outlined earlier and ignore other constructions (for example, the taboo NPI as a PP (*for shit*) as in *he can't sing for shit*).

All 13 examples of the Type 1 dismissive verb construction (the '*care/give* a X' frame) contained the negator *n't* (**I give a shit*).

(9) (laughs) Yeah n- the- the cops were like it's clear that they had to give the parents a call but **they didn't give a shit**. (UWA 2014: O1: Male: 19 years)

Versions with non-tabooed lexical material (for example, *I couldn't give a hoot/a toss*) were also always negated; similarly, the *could(n't) care less* construction:

(10) [RO] And I also go off my cup o' tea though it didn't worry me as much as I love my cup o' tea, **I couldn't care less**! (UWA 2013: O1: Female: 92 years)

While negative evidence is never 100 per cent conclusive, we can gauge the unacceptability of positive versions like *They gave a shit/I could care less* in AusE by the public discussion around these versions – overwhelmingly, they are condemned and dismissed as American English.[1]

Data evidence for constructions involving mass noun NPIs (for example, *dick*, *shit* or *jack shit*) showed up only examples with negators:

(11) I might have dented his chassis a bit but it was fine (Oh okay) or something. I don't know. It was a big old car, **didn't do jack shit to it**. But it fucked my car completely. (UWA 2015: H1: Male: 25 years)

While there were no examples like *It did jack shit to the car*, both of us (as native AusE speakers) find these versions perfectly acceptable. Certainly, the *Oxford English Dictionary* (*OED*) entries fluctuate (for example, 'They're not going to do shit'; 'That means you got shit'), from the 1940s through to the 2000s. Such variation would be a predictable spin-off if a reanalysis were in progress (as predicted by Jespersen's Cycle).

The 'X-all' structures (*damn/bugger/sod/fuck all*) in the UWA corpus data behaved differently again, only ever appearing without the negator *not*; in other words, there were no examples such as *I didn't do fuck all/bugger all*.

(12a) But, um, I would also love to – and again, I never could never do it, because I'm a weenie butt – but I would love to be able to, um, a) that, but b) um, go kayaking amongst glaciers, it would be like the most amazing thing ever, but y'know, **you need upper body strength for that, and I have fuck all**, so . . . (UWA 2014: C3: Female: 20 years)

(b) [1] Great . . . So, how's your day been? What've you been up to today?
[2] (Whispers) **I wanna say shit all**.
[1&2] (Laughing).
[1] That's fine you can say whatever you like. (UWA 2014: D1: Female: 75 years)

If what we are seeing here is the fall-out of Jespersen's Cycle, then these 'X-all' expressions appear to have completed one turn of the cycle, having moved from polarity item to negative quantifier, and given that the speaker in example (12b) is a 75-year-old female, the change would appear to be well entrenched. Compared with the other NPIs then, they are ahead of the game. The Type 1 constructions appear stuck at stage 1, with no evidence yet in AusE of any reanalysis taking place (**They gave a shit/I could care less*). The other Type 2 constructions, the 'verb X' frame (as in *I (don't) know shit/diddly squat*), are somewhere in the middle, manifesting the sort of variation one might expect of a construction undergoing reanalysis – these taboo items appear regularly with both negated and non-negated verbs.[2] Of course, the absence of structures like *He didn't know bugger all* in the UWA corpus could simply represent a gap in the data. To confirm this is not the case, we now report the results of a follow-up survey of judgement tasks testing the acceptability of taboo NPIs and negators (see Burke 2017 for details).

3.1 What the Survey Data Reveal

The survey was conducted with three different groups of native AusE speakers at a prominent Australian university.[3] The total number of participants was 170: the first group totalled 48 participants, the second 84 and the third 38. The students were presented with audio recordings of the sentences (to avoid the potential normative effect of written versions); hidden in a number of different sentence types were two 'bugger all' sentences – one in which *bugger all* was used as a negator (*This essay's due tomorrow and I've done bugger all*), and one in which *bugger all* was used in combination with another negator, intended to act as an NPI (*This essay's due tomorrow and I haven't done bugger all*). Students had two tasks – to rate the sentences 1–5, 1 being the least acceptable and 5 being the most acceptable (that is, no problem). They also performed a direct grammaticality judgement task: would you use this sentence in an everyday conversation, yes or no. Space was also provided for comments and the students were encouraged to write down why they felt the sentences were unacceptable or 'sounded odd'.

The graph in Figure 16.1 shows the results for the first sentence, in which *bugger all* is used as a negator. Most students rated it very highly, giving it the highest possible rating of 5.

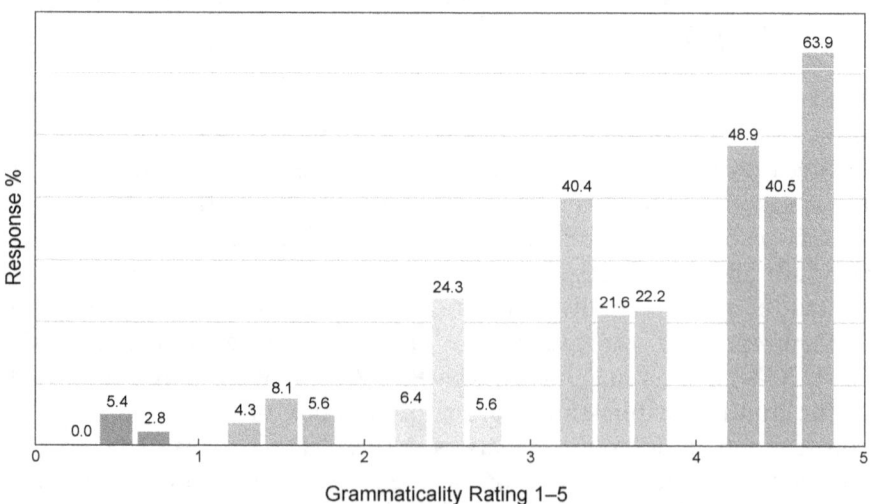

Figure 16.1 Grammaticality ratings 1-5 by participants of *This essay's due tomorrow and I've done bugger all*. A colour copy of this figure is available on the EUP website: edinburghuniversitypress.com/EcologiesofWorldEnglishes

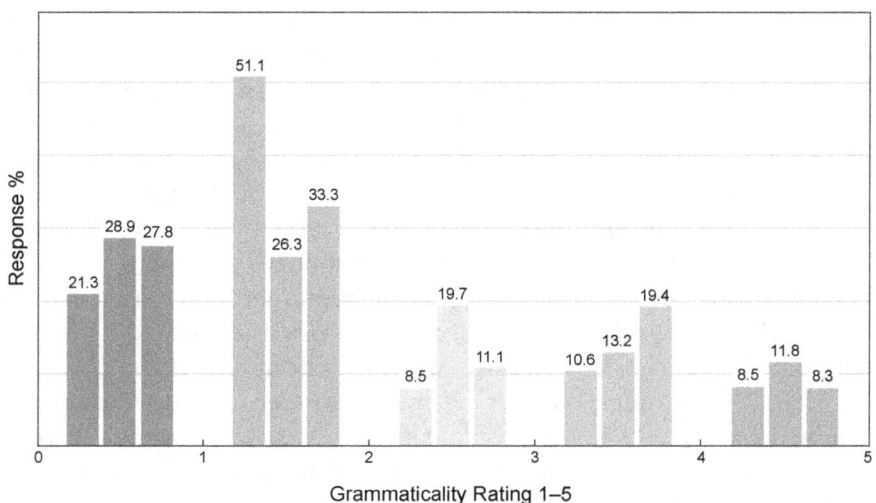

Figure 16.2 Grammaticality ratings 1-5 by participants of *This essay's due tomorrow and I haven't done bugger all*. A colour copy of this figure is available on the EUP website:
edinburghuniversitypress.com/EcologiesofWorldEnglishes

In stark contrast, *bugger all* used in combination with another negator was roundly condemned. Most students gave this sentence a '2' or a '1' (Figure 16.2).

The survey results nicely confirm the corpus data: these 'X-all' structures are different linguistic beasts, different even from the other Type 2 mass noun NPIs.

A necessary stage in the reanalysis of any NPI is double negation (or 'negative concord'); this must occur before the first inherently negative item is 'dropped'. Given the stigma that has attached to the use of multiple negation since the start of the early modern period (see Nevalainen 1998), however, it is difficult to imagine how another Jespersenian scenario like this could unfold. The negative evaluation of patterns like *You don't know nothing* would block any reanalysis from taking place. In this regard, taboo NPIs are interesting since we could imagine they would not be subject to the same degree of prescriptive scrutiny. In fact, Hoeksema (2009: 25) has argued exactly this, speculating that if speakers are using taboo vocabulary, then they are not likely to be censured for using multiple negation. In this regard, the survey commentary has something interesting to contribute.

Firstly, the written comments from the students who took part in the survey revealed that *bugger all* was so strongly interpreted as a negator that when it was combined with another negator, it was judged as multiple negation and corrected by the students ('you should use *have done bugger all*'). Moreover, so keen were these students to enforce the tenets of Standard English that they made such comments as: 'saying *bugger all* is fine ... but multiple negation? That's just not on'; 'double negative'; 'not a fan of double negation' or 'double negation – not really OK'; and, on one occasion, 'bogan' (= 'crude or unsophisticated person of low social status'). Such comments strongly suggest that these speakers were viewing *bugger all* as inherently negative and this was what led to the low acceptability ratings: 'comes across as a type of double negation because *bugger all* = nothing', '*Bugger all* means *nothing*, therefore there's a double negative'. The only objections these AusE speakers raised concerned the perceived outdatedness of the taboo negator – 'I would say *jack shit*', suggested one. In short, AusE speakers are perfectly happy to say *bugger* (or 'jack shit'), but not if the result is double negation.

These taboo NPIs do not seem to be flying under any prescriptive radar. Moreover, as Burke (2014: 479) shows, they are routinely found in the Australian print media; one of her many examples comes from the 81-year-old Australian broadcaster and social commentator Phillip Adams: 'I bought a toaster from Woolies. Home-brand, made in China. Only to discover that the Chinese, for all their wisdom and marvels of their regional cuisines, know bugger all about toast'.[4] Clearly, any development of the taboo NPIs cannot be attributed to the absence of standardisation. If speakers are rejecting multiple negation as completely unacceptable, even in the context of these taboo expressions, how is it then that NPIs ever undergo their transformation into negators? In fact, as we go on to explain, our contention here is that these 'X-all' structures did not begin life as an NPI and undergo reanalysis but have always had an inherently negative value. Before we examine the historical evidence, however, we present one more example from the UWA corpus that reveals Australian 'X-all' as having moved a further notch along the grammaticalisation trajectory.

3.2 From Negative Quantifier to Negative Adverb in Australian English

The following example (13) shows that *bugger all*, and we infer the 'X-all' construction more generally, has spread its wings and now can appear with a wider range of verb phrases – no longer confined to the functions of a nominal quantifier ('nothing') as in earlier examples (12a–b), it has evolved into a general negative adverb ('not').

(13) [1]: Do you think you'll ever work somewhere else or you happy pulling being a plasterer?
[2:] Umm yeah just depends I guess umm happy at the moment coz in summer it's got good money **but winter you just you work bugger all** so umm last year I considered the mines and ... (UWA 2013: D1: Male: 21 years)

This is a development that is not attested in any other English dialect (though we admit the research is scarce!). So, what drove this reanalysis in AusE? In particular, how was 'X-all' reinterpreted as a negative element when these are not particularly frequent constructions?[5] High frequency of a sequence of words is always a key player in grammaticalisation processes (Bybee 2007: 336), and yet, even for AusE speakers (who love their bad language), taboo NPIs are not exactly 'everyday'. We suggest that it is not so much frequency as the special socio-cultural status of the 'X-all' structures that earns them a special place in AusE. As Aitchison (1981: 92) describes, '[i]nteracting with frequency of use is another factor which is often indistinguishable from it, that of the importance of a word within a particular subculture'.[6]

4. THE AUSTRALIAN LOVE OF 'BAD' LANGUAGE – BUT NO DOUBLE NEGATION

> At my university, at the beginning of each semester, I am asked to speak to the new students from overseas. My task is to tell them what sort of society they have come to. Most of what I say is very conventional and would not surprise you. But one thing I say I ask them to keep secret from the Australians they will meet. I tell them that Australians are a very obedient people. I advise them to keep this secret because Australians imagine themselves to be the opposite of obedient. They think of themselves as anti-authority. They love a larrikin. (Hirst 2004)

Many have observed that modern-day Australians see their colloquialisms, nicknames, diminutives, insults and swearwords as important indicators of their Australianness and linguistic expressions of cherished ideals such as friendliness, nonchalance, mateship, egalitarianism and anti-authoritarianism (Lalor and Rendle-Short 2007; Wierzbicka 1992). This love affair with taboo vocabulary goes back to the earliest English-speaking settlements of the 18th and 19th centuries and continues to hold a special place in Australian culture. Of course, this is not to suggest that Australian culture has remained unchanged; as Wierzbicka (2002: 1179) outlines in her exploration of the so-called 'Great Australian adjective' *bloody*, 'change is not inconsistent with continuity' – students may no longer be happy negating with *bugger all*, but there is no shortage of other more 'colourful' substitutes for the 'X-all' frame. Moreover, the fact that words like *bugger*, *bullshit* and *bloody* now make regular appearances in the Australian parliament, on free-to-air television and in print media illustrates this socio-cultural change and continuity that Wierzbicka describes for Australia.

In the Australian language today, we continue to see both language internal and language external forces working in concert, the effect of which is to privilege vernacular phonology, non-standard morphosyntax and lexis. This goes beyond the colloquialisation that is accompanying globalisation and the electronic revolution and is a distinctive point of difference for AusE. Collins and Yao describe how the penchant for informality is considerably stronger in AusE compared with British and American English:

> Our results substantiate impressionistic comments in the popular literature regarding the relative popularity of colloquialism/ informality in AusE. Our comparative figures confirm that grammatical colloquialism is burgeoning in fiction and press reportage in Australia, by comparison with these genres in AmE and BrE. (Collins and Yao 2018: 273)

Similarly, Peters and Burridge (2012) in their study of areal features highlight that English in both Australia and NZ goes well beyond the kinds of vernacular and informal grammar and lexis noted for varieties elsewhere (see also Leitner 2004). This is supported by the shift we have observed in 'X-all' from negative quantifier ('nothing') to fully-fledged adverbial negator ('not').

If bad language is such an earmark of AusE, how do we explain the strongly normative attitudes in the survey feedback? Students appeared very willing to negate with *bugger* or *fuck* but not if there was any hint of double negation. Alongside a strong attachment to the vernacular in

Australia, there also exists a well-attested and thriving linguistic complaint tradition and there is evidence that this tradition even exceeds what has been observed in major English-speaking nations elsewhere. From letters to the editor collected from across the English-speaking world, Lukač (2018: 8), for example, observes 'that the practice of publishing letters on usage is the most popular in Australia and NZ, followed by Ireland and the UK, and, finally, it is least established in the US and in Canada'.

This oxymoronic behaviour is not confined to the linguistic conduct of AusE speakers. Australians generally place a high value on anti-authoritarianism and at the same time Australia is a society which is exceedingly rule-governed. In his discussion of Australian democracy, historian John Hirst (2004) describes how Australia was the first country in the world to have compulsory seat belts in cars and one of the first countries to introduce compulsory random breath tests for motor vehicle drivers, compulsory helmet laws for cyclists as well as motorcyclists, compulsory voting (and, before it, compulsory enrolment), and strict gun control laws. The laws against smoking in public are severe – as Hirst describes, at football games Australian spectators yell foul abuse at umpires and players and then at half time file obediently outside to have a smoke.

Hirst's observations have been backed up recently by the results of the 2018 World Values Survey (this tracks changes in the values and beliefs of citizens in 97 countries, including Australia). Researchers in its Australian component (the Australian Values Study) surveyed more than 1,800 Australians, and among the several key themes that emerged is the following: 'Despite our claims to larrikinism, we have a keen respect for *authority* and many of us are open to *"strongman" and technocratic styles of government*' (Social Research Centre 2020; emphasis original).

Severin and Burridge (2020) suggest urges to clean up the language are the likely hangover of something called *cultural cringe*, a distinctly Australian phrase referring to the feeling that other (typically anglophone) countries are somehow better. A convict past, coupled with the nation's beginnings as a British colony, has meant some Australians feel a need to prove that Australia is on par with other nations around the world – and a high standard of English would demonstrate this.

5. A HISTORICAL DETOUR – WHENCE THE 'X-ALL' CONSTRUCTION

Before we conclude, we would like to present historical evidence to back up our claim that expressions like *bugger all* and *fuck all* have always been negative in value. Certainly, the first citations for the terms *bugger all* and *fuck all* in the *OED* suggest this, as do entries in slang dictionaries (for example, Dalzell and Victor 2005; Green 2010):

(14a) The word 'nothing' was replaced in the Army by 'b—r-all' – 'I did b—r-all'; 'There was b—r-all to eat'. (1921, *Notes & Queries*. 19 Nov. 418/2)
(b) He then said, 'You are a fucking coward & you will go to the trenches – **I give fuck all for my life & I give fuck all for yours** & I'll get you fucking well shot.' (1916, *Rec. Trial H. Farr.* (P.R.O.: WO 71/509) f. 4)

All these entries date from the early 20th century. However, these are unlikely to be the earliest appearances of these structures, given that swearwords would have had a life on the street long before they appeared in print. Importantly, at the crucial time in this development of 'X-all' negation, these taboo expressions had been well and truly banished to the 'Dark Continent of the World of Words' (lexicographer John Stephen Farmer's description of where the invisible obscenities of early Modern English went; Farmer and Henley [1890] 1904: vi). They do not appear in dictionaries of the Modern English period, even Samuel Johnson's (and his dictionary was not 'a polite book', as Hudson points out; 1998: 89) or Grose's (1785) *Dictionary of the Vulgar Tongue*; occasional specialist dictionaries included the words but always disguised in Latin. In short, uncovering their grammatical behaviour is not easy.

Our investigation of taboo negators therefore took us to the Old Bailey Corpus (Huber et al. 2016), a corpus of approximately 14 million words from the criminal trials held at the Old Bailey (London's central criminal court) from 1720 to 1913 (all annotated for parts of speech and direct speech; Huber 2007). We also searched the full proceedings of the Old Bailey 1674–1913 (200,000 trials, totalling c. 134 million words; Hitchcock et al. 2018). Being more colloquial in nature, these texts are especially revealing – even taboo words make an appearance. Moreover, many of those whose voices we hear in the Old Bailey courtroom were transported to Australia as convicts – their voices formed a crucial part of the early linguistic melting pot. Nearly one in five of the convicts sent to Australia were tried at the Old Bailey in London (State Library NSW 2019). Robson's (1994) history of transportation estimates total convict numbers to be around 163,000 and, as colonial commentary makes clear, they were the ones who set the linguistic fashions at that time (Burridge 2020).

As evidence of the abundance of obscenities in these Old Bailey transcripts, we offer the following summary of the appearances for *bugger* (Table 16.1). We emphasise here that finding these taboo words has special challenges; the euphemistic smokescreens mean they appear in many different forms and they are often camouflaged by dashes. Even the array of different spellings in the *OED* was inadequate to catch all examples of *bugger*; we uncovered a number of other spellings and abbreviations but might well have missed other disguises.

Table 16.1 *Bugger* in the Old Bailey

Item	*Number of hits*
b–	782 (but could include *bastard* and *bloody*)
b – r	32 (swearwords, but one)
b–g	5 (swearwords)
b–gg–r	37 (swearwords)
bugger	9 (all the literal meaning)
bougre	9 (swearwords)
bouger	4 (swearwords, but one)
bougger	1 (swearword)
buggar	14 (swearwords)

Given the religious based idiom of swearing at this early time, *damn* would have been an even more likely supporting NPI for negation; hence, we widened our search and included appearances of *damn*. Examples in the transcripts of both taboo words as minimisers in the first frame (Type 1) were plentiful:

(15a) she told them she **would not give a d—n** for them (15 Feb 1804; t18040215-44)
(b) 'It cannot be helped now, **I should not care a b—dy b–gg–r** if I was going to be hung up for it'. I said the less he said of that sort the better. (12 Sep 1821; t18210912)

Significantly, however, the transcripts did not reveal a single appearance of *bugger all*, or even *damn all* (in any disguise). Of course, we cannot say with any confidence that the 'X-all' frame did not exist at this time, just because we find no evidence of it in the corpus data. Nonetheless, given the general flourishing of *buggers* and *damns* in the Old Bailey transcripts, the negative evidence is surely telling us something – at the very least these were not frequent constructions and we can accept as accurate dictionary evidence dating the 'X-all' construction as early 20th century. It is telling therefore that all these entries show *bugger all* as well as *damn all* as negators, with one exception (dated 2000) in the *OED*.

(16a) You **don't know bugger-all** about Dulston. (*OED* 2000 W. Self *How Dead Live* 178)

A Google Ngram search also showed 'X-all' structures appearing only late in Google books (again the 20th century); true, Google Ngram viewer is an extremely blunt instrument, especially given the nature of the vocabulary we are searching for, but it is nonetheless telling that all examples of *bugger all* and *damn all* were as negators, with one exception from a 1960s play (*Plays and Players*):[7]

(b) 'She **en't** saying **bugger all**' (p. 42)

These two rare examples in (16a) and (16b), we would argue, are cases of double negation. Certainly, the reply ('You en't gotter talk like that Rube') following the quotation in (16b) suggests the author's intention is to indicate non-standard usage here.

In short, there seems little evidence that the 'X-all' expressions originated as NPIs, and later underwent reanalysis as negators as described by Jespersen's Cycle. Elsewhere (Burke and Burridge forthcoming), we propose the 'X-all' negator had its origins in the noun *all* 'possessions, effort, interest', especially the noun modified pejoratively with *little* (for example, 'We are ambitious and wish to do our little all'; 1912 *OED National Rotarian*). Early grammarian Hendrik Poutsma describes how the depreciative meaning implied in *all* 'is often emphasised by *little* **or a word of like import**' (1916: 1017; emphasis added); he gives a number of examples (for instance, 'Finding, the wretched all they here can have').

We would not expect Poutsma or Jespersen to give examples with words from the 'Dark Continent', but it is not difficult to imagine how this 'word of like import' could encompass *damn, bugger* and later *fuck* (in line with the transition from the religious to the secular in patterns of swearing; compare *(God) damn you > bugger you/screw you* and so on). In short, we argue that taboo items like *bugger all* have never been NPIs; their (more recent) appearances with auxiliary negators are instances of double negation. The large number of participants in the survey who rejected double negation understandably therefore rejected *The essay's due tomorrow and I haven't done bugger all*. Others were just confused, one student asking: 'So you have worked, or you haven't?'

5.1 Janus-faced Taboo Negators

Before we finish this section, we feel there is another aspect to these constructions which potentially affects their development. In the case of the Type 1 constructions of indifference (the 'care/give a X' frame), positive forms are used where the lack of negator conveys an emphatic sense of concern or care; hence we find widespread slogans like *Give a Damn*. In Australia this is also well attested; for example, the campaign name for education reform – *I Give a Gonski*,[8] after the Gonski Review – and the Athlete's Foot (2019–20) advertising catchphrase *We Really Give a Fit* (Amato 2019).

Similarly, Modern English *damn all* also can have a positive meaning 'everything possible'. Consider the incident when language maven William Safire got into trouble in one of his 1988 essays for writing:

> George Bush has devoted the past decade of his life to winning the Presidency, and this sense of purpose has profoundly changed him. A few of the people who knew him in the 70's now marvel at how their gentlemanly friend **will do damn-all to win**. (Safire 1988: 22)

Later writing about his 'egregious error', Safire (1988: 22) admitted he meant here that George Bush would do 'everything possible' (not 'nothing at all'). Opposite meanings can sometimes co-exist peacefully, but only if different contexts are involved and there is no chance of a misunderstanding (*to dust* something removes the dust, unless fingerprints or cakes are involved; for example, *we dusted for fingerprints*). In something as crucial as negation, however, such ambiguity is hardly ideal. Time will tell what the language does with these Janus-faced constructions.

6. CONCLUSION

As earlier described, the conventional view of these negators in the 'X-all' construction is that they originated as NPIs then underwent reanalysis in accordance with Jespersen's Cycle (see Burke 2014; Hoeksema 2009; Lawley 1974). We have argued here that there is little support for this scenario; on the contrary, evidence suggests that expressions like *damn all* and *bugger all* began life with an inherently negative value, modelled, we suggest, on the depreciative phrase *little/wretched all* (for details of the journey from *little/wretched all* to *all damn/bugger/fuck all*, see Burke and Burridge forthcoming). We also gave evidence of a shift in the 'X-all' structure from negative quantifier ('nothing') to fully-fledged marker of negation ('not'). This development in AusE is along a well-trodden path of grammatical change, involving all kinds of interfering psychological, physiological, linguistic factors, the usual suspects associated with the processes of grammaticalisation. In this chapter, we have also emphasised the social and cultural pressures that have worked to coerce the language in this direction – a major force behind this change being the more informal character of Australian culture and its greater willingness to embrace colloquial styles. By this we are not suggesting that any one of the 'X-all' negators might be on its way to becoming the main exponent of negation in AusE – Australians might have a relaxed attitude to swearing but we are unlikely to see a taboo word become frequent enough to grammaticalise into the default negator.

NOTES

1. See the Australian Writers' Centre blog at <https://www.writerscentre.com.au/blog/qa-i-could-care-less-vs-i-couldnt-care-less-which-one/> (last accessed 13 January 2021).
2. There is another way of explaining this fluctuation, however. The taboo object gives the same amplified message in examples like *I don't know shit* and *I know shit* – with or without a negator, there is a trifling amount of knowing (compare the dismissive Type 1 construction earlier discussed). Taboo words emphasise whatever emotive force the speaker attaches to the speech act.
3. Two of the groups were undergraduates with little experience of syntax; the third group comprised Masters students in speech pathology who were more practised in analysing syntax.

4. *The Weekend Australian Magazine*, 6–7 October 2012.
5. Hoeksema (2009: 22) also ponders on how taboo items can move along the Jespersen trajectory when they are 'fairly infrequent in most people's speech, with the possible exception of the likes of Tony Soprano').
6. One example Aitchison (1981) gives shows how non-standard verb endings in the English of Reading adolescents tend to attach to words that are culturally important to these teenagers (for example, *We fucking chins them with bottles* 'We hit them on the chin with bottles'); the *-s* ending attached to these verbs 90 per cent of the time versus only 50 per cent for other verbs.
7. <https://books.google.com.au/books?id=RhgvAQAAIAAJ&q=%22bugger+all%22> (last accessed 13 January 2021).
8. <https://www.principleco.com.au/projects/i-give-a-gonski> (last accessed 13 January 2021).

REFERENCES

Aitchison, J. (1981). *Language change: Progress or decay?* Fontana Paperbacks.

Amato, S. (2019). The Athlete's Foot launches 'Give a fit' this back to school. B&T, 11 January. <https://www.bandt.com.au/athletes-foot-launches-give-fit-back-school/> (last accessed 13 January 2021).

Bolinger, D. (1975). *Aspects of language* (2nd ed.). Harcourt Brace Jovanovich.

Burke, I. (2014). 'Giving a rat's' about negation: The Jespersen Cycle in modern Australian English. *Australian Journal of Linguistics, 34*(4), 443–75.

Burke, I. (2017). *Wicked which and ninja never: Relative clauses and negation in modern Australian English conversation* [Doctoral dissertation, Monash University].

Burke, I. and Burridge, K. (forthcoming). *Bugger* and *damn* downunder: The development of taboo negators in Australian English.

Burridge, K. (2015). Historical linguistics and relationships among languages. In K. Allan (Ed.), *The Routledge handbook of linguistics* (pp. 344–65). Routledge.

Burridge, K. (2020). History of Australian English. In L. Willoughby and H. Manns (Eds.), *Australian English reimagined: Structure, fea-*

tures and developments (pp. 175–92). Routledge.

Bybee, J. (2007). *Frequency of use and the organization of language.* Cambridge University Press.

Collins, P. and Yao, X. (2018). Colloquialisation and the evolution of Australian English: A cross-varietal and cross-generic study of Australian, British, and American English from 1931 to 2006. *English World-Wide, 39*(3), 253–77.

Dalzell, T. and Victor, T. (Eds.). (2005). *A new Partridge dictionary of slang and unconventional English.* Routledge.

Danat, B. (1980). Language in the legal process. *Law and Society Review, 14*, 445–564.

Farmer, J. S. and Henley, W. E. (1904). *Slang and its analogues: Past and present* (Vol. 1). (Original work published 1890). <https://archive.org/details/slangitsanalogue01farmuoft/page/n7/mode/2up> (last accessed 13 January 2021).

Green, J. (2010). *Green's dictionary of slang* (3 vols). Chambers.

Grose, (Captain) F. (1785). *Dictionary of the vulgar tongue.* S. Hooper.

Hirst, J. (2004). The distinctiveness of Australian democracy. *Papers on Parliament No. 42.* The Senate Occasional Lecture Series. Parliament of Australia. <https://www.aph.gov.au/sitecore/content/Home/About_Parliament/Senate/Powers_practice_n_procedures/pops/pop42/hirst> (last accessed 13 January 2021).

Hitchcock, T., Shoemaker, R., Emsley, C., Howard, S., McLaughlin, J. et al. (2018). The Old Bailey proceedings online, 1674–1913 (version 8.0) [Online corpus]. <http://www.oldbaileyonline.org/> (last accessed 13 January 2021).

Hoeksema, J. (2009). Jespersen recycled. In E. van Gelderen (Ed.), *Cyclical change* (pp. 15–35). John Benjamins.

Hopper, P. J. and Traugott, E. C. (2003). *Grammaticalization* (2nd ed.). Cambridge University Press.

Horn, L. R. (2001). Flaubert triggers, squatitive negation, and other quirks of grammar. In J. Hoeksema, H. Rullmann, V. Sánchez-Valencia and T. van der Wouden (Eds.), *Perspectives on negation and polarity items* (pp. 173–200). John Benjamins.

Huber, M. (2007). The Old Bailey proceedings, 1674–1834: Evaluating and annotating a corpus of 18th- and 19th-century spoken English. In A. Meurman-Solin and A. Nurmi (Eds.), *Annotating variation and change* (*Studies in Variation, Contacts and Change in English, 1*). <http://www.helsinki.fi/varieng/series/volumes/01/huber/> (last accessed 13 January 2021).

Huber, M., Nissel, M. and Puga, K. (2016). Old Bailey Corpus 2.0. hdl:11858/00-246C-0000-0023-8CFB-2.
Hudson, N. (1998). Johnson's 'dictionary' and the politics of 'Standard English'. Eighteenth-century lexis and lexicography [Special issue]. *The Yearbook of English Studies, 28*, 77–93.
Jespersen, O. (1914). *A Modern English grammar on historical principles (Part 3: Syntax)*. (Vol. 2). George Allen & Unwin.
Jespersen, O. (1917). *Negation in English and other languages* (2nd ed.). Munksgaard.
Lalor, T. and Rendle-Short, J. (2007). 'That's so gay': A contemporary use of *gay* in Australian English. *Australian Journal of Linguistics, 27*(2), 147–73.
Lawley, J. (1974). Ample negatives. In *CLS 10: Papers from the Tenth Regional Meeting*. Chicago Linguistic Society.
Leitner, G. (2004). *Australia's many voices. Vol. I: Australian English – the national language*. Mouton de Gruyter.
Lukač, M. (2018). Grassroots prescriptivism: An analysis of individual speakers' efforts at maintaining the standard language ideology. Prescriptivism [Special issue]. *English Today, 34*(4), 5–12.
Nevalainen, T. (1998). Social mobility and the decline of multiple negation in Early Modern English. In J. Fisiak and M. Krygier (Eds.), *Advances in English historical linguistics (1996)* (pp. 263–91). Mouton de Gruyter.
Peters, P. and Burridge, K. (2012). Areal linguistics in the South Pacific. In R. Hickey (Ed.), *Areal features of the anglophone world* (pp. 233–60). Mouton de Gruyter.
Postal, P. (2004). *Skeptical linguistic essays*. Oxford University Press.
Poutsma, H. (1916). *A grammar of late Modern English, for the use of continental, especially Dutch students (Part 2)*. P. Nordhoff.
Robson, L. L. (1994). *The convict settlers of Australia: An enquiry into the origin and character of the convicts transported to New South Wales and Van Diemen's Land 1787–52*. Melbourne University Press.
Safire, W. (1988). On language; hit my hot button. *The New York Times Magazine*, 6 November, section 6, p. 22. <https://nyti.ms/29zpRwS> (last accessed 27 January 2021).
Severin, A. and Burridge, K. (2020). What do 'little Aussie sticklers' value most? In D. Chapman and J. D. Rawlins (Eds.), *Language prescription: Values, ideologies and identity*. Multilingual Matters.
Smith, T. (2018). 15 Australian slang words to help you speak like a

local. *Culture Trip.* <https://theculturetrip.com/pacific/australia/articles/the-australian-slang-terms-you-need-to-know/> (last accessed 13 January 2021).

Social Research Centre. (2020). *Australian Values Study.* <https://www.srcentre.com.au/ausvalues> (last accessed 13 January 2021).

State Library NSW. (2019). Convicts: Bound for Australia. Trial & court records [Research guide], 11 September. <https://guides.sl.nsw.gov.au/convicts-bound-for-australia/trial_court_records> (last accessed 13 January 2021).

Vennemann, T. (1974). Topics, subjects and word order: From SXV to SVX via TVX. In J. Anderson and C. Jones (Eds.), *Historical linguistics 1* (pp. 339–76). North-Holland.

Wierzbicka, A. (1992). *Semantics, culture, and cognition: Universal human concepts in culture-specific configurations.* Oxford University Press.

Wierzbicka, A. (2002). Australian cultural scripts – *bloody* revisited. *Journal of Pragmatics, 34*(9), 1167–209.

CHAPTER 17

The Auckland Voices Project: Language Change in a Changing City

Miriam Meyerhoff, Elaine Ballard, Helen Charters, Alexandra Birchfield and Catherine I. Watson

1. INTRODUCTION

Given the relatively small number of speakers of NZ English (NZE), the structure and history of NZE is surprisingly well-known (for example, Bauer and Warren 2004; Bell and Kuiper 2000; Gordon et al. 2004; Watson et al. 1998). It has been axiomatic that NZE shows minimal regional differences (but see Trudgill 2004 and Bauer 2008 on lexical differences and Bartlett 1992 on accent in the far South). Other previous studies of NZE (Holmes et al. 1991; Gordon et al. 2004; Hay et al. 2008; Warren 2018) take little account of Auckland, the largest and most socially and ethnically diverse metropolitan area in New Zealand (NZ).

In 2020, a third of NZ's population were Aucklanders (Stats New Zealand 2020a[1]); Auckland accounts for more than 50 per cent of NZ's total population growth since 2006 (Stats New Zealand 2020b); and in the 2018 Census, the proportion of Aucklanders born overseas was 48 per cent, compared with 31 per cent nationally (Stats New Zealand 2020a). Ethnic heterogeneity is thus greater in Auckland than elsewhere in NZ, as shown in Table 17.1.

There is also good reason to believe that Auckland English is itself internally heterogeneous. Duhamel and Meyerhoff (2014) found that, within a sample of 247 New Zealanders living in Auckland, there were strong perceptions that distinctive ways of speaking characterise speakers from West Auckland, South Auckland and the North Shore and in the case of last two, respondents' comments often linked perceptions of speech differences to perceptions of the different ethnic composition in those areas.

Table 17.1 Ethnic diversity in Auckland and in New Zealand according to the 2013 New Zealand Census

	European	*Māori/Pacific*	*Asian*
New Zealand's total population	70%	nearly 20%	10%
Auckland's population	56%	24%	21%

However, speech studies that have been conducted in Auckland have looked only at specific ethnic or identity-based communities, investigating language maintenance and change in the Pacific community in South Auckland (Bell et al. 2000, 2001; Taumoefolau et al. 2002; Bell and Gibson 2008) or gender liminality in Auckland English (Hazenberg 2017). While noteworthy in their own right, these studies cannot provide insight into the nature of Auckland English more generally, its relationship to NZE norms or mechanisms of its emergence and change.

This means that there is a tremendous gap in the descriptive adequacy of what we know about 'NZ English', and in particular what might be happening to NZE in Auckland today under the influence of substantial migration.

The Auckland Voices Project was designed to fill this gap, and in doing so, allow us to test the emerging idea that the increasing heterogeneity of urban speech communities necessitates a re-examination of our theories about the progress and diffusion of language variation and change (Labov 1994, 2001, 2010; Smakman and Heinrich 2015).

Whether migration influences regional speech patterns or not was a fundamental question for Auckland Voices. Additionally, the project sought to discover whether any innovations emerging from more heterogeneous parts of the city might be spreading and if so whether younger speakers appear to function as the vectors of change. Auckland Voices therefore recorded speakers in two broad age groups from three different parts of the city and investigated features on multiple levels of linguistic structure including vowel quality (Ross 2018; Watson et al. 2018), relative clause formation (Birchfield 2019; Meyerhoff et al. 2020), quantifiers (Charters and Ballard 2018) and pronunciation of the definite article (Meyerhoff et al. 2019).

This chapter provides the first definitive outline of the methods and scope of Auckland Voices. It also expands on Meyerhoff et al. (2019) with an examination of the variable realisation of the definite article. We will show that the behaviour of the definite article is distinctive and not part of a general levelling of the allophonic article system in English.

The methods and results outlined in this chapter also afford connections with Schneider's proposed research framework (this volume), exploring connections between migration, diversity, change, community, regional and ethnic identities, with linguistic features at all levels of analysis (lexical, phonetic, phonological and structural).

2. MIGRATION, MULTI-ETHNIC COMMUNITIES AND LANGUAGE VARIATION AND CHANGE

Conventional thinking in sociolinguistics is that changes in pronunciation and language structures are led by adult women and then accelerated in the speech of teenagers (Labov 2001; Tagliamonte and D'Arcy 2009). However, work by Cheshire et al. (2011) suggests that in today's ethnolinguistically diverse urban communities, the patterns of change discussed by Labov (2001) do not hold. Rather, the leaders of change in their London study tended to be younger males. Hazenberg's (2017) work indicated that changes in Auckland English might no longer fit the conventional model either. This highlights how little we understand about the impact of diversity on the typical profile of language change.

Many classic sociolinguistic studies explicitly excluded recent community migrants from study. What little research has been done on the language of migrants has supposed that they are largely engaged in copying indigenous speech norms (Regan et al. 2009; Meyerhoff and Schleef 2012; Daleszynska and Meyerhoff 2020), but this perhaps depends on the ratio of migrants to locally born families. For instance, in Schleef et al. (2011), Meyerhoff and Schleef (2012), Truesdale and Meyerhoff (2015), and Daleszynska and Meyerhoff (2020), Polish teenagers seemed extremely well-attuned to variation in the speech of their locally born peers, replicating quite subtle and regionally distinctive patterns of variation. But the Polish migrants were a very small minority within an otherwise largely homogeneous ethnolinguistic context.

By contrast, in inner city London, ethnolinguistic heterogeneity is extreme and there is no demographically dominant locally born group. Here, the first- and second-generation migrant youths are leading language change, and among them, younger males seem to be most advanced. This upsets the usual association between upper working-class/lower middle-class women as the leaders of language change that has emerged from previous work on urban sociolinguistics.

The Auckland Voices Project was designed to explore the extent to which the London findings might apply to other communities where there is highly heterogeneous linguistic input. The project, therefore, hypothesises that the children and grandchildren of immigrants might be central, not peripheral, to innovations and change working their way through the larger speech community.

However, the Auckland Voices Project did not simply replicate the London study's design. In addition to contrasting a young community close to the city centre with a relatively short history of demographic mixing with a more homogeneous White community further out, it also included speakers from a part of the city that has been demographically mixed for decades. This allows the project to test the hypothesis that the effects of diversity will be most apparent in language variation at critical points, specifically when there is an ethnic and linguistic plurality in the make-up of the sub-community and no single group predominates.

Our specific research questions were:

1. Do high levels of diversity in communities favour the emergence of new and distinct regional varieties?
2. Do innovations spread from highly diverse communities to more homogeneous communities and if so, do younger speakers spearhead this change?
3. Are these changes likely to become entrenched as part of a new Auckland English? If so, how does the direction of change compare with the direction of historical changes in NZ English?[2]

The results of the analysis of the definite article presented in this chapter speak primarily to (1) and (2) above, though we have some thoughts about their possible future entrenchment.

3. AUCKLAND VOICES PROJECT: PROFILE OF THE COMMUNITIES AND PROJECT DESIGN

Auckland Voices is a multi-site investigation of the impact of migration on NZE. It focused on data collection in three communities.[3] In Auckland terms, our three field sites are quite close to each other, as shown in Figure 17.1, but they are markedly distinct in history and present-day demographic make-up.

Distribution of ethnic groups across Auckland's suburbs is not uniform. In some suburbs the proportions of different ethnic groups

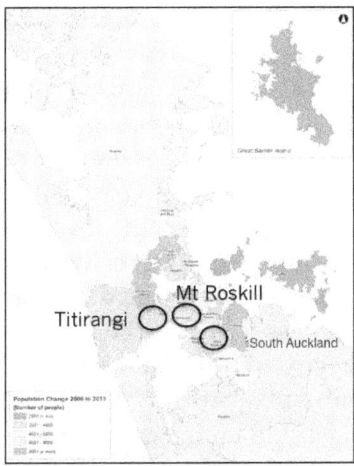

Figure 17.1 Fieldwork locations for the Auckland Voices Project (2016–18). A colour copy of this figure is available on the EUP website: edinburghuniversitypress.com/EcologiesofWorldEnglishes

resemble national averages, but in 35 per cent of Auckland's suburbs, no single ethnic group represents more than 50 per cent of the population. In these parts of the city, many speakers were born elsewhere and many more have grown up using or hearing different varieties of English (Stats New Zealand 2013), as well as numerous heritage languages from very different language families. This should favour rapid language change (Cheshire et al. 2008, 2011). Moreover, different suburbs have become ethnically diverse at different times. Table 17.2 shows how our selected communities reflect urban diversity within Auckland and allow us to test our hypotheses about the effects of migration and age on language variation and change.

Table 17.2 Age and social demographics in three Auckland communities

	Younger speakers	*Older speakers*
Titirangi	Predominantly Pākehā	Predominantly Pākehā
South Auckland	Ethnically mixed	Ethnically mixed
Mount Roskill	Ethnically mixed	Predominantly Pākehā

Pākehā are New Zealanders of predominantly European descent.

Titirangi in West Auckland has been, and remains, a very ethnically homogeneous community. Before British settlers arrived in the

19th century, Māori utilised this remote and forested region with both sheltered and wild surf beaches. The British established a school there as early as 1845 and there has been a recognised Anglo settlement since the late 19th century (Sollitt-Morris 2015). The Titirangi of today remains a popular recreational destination and is older, wealthier and whiter than Auckland is on average, being about 80 per cent Pākehā.

Today's 'South Auckland' includes the adjacent suburbs of Papatoetoe, Manurewa and Ōtara, but people have lived here since people first settled in NZ, the area being highly valued by Māori for habitation, horticulture, seafood and access to two harbours. In 1861, the Great South Road opened the new city of Auckland to horticultural lands further south, and the township of Papatoetoe, lying on this road, was founded in 1862, also furnishing a stop on the early railway line. These transport routes brought White settlers to the region throughout the 20th century (O'Malley 2016: 162), and in the 1960s and 1970s many immigrant workers from the Pacific Islands also settled here. More recently, climbing house prices in central Auckland have seen young Southeast Asian families moving to Papatoetoe to join its long-time residents of Pākehā and Pacific Island descent. Neighbouring Manurewa and Ōtara remain important hubs for the Pacific Island diaspora, preserving traditional arts, culture, language and food through markets and religious practices. South Auckland, then, has been ethnically diverse for many decades; the 2013 Census showed there was no single ethnic majority in the area.

In contrast to Titirangi and South Auckland, the demographics of Mount Roskill have changed recently and rapidly. Little more than farmland until the 1950s, when Mount Roskill became a site of major government housing builds, by the 1960s it was a predominantly Pākehā community with a sizeable Pacific Island minority. Only since the 1990s and intensified housing development has Mount Roskill seen the arrival of a very large, internally diverse Asian community and quite a number of refugee households. In the Roskill Youth Zone (RYZ, pronounced 'rise'), ads for 'bootcamp with Ming' jostle with ads for Free Yoga offered by Fleur; 'RYZ above the Rim' classes in basketball alternate with Bollywood fitness classes and boys- and girls-only Polynesian dancing classes. Mount Roskill now has a very mixed high-density population. Here too, the 2013 Census recorded no single ethnic majority.

The demographic contrasts between these three communities allow us to build up a measured picture of how language change takes hold and diffuses across different groups of speakers.

3.1 Details of the Speech Recordings

Recordings with speakers in all three areas took the form of classic sociolinguistic interviews (Labov 1984; Meyerhoff et al. 2015). Speakers in two age groups were recorded: 25 years and under and 40 years and over. While this gap was a necessary expedient given available resources, it provides two clear benchmarks in all three communities, particularly relevant to the Mount Roskill community where speakers over 40 and under 25 have grown up in communities with markedly different ethnic and linguistic profiles. The mean age for the younger speakers across all three communities was 22 years and the mean age for the older speakers was 69 years.

The interviewers were local residents with strong ties in the communities, age matched as much as possible with the interviewee.[4] Recordings lasted at least an hour with some lasting over three hours. Most were close to two hours in length.

Table 17.3 shows the make-up of our corpus.

Table 17.3 Speakers recorded for the Auckland Voices Project

	Younger		Older		
	Female	*Male*	*Female*	*Male*	**Total**
Mount Roskill	6	8	6	5	25
South Auckland	7	6	3	4	20
Titirangi	7	7	8	3	25
					70

The interviews involved conversation structured loosely around topic prompts (for example, What is the (best/worst) thing about living in this neighbourhood? Does your family have any superstitions? What do you say when someone asks where you are from? What would your fantasy holiday be?), a reading passage from Holmes et al. (1991) and semantic differential tasks.

Semantic differential tasks are a more naturalistic way of eliciting very careful speech than word lists or minimal pairs. In the Auckland Voices Project, participants were asked to specifically comment on the difference between a *deck* and a *verandah* (to elicit careful tokens of the DRESS and TRAP vowels), between *nits* and *cooties* ('head lice', to elicit careful tokens of KIT and GOOSE), and between *listening* and *hearing* (to elicit careful tokens of the NEAR diphthong). As in other studies, these tokens can then be compared with tokens produced in more conversational speech and the reading passage to infer different levels of awareness associated with these known vocalic variables.

The analysis presented here is based on this core data, but our corpus has been augmented from other sources. We were granted access to parts of older oral history recordings of Aucklanders gathered by Auckland Libraries and by the University of Auckland Faculties of Education and Engineering, as well as 60 original narratives told by school children and recorded by Auckland Museum as part of the Tāku Tamaki ('My Auckland') project. Since some of the schools that participated in Tāku Tamaki fall within or match the demographics of our three primary research sites, this extended our corpus into much younger speakers than we had originally planned or had the resources to sample. The overall distribution of speakers in the three sub-corpora that now make up the Auckland Voices corpus is shown by year of birth in Figure 17.2.

In short, the Auckland Voices Project assembled an unparalleled record of Auckland English, one that goes some way to filling in the historical gaps about how locally born residents and migrants to the city have sounded over time.

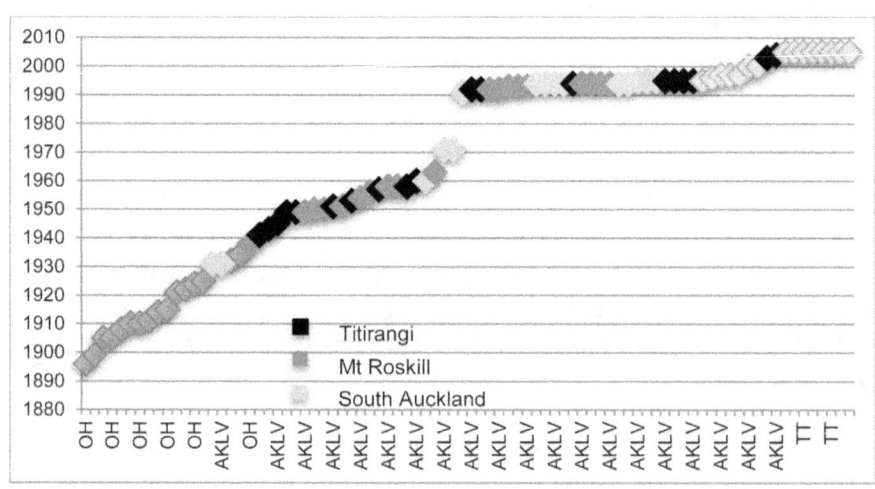

Figure 17.2 Recordings collected in the Marsden-funded component of the Auckland Voices Project (AKLV), the Auckland Libraries oral history archives (OH) and the Auckland Museum Tāku Tamaki (TT) project. Individual speakers plotted by year of birth.

We turn now to an investigation of the pronunciation of the definite article in Auckland Voices. Previous research suggests the pronunciation of articles is a variable likely to be sensitive to an increase in the number of multilingual speakers or speakers for whom English is not their primary language. Hence, the contrast between the norms of younger and older speakers is of interest, not just the contrast between the three communities as a whole.

4. DEFINITE ARTICLE: ALLOPHONIC VARIATION MEETS LANGUAGE VARIATION AND CHANGE

Standard English is characterised by allomorphic variation in the realisation of the definite article, depending on whether the following word is vowel-initial: the definite article *the* is [ði] before vowels and [ðə] elsewhere.

In practice, however, there are many speakers who tend to pronounce *the* as [ðə] even before vowels. Second-language speakers of English of all ages have been reported to generalise [ðə] before vowels and this is also a feature of contact varieties of English in North America, the United Kingdom, South Africa, Asia and the Caribbean (Fox 2015: 151–3 reviews this literature).

Fox (2015) documents the generalisation of [ðə] in London English where the change appears to be led by what is (sociolinguistically) a surprising group of speakers. The highest frequency of these incoming forms is in the speech of young Bangladeshi males, and young Anglo males are following, with young female speakers lagging. Cheshire et al. (2011, 2013) examined the use of [ðə] before vowels in their larger corpus of inner city London English and corroborated Fox's finding. This generalisation has also been reported as a feature that persists in the speech of third-generation descendants of Italian migrants to the UK (Guzzo et al. 2008, in Cheshire et al. 2011). This fact together with the patterns in the Multicultural London English project led Cheshire and her colleagues to conclude that this is a feature of group second-language acquisition. People growing up in a community like inner city London, where there is no longer any ethnic/ethnolinguistic majority, are being exposed to a large number of different input varieties from a very wide feature pool (Mufwene 2001; Aboh and Ansaldo 2006). In London, Cheshire and her colleagues (2013) have suggested that this is what leads to the emergence of 'ethnically neutral' forms. That is, the regularisation of the allomorphic variation of the article here cannot be dismissed as a developmental phenomenon, nor can it easily be claimed to be a marker of a particular ethnic group's English.

Our study investigated the use of [ðə] before vowel-initial nouns in only the conversational speech corpus of the Auckland Voices Project, that is, the older and younger speakers in the three communities of South Auckland, Titirangi and Mount Roskill.

4.1 Definite Article

The dependent variable was the use of the centralised vowel instead of the (prescribed) peripheral vowel, that is, [ðə] vs [ði], as shown in examples (1)–(6). (We use the symbol [ə] to represent the centralised vowel in NZ English, since the general consensus among NZ phoneticians is that this is most appropriate for KIT and COMMA vowels.) Tokens were identified by a grep search in ELAN (Sloetjes and Wittenburg 2008) that searched for strings of <the> followed by any vowel or <h>. These were then individually checked against the audio file.[5]

(1) But that's the [ðə] only thing. (Adrian, younger, South Auckland)
(2) I was the [ði] only one that I know in my school that went off to do a BA. (Vivian, younger, South Auckland)
(3) at the [ði] end of school. (Nicholas, older, Mount Roskill)
(4) Having a mother . . . might have softened the [ðə] edges to the personality. (Nicholas, older, Mount Roskill)
(5) The [ðə] odd job here and there. (Charlotte, older, Titirangi)
(6) I must admit I'd be like so the [ði] opposite. (Chloe, younger, Titirangi)

Unclear tokens were excluded, for example, cases where the definite article occurred before a high tense vowel since this often results in ambiguous forms such as [ði:ziəst].

The independent variables modelled were: the following vowel, stressed versus non-stressed NP (examples (7)–(9)) and three social factors – age of the speaker (older versus younger), gender of the speaker and community.

(7) It's not about **the individual**, it's more about how [. . .] we're gonna keep the reputation of the school. (Arush, younger, Mount Roskill)

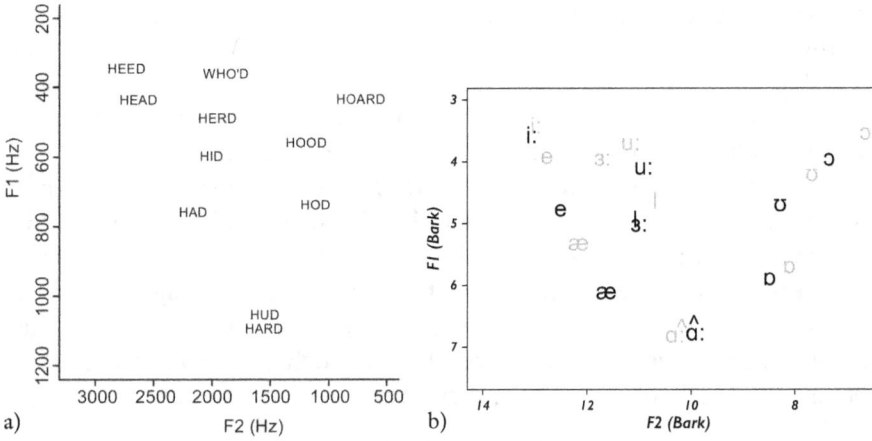

Figure 17.3 The canonical New Zealand English vowel space, monophthongs (adapted from Watson et al. 1998) compared with the vowels in read speech in Auckland Voices, grey = older speakers, black = younger speakers (Watson et al. 2018).

(8) And I'm thinking, **the other two** have got away with a few things, so I can try that. (Ellen, older, Mount Roskill)
(9) Yep, this was **the original** and the rest were mainly farms. (Jemaine, younger, South Auckland)

The coding of stressed vs unstressed was based on the presence or absence of prosodic stress or emphasis, an advantage of coding directly from the audio in ELAN (Nagy and Meyerhoff 2013).

Similarly, the following vowel was coded as uttered rather than according to its canonical class; mostly realisations were as expected. The analysis of following vowels was done auditorily with spot-checking of coding to ensure agreement. The canonical NZ English vowel space is shown in Figure 17.3a, and the vowel space for our older and younger speakers in all three communities in Figure 17.3b (see Watson et al. 2018 for the statistical methods allowing the presentation of male and female speakers in one plot).

We undertook a multiple regression analysis of the data using Rbrul (Johnson 2009), in which we modelled the speaker as a random effect. We compared results for all three communities as a whole and then compared the linguistic constraints on the use of [ðə] before vowels in the different age cohorts of each community. This allowed us to determine not only whether the overall frequency of [ðə] generalisation is the same in the three communities and within the different age groups, but also whether the 'grammar' of the variation (what contexts favour or disfavour the innovative use of [ðə]) is similar across different communities and age cohorts (Tagliamonte 2002; Meyerhoff 2009).

Our overall findings were that [ðə] is favoured much more strongly by speakers in South Auckland than it is by speakers in Mount Roskill, and that Mount Roskill speakers favour [ðə] rather more than Titirangi speakers. In all three communities, there were only two significant predictors: the following segment and the speaker's age group. In each community, older speakers were always much less likely to use [ðə] before vowels than younger speakers were.

4.2 Following Vowel

In all three communities, the nature of the following vowel had a significant effect on the probability of [ðə]. A following high front vowel (FLEECE and, in Titirangi, also NEAR) favoured speakers' use of [ðə]. This suggests that the use of [ðə] prevocalically in Auckland English might have initially been a phonetic dissimilation phenomenon: an avoidance of two high front vowels adjacent to one another. This propensity holds even when we break the three communities down into the younger and older speaker cohorts. Following FLEECE is always the strongest (or, for older Titirangi speakers, second strongest) context favouring use of prevocalic [ðə]. This can be seen in Tables 17.4 and 17.5.

The motivation here is not to allow a direct comparison of how speakers in the three communities treat different following vowels. Rather, it is an attempt to first find the most economical explanatory model for speakers in each community.[6] This results in different sub-groupings of following vowels, depending on their (chance) distribution in the conversational corpus. Because the number of tokens of any following vowel can fall quite low when we divide the corpus up by age group and community, it is necessary to combine some vowel classes in order to still be able to conduct some form of quantitative analysis. This has always been done in ways that make sense given the phonetics of NZE (compare Figure 17.3); however, it will differ across sub-groups of speakers according to the vagaries of what individuals chose to talk about. The combination of KIT and comMA in all six partitions of the corpus follows the usual treatment of these vowels as being phonetically very similar in NZE. Likewise, the combination of STRUT and START when there are very few tokens of one or the other, following Warren's (2006) conclusion that these differ phonetically only in length. Nouns with an initial diphthong can be infrequent in conversation, so where there were few tokens of these, they were grouped as closing or centring diphthongs. (Where there was no data on a particular following vowel in any given group of speakers, this is not represented in Tables 17.4 and 17.5.)[7]

The figures in Tables 17.4 and 17.5 should be interpreted as follows. The input probability represents the overall likelihood that the definite article will be realised as [ðə] with any following vowel in the data for that sub-group of speakers. The probabilities associated with an individual vowel class or classes indicate how much more, or less, likely it is for *the* to be realised as [ðə] with those following vowels. Because these probabilities are centred on 0.5, values over 0.5 indicate that with a following vowel of this class, *the* is more likely to be realised as [ðə] (relative to the overall input probability) and values under 0.5 indicate that with a following vowel of this class, *the* is less likely to be realised as [ðə]. Probabilities close to 0.5 indicate a weak effect, and values close to 0.1 and 0.9 indicate strong effects, while values of 1.0 and 0.0 indicate categorical use/non-use of [ðə].

If a following high front vowel disfavours use of the high front vowel variant [ði], we might ask whether a following low centralised vowel disfavours the generalisation of the centralised variant [ðə]. This appears to be weakly the case. That is, following STRUT is when speakers are likely to continue to use [ði], if they use it at all (notice that the input probability for use of [ðə] is very high for younger speakers in South Auckland and Mount Roskill, that is, they generally favour use of [ðə]). This strengthens the sense gained from the effect of following FLEECE, namely, that there is a phonetic, dissimilatory basis for the emergence and diffusion of [ðə] prevocalically. However, it is clear from the ranking of which following vowels most favour the use of [ðə] to those which favour it least that diffusion of [ðə] does not roll out purely on a phonetic basis. It seems, rather, that the dissimilation effect establishes benchmarks circumscribing the boundaries of the variation, but that after that, there is considerable latitude in how groups of speakers systematise the alternation.

Given that, as Figure 17.3 showed, there is considerable phonetic overlap between STRUT and START vowels in NZ English (START being distinguished from STRUT by length; Warren 2006), the fact that STRUT and START do not both always favour the continued use of [ði] requires some comment. Watson et al. (2018) analysed the read speech

Table 17.4 Effect of following segment on older speakers' use of [ðə] in three Auckland communities

	Titirangi		South Auckland		Mount Roskill	
	N = 329		N = 260		N = 385	
Input prob.	0.02		0.06		0.008	
Following segment	Following segment	Prob.	Following segment	Prob.	Following segment	Prob.
THOUGHT	FLEECE	0.95	FLEECE	0.92	FLEECE	0.98
FLEECE	CHOICE	0.84	CHOICE	0.73	GOAT	0.65
TRAP	THOUGHT/NURSE	0.78	THOUGHT/NURSE	0.69	MOUTH/FACE	0.64
FACE	SQUARE	0.76	SQUARE	0.67	PRICE	0.62
START	MOUTH	0.75	MOUTH	0.67	SQUARE	0.58
KIT/comMA/NURSE	DRESS	0.62	DRESS	0.55	THOUGHT	0.56
PRICE	KIT/comMA	0.60	KIT/comMA	0.48	DRESS	0.50
LOT	PRICE	0.29	PRICE	0.45	CHOICE	0.45
CHOICE	LOT	0.28	LOT	0.41	NURSE	0.42
NEAR/SQUARE/MOUTH/GOAT	TRAP	0.19	TRAP	0.41	KIT/comMA	0.34
DRESS	FACE	0.08	FACE	0.4	TRAP	0.24
STRUT	MOUTH	0.05	MOUTH	0.15	LOT	0.21
	STRUT/START		STRUT/START	0.06	STRUT/START	0.08

Table 17.5 Effect of following segment on younger speakers' use of [ðə] in three Auckland communities

	Titirangi		South Auckland		Mount Roskill	
	N = 150		N = 297		N = 347	
Input prob.	0.53		0.88		0.78	
Following segment	Prob.	Following segment	Prob.	Following segment	Prob.
FLEECE/DRESS/NEAR/SQUARE	0.95	FLEECE	1	FLEECE	0.95
CHOICE	0.87	SQUARE	0.87	FACE	0.72
TRAP	0.68	LOT/THOUGHT	0.77	CHOICE	0.70
START	0.66	MOUTH/FACE	0.73	THOUGHT/NURSE	0.70
MOUTH	0.58	PRICE	0.61	START	0.63
LOT	0.41	CHOICE	0.51	LOT	0.61
GOAT	0.41	TRAP	0.44	DRESS	0.53
THOUGHT/NURSE	0.31	KIT/comMA	0.39	TRAP	0.53
KIT/comMA	0.29	START	0.36	GOAT	0.43
PRICE	0.24	GOAT	0.31	FACE	0.42
STRUT	0.19	DRESS	0.22	KIT/comMA	0.39
FACE	0.17	STRUT	0.22	SQUARE	0.28
				STRUT	0.15
				MOUTH	0.04

collected in the Auckland Voices project and found, as with previous studies of NZE (Maclagan 1982; Watson et al. 1998; Warren 2006), that there was no significant difference in the F1 and F2 values for STRUT and START. However, recent, independent work on Auckland English by Hazenberg (2017) suggests that there may be change taking place and that for some speakers of Auckland English there is a significant difference in F1. Indeed, the possible re-separation of STRUT and START was foreshadowed in Watson et al. (1998) and Warren (2006) who found evidence that there might be greater separation of the vowels in continuous speech (rather than read speech) and among younger speakers, respectively. Hazenberg (2017) found that STRUT vowels were significantly raised relative to START in the conversational speech of 45 Aucklanders (recorded in 2013–15) and this raising was most marked among younger speakers and queer speakers. Moreover, Hazenberg (2017) observed that the realisations of START were much more homogeneous than the realisations of STRUT among the different cohorts of speakers he recorded. The ongoing raising of STRUT renders it phonetically much closer to [ðə] than START is. In other words, the divergence in how STRUT and START behave as conditioning factors with [ðə] may strengthen the dissimilation argument.

4.3 Stressed vs Unstressed NP

The stressed/non-stressed NP predictor did not show up as significant, except in one group of speakers. It seems that for the older Titirangi speakers, the alternation between [ði] and [ðə] is predictably conditioned by following vowel vs consonant and the only context in which [ðə] is favoured before vowel-initial NPs is when the NP has contrastive stress. Since stressing a vowel-initial NP often involves insertion of a glottal stop, this effectively transforms the context from a prevocalic one to a preconsonantal one. Hence, the use of [ðə] among older Titirangi speakers seems to be consistent with the prescriptive norms of Standard English.[8]

4.4 Age

In general, the effect for age group was such that [ðə] is generalised more among younger speakers across the three communities and in some communities the amount that individuals generalise [ðə] before vowels has changed dramatically across the two age groups: the overall rate of [ðə] before vowels among older speakers in Mount Roskill ranges between 0 per cent and 33 per cent for individuals, whereas among the younger speakers the range does not overlap at all: 33–100 per cent.

4.5 Implications

There are broader implications of this finding. Most analyses of English vowels do not look at the realisation of unstressed vowels, as in function words like *the*. If we are correct in suggesting that the distribution of [ðə] is influenced by the quality of the following vowel, and if we are correct in suggesting that younger speakers exhibit a stronger dissimilatory effect with STRUT because STRUT has raised from START, then this suggests that the phonemic representation of *the* may be changing over time. The evidence is that older speakers have a strong and consistent dissimilation effect with following START and STRUT, but younger speakers have a clear dissimilation effect only for strut. This suggests that the underlying vowel in *the* is more raised for younger speakers than for older speakers. That is, the younger and older Aucklanders we interviewed may have different phonemes associated with *the*. In line with this, we also note that the disfavouring effect of following KIT/COMMA also appears to become more consistent among the younger speakers.

Further detailed analysis of the realisation of vowels in conversational speech in all three Auckland Voices communities may shed light on the extent to which the distribution of [ðə] is conditioned by the phonetics of the following vowel.

In short, the data in the Auckland Voices interviews confirms that the same variables (with the same variants) are in play in the highly mixed urban settings of both London and Auckland. But the specificities of them differ within Auckland and differ from what has been found in London.

5. DISCUSSION

In Auckland, the levelling of the allomorphic distinction between [ði] and [ðə] seems to be driven by phonetic considerations.

We suggested at the outset that the Auckland Voices corpus was designed to explore whether some of the sociolinguistically surprising findings from the Multicultural London English project emerge as a consequence of the extreme levels of ethnic mixing typical in inner city London and communities like Mount Roskill or whether it was a distinctive feature of London alone.

Our exploration of the use of [ðə] before vowels in Auckland English suggests that there is change taking place and the use of [ðə] is becoming more typical before vowels in all three communities across Auckland. However, we did not find evidence that there was any significant gender effect. When we drill down into the data of individual communities, to the extent that we find any effect for gender, young women seem to be leading the change, as would be predicted (Labov 2001).

We suggested that phonetic dissimilation is an important factor constraining the distribution of [ðə] and if this is correct, then it would seem that the effect of the following segment as a trigger for dissimilation is more advanced in precisely the speakers who live and have grown up in ethnically mixed communities. These are comparable to the speakers that the Multicultural London English project found to be leading change in London. This pattern is clearest in the older speakers in South Auckland and Mount Roskill. The evidence for a phonetic basis underpinning the expansion of [ə] before vowels is less clear, partly by virtue of the much smaller number of tokens.

6. CONCLUSION

This chapter outlined the structure and goals of the Auckland Voices project, looking at the trajectories of variation and change in the urban English of NZ's largest city. The increasing ethnic diversity in some parts of Auckland places the city within larger global trends in urban migration and urban heterogeneity, typical of many cities in the Indo-Pacific region and across the globe. Auckland Voices has already looked at variation and change across three different communities in Auckland, examining aspects of pronunciation, morphophonemics, syntax and semantics/lexicon. In this chapter, we reported on our findings with respect to the phonetic realisation of the definite article in these three communities and in two major age groups.

The data on the pronunciation of the definite article as [ðə] before vowel-initial NPs does suggest that this generalisation is more advanced in South Auckland, the community that has been most ethnically diverse for the longest. It also seems to be spreading quite rapidly among younger speakers in the other two communities, though the younger speakers in the more middle-class and predominantly White community in West

Auckland appear to be lagging in the adoption of this variant. This provides some affirmative support for our first two research questions about whether more diverse communities might favour the emergence of new variants and whether these may spread among younger speakers across the city. The sociolinguistic distribution of prevocalic [ðə] strongly suggests this feature is already well entrenched in Auckland English and there is every chance that it will continue to generalise (perhaps with a reassignment of linguistic constraints on the use of prevocalic [ði] in the future).

Culture is, as Schneider notes, a problematic concept on many levels, and we need not commit ourselves to labelling the three communities we have investigated here as fundamentally different in culture. Indeed, as a team, what so far strikes us as notable is the extent to which younger speakers across all three Auckland communities seem to be able to converge on similar linguistic norms, despite the demographic and sociohistorical differences between their communities. Schneider concedes that for more abstract linguistic variables, evidence of cultural impact on language is 'partial and tentative rather than definitive ... and awaits further testing' (p. 000). We believe that in this chapter we have shown that the testing of this proposal can be readily extended using the traditional methods and analytic tools of language variation and change. We look forward to sharing further such investigations of additional abstract forms of variation in Auckland English with the wider linguistic community in the future.

NOTES

1. NZ.Stat search 15 January 2020: Population of Auckland region 1.571 million; total NZ population 4.699 million.
2. The second sub-question here is more directly relevant to previous studies of change in progress in New Zealand English pronunciation, rather than the novel morphological variable investigated here.
3. This core data collection was funded by the Royal Society of New Zealand Te Apārangi.
4. In Titirangi, interviews with younger speakers were conducted by a long-term Pākehā resident in her twenties; older speakers were recruited by a Pākehā woman in her 60s who is a long-term resident in West Auckland. Interviews with speakers in South Auckland were conducted by two Samoan women in their 20s and in Mount Roskill by two Indian women in their 20s. Meyerhoff interviewed all the

older speakers from Mount Roskill (with whom there was an overlap in age and, for most speakers, ethnicity), some of the older South Auckland speakers (who were recruited by family members, close friends or through a community presentation) and three younger speakers in Mount Roskill, who were recruited by Ballard through university networks.
5. This was principally done by Birchfield with random cross checking by Meyerhoff and joint discussion of any problematic following vowel tokens.
6. Direct quantitative comparison of different following vowels would require a much larger corpus than we have here. It also explores a slightly different question than this approach does. Direct comparison of individual vowels presumes the phonetics of the vowel space is fundamentally the same for all speakers. Since Catherine Watson's and Evan Hazenberg's previous work on Auckland English questions the phonetic uniformity of NZ English and the phonetic details of Auckland English in particular, our approach is preferable as a heuristic. It allows us to explore the vowels as evidenced in the conversational data collected.
7. Following GOOSE cannot occur – initial /u/ triggers a jod-onglide (which plausibly is related historically to the peripheral vowel in [ði] and further strengthens the case for a broader analysis of the prevocalic realisation of *the* that includes other hiatus resolution options, such as glottal stops. That lies beyond the scope of this chapter).
8. We did not systematically check whether the use of [ðə] prevocalically in non-stressed contexts was also associated with glottal insertion, but this is clearly an avenue worthy of further exploration. As we will suggest shortly, we believe the fine phonetic conditioning of [ðə] suggests a somewhat different process might (also) be at work.

REFERENCES

Aboh, E. O. and Ansaldo, U. (2006). The role of typology in language creation. In U. Ansaldo, S. Matthews and L. Lim (Eds.), *Deconstructing creole* (pp. 39–66). John Benjamins.

Bartlett, C. (1992). Regional variation in New Zealand English: The case of Southland. *New Zealand English Newsletter*, 6, 5–15.

Bauer, L. (2008). Homogeneity, heterogeneity and New Zealand English. *New Zealand English Journal*, 22, 1–8.

Bauer, L. and Warren, P. (2004). New Zealand English: Phonology. In B. Kortmann, E. W. Schneider, K. Burridge, R. Mesthrie and C. Upton (Eds.), *A handbook of varieties of English* (pp. 580–602). Mouton de Gruyter.

Bell, A., Davis, K. and Starks, D. (2000). Languages of the Manukau region: A pilot study of use, maintenance and educational dimensions of languages in South Auckland. Woolf Fisher Research Centre, University of Auckland.

Bell, A., Davis, K. and Starks, D. (2001). Maori and Pasifika voices in Manukau: A preliminary study. *Many Voices, 17*, 8–13.

Bell, A. and Gibson, A. (2008). Stopping and fronting in New Zealand Pasifika English. *University of Pennsylvania Working Papers in Linguistics, 14*(2), 44–53. <https://repository.upenn.edu/pwpl/vol14/iss2/7> (last accessed 13 January 2021).

Bell, A. and Kuiper, K. (Eds.). (2000). *New Zealand English*. John Benjamins.

Birchfield, A. M. (2019). *'All the people who live in Auckland': A study of subject and non-subject relative clauses in Auckland English* [Master's thesis, Victoria University of Wellington].

Charters, A. H. and Ballard, E. Y. (2018). *Not much changes: Quantifier use in Auckland English* [Paper presentation]. New Zealand Language in Society Conference, 14–16 November, Victoria University of Wellington, Wellington, New Zealand.

Cheshire, J., Fox, S., Kerswill, P. and Torgersen, E. (2008). Ethnicity, friendship network and social practices as the motor of dialect change: Linguistic innovation in London. *Sociolinguistica, 22*, 1–23.

Cheshire, J., Fox, S. Kerswill, P. and Torgersen, E. (2013). Language contact and language change in the multicultural metropolis. *Revue française de linguistique appliquée, 18*(2), 63–76.

Cheshire, J., Kerswill, P., Fox, S. and Torgersen, E. (2011). Contact, the feature pool and the speech community: The emergence of Multicultural London English. *Journal of Sociolinguistics, 15*(2), 151–96.

Daleszynska, A. and Meyerhoff, M. (2020). The voice of Polan[t]: Modelling L1 interference in the acquisition of (t, d) variation by Polish migrants in Edinburgh. *Sociolinguistic Studies, 14*(1–2), 107–30.

Duhamel, M. and Meyerhoff, M. (2014). An end of egalitarianism? Social evaluations of language difference in New Zealand. *Linguistics Vanguard, 1*(1), 235–48. <https://doi.org/10.1515/lingvan-2014-1005> (last accessed 13 January 2021).

Fox, S. (2015). *The New Cockney: New ethnicities and adolescent speech in the traditional East End of London*. Palgrave.

Gordon, E., Campbell, L., Hay, J., Maclagan, M., Sudbury, A. and Trudgill, P. (2004). *New Zealand English: Its origins and evolution*. Cambridge University Press.

Guzzo, S., Britain, D. and Fox, S. (2008). From L2 to ethnic dialect: Hiatus resolution strategies in Bedford Italian English [Paper presentation]. International Conference on Global English, 14–16 February, University of Verona, Italy.

Hay, J., Maclagan, M. A. and Gordon, E. (2008). *New Zealand English*. Edinburgh University Press.

Hazenberg, E. (2017). *Liminality as a lens on social meaning: A cross-variable analysis of gender in New Zealand English* [Doctoral dissertation, Victoria University of Wellington].

Holmes, J., Bell, A. and Boyce, M. (1991). Variation and change in New Zealand English. Project report to the Social Sciences Committee of the Foundation for Research, Science and Technology. Victoria University Department of Linguistics.

Johnson, D. E. (2009). Getting off the Goldvarb standard: Introducing Rbrul for mixed-effects variable rule analysis. *Language and Linguistics Compass*, $3(1)$, 359–83.

Labov, W. (1984). Field methods and the project on linguistic change and variation. In J. Baugh and J. Scherzer (Eds.), *Language in use* (pp. 28–53). Prentice Hall.

Labov, W. (1994). *Principles of linguistic change: Internal factors*. Blackwell.

Labov, W. (2001). *Principles of linguistic change: Social factors*. Blackwell.

Labov, W. (2010). *Principles of linguistic change: Cognitive factors*. Wiley-Blackwell.

Maclagan, M. A. (1982). An acoustic study of New Zealand vowels. *The New Zealand Speech Therapists Journal*, $37(1)$, 20–6.

Meyerhoff, M. (2009). Replication, transfer and calquing: Using variation as a tool in the study of language contact. *Language Variation and Change*, $21(3)$, 297–317.

Meyerhoff, M., Birchfield, A., Ballard, E., Charters, H. and Watson, C. (2019). Definite change taking place: Determiner realization in multiethnic communities in New Zealand. *University of Pennsylvania Working Papers in Linguistics*, $25(2)$, 71–8. <https://repository.upenn.edu/pwpl/vol25/iss2/9/> (last accessed 13 January 2021).

Meyerhoff, M., Birchfield, A., Ballard, E., Watson, C. and Charters, H. (2020). Restrictions on relative clauses in Auckland, New Zealand. In K. V. Beaman, I. Buchstaller, S. Fox and J. A. Walker (Eds.), *Socio-grammatical variation and change: In honour of Jenny Cheshire* (pp. 115–33). Routledge.

Meyerhoff, M. and Schleef, E. (2012). Variation, contact and social indexicality in the acquisition of (ing) by teenage migrants. *Journal of Sociolinguistics, 16*(3), 398–416.

Meyerhoff, M., Schleef, E. and Mackenzie, L. (2015). *Doing sociolinguistics: A practical guide*. Routledge.

Mufwene, S. S. (2001). *The ecology of language evolution*. Cambridge University Press.

Nagy, N. and Meyerhoff, M. (2013). Extending ELAN into variationist sociolinguistics. *Linguistics Vanguard, 1*(1), 271–81. <https://doi.org/10.1515/lingvan-2015-0012> (last accessed 13 January 2021).

O'Malley, V. (2016). *The great war for New Zealand: Waikato 1800–2000*. Bridget Williams Books.

Regan, V., Howard, M. and Lemée, I. (2009). *The acquisition of sociolinguistic competence in a study abroad context*. Multilingual Matters.

Ross, B. (2018). *An acoustic analysis of New Zealand English vowels in Auckland* [Master's thesis, Victoria University of Wellington].

Schleef, E., Meyerhoff, M. and Clark, L. (2011). Teenagers' acquisition of variation: A comparison of locally-born and migrant teens' realisation of English (ing). *English World-Wide, 32*(2), 206–36.

Sloetjes, H. and Wittenburg, P. (2008). Annotation by category – ELAN and ISO DCR. In N. Calzolari, K. Choukri, B. Maegaard, J. Mariani, J. Odijk, S. Piperidis and D. Tapias (Eds.), *Proceedings of the 6th International Conference on Language Resources and Evaluation (LREC 2008)* (pp. 816–20). European Language Resources Association.

Smakman, D. and Heinrich, P. (Eds.). (2015). *Globalising sociolinguistics*. Routledge.

Sollitt-Morris, L. (2015). *Atkinson Park and life at Paturoa Bay*. Lynette Sollitt-Morris.

Stats New Zealand. (2013). *New Zealand Census*. <http://www.stats.govt.nz/Census/2013-census/data-tables/meshblock-dataset.aspx>; <http://www.stats.govt.nz/Census/2013-census/profile-and-summary-reports/quickstats-culture-identity/languages.aspx>; <http://www.stats.govt.nz/Census/2013-census/profile-and-summary-reports/quickstats-culture-identity/languages.aspx> (all last accessed 13 January 2021).

Stats New Zealand. (2020a). NZ.Stat. [includes 2018 Census data] <https://www.stats.govt.nz/tools/nz-dot-stat> (last accessed 13 January 2021).

Stats New Zealand. (2020b). Northern regions lead population growth. <https://www.stats.govt.nz/news/northern-regions-lead-population-growth> (last accessed 9 February 2021).

Tagliamonte, S. A. (2002). Comparative sociolinguistics. In J. K. Chambers, P. Trudgill and N. Schilling-Estes (Eds.), *The handbook of language variation and change* (pp. 729–63). Blackwell.

Tagliamonte, S. A. and D'Arcy, A. (2009). Peaks beyond phonology: Adolescence, incrementation, and language change. *Language, 85*(1), 58–108.

Taumoefolau, M., Starks, D., Davis, K. and Bell, A. (2002). Linguists and language maintenance: Pasifika languages in Manukau, New Zealand. *Oceanic Linguistics, 41*(1), 15–27.

Trudgill, P. (2004). *New-dialect formation: The inevitability of colonial Englishes.* Edinburgh University Press/Georgetown University Press.

Truesdale, S. and Meyerhoff, M. (2015). Acquiring some like-ness to others: How some Polish teenagers acquire the Scottish pragmatics of *like. Te Reo, 58,* 3–28.

Warren, P. (2006). Oops, I've done a futt: Quality and quantity in a New Zealand vowel contrast. *Te Reo, 49,* 125–43.

Warren, P. (2018). Quality and quantity in New Zealand English vowel contrasts. *Journal of the International Phonetic Association, 48*(3), 305–30.

Watson, C. I., Harrington, J. and Evans, Z. (1998). An acoustic comparison between New Zealand and Australian English vowels. *Australian Journal of Linguistics, 18*(2), 185–207.

Watson, C. I., Ross, B., Ballard, E. Y., Charters, A. H., Arnold, R. and Meyerhoff, M. (2018). Preliminary investigations into sound change in Auckland. In J. Epps, J. Wolfe, J. Smith and C. Jones (Eds.), *Proceedings of the Seventeenth International Australasian International Conference on Speech Science and Technology* (pp. 17–20). Australasian Speech Science and Technology Association.

Index

abduction, 283
AbE *see* Aboriginal English
Aboriginal education, 280, 293
Aboriginal English/AbE, 2, 9, 11, 144, 280, 284–96
Aboriginal English: contexts of use, 285
Aboriginal listener context, 286
Aboriginal meanings for English words *see* conceptual relevance
acculturation, 18, 130, 144, 165
acrolectal, 197, 218, 219, 268
address term *see* term of address
adoption (of children), 8, 135–44
adoption (of language), 283–4
adstrate language, 1, 5, 13, 209
adverb, position of, 57–9
affirmation, 294, 296
Afrikaans, 47–61
Afrikaans, camouflaged, 47, 48, 57, 60
age of speaker, younger/older (speaker's age group), 356
age stratification, 160
agreement (grammatical) 37; *see also* concord
agreement/disagreement, 121, 263, 310, 312, 320, 355

alternative choice/form/term, 36, 91, 102
alternative explanation/interpretation/ perspective, 39, 182, 251
American English/AmE, 27, 39, 109, 111, 114, 121, 171, 194–7, 201, 208, 247–9, 263, 326–8, 334
Americanisation, Americanise, 130, 144
Anglo-Indian (dictionaries), 87, 91–2, 95
angloversal, 11, 260, 263
animacy, 252, 253, 255
AntConc, 21, 28, 67, 138, 243
anthropology, 16, 25, 108, 129, 146
anti-authoritarian, 334, 335
Arabanoo, 283
Arabic language, 1, 5, 88–9, 91–4, 110
Arabic loanword 6, 88–9, 91–3, 96–8, 100, 102, 6, 88–9, 91–3, 96–8, 100, 102
archaic language, 59, 66, 113, 115, 120, 319
areal feature, 262, 272, 334
areality, 261, 266, 267, 272
areoversal, 260, 274
artefact, 14, 16, 19, 22, 24, 40, 81
arts, crafts and costume, 73
assertive modal, 245, 255

Auckland, 12, 345–63
Auckland Voices project, 12, 345–9, 351–2, 354, 360, 362
AusE *see* Australian English
Australia, 8, 11, 13, 158, 165, 280–2, 284, 293, 334–5
Australian English/AusE, 11–12, 86, 152, 263, 280, 284, 285, 287, 291, 292, 296, 324, 327, 328–30, 332–5, 340
authoritarian, 2, 317
authority, 10, 29, 98, 302, 333, 335

Babu English, 90, 91, 97
backshifting, 240
behavio(u)r, 4, 17, 25, 30, 64, 67, 68, 71, 112, 113, 116, 121, 135, 141, 166, 261–3, 313, 335, 336, 346
Beijing, 8, 10, 172–86, 238, 239, 241, 243–55
Bennelong, 283
bhai, 93, 95, 101–2, 104
bicultural education, 11, 293, 295, 296
biculturalism, 281, 295
bidialectalism, 11, 291, 296
bilingual education, 296
bilingualism, 152, 194, 206
Black South African English, 116, 120
blend/portmanteau word, 71, 81
bookish/bookishness, 90, 217, 231
borrowing, 2, 5, 6, 40, 48, 64–6, 68, 70, 71, 73–6, 78–80, 82, 83, 121–3, 132, 274
boyfriend, 34, 117, 138, 142, 272
British English/BrE, 9, 18, 21, 40, 86, 111, 114, 115, 144, 171, 172, 195–7, 201, 208, 217, 226, 231, 241, 247, 334
British Raj, 6, 90, 91, 95, 97
broadcasting, 12, 111, 302, 315, 319–21

brother, 8, 30, 31, 73, 76, 77, 93, 102, 117–19, 132, 135, 138–40, 145, 159, 162, 271, 286, 292
bugger (all), 12, 325, 327, 329–40

calque, 2, 5, 47, 90, 109, 113, 121, 123, 267
care/give a X, 324–5, 327–8, 337, 339
Caroline Islands, 130
Carolinian, 130, 133–5, 140, 143
Chamorro, 130–5, 138, 140, 141, 143, 145
Chinese culture, 21–2, 31, 32, 34, 41, 171, 245
Chinese ethnicity, 10, 194, 196–9, 202–4, 208
Chinese language/dialect, 2, 8, 27, 65, 82, 94, 98, 172, 187, 195, 200, 203, 204
civil administration, 97
CKI (Cocos-Keeling Islands), 8, 151–6, 157–8, 160–8
CKI English, 154, 157, 160–2, 164, 167
CLAWS, 220
clusivity, 261, 267
Cocos (Keeling) Islands *see* CKI
Cocos Malay, 8, 152, 154, 156–8, 160, 161, 163–7
code-switching, code-switched, 90, 121, 122
collective nouns, 4, 37, 275
collective responsibility, 302, 309, 314–16, 320
collectivism, 4, 8, 25–8, 34, 36, 41, 153, 159, 161, 167, 261
collectivist culture, 8, 19, 37–9, 54, 165
collectivist term, 8, 27, 166
collectivity, 11, 36, 267, 269, 275
colloquialisation, 301, 321, 324, 334
colloquialism, 333–4
colonial, 1, 5, 6, 11, 15, 48–9, 66, 87,

89, 98, 101, 130–1, 133–5, 152, 187, 217, 280–4, 287, 293, 295–7, 303, 305, 337
colonialism, 5, 11, 171, 280, 293, 295–6
colonisation, colonise, 65, 133, 151, 194, 280–3, 292
communicative function, 64
conceptual metaphor, 18, 170–3, 178, 180, 183, 184
Conceptual Metaphor Theory, 170
conceptual relevance, 285
concord, 4, 37–9, 275; *see also* agreement (grammatical)
conditional inference tree, 202, 221–4, 226, 228, 231–2, 244, 252–4
Confucian, 20, 21, 28, 31
contact-based English, 264
contact variety, 154, 157, 167, 200, 260, 262, 266, 274, 353
context: high vs. low, 33, 159
contextual appropriateness, 291
conversion to verb (of noun, adjective, adverb), 288
Cook Islands, 11, 268–71
Cook Islands English/CookE, 266, 268–71
core borrowing, 6, 71, 78
corpus linguistics, 18, 49, 86, 109, 145, 147
could, 240, 242–7, 251, 327–9
courtship, 34, 142
cousin, 8, 30, 31, 132, 135, 138–40, 146, 159, 162, 286, 292
crore, 93, 95–6, 104
cross-cultural analysis, 3, 16, 19, 24, 171, 180, 183, 184
cross-cultural psychology, 25, 26, 32, 40
cultural borrowing, 6, 66, 68, 70, 71, 73–6, 78, 80
cultural framing, 80
cultural identity, 130, 152, 232, 263

cultural keyword, 3, 6, 86–7, 93, 95, 97, 171, 232
cultural linguistics, 3, 18, 34, 153
cultural object, 3, 5, 16, 20, 22, 24, 40, 48, 54, 66, 82, 122
cultural practice, 3, 57, 60, 74, 129, 143–4, 157, 262
cultural shift, 154, 167
cultural studies, 16
culture *see* dimensions of culture
culture-grammar relationship, 266, 272
customised corpora, 3, 243

decolonisation, 11, 280–1, 283, 291, 292, 295
decolonised English, 280, 285, 295
definite article, pronunciation of, 12, 346, 352–4, 357, 362
democracy, 7, 8, 171–86, 335
democratisation, 242, 301, 313, 321
demonstrative, 286, 289
descent (ethnicity), 24, 134, 194, 196, 201, 203, 274, 282, 349–50
de-voicing, 296
diachronic, 6, 9, 11, 13, 87, 104, 184, 218, 309
diaspora, 158, 350
dictionaries, Indian English, 93, 94
diglossia, diglossic, 157, 195
dimensions of culture, 3, 7, 19, 24, 25, 48, 54, 151
discourse culture, 217–20, 222, 225, 226, 230–2
discourse marker, 6–7, 103, 108, 109, 111, 120–3, 157, 216, 286
distance, 3, 28–30, 141, 145, 159, 242, 256, 263
distance/intimacy, 145
distributional analysis, 151, 159
diversity, 13, 72, 104, 151, 194, 208, 294, 311, 346–9, 362
dominant culture, 11, 284, 294–6
durability, 5, 105

East India Company, 89
ecolinguistics, 1, 3
ecology, 1, 2, 14, 65–6, 87, 91, 193, 195, 261–2
editorial *see* newspaper editorial
effect plot, 225, 227, 229
EFL, 9, 10, 13, 109, 215–20, 222, 225, 226, 228, 231–3, 241
elder, 52, 56, 132–3, 140–1, 269, 286
embodiment, embodies, 18, 35, 74, 262, 272, 288–9
emotion, expression of, 3, 7, 153
end-focus, 36, 38
English as a lingua franca *see* EFL
English as a native language *see* ENL
English as a second language *see* ESL
English-dominant, 4, 9
English editorials, 170, 172–4, 238, 243–4, 255
ENL, 2, 9, 10, 11, 13, 215–20, 225, 228, 231–3, 272
entertainment, 75, 99–100, 105
epistemic, 240, 244, 311, 319
ESL, 2, 9, 10, 13, 109, 215–20, 225–6, 228, 230–3, 241, 260, 272
ethnic, 9, 10, 13, 51, 54, 110, 133, 152, 154, 164, 194, 205, 207, 208, 270, 271, 276, 345–51, 354, 361, 362
ethnicity/ethnicities, 2, 9, 23, 130, 137, 146, 157, 193–4, 196, 198–9, 202–5, 208–9, 270, 364
ethnosyntax, 35
evolutionary status (incl. political status), 109, 124, 152, 193–4, 205, 231, 240–1, 250, 256, 321
exonormative, 6, 66, 89–90, 108, 109, 123, 124, 231, 241
expanding circle, 3, 172, 225, 238, 241, 250, 251, 255
exploratory, 129, 137, 217, 247, 251, 255, 284
extended family, 132, 136, 139, 285

extended reference, 210, 285–6
extrinsic/intrinsic, 238–40, 252

family relations, 31; *see also* kinship
family term *see* kinship term
family/families, 2, 7, 11, 37, 100, 102, 116, 118, 129–46, 154, 156, 163, 166–7, 201, 206, 264, 267–71, 282, 285, 287, 292, 347, 351, 364
farming, 62, 88, 105
fashion, 98, 100
Federated States of Micronesia/FSM, 130
Fiji, Fijian, 268, 271, 275, 276
Fiji English, 268
Filipino, Pilipino, 73, 83
first person pronoun, singular/plural, 27, 28, 40, 41, 54, 61, 72, 159, 160, 161, 243, 247, 250, 265, 267, 269, 221, 272, 304, 311, 315; *see also* *I*, *we*
Fisher's Exact test, 21, 41
fixed expression, 321
flora and fauna, 3, 65, 74
food (and drink), 19, 22, 23, 53, 54, 65, 74, 79, 94, 98, 99, 105, 119, 135, 136, 253, 286, 350
foreigner talk, 282
formal, 15, 18, 40, 74, 96, 109, 122, 167, 206, 218, 295
formal writing/discourse, 9, 12, 97, 112, 116, 117, 120, 122, 141, 196, 218, 219, 230, 242, 302, 319
formality, 67, 112, 138, 145, 256, 302, 319
friendship, 6, 77, 86, 104, 117, 134

GB *see* British English
generation, younger/older, 47, 132, 156, 160, 161, 165, 241, 287, 274, 295, 347, 327, 353
generational, 8, 13, 12, 160, 161, 167
girlfriend, 34, 138, 142

globalisation, 115, 123, 130, 165, 167, 194, 334
GloWbE corpus, 6, 66, 87, 92, 93, 94, 95, 96, 98, 100, 101, 102, 103, 104
governance, 76, 177
government, Government, 12, 37, 76, 86, 88, 89, 91, 94, 96, 98, 105, 109, 110, 135, 156, 172, 173, 176, 177, 182, 187, 206, 240, 273, 287, 292, 335, 356
government as grammatical subject, 304, 305, 313–17, 319
grammar, 12, 13, 35, 39, 57, 60, 64, 108, 240, 260–3, 265, 266, 268, 272, 334, 356
grammaticalisation, 239, 275, 301, 326, 332–3, 340
grandparent, 138, 140
greeting, 2, 6, 23, 24, 108–15, 120, 122, 123
group orientation, consciousness, 51, 283, 285, 286
Guam, 7–8, 129–33, 137–46

habitat, 232, 274
Hansard, 9, 11, 12, 118, 242, 301, 303–9, 312–13, 315, 317, 320–1
have to, 2, 11–12, 248–9, 301–3, 305–8, 311–12, 314–19
hegemony, hegemonic, 294, 296
high-contact, 207
Hindi, 88–90, 91–5, 105
Hindi-Urdu, 6, 89
Hindustan, 88
Hindustani, 6, 94–5
Hinglish, 90
HK *see* Hong Kong
Hobson Jobson, 91–5, 105
Hofstede, Geert, 17, 25–9, 31, 32, 151, 153–4, 158–9, 164
Hong Kong (HK), 6, 8, 10, 13, 16, 20, 22–4, 27–31, 33–4, 38–9, 41, 131, 151–2, 160–4, 171–9, 181–7, 217–18, 220, 222, 225–6, 228, 230–1, 238–9, 241, 243–53, 255, 258
Hong Kong English (HKE), 10, 153, 230, 241
Hongkong *see* Hong Kong
honorific (term), 71, 73, 77, 103, 116
hono(u)r, 116, 136
housing, 52, 156, 350
humiliation, 297
husband, 116, 138, 142–3, 271
hyperdialectalism, 263, 274

I, 8, 115, 199, 208, 240, 242, 250–1, 253, 261, 267, 271–2, 312
ICE, 240; *see also* International corpus of English
ICE-GB, 20–4, 27–31, 33, 38–9, 61
ICE-HK, 20, 22–4, 27–31, 33, 38–9
ICE-IND, 20, 22–4, 27–31, 33, 38–9
ICE-NZ, 20, 22–4, 27–31, 33, 38–9
ICE-PHI, 5–6, 20, 66, 68–83
ICE-SA, 61
ICE-SING, 20, 22–4, 27–31, 33, 38–9
ICE-UG, 6–7, 111, 114–15, 117–19, 121–2, 124
inclusive-exclusive *see* clusivity
Indian entertainment, 99–100
Indian food, 90, 94, 98–9
Indian language, 90, 93, 194, 195
Indian Ocean, 152, 154
Indian Singaporean, 207
indicator construction/structure, 4, 19–20, 36, 38, 256, 261, 285
indicator term, 3–4, 7, 19–21, 24–30, 33–4, 40–1, 104, 145–6, 153, 159, 161–7, 171–84, 243, 261, 285
indigenous language, 3, 5–7, 11, 19, 22, 40, 50–2, 64–75, 78–80, 82–3, 91, 110, 113, 122–3, 131–3, 141, 154, 280–1, 292–3, 347

Indigenous people, 8, 11, 52, 56, 61, 77, 82–3, 130, 133–5, 151, 280–5, 292–7
individualism, individualistic, 4, 8, 25–9, 34, 36–7, 39–41, 61, 153, 159, 161, 165–7, 261
individuality, 4, 9, 36, 255, 267
Indo-Pacific, 14–16, 28, 41, 362
informal (language), 9, 12, 61, 71, 91–2, 112, 114–15, 117–18, 121–2, 158, 242, 256, 334
informal (system), 95–6, 137, 142, 241, 340
inner circle (English), 217, 225, 240
input, 9, 20, 40, 193–7, 200, 205–8
insider–outsider, 11, 264–5
interactive language, 95, 226, 242, 247–8, 250–3, 255–6
interconnected, 92, 287
intercultural communication, 17, 25
interjection, 77, 81
International Corpus of English/ICE, 6–8, 10, 16, 20, 22–4, 27–31, 33, 38–9, 55, 67, 145, 154, 159, 164, 166–7, 219–20, 239–40; *see also* ICE-GB, ICE-HK, ICE-IND, ICE-NZ, ICE-PHI, ICE-SA, ICE-SING, ICE-UG
intrinsic *see* extrinsic/intrinsic

Jespersen's Cycle, 325–9, 338, 340

Kachruvian circle, 10, 215, 216, 218, 221, 225, 228, 230
keyword, 50, 85, 103, 175, 180, 241, 243
kinship, 2, 34, 40–1, 115–16, 129, 130–2, 134–5, 137, 146, 159, 162, 168
kinship term, 8, 29–31, 47, 55, 71, 73, 76, 101, 103, 115, 116, 123, 129, 131–2, 134, 138–9, 142, 145, 159, 162–4, 171, 285

Koorified, 291
Kosrae/Kosraean, 7, 8, 130–1, 135–7, 139, 141–4, 146–7

L1, 9, 38–9, 103, 108–9, 113–15, 118–19, 122–4, 193–4, 196–203, 205, 207–8, 216–17, 255, 260, 267–8
L1 English, 115, 260
L2, 39, 109, 123–4, 152, 167, 193–4, 196, 198, 207, 247, 257, 266–7, 272, 274
L2 Englishes, 109, 267
landscape, 49, 52, 54, 56, 61
language adoption, 283–4
language and culture, 3, 4, 15–16, 18, 21, 47–8, 65–6, 83, 109, 208–9, 232, 269, 283
language contact, 7, 19, 64–6, 82, 93, 265
language family, 110, 113, 349
language planning, 293
letters, social and business, 67, 69–72, 117–19, 335
level (of language), 2, 9, 40, 49, 67, 68, 110, 120, 124, 145, 152, 156, 218, 219, 232, 233
lexeme, 140
lexical unit, 76–7, 80–1, 167
lexical-conceptual (dimension), 40, 171, 180, 183–4
lexicon, 57, 66, 93, 108, 123, 167, 328, 362
lexicopragmatic, 2, 13
lexicosemantic borrowing, 64–5, 67–70, 72, 74, 76, 78–83
lexis, 47, 110, 131, 160, 233, 334
lifestyle, 90, 134, 145, 158
linear regression model, 220–1, 225
linguistic innovation, 13, 81, 273
linguistic relativity, 17
long-term, 32, 153, 159, 321, 363

Malay, 8, 23, 65, 82, 152, 154, 156–8, 160–1, 163–7, 194–5, 209
Malaysia, 8, 151, 153, 157, 165, 194, 310
Mapping Principle, 184
marginalisation, 296–7
married, 47, 55, 116, 138, 142–3
masala, 98–9
material culture, 98, 100, 104
medium (of communication), 91, 172, 219–22, 225–33, 241, 243
metaphor, conceptual, 8, 170–3, 176, 178, 180–5
Metaphor Pattern Analysis, 174
metaphor, source domain:
    building, 178–9, 180, 183, 186
    competition, 8, 178, 183, 186
    democracy, 8, 171–86
    journey, 8, 170, 178–80, 183–4, 186
    living being, 178–9, 183, 186
    physical object, 177–80, 183, 186
metaphorisation, 176, 183
Micronesia, Micronesian, 13, 129–30, 136
Micronesian English, 129
Middle English, 325
might, 240, 242–8
migrant/migration, 12–13, 201, 346–9, 362
minimiser, minimal direct object, 324, 326
mobility, 137
modal of necessity/obligation, 240, 242, 244–5, 247–8, 256, 301–6, 308–9
modal (tentative), 245, 255
modal verb, 10, 220, 238, 241–3, 238–46, 250, 255, 275, 301, 316, 318
mode *see* medium
monetary, 6, 22, 95, 96, 104
morphosyntax, morphosyntactic, 2, 4, 9, 260, 265, 274, 285, 334

mother/mom/mum, 73, 75–6, 116–19, 134, 136, 138, 140–1, 146, 285, 292
mother tongue, 137, 266, 271
Mughal, 6, 23, 87–9, 91–3, 95–6
Multicultural London English project, 353, 361–2
multifactorial analysis, 238, 252
multilingual speaker, 1, 5, 14, 67, 353
multiple negation, 325, 331–2
music, 22, 75
must, 11–12, 240, 242, 244, 246–8, 251, 253, 289, 301–3, 305–6, 308–20

nativisation/nativise, 90, 108, 280–1
nativization/nativize, 215, 282
need to, 248–9, 301–3, 305–9, 312–15, 320
negative polarity item (NPI), 324–5, 327–8, 330–2, 337
negative quantifier, 326, 329, 332, 334, 340
negator, 12, 325–32, 334, 338–40
neo-colonialism, neo-colonial, 11, 280–1, 293, 295, 297
neologism, 6, 80, 82
New South Wales Pidgin, 284
New Zealand English/NZE, 9, 123, 273, 301, 345–6, 348, 354–5, 357, 363–4
newspaper editorial, 2, 8, 10, 69, 72, 170, 172–4, 175–84, 188, 238–9, 242–5, 247–8, 250–3, 255–6
nexus, 3–5, 7, 9, 11, 13, 18–19, 22, 24, 35, 40, 49, 54, 57, 104, 115, 120, 122, 151, 153, 164, 167, 239, 241, 243, 256, 261, 283, 285, 324
Nigerian English, 116, 118
node (terminal), 221, 222, 225, 253
nominal (relating to nouns), 10, 115, 217–20, 225–6, 228, 230–2
norm-dependent, 215, 232
norm-developing, 215

Northern Mariana Islands, 133
noun, 18, 36, 55–6, 67–8, 94, 96, 221, 222, 225–6, 228, 230–3, 253, 265, 275, 288, 303, 304–5, 312, 316, 319, 325–8, 331, 338
NPI *see* negative polarity item
NSW Pidgin *see* New South Wales Pidgin
null object pronoun, 264, 266
number contrast (for pronoun), 260, 264, 266
Nyungar, 287, 291, 292
Nyungarisation, 291
NZE *see* New Zealand English

observation, 25, 86, 289
official language, 89, 135, 172, 241
Old Bailey Corpus, 336–7
Old English, 325
older person, 71, 73, 76, 117, 132, 136, 138, 141, 156, 160, 165, 194, 201, 273
older speaker, 8, 12, 160–2, 349, 351, 353, 355–6, 358, 360–4
Oom Schalk, 47, 50–5, 57–8, 60–1
oral (discourse), 46, 218–19, 222, 225, 231, 291, 352
orthography, 65, 73, 75
outer circle, 171, 219, 225, 238, 240–1, 250–1

Pacific Islander/community, 144–5, 261–2, 266, 268, 270, 346, 350
Pākehā, 24, 349–50, 363
Pakistan, 6, 88–9
paradigm gap, 215–16, 233
parliamentary discourse, 11, 302, 304, 306, 309, 320–1
participant-differentiated identification, 292
part-of-speech (POS), 10, 215, 218, 220, 226, 231–3, 336
passive, 4, 37–9, 252, 289

past tense, 2, 9, 61, 193, 195–6, 199–204, 240, 243, 262
past tense context, 195
past tense marking, 193, 196, 199–204
people (types of), 11, 17, 49, 52, 54, 56, 76, 88, 89, 96, 112–13, 131, 133, 154, 157–8, 166, 176, 263, 270, 281–4, 286–7, 291–3, 296–7, 304–5, 310–11, 314, 333, 353
Persian-Arabic loanword, 92, 98, 102
persuasive writing/discourse, 69, 242, 247, 255, 291, 302
Philippine English, 5, 6, 10, 64–7, 79, 81–3
Philippine learner-writer, 231
Pitkern-Norf'k, 264–5, 267, 268, 273
politeness, 17, 28–30, 34, 104, 108, 115, 123, 152, 242–3, 263, 318, 319
politics, 20, 65, 76, 81, 82, 99, 151, 182, 242
Polynesian, 268, 350
portmanteau word *see* blend
POS (part-of-speech) tag, 220, 232
postcolonial biculturalism, 281, 295
postcolonial English, 13, 151, 217, 281
post-creole, 284
postnominal, 102–3
post-protectorate, 108, 109, 124
power, 3, 5, 7, 28–31, 34, 100, 116, 122, 130, 131, 133, 136, 159, 181, 182, 184, 231, 247, 248, 255, 256, 263, 283, 284, 290, 302
Prakrit, 88, 92–3
prenominal, 103
pronominal feature/system, 11, 34, 263–4, 267–8, 272–3, 275
pronoun, first person, 11, 27–8, 40, 41, 54, 61, 160, 250, 265, 267, 272, 304, 309, 315, 316, 318
prosodic stress, 355

quasi-modal, 238–43, 247–50, 252, 255, 256; *see also* semi-modal

recipientless construction, 35, 37–9, 41
regional difference, 10–11, 240, 253, 272, 345
regional variation, 255; *see also* variation
register (spoken, written), 61, 217–18, 231, 302, 306, 321
regression modelling, 220
relations *see* social relations
religion, religious practice, 23, 52, 88, 102, 135, 157; *see also* spiritual
reporting, 55, 289, 321
respect, 6, 29, 76, 93, 102, 104, 116, 133, 135–6, 140–2, 145, 159, 291, 297, 335
respectful term, 41, 90, 94–5, 102–4, 116, 141, 313
rhetoric, rhetorical, 12, 238–9, 243, 245, 247, 250–1, 255, 265, 282, 302–3, 310, 314–16, 320–1
rights, 26, 130, 146, 177
romantic partnership *see* courtship

sabzi, sabji, 94, 98–9, 101
sahib, saheb, sahab, 93, 95, 101–2, 104
Saipan/Saipanese, 7–8, 129–31, 133–5, 137, 138, 139–44, 146
Samoa, Samoan, 111–12, 264, 266, 268, 275–6, 363
Sanskrit, 65, 82, 88, 91–3, 102
Sapir-Whorf hypothesis, 17
schematic construction/structure, 4, 17, 35, 38, 40, 49 ; *see also* indicator construction
second-language varieties of English *see* ESL
second-person (pronoun), you, 2, 242, 250–1, 256, 260–1, 263
self (the) *see* individuality
semantic category, 73–6
semantic domain, 52–3
semantic field, 5, 86–7, 95, 105

semi-modal, 2, 10–11, 256, 301–2, 312, 314–15, 320; *see also* quasi-modal
Setswana, 5, 50–3
shall, 2, 240, 242–6, 312, 315–16
shalwar, salwar, 94, 98, 100–1
shared neocolonial history *see* interconnected
short-term, 32, 153, 154
should, 11–12, 240, 242–8, 250–1, 255–6, 301–3, 305, 308, 313–15, 317–20
sibling, 76, 132, 134–6, 138–9, 145–6
Singaporean children/society 193, 195–6, 201, 207–8
Singapore English/SingE, 9, 120, 154, 193–6, 198–202, 204–5, 207–8, 210, 215
Sinosphere, 238–9, 243–4, 248, 255–6
sister, 71, 73, 76, 105, 117–19, 135–6, 138–40, 145, 271, 286, 292
SLE *see* Sri Lankan English
social, 32, 48, 79, 87, 90, 98, 104, 112, 120, 130–1, 145–5, 156–7, 205, 208, 261, 262, 265, 281–2, 341, 354
social media, 157, 166
social letters, 67, 69, 70–2, 117, 119
social relation(ship)/density, 2, 6, 29–30, 76–7, 101, 104, 110, 115, 122–3, 129, 140, 153, 228, 263, 267, 276, 332; *see also* social status
social status, 4, 7, 10, 11, 29, 40, 113, 115–16, 117, 133–4, 145, 207, 263, 332–3
sociolinguistic interview, 3, 7, 9, 130, 145, 147, 158–9, 351
sociosexuality, 34, 40
solidarity, 11, 28–9, 31, 104, 117, 164, 180, 263, 265, 267; *see also* interconnected
source domain *see* metaphor
South African, 1, 5, 49–51, 112, 157, 302, 320

South Pacific, 11, 13, 260, 262, 264, 266–7, 275
South Pacific English, 262, 275
Spanish colonial influence, 5, 64, 65, 82
Spanish language/loanword, 5, 64–6, 73–9, 132–3, 135, 140
SPE *see* South Pacific English
speaker attitude, 113, 121, 141, 143, 144, 161, 267, 269, 275, 310, 312–13, 340
Speaker (parliamentary), 114, 118, 305, 313–14
speaker variation, 10, 13, 123, 162, 164, 194, 196, 205, 207–8, 216, 218–19, 222, 225, 231–3, 242, 329, 354–6
speech/spoken corpus, 12, 20, 50, 61, 66–7, 83, 151, 164, 219, 220, 226, 228, 230
spiritual, 31, 290, 296
spoken vs written, 2, 7, 9–10, 82, 93, 105, 110–11, 115, 119, 121, 151, 153, 157–8, 194–5, 216–20, 226, 228, 230–1, 241–2, 247, 257, 260, 302
Sri Lankan English (SLE), 86, 102, 216
standard corpora, 239; *see also* International Corpus of English
status *see* evolutionary status; social status
structural schema *see* schematic construction
structure (grammatical), 262, 268, 272, 274–8; *see also* indicator construction
style, 10, 46, 56, 158, 218, 232, 242, 247, 250, 255, 321
stylistic variation, 217, 231–2
subject (grammatical), 59, 193, 195–6, 199–203, 208, 240, 250, 252–3, 303–5, 308–9, 312, 314, 316, 319
substrate language, 1, 2, 5, 10, 13, 272
synchronic evidence, 13, 87
syntax, 2, 5, 39, 48, 60, 240, 324, 362

taboo, 12, 16, 61, 142, 324–9, 331–4, 336–7, 339, 340–1
Tagalog, 5–6, 54, 65, 67–8, 71, 73–81, 83
Tahitian, 267, 272
Taipei, 8, 10, 172–5, 177–86, 238–9, 241, 243–53, 255
target domain, 171, 173–5, 178–81, 183–4, 187
tense (past), 2, 9, 193, 195–6, 199–204, 240, 243, 262, 275, 287; *see also* unmarked past verb
tense (present), 61, 217
terminal node, 221, 222, 225, 253
term of address, 55, 77, 102, 117–18, 123
term of reference, 97, 140
terra nullius, 282
text type/text-type, 20, 65, 67, 68–72, 218, 226, 238–9, 241, 243, 255
the (definite article), 12, 346, 348, 353–4, 357, 362
think out, 57–8
time orientation (short–term vs. long–term), 3, 32, 153, 154, 159, 321, 363
time reference, 287, 290
title (personal), 29, 55, 78, 93, 97, 102; *see also* honorific
topicalisation, 59
transcendent meaning, 290–1
transfer (cross-linguistic), 60, 90, 113, 194, 203, 205, 231
transition, 95, 97, 100, 112, 131, 327, 339
type-token ratio (TTR), 220–2, 225, 228

Uganda, Ugandan, 7, 13, 109, 110–11, 113–14, 118–19, 122
Uganda Web *see* Web-UG
Ugandan English, 2, 5–6, 109, 120, 122
unmarked (bare) past verb, 193, 200–4

Urdu, 88–90, 92–5, 102, 105
UWA corpus (University of Western Australia), 328–9, 332

variation (linguistic), 3, 36, 50, 154, 158, 160, 163, 165–7, 194, 196–8, 202, 205–6, 217, 219, 231–2, 239, 255, 264, 309, 320, 329, 346–9, 353, 356–7; *see also* speaker variation
variety of English, 3, 9–10, 19–20, 40–1, 51, 104, 108–9, 111, 116, 120, 152–4, 162, 171, 178, 180, 184, 193, 218, 238–9, 241, 255–6, 260, 263, 274–5, 281, 281, 301, 348–9, 353
varioversal, 260
verb, verbal style, 219–22, 224–6, 228–31, 232
vocabulary, 48–50, 51–2, 55–7, 60, 64, 81, 86, 91–3, 124, 136, 163, 165, 167, 331, 334, 338
vowel, 152, 193, 196, 198–9, 208, 288, 346, 353–7, 360–2, 364
vowel following, effect of, 12, 354–7, 360–1, 364

want to, 239, 247–9
we, 8, 11–12, 115, 151, 159–61, 240, 242, 250–3, 264–5, 267–73, 286, 291, 293, 309–11, 313–16, 318, 320
Web-UG, 6, 7, 111, 113–15, 118–19, 121–2
welcome, 7, 114–15, 133
Western/Westernise/Westernisation, 7, 8, 20–1, 26, 29–32, 35, 41, 99–101, 112, 116, 129–31, 133–4, 141, 152–4, 158, 171, 182, 245, 270–2
wife/wives, 94, 103, 138, 142–3, 271
will, 2, 10, 240, 242–8, 250–6, 289, 315
word order, 57–9, 61
World English, 1, 2, 5, 8, 13–14, 15, 18, 20, 35, 37, 108, 113, 116, 120, 153–4, 168, 193, 216, 219, 263
would, 240, 242–7, 250–5

X-all structure, 12, 325, 329, 331–4, 336, 338, 340

Yoruba, 112, 116, 124
you see second-person
younger speaker, 132, 140, 346, 348–9, 351–2, 354–7, 359–64

zero subject, 196, 199–202, 208

EU representative:
Easy Access System Europe
Mustamäe tee 50, 10621 Tallinn, Estonia
Gpsr.requests@easproject.com

www.ingramcontent.com/pod-product-compliance
Lightning Source LLC
Chambersburg PA
CBHW071224230426
43668CB00011B/1300